KEITH
RICHARDS

BEFORE THEY MAKE ME RUN

KRIS NEEDS

Plexus, London

Copyright © 2004 by Kris Needs and Plexus Publishing Limited
Published by Plexus Publishing Limited
55a Clapham Common Southside
London SW4 9BX
Tel: 0207 622 2440
Fax: 0207 622 2441
www.plexusbooks.com
First Printing 2004

British Library Cataloguing In Publication Data

Needs, Kris
Keith Richards : before they make me run
1. Richards, Keith, 1943 – 2. Rock musicians – Great Britain –
Biography
I. Title
782.4'2166'092

ISBN 0 85965 344 7

Printed and bound in Great Britain by Bell & Bain Ltd., Glasgow
Cover design by Phil Gambrill
Book design by Rebecca Martin

For Michelle; Alan, Jackie and Paul Clayton; Robin Pike; Mick Jones; Keith Richards, and my son, Daniel Lee Needs.

Dedicated to the memory of Bert Richards, David Needs and Barrie Clayton ('MC Kendo').

ACKNOWLEDGEMENTS

Special thanks to Alan Clayton, Keith's old mate, whose stories and contact with the man kept the juices flowing while the 'Licks' tour raged and this book kept growing. Robin Pike, my old chemistry teacher, who sorted me out seeing the Stones in 1968 and through the seventies. His advice and memories proved invaluable. Michelle Long, my long-suffering girlfriend, who had to put up with an obsessed maniac for a year: I love you. Bernard Doherty, Lucy Hopkins and staff at LD Publicity for sorting me out with Stones goodies and tickets since 1990. Plexus Publishing for putting up with the monster I unleashed – very late and too huge. Thanks to Sandra Wake, Terry Porter, Chloe Lola Riess, Rebecca Martin and Louise Coe. Special thanks to Paul Woods for taking on the unenviable task of editing the bastard. And thanks of course to Keith for living this story in the first place.

Thanks and shouts to my mum, Joan Needs; the kids: Abbey, Chloe, Jamie and Ellie; the Richards family; Jane Rose; Bill Bolton; Tony Russell; Ronnie Wood; David, Sara, Joseph, Nik and Jeanette at FML Management; Primal Scream; Jim 'Midnight Rambler' Fyffe; Aron, Geezer and all at Stay Up Forever; Richard Sen and the gents at Record and Tape Exchange, London; Lol Hammond and Caro; Rob and the Breakin' Even Crew, Reading; Stoke Mandeville Hospital; KT and Jerry the Postman; Colin 'Nuclear Waste' Keinch; Claire and Michael; Richard Norris and Simon Marshall.

Thanks to the following photographers, magazines and publications and photographic agencies: Harry Goodwin/All Action; Gered Mankowitz; Henry Diltz/Corbis; Michael Putland; Judie Bernstein/Topix; Bob Gruen/Topix; Alan Clayton; Neal Preston/Corbis; David Koppei/All Action; Dave Hogan/All Action; Ebet Roberts/Redferns; Justin Thomas/All Action; Mitchel Sams/All Action; Robert Altman/Retna; Bettman/Corbis; Luis Sanchis/LD Publicity; Scarlet Page/LD Publicity; Rankin/LD Publicity; Cecil Beaton/Sothebys; Monitor Picture Library/Retna; David Macho/Keith Altham PR/Rolling Stones Archive; Michael Putland/Keith Altham PR/Rolling Stones Archive; *The Rolling Stones Book*; *The Times*; *Sunday Express*; *Rolling Stone*; *Zig Zag*; *Aylesbury Roxette*; *Beggars Banquet*; *Daily Express*.

CONTENTS

INTRODUCTION

Yeah, just what the world needs – another book about Keith Richards and the Stones. But that was never the intention. This has got to be *more* than that.

I'd better put my cards on the table from the start. This is not an Authorised Biography – that simply won't happen.

I've spent the last 40 years nurturing this celebration of the greatest rock 'n' roll star on earth. I've loved the Rolling Stones, to the point of near-obsession, from the moment when, as a nine-year-old in 1963, I saw them playing 'Come On' on TV. Since then, I've followed their every move. Particularly Keith's.

Keith was always my man – even back in the sixties, when most of the attention was on Mick Jagger and Brian Jones. The first thing that hit me was the cut-throat raunch and innovative attack of his guitar-playing. Then, as I grew up, Keith emerged as the most charismatic Stone of all. By the time I was sixteen his delectable flowers of evil were in full bloom, the spirit of the blues personified. His guitar playing was by now a metronomic wrecking machine, and he'd been dubbed with titles like 'the Human Riff' and 'the World's Most Elegantly Wasted Human Being'.

It made me look deeper into the music, into what fuelled Keith's fire. A nine-year-old isn't going to know about Chuck Berry, Jimmy Reed, John Lee Hooker, Bo Diddley and Muddy Waters, but I made damn sure I checked them out after they became known as Stones influences. Then came country music and reggae, as Keith got heavily into them in the seventies. In the eighties, after hanging out with Keith, I checked out albums by Hoagy Carmichael, and even music hall comedian Max Miller! Keith wants his gravestone to bear the legend, 'He Passed It On.' He certainly did in my case.

Over the last 36 years, I've caught the Stones live as often as I could and encountered Keith on several occasions. I've done interviews with him that have gone on for two days and have simply hung out with him as mates. In early '77, I sat in court as a reporter for the duration of his three-day drugs trial, but a few years later perched three feet away from him in a hotel room while he thrashed out 'Wild Horses' and some of his favourite blues. I've collected every studio emission I could get my hands on – official and unofficial – and stocked up on memorabilia ever since joining the Stones fan club in '64. Keith and the boys never cease to amaze me. To turn out something as awe-inspiring as the *Licks* show after 40 years is hard to believe. But then Keith would be equally happy playing to a few people in a room somewhere – or even back in his bedroom, where it all began.

Keith's story has been told before, usually in cold, factual terms or through his own oft-repeated words. My take on it is that I've grown up, then grown older, with the guy. This book is a labour of love. I built it up like a Stones record – starting

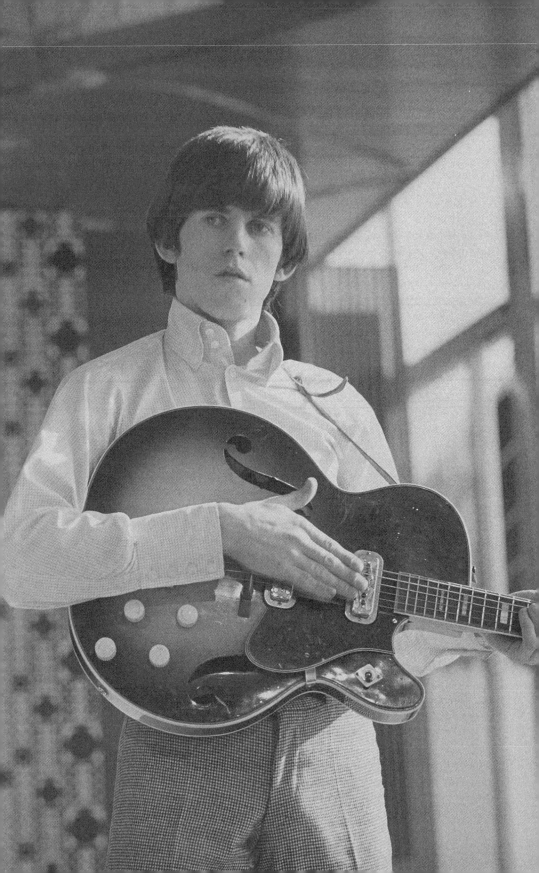

with some basic ideas, enlarging it into a sprawling mass, then honing it into shape. There was a bottomless well of myth, truth and incidents to draw from. If my long-suffering editor hadn't stepped in with his trusty machete, I'd be writing it forever. To quote a phrase of Keith's, 'It'd be like painting the Sistine fucking Chapel!'

Or, as Keith's mate Alan Clayton says, 'It's one man's chronicle of his life and his thoughts on Keith Richards and the Rolling Stones as he grows up . . . Keith deserves a bit of a tribute.'

This book also deals with the music that has turned Keith on, and that he has subsequently turned me onto. There are some historic guidelines, classic quotes, musical interludes and accounts of our personal encounters. When I interviewed Keith for the mag I was running in the eighties, he considered the feature one of the best things that had been written about him. He was subsequently up for another interview, which turned out to be an exclusive.

During the course of this two-day marathon, which carried on way after the interview was done, Keith confessed, 'Thing is, you're one of the Rolling Stones and you play that game to a certain extent, because it's what you have to do. As long as *I* ain't bullshitted by being Keith Richards of the Rolling Stones, I don't give a damn. I don't mind bullshitting other people! You want this Keith Richards? You want that Keith Richards? Then *there's* your Keith Richards!'

The interviews were more like open-ended conversations, and were crucial in my quest to understand Keith's essence. He talked candidly about his struggle with heroin, but more happily expounded for hours on his favourite obsession – music. 'That's my real addiction,' he concluded.

Inevitably, the spirit of Chuck Berry hangs over this book and occasionally lands a lucky punch. Muddy Waters and Robert Johnson are never further away than Keith's boom-box. Other factors loom large in Keith's life:

The huge influence and sad losses of Ian Stewart and Gram Parsons. The heavy dope period, when he was top of the Next-To-Die chart. The eternal friction with his partner-for-life, Mick Jagger. The roots culture of Jamaica. The great comedians. Hoagy Carmichael's romantic ballads. Shepherds pie and bangers & mash. His best mate, Ronnie Wood. And, not least, domestic bliss – well, Keith's version anyway.

Keith hit 60 last year, on the twentieth anniversary of his wedding to Patti Hanson. Keith Richards in 2004 is a fulfilled and much-loved man, with the recent *Licks* tour showing that he's yet to reach the peak of his powers. In telling his story, I've tried to pass on the excitement and the joy of his music, his innate sense of humour and love of comedy.

Ultimately, I agree that Keith deserves a rightful tribute, as he's the biggest fan of all. As he says, 'You couldn't write this story.' But you can sure have a lot of fun trying.

CHAPTER ONE

THE BLUES HAD A BABY

School Daze

Keith Richards was born on Saturday 18 December, 1943, at Livingstone Hospital, Dartford, Kent.

The family of Keith's father, Bert, who was born in 1915, had moved from Wales to Walthamstow, east London, in the 1800s. Bert's mum was the Mayoress of Walthamstow during the Second World War, while Bert was in the Army. Theirs was undoubtedly the straight and narrow side of the family.

In 1933, Bert had met Doris Dupree, one of seven sisters who were also natives of Wales. They went out together for five years, before getting married in '38. Doris claims she got pregnant so she wouldn't have to work.

Keith's first vague memory is of air-raid sirens and fighter planes in the sky. Dartford was located in what was nicknamed 'Doodlebug Alley', a section of the River Thames that acted as a landmark when the Luftwaffe targeted the docks. For a few months towards the end of the war, the Germans were sending V2 rockets – unmanned missiles, nicknamed 'doodlebugs' – that flew over the target area until their engines cut out, then plummeted directly to the ground.

When he was one year old, Keith spent the last part of the war in the relative safety of Mansfield, Nottinghamshire, where Bert was getting over having his leg blown up on D-Day. When they returned they found that a doodlebug had land-ed on their house, damaging Keith's bedroom. He likes to claim that it landed in his cot, and admits to still getting the odd shiver when he sees an old Second World War movie.

In mid-1964, the Stones' Fan Club would begin a monthly magazine called *The Rolling Stones Book*. Obviously inspired by Beatles and Elvis fan mags, the book was packed with photos of the Stones at work and play, plus comments from a fan's perspective. From issue four, they started running the Stones' own stories, the very first time they were ever told.

Looking back, it's funny to see how all the group had a year taken off their ages. As Keith's birthdate is given as one year later, he's effectively missed the war, and thus recalls: 'We were sitting out on the lawn, just my mum and I. The war was over, actually, but I knew what had gone on. My mother says I was scared when planes went overhead. I remember her telling me it was one of ours, a Spitfire. But nothing else about the war . . .'

Out of the army, Bert worked long hours as an electrical engineer, while Doris demonstrated washing machines at the Dartford Co-Op. They lived a short walk from where young Michael Jagger, a mere five months older, resided with his more middle-class parents, Joe and Eva. His dad was a TV sports presenter, and would encourage little Mick to pursue physical education as a career. Keith and Mick knew each other from the neighbourhood, but only ever played together in the way that groups of five-year-olds do.

Doris came from the musical side of Keith's family. Her dad, Theodore 'Gus' Dupree, played guitar, piano and fiddle, led dance bands in the thirties, and played in a country swing band in the fifties. He was billed as 'Gus Dupree, King of the Country Fiddle', and played mainly at air force bases around London. To this day, Keith cites Gus as a major reason that he got into music at such an early age. It also explains how the first music he got into was country – before rock 'n' roll had even come along. His hero was Roy Rogers, the guitar-toting cowboy, who Keith would see at the Saturday morning movies. The glamour of Roy's Wild West beat the shit out of the grey post-war reality he was growing up in. (Of course, young had Keith had his own cowboy outfit too.) Meanwhile, Doris would play her son music by Nat King Cole, Duke Ellington, Count Basie and various jazz singers.

Keith started at Westhill Infants School in January '48. In Bill Wyman's voluminous and painstaking *Rolling with the Stones* tome, Doris says that Keith 'was in a terrible state all day' when he first started school. 'I had to carry him home. He was frightened that maybe I wasn't coming to get him. With six aunts, he was a bit spoiled . . . He was a funny kid. He never seemed to want to go out like other kids . . . A timid, introvert boy, he didn't like football. If a ball came near him, he'd run away.'

David Dalton's 1981 collection of Stones facts – *The Rolling Stones: The First Twenty Years* – reprinted several articles from old magazines, including 'The Stones By Their Mums', lifted from a Sixties publication called *Everybody's*. It could be a foretaste of *Hello!*, as Doris comes 'out of the canteen at the Dartford store where she works as a demonstrator to talk about her son'.

'I was one of a family of seven girls, and Keith was the first boy. With six aunts, he was a bit spoiled, and he really was a sweet-looking kid. Chubby and sturdy – and always with a red nose.' Doris also mentions how the grown-up Keith would shower her with gifts, such as an Austin 1100 car for her birthday, an antique watch and a gold cigarette lighter.

'He was just the same as a child. Always giving people presents. He would save up his pennies until he had enough money, and then buy me a box of chocolates. Rather spend money on others than himself.'

In September '51, Keith went on to Wentworth County Primary School where he once again met the then-Mike Jagger, who was in the year above. Keith was quite the opposite to Mick even then – he hated schoolwork, only doing well in English, art and history. Jagger would go on to get seven 'O' levels, three 'A's and was fond of sports, even becoming a school prefect. As he grew up, Keith would be more interested in sneaking a quick fag while skiving off of the cross-country races.

But Keith loved the frequent visits to see Gus and his guitar, which he would brazenly display with a 'don't touch until you're ready' rule. Gus finally let Keith hold it when he was ten, and it was love at first sight. Gus would take his grandson to West End guitar shops, where he'd stare at all the instruments and marvel at the 'Santa's workshop'-style repair activity going on.

Keith also reckons that it's from Gus – 'one of the great dirty old men' – that he inherited his sense of humour. Gus turned Keith on to the great British music-hall humour of nutters like Max Miller, Stanley Holloway, Jimmy James and the Crazy Gang. These men sowed the seeds of British comedy, from the *Carry On* films to the greats like Tommy Cooper. And Keith would carry on Gus's mission. Over 30 years after his indoctrination into the joys of music hall, Keith would sit in a London hotel room playing his beloved tapes to yours truly, cackling his bollocks off as he pointed out the good bits. It's the same 'pass it on' ethic that he's always had about music.

Keith would later describe himself as something of a 'hood' at school. If he'd started off as a 'mummy's boy', then by his early teens he was turning into quite 'a yob' – though mostly out of boredom with schoolwork, and to avoid bullying. But he still made it into the school choir as a boy soprano, even if it was only to get out of lessons. Making up an angelic, be-cassocked trio with two of his reprobate cronies, Keith sang at Westminster Abbey, the Royal Albert Hall, and even the Royal Festival Hall in front of the Queen. But that all finished when his voice broke. The mummy's boy started to evolve into a degenerate and began retaliating when he got picked on, which happened all too often.

His surroundings weren't exactly conducive to a hassle-free childhood. In '54, the local council granted the family a replacement home for their bomb-damaged house at Chastillian Road. Spielman Road was on a new post-war estate called Temple Hill. It was one of hundreds of hastily-erected little boxes, which would be crime-ridden and rotten within years.

Keith later reflected on his dead-end estate adolescence, which was eventually saved by rock 'n' roll: 'Working class, English working class . . . struggling, thinking they were middle class. Moved into a tough neighbourhood when I was about ten . . . to what they'd call in the States a housing project. Just been built. Thousands and thousands of houses, everyone wondering what the fuck was going on. Everyone was displaced, they were still building it and already there were gangs everywhere. Coming to teddy boys. Just before rock and roll hit England. But they were all waiting for it. They were practicing. Rock and roll got me into being one of the boys. Before that I just got me ass kicked all over the place. Learned how to ride a punch.'

Keith hated the scary rows of houses and the thug kids who'd pick on him as he scarpered home from school. Meanwhile, his mum resented the fact that set-in-his-ways Bert wouldn't take a chance on finding somewhere better to live. In 1955, life looked bleak for Keith. All that was about to change, but first he had to fail his eleven-plus examination. This unscrupulous ritual, which took the form of basic English and maths tests, could dictate what happened to the pupil for the rest of his life. If you passed – like Mick – you went up to grammar school. If you failed – like Keith – you went down to technical college or secondary modern school. This could become a lifelong defining moment for a person's class and social status – though it was the lower-class 'thickos' who seemed to have more fun.

In September, Keith went to Dartford Technical College. He hated that, too, and was made to retake his third year studies. Still something of an aimless loner, Keith joined the Boy Scouts for two years and made it to leader of the Beaver Patrol (quiet at the back there), but got thrown out for whacking a kid he took a particular dislike to. Despite peer pressure, however, he never had the inclination to hitch up with one of the local gangs. As a result, he was still picked on at school and turned to music almost as a desperate form of solace.

The Blues Come Around

Keith has always worn his major influences on his sleeve. As he's fond of saying, 'When we started the Rolling Stones our aim was to turn the world on to Muddy Waters.'

So it came as a small surprise when he told me his first musical hero had been country music's tragic giant, Hank Williams. I always assumed it was Elvis, or Chuck Berry, and that country had come in years later when he hooked up with Gram Parsons.

Not so though, because even if you go back to the Stones pop of *Aftermath*, there are several tracks inflected with country-style harmonies and strumming.

'If I own up, Hank Williams is probably one of the first people that turned me on,' he testified when we talked in mid-1980. 'Way before rock 'n' roll and Chuck Berry, I was listening to country music. Just because I happened to hear a couple of songs and I got into it.' And Hank had the same relationship to country that Elvis or Chuck had to rock 'n' roll, blowing its staid, redneck blandness out of the water with his intense, emotional laments.

It's not hard to see why Keith was smitten. Born in Alabama in 1923, Hank Williams was one of the early musical outlaws, coming from poverty and learning guitar from a black street musician. After the Second World War, he took country music from its rural roots and thrust some emotional reality into the burgeoning Nashville scene. Already building a reputation for heavy drinking, Hank still became country's first superstar, busting the music out just like the Stones would later do for the blues. Country music at the time meant cowboys trotting out bland lyrics over syrupy pedal steel backings. You had to dig hard to find the bare emotional seam that would later come to the fore via the likes of George Jones, and reach their logical conclusion with the heart-wrenching songs of Gram Parsons.

Hank was the first. He was the original tortured artist, surviving on prescription drugs to combat the lifelong pain of a back injury – sustained when he was thrown from a horse. Classics like 'You Win Again', 'The Blues Come Around', 'I'm So Lonesome I Could Cry', 'Your Cheatin' Heart' and 'I Heard That Lonesome Whistle Blow' were pure bared soul, although he could still dash off a pop hit like 'Jamabalaya'. But Hank's private life was all turmoil and excess. It wasn't surprising when he met an early death at the age of 29 – suffering a massive heart attack in the back of his Cadillac on the way to a gig.

To indulge in such a pained legacy in early adolescence partly explains how Keith would later create his poignant ballads with the Stones.

When Keith was fourteen, he managed to persuade his parents to buy him a gramophone player – the sort you had to wind up. The first record he bought was a cheap imitation of a Rick Nelson song, but, like many kids at the time, he got the rock 'n' roll bug from the seismic impact of Bill Haley and the Comets' 'Rock Around The Clock'.

But Keith soon moved on to something bigger and more raunchy when Elvis Presley appeared, the sex-on-legs icon from the wrong side of the tracks, with his 1956 hit 'Heartbreak Hotel'.

'It's funny,' he reflected. 'You always know it. Mick and I talked about it a lot. I knew from the minute I first heard Elvis that that's what I wanted to do. Once you've decided that you want to be the best rock 'n' roller in the world, you go ahead and try it.'

Then came the manic, piano-bashing, revival-meeting holler of Little Richard. Suddenly, Keith had a purpose in life. He settled into being a teenager, and even started going out. 'I was into Little Richard. I was rocking away, avoiding the bicycle chains and the razors in those dance halls . . . "Lucille" is the one that first turned me on, that made me think, rock 'n' roll's here. Suddenly my world went from black and white to Technicolor.'

Keith took to wearing winklepicker shoes, pink socks and drainpipe jeans, and hanging out at the snooker hall and fairgrounds with the local teddy boys. He was the school rocker, and started investigating the speedy possibilities of slimming pills, or whatever cheap buzz you could find at the local chemist's shop.

If Hank Williams had infected the young Keith with an aching soul, Chuck Berry loaded up his arsenal of guitar licks with deadly ammunition. Chuck's driving guitar style mixed engine-purring sex with precision impact. It grabbed Keith where it counted most.

Berry was born in St Louis, Missouri in 1931. Most of his family sang in the city's Antioch Baptist Church Choir, whereas Chuck was assigned to the bass section of his High School Glee Club. He became enamoured of the guitar when he encountered it during a school revue and taught himself to play with the aid of instruction books. Soon he was supplementing his income while still at school, playing house parties and church socials, while assisting in his father's carpentry business. In '52, Chuck formed his own group and started playing in clubs.

Unsurprisingly, there is a Chuck Berry-Muddy Waters connection. The pair met when Chuck was playing a stint at the Cosmopolitan Club. Muddy sent him to his label, Chess Records, for an audition. They signed him up and recorded 'Maybelline', which went straight up the American charts. Soon Chuck was playing everywhere from clubs to arenas with touring rock 'n' roll shows, while classic anthems like 'Let It Rock' and 'Johnny B. Goode' provided the ultimate teenage cars-and-girls soundtrack. Chuck came up with the lyrics, while a lot of the musical ideas came from his underrated piano player, Johnnie Johnson. Okay, so many of the songs sounded similar, revolving around that inimitable clipped guitar drive that so influenced the young Keith. But it worked.

While Chuck's first dent on the UK charts was made by 'School Days' in June '57, he wouldn't tour the country until May '64 – mainly on the back of the massive exposure he received via the Stones.

Keith, meanwhile, was becoming increasingly obsessed with music: 'I used to pose in front of the mirror at home. I was hopeful. The only thing I was lacking was a bit of bread to buy an instrument. But I got the moves off first, and I got the guitar later.'

'Keith was always worrying for a guitar of his own,' recalled Doris. 'When he was fifteen, I bought him one for ten pounds. From that day, it has been the most important thing in his life. My father taught Keith a few chords, but the rest he has taught himself.'

Keith reflected about those formative times when we were chatting in '83: 'First off, nobody becomes a musician with just the idea of making money. You don't learn an instrument with the idea that this is going to make you money. You only learn how to play an instrument because – fuck it – that's what you wanna do. That's the only drive that makes you figure out this weird game. Whether it's a guitar or a piano – work your way around that maze and actually learn how to play the thing. Money ain't the drive. You don't think about that. When you start, you don't even know what you're doing. You do it because you wanna do it. You don't worry about making money. You'll make money some other way. Be a panel beater or something, y'know. You just really, dearly wanna be able to sound like that bloke on that record that you really love. You wanna learn to play that.

'It's a real obsession because it takes the place of everything else. Sometimes it's an excuse. You're a shy boy – "Shit, I'd rather sit here and play guitar rather than go out and make a fool of myself trying to pull chicks." A lot of it's that. A lot of it's also watching yourself in your mum's wardrobe mirror, posing and getting the moves off. It's all strange little things like that. The least of it is, "How I wanna be a millionaire." Later on, maybe that comes and that's where most of the guys get screwed up.'

So, after December 1958, the adolescent Keith Richards shut himself away in the bedroom with a guitar and some Chuck Berry records. He talked again of his lone self-tuition in an interview with *Guitar World*'s Jas Obrecht, in December '92: 'Chuck was my man. He was the one that made me say as a teenager, "I want to play, Jesus Christ!" And then suddenly I had a focal point, but not that I was naïve enough, even at that age, to expect it to pan out. But at least I had something to go for, some way to channel the energies that you have at that age. And, definitely with rock 'n' roll, you have to start somewhere around then.'

When the hormones boot in.

'Yeah, yeah. Exactly. That's it. If you don't have the juice then, you never will. And then it's a matter of sustaining the juice.'

Another major influence on the teenage Keith was Bo Diddley, who first appeared on Chess Records with his eponymous monster hit in 1955. 'Bo Diddley' immediately established the man's sound – a shimmering voodoo shuffle with its beat greatly influenced by African rhythms and the pre-war jump music of Louis Jordan and his Tympani Five.

Diddley was born Ellis McDaniel in a small town called St Comb, Mississippi, in 1928. By the age of seventeen he was playing guitar in a band semi-professionally, before going to Chicago and forming a full-time trio. Part of the reason for his otherworldly sound was the fact that he customised his own guitars and amplifiers. While his two accomplices played washboard and maracas, Bo thrashed out a coruscating wall of rhythm.

As he put it, 'Man, when I used to tramp them streets looking for work, everybody was singing like T-Bone Walker and them old-time blues cats. So I figured that, to make the scene, I had to think up something different.'

It was all rubbing off on Keith – from the seventies onwards, he became a great believer in customising guitars to fit particular needs and create unique sounds. As he favours five strings for his open tunings, it's often been a necessity. Bo and his huge wooden suit-box paved the way for such previously unheard-of innovation Within a couple of years, Keith had his Chuck and blues licks boiling down into the deadly hybrid that's been his trademark ever since. He doesn't seem to have gone out much in his mid-teens, but the end result of his relentless practising was that he got every Berry lick down like the master. This was Keith's education. He certainly wasn't into pursuing a career with a view to making money, like Mick at the London School of Economics. In April 1960, aged sixteen, he was booted out of Dartford Technical College for his constant truancy and a few pranks.

It turned out to be the best thing that could have happened to him. Fortunately, Keith's headmaster thought he had some artistic talent and enrolled him in Sidcup Art College. This was the popular late fifties/early sixties disposal system for students of an artistic and rebellious nature. Here, they could be as outrageous as they wanted. Keith spent a lot of the time hanging out with fellow guitar enthusiasts in the gents' toilets – the only place they could practice in peace – and found he was learning more about music than anything else, particularly the blues. Big Bill Broonzy, Muddy Waters and John Lee Hooker were the first blues artists he slavishly copied in order to learn from. From this point he knew what he wanted to do in life, and it didn't involve regular job hours or wages. He simply wanted to play guitar like his heroes.

Keith may have got his first teenage kicks from a rock 'n' roll jump-start, but it was the blues that truly set his soul on fire. As Bill Wyman has said, before the Rolling Stones hardly anybody knew about the music, which was only available on hard-to-find import albums. What allowed the blues to bust out of the confines of a purist movement was the Stones' ability to mate it with other forms of music. Keith initially came up through country 'n' western before getting into rock 'n' roll through Elvis, Chuck, and, later, Little Richard and Jerry Lee Lewis. He was an out-and-out rocker with a taste for certain bluesmen like Jimmy Reed. Then Mick and Brian Jones turned him on to Muddy Waters and Robert Johnson, and opened up a whole new spectrum. The Stones would mix scholarly respect for classic blues music with rock 'n' roll's animal attack – all shot through with teenage hormones on the rampage.

Nine years after they first met at primary school, Keith and Mick remembered each other when Keith bought an ice cream from Mick, who had a holiday job selling cornets outside Dartford Library. Keith later met Mick on his train to Sidcup Art School, while Mick was on his way to classes at the London School of Economics. This story has been retold to the point of becoming a rock legend. Keith homed in on the albums under Mick's arm – Chuck's *One Dozen Berries* or *Rockin' At The Hops*, depending on which story you believe, and *The Best Of Muddy Waters*.

Muddy rapidly became as big an obsession as Chuck. Jas Obrecht suggested to Keith that – like Muddy Waters – Keith approaches rhythm guitar 'with the primal energy of a sex drive'. Spot on. Even in the sixties, the little girls understood.

'Well, that's a compliment. Thank you . . . He's my man. He's the guy I listened to. Maybe I just picked it up off him. I recognised it. It was just the same as my drive. I felt an immediate affinity when I heard Muddy go [plays the intro to 'Rollin' Stone']. You can't be harder than that, man. He said it all right there. So all I want to do is be able to do that.'

'When I eventually got to hear Muddy Waters, it all fell into place for me,' Victor Bockris quotes him in his *Keith Richards: The Unauthorised Biography*. 'He was the thing I was looking for, the thing that pulled it all in for me. When I heard him I realised the connection between all the music I'd heard. He made it all explainable. He was like a codebook. I was incredibly inspired by him as a musician. He was more than a guitar player, more than a singer, more than a writer. It was all him. He was the hoochie coochie man.'

While the teenage Keith was bent over that guitar, getting hot with Muddy, he could never in his wildest dreams have imagined that one day he'd be jamming with the man. He'd fantasise about it, sure, but he could never have imagined himself on the same level. Or to be in a position where he was asked to write the foreword for Muddy's biography, *Can't Be Satisfied* by Robert Gordon, published in 2002. One listen to 'Rollin' Stone' is all you need to understand the depth of Muddy's influence. The guitar is stark, sparse, and spitting daggers. No flash solos, just lethal rhythm oil. Pure essence of Keef.

Keith starts his foreword with a definition of the blues: 'There's a demon in me. I think there's a demon in everyone, a dark piece in us all. And the blues is a recognition of that and the ability to express it and make fun out of it, have joy out of that dark stuff. When you listen to Muddy Waters, you can hear all of the angst and all of the power and all of the hardship that made that man. But Muddy let it out through music, set the feelings loose in the air. The blues make me feel better.'

Keith goes on to explain how he first heard Muddy via Mick, after that fateful train meeting in '61. 'I was going to mug the guy for the Chuck Berry because I wasn't familiar with Muddy. We started talking, went 'round to his house, and he played me Muddy and I said, "Wow. Again." And about ten hours later I was still going, "Okay, again." When I got to Muddy and heard "Still A Fool" and "Hoochie Coochie Man" – that is the most powerful music I've ever heard. The most expressive.'

'Rollin' Stone' is cited by Keith as the song from whence the band took their name for their first proper gig. 'We basically wanted to turn the whole world on to Muddy and his like,' he continues, adding, 'I always felt that Muddy ran the band, that there was a real connection.'

If Chuck Berry had provided the wheels, then Muddy Waters was Keith's ultimate destination. The gateway to the blues. 'Muddy was like a map, he was really the key to all of the other stuff. I found out Muddy and Chuck were working out of the same studio and on the same Chess label and there was the Willie Dixon connection too. Then I had to find everything of Muddy's that I could and at the same time find where Muddy got it from. So I sat and listened to Robert Lockwood Jr. and to cousins and relations. Via Muddy, I found Robert Johnson, and then it all started to make sense.'

He winds up with his whole *raison d'etre*: 'This music got called the blues about a hundred years ago, but the music is about a feeling and feelings didn't start just a hundred years ago. Feelings start in the person and I think that's why the blues is universal, because it's part of everybody. Muddy is like a very comforting arm around the shoulder. You need that, you know? It can be dark down there, man.'

Muddy came up the hard way, playing the Chicago blues bars and neighbourhood dives to make ends meet. It wasn't until he visited the UK for the first time in '58 that he realised he meant something more than a Saturday night drinking soundtrack. Muddy was special, and it took Mick Jagger to grab that hard-to-find blues booty by mail order. Once Keith was bitten, forget about it.

Muddy Waters was born McKinley Morganfield in Rolling Fork, Mississippi, in 1915. He was nicknamed Muddy because he liked to play in the creek. Muddy came up playing Saturday night fish fries, jook joints and, somewhere along the line, witnessed the great Son House, who bowled him over. Son House had taught guitar to Keith's other main blues inspiration, Robert Johnson. As Muddy said to Peter Guralnik in his classic book *Feel Like Going Home*, 'I consider myself to be what you might call a mixture of all three. I had part of my own, part of Son House, and a little part of Robert Johnson.'

Muddy hated Mississippi and rarely went back once he relocated to Chicago in 1943. But the blues scene wasn't thriving then, so he took on driving jobs while playing the clubs at night. Around '45, Muddy was hanging out with Big Bill Broonzy and – having been given his first electric guitar by his uncle – got to record some unreleased tunes for Columbia. In '47, he caught the ear of Sammy Goldstein, black talent scout for Aristocrat Records – later Chess. He was sought out on his truck and sent to play a session that had been arranged by in-house piano player Sunnyland Slim.

For a solid six-day week working on the job, plus seven nights spent playing, Muddy was making around $50 a week. When Aristocrat changed its name to Chess, Muddy was in there and immediately scored a hit with 'Rollin' Stone'. It wasn't a national hit – it was distinctly for the Southern 'race market'. But all the same, 60,000 sales was okay. By the end of the decade, Muddy had managed to give up the day job and live on a healthy influx of club dates. Previously, he'd been backed by Little Walter's harmonica and Willie Dixon on bass, but he was now expanding the line-up, enjoying an ongoing rivalry with Howlin' Wolf and rising to the top of the blues field. He was really breaking through by '54, with hits like 'Hoochie Coochie Man' and 'I Just Want To Make Love To You', which the Stones covered on their first album.

'It was sex,' commented Marshall Chess. 'If you had ever seen Muddy then, the effect he had on women . . . On Saturday night they'd be lined up ten deep.'

Little did Muddy know, but a few years later he'd be accorded a kind of worldwide respect that would boost his reputation and keep him for the rest of his life, until his death in '83, largely thanks to the Stones.

As Muddy himself commented in Robert Gordon's book, 'The Rolling Stones created a whole wide-open space for the music. They said who did it first and how they came by knowin' it. I tip my hat to 'em. It took the people from England to hip

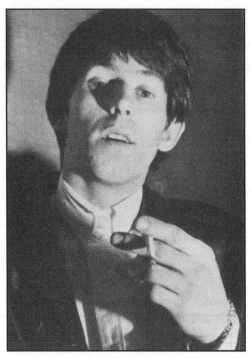

The trademark fag makes an early appearance.

my people – the white people – that a black man's music is not a crime to bring in the house.'

Unlike Mick, Keith has never wavered from his blues crusade. When I got to know him in the eighties, he explained, 'It's like breakfast. Eggs and bacon every morning and then blues. Always. I carry it around . . . I go around with one suitcase full of clothes and two suitcases full of cassettes. I've got 2,000 cassettes that I daren't let out of my sight!'

Keith talked about the blues while picking sympathetically on a large acoustic guitar. 'The blues is a nice constant thing. I get exactly the same thing that I did when I first heard it. It's timeless, and that's what's important about that music for me. I find that I can not only still appreciate it, but appreciate it more listening to it after twenty years. I understand a little more about it. You never stop finding out about things that are that good. Robert Johnson is probably the ultimate apex of the blues singer, writer, guitar player – everything wrapped up in one. There's nothing the guy could do that was wrong. He was just too brilliant to live.'

Robert Johnson remains the most enigmatic figure in the history of the Delta blues. He only made a handful of recordings, but they were enough for Keith to place him on the highest pedestal amongst his influences.

Johnson's high voice was pitched against atonishingly innovative guitar playing which Keith holds up against the great classical composers. A child prodigy whose path, legend had it, took him past a Mississippi crossroads where he was said to have sold his soul to the Devil, in exchange for his unearthly guitar skills. Keith has been to the supposed location and carries around a little bottle of sand that he scraped up there.

'Little Robert' hailed from Tunica County, Mississippi, and was a pupil of Son House, who himself learned his idiosyncratic picking style from 1920s country blues giant Blind Lemon Jefferson.

Muddy Waters had played with Robert Johnson, which urged Keith to track down the Johnson anthology *King Of The Delta Blues Singers*. When Keith was sharing a flat with Brian Jones, the pair tried to unravel and copy Johnson's unique style of playing. The Stones went on to cover 'Love In Vain' and 'Stop Breaking Down', while the legendary damned bluesman had his mystique reinforced by the Stones. His legend suited the group perfectly: tragic, damaged, an early casualty in the American lineage that spawned Hendrix.

Robert Johnson's intricate and emotional style of playing stood out among the wave of hopeful blues artists coming out of the cotton-fields in the thirties. But it was years after he died before he achieved recognition, and the myths started growing up around his death.

Johnson had been booked for his first high-profile New York appearance at Carnegie Hall in December '38, as part of the 'Spirituals-To-Swing' concert. In a TV documentary called *In Search of Robert Johnson*, commentator John Hammond Jr. says that Johnson 'died at the moment of booking'. Legends abound as to the reason. He's commonly thought to have been poisoned by a jealous girlfriend – the same way that Blind Lemon met his maker. But other theories have included stabbing, shooting and Hammond's rather dramatic theory that he 'spent his life escaping the hounds of hell', having sold his soul to the Devil: 'He died on the lines, barking like a mad dog.'

As time went on, people would tell Keith that he was pretty good at reproducing Johnson's unique style. 'I say I'm only a third of the way there,' he told *Guitar World* in '96. 'He's like Bach on that thing; he has different licks, very different sounds and different systems of picking, different tunings. What a hell of a guy. I wonder if he would have told you his secrets?'

Keith put all this eulogising into perspective in Hammond's documentary: 'You think you're getting a handle on the blues and then you hear Robert Johnson, some of the rhythms he's doing and playing at the same time, you think, "This guy must have three brains!" To me he was like a comet or a meteor that came along and BOOM, suddenly he raised the ante, suddenly you had to aim that much higher.'

Let It Rock

At Sidcup, Keith also met a fellow blues enthusiast called Dick Taylor, who had the same ideals and would jam with Keith at lunchtime. Keith's first ever gig was at a sports dance in Eltham with a country 'n' western band, which also included fellow art student Michael Ross. They did Johnny Cash songs, 'Blue Moon Of Kentucky' from the first Elvis album, and other rockabilly favourites.

Keith already had his style down when he ventured out of his bedroom with his new licks. On his first foray into the jam sessions he'd enjoy for the rest of his life, he simply moved to someone else's bedroom: often Mick's, or Dick Taylor's, or a bloke called Alan Etherington's, who used his parents' radio as an amplifier.

Taylor reminisced about those formative days in *The Rolling Stones Book*: 'I first knew old Mick at Dartford Grammar School when we were both eleven years old. I got to know Keith Richard at Sidcup Art School [where he was known as 'Ricky'] about four years later . . . Keith had pretty long hair when I first met him and he was always telling people about how crazy he was about rhythm 'n' blues. Even at fifteen he could play all Chuck Berry's solos. His first electric guitar was a Spanish Rosetti. It cost about ten quid. His amplifier was obviously home-made.'

In 1995, a senior civil servant from Dartford talked to *Record Collector* about a rather special reel-to-reel tape in his possession. It featured his former classmate at Dartford Grammar School, Mick Jagger, plus his mate Keith Richards, jamming with a floating group of like-minded chums in someone's bedroom sometime in late '61.

Mick and Keith would get together with fellow ex-grammar school blues aficionados Taylor, Etherington and Bob Beckwith, and plough through their favourite blues and rock 'n' roll tunes. At the time they called themselves Little Boy Blue and the Blue Boys. Apart from Keith, they'd gravitated towards each other while at school, bonded in a kind of subterranean blues appreciation society.

Keith joined up after his train meeting with Mick, in late October '61. They talked about music for about twenty minutes and arranged to meet up to play records and jam.

Keith's mum, Doris, recalled that day in the Record Collector piece: 'I remember the night Keith came in from art school and told me he'd met Mick at the station that morning. He was really excited about that meeting. He'd been playing guitar for ages, but always on his own. He was too shy to join in with anybody else, although Dick Taylor had often asked him.'

The guy with the tape, who wished to remain anonymous, agreed: 'He struck me as an introvert when I first met him. He seemed more interested in his guitar than anything else.'

The serious jamming started in November of that year, although the lads didn't initially think of taking it further. They thought they were the only blues fans in the world.

'Keith sounded great,' recalled Dick Taylor, 'but he wasn't flash. When he came in, you could feel something holding the band together.'

The anonymous friend took his parents' tape recorder and captured two of the sessions, which were probably recorded in Mick's bedroom. *Record Collector's* Peter Doggett heard the tape – 'the earliest existing record of the sound that revolutionised sixties rock' – and described it as rough and ready, but 'utterly compelling ... what never changes is the reckless sense of wonder and adventure.'

The list of tracks is fascinating, especially as several of the tunes later made it onto Stones albums, mainly the Chuck Berry covers: 'Around And Around', 'Little Queenie', 'Down The Road Apiece' and 'Beautiful Delilah', which can be found on various bootlegs. They also have a go at Ritchie Valens' 'La Bamba', Billy Boy Arnold's 'I Ain't Got You' and Elvis Presley's 'You're Right, I'm Left, She's Gone'.

The last one must have come from Keith, who's been quoted as saying his favourite guitar solo of all time is Scotty Moore's killer salvo in the middle. There are also a couple of obscure blues songs and some of the numbers are played twice.

As confirmed by Bill Wyman, the tape was eventually auctioned at Christie's on 25 May, 1995. It went for £55,250 to an anonymous buyer – who turned out to be one M. P. Jagger.

Come On

After the initial exposure, it's no wonder Keith was obsessive enough to sit in his bedroom and master what was a new concept back then. Up until the early sixties, country, blues and rock 'n' roll had all existed in different boxes. Now Keith was slinging it all into his emergent style, marrying roots music with the world of white pop. Even in those early days, Keith didn't see musical barriers as relevant.

'R&B is a bit of a giggle,' he would say in '64. 'It's hard to say what R&B is. So many people say Chuck Berry is R&B, then he says he is rock 'n' roll, so where do you go from there? Still, I don't mind what you call it at the moment and for the next ten years. I'm happy.'

On the Scene with Rhythm & Blues was one of the magazines which appeared in the wake of the R&B boom kickstarted by the Stones around '64. It endeavoured to explain this new phenomenon, which sprang from the American race market into the clubs and homes of musically malcontent British youth:

'Two years ago, Rhythm-and-Blues was something you heard on rather kooky imported discs. A year ago, two London clubs featured it once a week, and the people who went there kidded you that they were the only ones in the whole world who knew anything about it. Today, it's rivalling beat music as the most pop thing on the pop scene.

'R&B is fab.

'It's gear.

'It's the greatest; it's a gas; it's way-out and with-it.

'But what is it? Simple, really. Rhythm-and-Blues is exactly what it says it is: the Blues, with rhythm – more exactly a rhythm section or, in today's talk, The Beat, added.

'Time was, pre-Trad, before Hipsters and Squares, before the Cool Cats had jumped, when the world was divided, not into Mods and Rockers but into Jazzers and Boppers, R&B was a kind of music you only heard in America – mainly in the big cities: New York, Chicago, Detroit and on the West Coast. You heard it in the

On a mission: the Glimmer Twins, around 1963.

coloured clubs; you could buy it on so-called "race" records – discs made specially for the Negro market only. It was a mixture of the blues, the ballads and laments of the poverty-stricken country Negroes, and the gutty, driving music their cousins danced and jived to. It swung like a bomb, because Negro always does. And it was usually played on harmonicas, guitars and drums. This was for a very practical reason: the people who played it had very little money – and harmonicas are cheap, guitars are sometimes cheap, and drums can be improvised from almost anything.'

The feature goes on to talk about Bill Haley and the dawn of rock 'n' roll, before diving into such seminal names as Muddy, John Lee Hooker, Jimmy Witherspoon, Sonny Terry and Brownie McGhee, as well as Ray Charles and the pre-army Elvis. It mentions Lonnie Donegan and the short-lived skiffle craze, which was derived from mating strains of blues and country, before alighting on the contemporary R&B boom with Chuck, Bo, Little Richard and Motown stars like Marvin Gaye and the Miracles.

Enter Alexis Korner, who's since become known as 'the father of British blues'. Bill Wyman reckons that 'without Alexis, it is arguable that there would be no Rolling Stones.' Alexis would look after, and often play with, visiting American artists like Big Bill Broonzy, Memphis Slim, Champion Jack Dupree, Roosevelt Sykes and Little Brother Montgomery. He started Blues Incorporated – initially as a duo with harmonica wiz Cyril Davies – around '53. They started off by playing a blues section during sets by Chris Barber and his Jazz Band, who were riding the 'trad' wave hitting the shore at the time.

'Trad jazz was the big pop music here,' said Alexis in an interview reproduced in David Daltons's book. 'Chris Barber was the big trad jazz band. Chris used us as an electric rhythm and blues unit within the band. He also started bringing over electric blues players from the States: Otis Spann, John Lee Hooker, Muddy, people like that. And was cutting his throat and killing the trad jazz scene by having this R&B unit within the band. He knew exactly what he was doing, fostering the thing that was going to come next in music.'

Then Blues Incorporated expanded and struck out on their own. When they needed somewhere to play, Alexis felt the best way would be to start his own club. The Ealing Jazz Club was opened by Korner in a basement on Ealing Broadway, west London, in March 1962. It rapidly caught on, and within four weeks was cramming in its 200 capacity.

Keith and Mick first checked out the club on 7 April. Headlining were Blues Incorporated, who were becoming the pivotal outfit in the growing UK blues movement and its first electric exponents. Their drummer was Charlie Watts, then a commercial designer, already sporting a dapper dress sense.

Keith later said he felt at home at the place: 'Heavy atmosphere. Workers and art students, kids who couldn't make the ballrooms with supposedly long hair then. Forget it, you couldn't go into those places. You gravitated to places where you wouldn't get hassled.' The small, smoky basement packed with blues aficionados thrilled Keith to the bone. The crowd included like-minded individuals like Ronnie Wood and Eric Clapton, plus a horde of other enthusiasts who would go on to make up the British R&B movement.

Also appearing was a blonde kid from Cheltenham, who called himself Elmo Lewis and played wicked slide guitar for singer P. P. Pond, later to be known as Paul Jones of Manfred Mann. Elmo's real name was Brian Jones.

Much later, Keith was reported as saying: 'As I saw Brian Jones playing I said, "What the fuck? Playing bar slide guitar!" We get into Brian Jones after he finishes "Dust My Blues". He's really fantastic and a gas . . . He's been doin' the same as we've been doin' . . . thinkin' he was the only cat in the world who was doin' it.'

Brian's band included a fierce boogie-woogie piano player called Ian Stewart. Keith met the man who would become one of the most important figures in his life when he started checking out Brian's gigs around Soho with Mick. 'He blew my mind, when he started to play,' he later reminisced. 'I never heard a white piano like that before.'

Bill Wyman begins his *Rolling with the Stones* book by acclaiming Lewis Brian Hopkin Jones: '. . . we were his brainchild and it was Brian who named us. He was the driving force behind the band in the early days. Brian was the original Rolling Stone.'

Indeed. Brian was living the life of a Rolling Stone well before the group's rise to infamy. But he was born in the sedate Gloucestershire town of Cheltenham into a middle-class family on 28 February, 1942. Like Keith, he had Welsh blood – his parents both met and married in their native Wales.

Around the same time that he started school, Brian contracted croup, which left him suffering from asthma attacks for the rest of his life. Good at music lessons, he passed his eleven-plus and went to Cheltenham Grammar School. Brian got his first guitar for his seventeenth birthday in '59. The same year saw him father an illegitimate baby boy with a fourteen-year-old schoolgirl, who had him adopted.

At this time Brian was frequenting the London jazz clubs regularly, but still found time to father another child by a one-night stand in Guildford. He drifted in and out of work and, when he was nearly nineteen, fathered a third child with girlfriend Pat Andrews. Brian continued to drift in and out of jobs and tried hitchhiking around Europe. His life was changed on the night in 1961 when he went to see Chris Barber's jazz band performing at Cheltenham Town Hall. Or rather, Alexis Korner's blues section in the middle. He talked to Alexis afterwards, quizzing him about the blues, then tracked down all the records by Elmore James and Robert Johnson he could find, and diligently set about learning how to play the blues.

Brian had met Paul Pond (later Paul Jones) while stopping over in Oxford, and the pair would regularly frequent Korner's new club in Ealing. By early '62, Brian would sit in with the house band, Blues Incorporated, eventually getting his own spot with Paul and piano player Ian Stewart.

After that night of 7 April, Brian was on Keith and Mick's 'Most Wanted' list, along with Charlie Watts and 'Stu'. In the end, they would effectively end up joining Brian's band which, in turn, would become the Rolling Stones.

The Birth Of The Stones

Before the end of April, Mick and Keith, along with Alexis and Charlie, got up for a version of 'Around And Around' at the Ealing Jazz Club. They received polite applause, but also got a few bemused looks when Keith flew into his patent

Men in uniform: one of the earliest promotional shots of the Rolling Stones. From left: Charlie Watts, Bill Wyman, Mick Jagger, Brian Jones, Keith Richards.

Chuck Berry onslaught. Basically, they were inflicting a style of music on the jazz and blues buffs that was more associated with teddy boys.

To some of the purists, who were quite precious about 'their music', this was like farting in church. The blunt Cyril Davies was downright hostile. Apparently, even Alexis was a trifle bemused by Keith's raunchy onslaught, and tried to restrict his jam session appearances. At the same time, he was trying his best to seduce Mick into expanding his guest role in Blues Incorporated. Keith, who didn't particularly like Blues Incorporated, reckons that Alexis simply wasn't into rock 'n' roll.

Ironically, the future Stones had caused ructions in the movement that supposedly spawned them. This intolerance of Keith's rock 'n' roll leanings goes against Alexis's later comment that, 'The fact that audiences don't want to hear the kind of music you're playing, doesn't mean they're right and you're wrong.' It was also quite surprising when he said, 'I felt a very strong sense of responsibility towards the cats [Mick, Keith and Brian] because they were ten or fifteen years younger than I. I considered that my job was to look after the cats so they could start properly. After that, it's their own business. You've got to try and point them in the right direction and let them run, because they're gonna run faster than you anyway.'

Whatever was said in generous hindsight, it's apparent from most recollections that Korner did indeed cast the first Stone. But it wasn't Keith – although, fastforward about ten years, and you have Keith guesting on an Alexis Korner solo album, playing a raucous version of 'Jumpin' Jack Flash'.

Harold Pendleton of the Marquee Club checked out Ealing and offered Alexis a regular Thursday night spot at his club, which was then situated in Oxford Street.

This also built up into a packed sardines situation, with Blues Incorporated as house regulars.

Mick sent Korner a tape of Little Boy and the Blue Boys playing 'Around And Around', 'La Bamba', 'Reelin' And Rockin'' and 'Bright Lights Big City'. Shortly afterwards, Brian Jones, his guitarist Geoff Bradford and Ian Stewart ended up joining forces with Keith, Mick and Dick. They still didn't have a proper drummer. They tried Mick Avory – later of the Kinks – at one point, but Keith thought he was terrible. Bradford wasn't into rock 'n' roll and left, while Mick had his stint with Blues Incorporated.

They would play every week at the Marquee. Twice a week, the fledgling Stones would rehearse above the Bricklayers Arms pub in Broadwick Street, Soho. While Mick moonlighted with Alexis, Keith found himself playing a lot more with Brian. This first came about when Keith ventured to the pub one evening to meet up with Ian Stewart and Brian. He was immediately smitten by Stu's boogie-woogie piano expertise. Keith told me in mid-'80 of how he sneaked into the rehearsal room a few minutes before Stu knew he was there: 'He was just sitting there playing, wearing little black leather shorts. Oblivious. I was already nervous because I was the Chuck Berry guy.' To Keith, Stu gave the outward impression of being a Cyril Davies-type – blunt, to the point, and maybe downright aggressive if he didn't like something.

'He was just sitting there playing but every now and again he'd stand up and look out of the window. Then he'd [Keith stands up and leans by the window of the Stones' office, while lifting a cocked forearm] go, "Phwoaar! Look at that!" Ha ha ha! It was the strippers down in the street going from job to job! Also, his bike was parked over the road and he kept checking on that.'

Regular rehearsals with Brian and Stu started soon after. Mick was still dividing his time between the two groups, but Keith and Brian found their guitars sparking into a formidable double-barrelled clash of the blues.

In October '62, it was time for Keith to leave the nest. He knew his ambitions and vocation were far from what his hard-working father envisaged for his son. 'I never consciously thought about leaving Dartford, but the minute I got out I had pretty strong instincts that I'd never go back,' he's said.

So Keith, Mick and Brian moved into the now infamous 102 Edith Grove, Chelsea. It might be fashionable now, but back then this was the wrong end of the Kings Road. They were broke and, apart from the all-important record player, the tiny space was as spartan and grubby as can be. Dare to sit in a chair and the odds were it would collapse. And they had to take in boarders to pay the rent. There was just one light bulb, a shared toilet and only their parents' food parcels, plus Mick's college grant, to survive on. Doris later reckoned it cost her about a pound a day to keep Keith going.

'Looking back on it all, I suppose we can really see the funny side of it now,' recalled Keith in the November '64 *Rolling Stones Book*. 'We can boost this so-called "home" of ours into calling it a haven of rhythm 'n' blues, or something. But times really were bad.'

'You wouldn't have liked to have fucking lived there,' said Keith in the late eighties, with an unsanitised memory. 'It was disgusting. Mould growing on the walls and no-one was ever going to clean the joint up. We lived on the second floor.' He's often told of how he used to mike up the communal toilet and record people: 'I had these amazing tapes of people on the john which I'd play the next day. It's incredible what people do while they're taking a crap. It was the funniest . . . you'd get people muttering, "Whoah, I need that. Ooaah! Just made it! Mmmm! Larvely!" Ah, youthful high jinx.'

When not wiring up the crapper, Keith and Brian would sit around all day playing their guitars and listening to Muddy Waters. With Mick at college, feeling a bit left out, they'd painstakingly try and work out exactly how Muddy, Robert Johnson and Chuck did it – '. . . just trying to figure out how in the hell these guys from Chicago got this beautiful sound and interplay,' while unaware of the sometimes unique tunings and recording techniques employed.

This relentless focus on perfecting guitar styles was what spawned Keith's mission to mesh twin guitars into a rhythmically lethal whole. 'The Rolling Stones are a two-guitar band,' would later be his credo, and those sessions with Brian did more to originate that immortal Stones sound than anything else. Keith, who admired Brian for having packed so much into his life, turned him on to Chuck Berry and Jimmy Reed. Brian retaliated with Robert Johnson, a life-changing experience for Keith.

Whereas Muddy, Chuck and Bo are usually held up as the pivotal influences on Keith and the fledgling Stones, there is one name who played more part in the group sound than anyone. Jimmy Reed had a unique twin guitar sound, which Keith tried to emulate with Brian in the early days and would finally nail down in the seventies with Ronnie Wood. And his drummer, Earl Phillips, had the jazzman's swing that inspired Charlie Watts to give the Stones their unique downstairs funk.

Reed hailed from Mississippi and moved to Chicago in 1950. His style is low-slung, understated and shot through with funk. Albums like his seminal *Rockin' With Reed* hum with that same buzz that you get from the Stones. They must have read the sleevenotes of *Rockin' With Reed*: '. . . the drums are loud, the bass is whamming, the harmonica is trying to blow everybody out of the studio, and the guitar is playing that old boogie-woogie . . . On top of all this, Jimmy Reed is singing at the top of his voice. Really now, nobody's putting on here. These folks are playing real blues, and they don't care who knows it.'

Stuff like that gave the Stones the attitude and motivation to try to recreate the electric, sex-charged atmosphere of the American blues clubs. This was an impossibly alien concept back in 1963, but it struck a universal chord situated well below the belt. The Stones' earliest studio forays are uncannily closer to the slinky, echoey ambience of Jimmy Reed than anyone else.

In *According to the Rolling Stones*, Keith talked about the way Brian and he built on Reed's twin-guitar firepower in the freezing winter of '62-'63: 'The two-guitar thing on Jimmy's records is so laid out, so stark and beautifully consistent . . . From there we moved on to Little Walter and Louis and David Myers, who were members of his backing band – and then, of course, the Muddy Waters stuff along with Jimmy Rogers, Howlin' Wolf and Hubert Sumlin. We listened to the team work, trying to work out what was going on those records: how you could play together with two guitars and make it sound like four or five.'

From left: Mick, Brian and Keith perform 'Come On' on Ready Steady Go *in 1963.*

Shortly after Keith moved out, Doris split up with Bert. Keith wouldn't see his father again for another twenty years. She eventually remarried – a bloke called Bill Richards, who Keith didn't take to, shared surname or not. (According to Keith, Richards was a common name around those parts.)

On 12 July, Blues Incorporated were booked to record a BBC radio session for *Jazz Club*, which meant they couldn't do their regular Thursday night spot at the Marquee. They also couldn't afford to pay Mick, and asked if his other band would fill in. With Long John Baldry as the headline act, they were booked to support. Needing a name quickly, they came up with the Rolling Stones – from Muddy's 'Rollin' Stone' blues.

Jazz News carried the first Stones news story: 'Mick Jagger, R&B vocalist, is taking a rhythm and blues group into the Marquee tomorrow night, while Blues Inc is doing its Jazz Club gig. Called "the Rolling Stones" ("I hope they don't think we're a rock 'n' roll outfit," says Mick), the lineup is Jagger (vocal), Keith Richards, Elmo Lewis (guitars), Dick Taylor (bass) and Mick Avery [sic] (drums).'

The set list for the first ever Stones gig included 'Honey What's Wrong?', 'Confessin' The Blues', 'Kansas City', 'Bright Lights Big City', 'Dust My Broom', 'Down The Road Apiece', 'I'm A Hoochie Coochie Man', 'Ride 'Em On Down', 'Back In The USA', 'Big Boss Man', 'Bad Boy', 'I Ain't Got You' and 'Tell Me That You Love Me'. Apart from a much-needed twenty quid, the band were granted further dates by Alexis at the Marquee and Ealing Jazz Club.

In August Mick Avory departed, to be replaced by Tony Chapman. In September Dick Taylor also left, to continue his studies at the Royal College of Art. Of course, he must have inflicted some boot-prints on his own buttocks later on, but also went on to enjoy some success with the Pretty Things – a raucous

R&B ensemble who once boasted longer hair than the Stones! Keith and Brian were still trying to get the academic Mick to throw in his full lot with the Stones, but Brian's insecure inter-band power struggles were already coming to the fore. At this time though, Keith was his best mate, and Brian considered himself the undisputed leader of the Rolling Stones.

In October the Stones went into the studio for the first time, recording three tracks at Curly Clayton Sound Studio. They did 'Soon Forgotten', 'You Can't Judge A Book (By Looking At The Cover)' and 'Close Together'. But they still needed a bass player, and placed an ad in Melody Maker. This was answered by Bill Perks from Beckenham, who was immediately at an advantage as he owned an amp. After some rehearsals at their new spot at Chelsea's Wetherby Arms, Bill was in – with the adopted surname of Wyman. Still no suitable drummer though. Tony Chapman came and went, while a guy called Steve Harris rehearsed with them but basically didn't have the time.

They still wanted Charlie Watts, who by then had left Blues Incorporated because he only wanted to play at weekends, and was unhappy in a group called Blues By Five. Finally, after much pestering, he agreed to join the Rolling Stones, who were now also playing regular gigs at the Flamingo in Wardour Street. 'I liked their spirit and I was getting very involved with rhythm 'n' blues,' remembered Charlie. 'So I said, OK, yes, I'd join. Lots of my friends thought I'd gone raving mad.'

Through the freezing winter of '62, the Stones encountered hostility and opposition from the jazz scene's old guard. They were seen as no-hope upstarts and, when they'd been granted a spot at the Marquee, were publicly slagged off by a drunken top-of-the-bill Cyril Davies. Marquee boss Harold Pendleton hated the Stones and loved it when Davies told them to fuck off. It got Keith's goat to the extent that he swung his guitar at Pendleton's chortling head. The Stones were not to play the Marquee again for several years.

At the end of January, the Rolling Stones – now in their famous early line-up of Mick, Keith, Brian, Ian, Bill and Charlie – went into IBC Recording Studios at Portland Place and cut five songs with Glyn Johns as engineer: 'Roadrunner', 'Honey, What's Wrong?', 'Diddley Daddy', 'I Wanna Be Loved' and 'Bright Lights Big City'. But no record labels were interested.

Then came a turning point. The Stones began a residency at the Crawdaddy Club, at the Station Hotel, Richmond. It was run by Giorgio Gomelsky, a documentary film-maker, who turned out to be an essential figure in the Stones' early history, coming within a hair's breadth of being their manager. Gomelsky was a larger-than-life figure of Russian and French parentage, who'd hitchhiked around the world and discovered the blues while staying in Chicago. He first caught the Stones at a pub in Sutton, Surrey and tried them out at the Crawdaddy after his regular outfit didn't show one week. The door money was split between himself and the band – on the first night, the six-piece Stones made £2 each.

The club was actually a pub's back room. No stage, two lights – one red, one blue. Gomelsky remembers how he'd encourage the crowd to dance and they would 'go berserk' as the Stones hammered out a hypnotic 'tribal ritual' for twenty minutes at a time. All this and no violence, at a time of rising youth gang warfare.

The weekly sessions were a growing success, with each gig more jammed than the week before. The Stones were honing their set, working in the new line-up and spreading shockwaves through London's underground rhythm and blues scene. Giorgio described in broken English the impact to David Dalton: 'The beginning of that whole real Stones thing, that Crawdaddy thing, was that audience participation, opening that scene between the band and the audience . . . I cannot tell you the excitement the place was in those months . . . The energy was incredible. It gave everybody courage for years and years and years.'

Gomelsky also spoke about Keith's trademark killer rhythm guitar, and how it made its mark at those first gigs: 'They did Jimmy Reed really well . . . it's the timing, the tempo, the beat is very important: it's got to be fast/slow . . . To keep the tension is not easy, and Keith knew that inside out . . . Keith is not a great guitar player by any stretch of the imagination, but he is a great rhythm guitar player because he always gets on the right feel . . . And that's what it's all about, the magic of a song working or a piece of music working.'

On 21 April, the Beatles went to check the Stones out at the Crawdaddy, after Giorgio had persuaded them to see this new group. They turned up for the second set, and afterwards went back to the Edith Grove flat, where the two groups spent the night playing records and talking.

The buzz continued to spread. A week after the Beatles' visit, nineteen-year-old publicist Andrew Oldham and agent Eric Easton went to see them, on the advice of *New Musical Express* editor Peter Jones. The pair offered a management contract on the spot, which was duly accepted, then set up Impact Sound to manage the Stones and produce their records. Within days Oldham had secured a record contract with Decca, through Dick Rowe – the man doomed to be known as the record executive who turned down the Beatles.

Giorgio Gomelsky himself would be regarded as the guy who let the Stones slip through his fingers. Not being overly ambitious or familiar with business tactics, he only had a handshake arrangement with the Stones. Andrew Oldham got their signatures before he even knew what was going on.

'I was probably 48 hours ahead of the rest of the business in getting there,' recalled Oldham in an *NME* interview. 'But that's the way God planned it.' He was asked what excited him about the Stones. 'Music. Sex. The fact that in just a few months the country would need an opposite to what the Beatles were doing. The Stones were gonna be that opposite . . . In the early days, the way the media was running was that you could invite the Beatles in for tea, but you couldn't invite the Stones.'

If Brian Epstein was often referred to as 'the fifth Beatle', then Oldham was undoubtedly the seventh Stone – after Ian Stewart. But one initial Oldham move was to relegate Stu to the post of road manager. Six band members seemed too many, and he just didn't have the right look with his conventional haircut. There are many varying opinions on this but, although Stu put on a brave face, it obviously hurt him deeply until the very end. He would continue to play piano for the Stones – but from the side of the stage, or on record. In reality, Stu never left. In spirit, he still hasn't.

'If I'd been Stu I'd have said, "Fuck it, fuck you,"' said Keith. 'But he stayed on to be our roadie, which I think is incredible, so big-hearted.'

Another move was getting Keith to drop the 's' from his surname. Keith still talks about Loog Oldham with affection and they keep in touch, even though he ceased to be the Stones' manager in '67. He was one of the first 'super-managers', who found themselves almost as well-known as the band. When we were talking about the Sex Pistols once, Keith described their svengali, Malcolm McLaren, as 'a half-assed Andrew Oldham'. And it's true that Oldham – who worked as a music biz press agent in the early sixties and did the PR for the first two Beatles singles – did an amazing job of boosting the Stones' anti-Beatle bad-boy image. He littered the papers with scams, bullshit and incidents calculated to spark outrage in the older generation, and rebellious devotion in the young. In retrospect, my own adolescent Stones obsession during those vital, formative years was proabably a lot to do with Oldham.

Many people believe he transformed and moulded the Stones into the anti-establishment insurrectionists they became. Not entirely true. All of that was there already, albeit mainly in the forms of Keith and Brian. Oldham himself even denied it, in a June '78 interview with US fanzine *Trouser Press*:

'Everything was pretty much a two-way street. We had our own little fantasies that we would run in-between each other – this or that shtick or the *Clockwork Orange* thing – but if you're asking me if I created the whole image, the answer is "no". Those things were us rehearsing between each other and hyping each other up. The only time I changed them was when I got them to wear a particular costume for a particular television show like *Thank Your Lucky Stars*.'

After the Decca deal was signed, Oldham took the band into the studio with himself in the producer's chair – even though he'd never produced a record in his life. They went into Olympic Studios, with a £40 budget at £6 an hour, and cut Chuck Berry's 'Come On' and Willie Dixon's 'I Wanna Be Loved'.

Andrew described the session in the Stones monthly, 'We're all very tense. This was understandable because, come what may, the disc had to be brought out in a hurry. And it's never good to make records in a rush, feeling that you've got to beat the clock . . . So we all felt a bit of panic through that three-hour session. We got both sides in the can but didn't have time to do anything else. I remember we kept rushing out to have a drink in an effort to keep the nerves down. Incidentally, all the Stones had got over all their personnel changes. This was the lineup as it is today . . . Mick, Brian, Bill Wyman, Charlie Watts, Keith Richards. Ian Stewart was there but he didn't play.

'Right! So that was the picture. Quite honestly we thought the song was a bit weak to put out as an A side. Somehow it wasn't melodic enough . . . and we had this feeling that people wouldn't want to buy it. 'Course it was never a particularly big hit . . . the trouble was clearly about material. I knew these boys could make the grade on the strength of their sound, but we spent hour after hour looking for the right sort of song for them. And when the doubts started being expressed about "Come On" . . . well, you can imagine the atmosphere.'

Oldham paints a picture of a group that had it all sewn up live, but were scuppered in their initial attempt to get it down in the big bad studio. They were nervous and, without a crowd to feed on, not cooking with their usual gas. 'Nobody really had a go at me but it was obvious they felt there was still something wrong. Either the actual song, or the finished product.'

Then Decca didn't like the Olympic tracks, so the group duly recut them at the label's own West Hampstead studio. 'It was hopeless in those studios,' recalled Oldham. 'The boys didn't enjoy the atmosphere, I couldn't do anything . . . it just wasn't worth it. Recording the Stones needs a very special recording technique . . . and it wasn't there.'

By now the press were starting to take notice. Giorgio invited down *Record Mirror*'s Norman Jopling, who wrote a good review in the 11 May issue: 'At the Station Hotel, Kew Road, the hip kids threw themselves about to the new "jungle music" like they never did in the more refined days of trad. And the combo they writhe and twist to is called the Rolling Stones . . . Three months ago only 50 people turned up to see the group. Now promoter Gomelski has to close the doors at an early hour with over 500 fans crowding the hall.'

'Come On' was released on 7 June and got to number twenty in the charts. The Stones made their first TV appearance on the popular Saturday teatime show *Thank Your Lucky Stars* on the day of release. I remember it well – your nine-year-old author was perched on a sofa, watching the procession of bland pop idols of the time with a big yawn. Then these five geezers materialised. They might have been sporting matching velvet-collared jackets and black trousers with ties, but their hair was longer than any I'd seen before, plus they rocked. It was short, sharp and loaded with attitude. I knew then this group was different from the rest. 'I think I like this,' I remarked. My dad groaned. It was the start of a very long and beautiful obsession.

The jackets were the 'costume' Oldham referred to. 'The guy who did *Thank Your Lucky Stars* was some 50 year old guy who was, as we say in England, educated in the RAF. There was no way he was going to have them on . . . if it didn't look like they had made some effort to show their appreciation . . . Gradually, over the course of a few shows, the costumes disappeared anyway, but faced with the prospect of either wearing the costume or not getting on they went and did it.'

Keith – who, in particular, couldn't be arsed with the uniform – used the incident to illustrate how the Stones had been their own men even before Oldham came in. 'It's funny . . . people think Oldham made the image, but he tried to tidy us up . . . . There are photographs of us in suits he put us in, those dogtooth checked suits with the black velvet collars . . . the press picked up on us only when we'd personally got rid of those dogtooth jackets and the Lord John shirts. It was only then that Andrew suddenly realised the full consequences of it all and got fully behind it.'

Record Mirror was on the case again, describing the single as 'catchy, punchy and commercial', while observing 'it's not the fanatical R&B sound that audiences wait hours to hear.' They were echoing the popular opinion that the Stones had tailored their sound for the single, and hadn't captured the live excitement that was making their name. Or, as Andrew Oldham put it, 'I don't think they were actually compromising. I think they thought the record sucked, which it did.' In fact, the main reason the group covered 'Come On' was that the song hadn't been released in the UK, so no-one else had done it already.

As Keith said in '89: 'As a first record we knew that something like "Come On" was needed to start with. We had no intention of that leading the way to what we were going to do next. We did "Come On" because it was the most commercial sound we were capable of making at the time. And the song had some

The Rolling Stones on HMS Discovery, London Embankment, 1963.

kind of affinity to what we were used to doing.' They wouldn't play it as part of their live R&B onslaught, though. 'It was too embrassing, man.'

As the weeks rolled on, 'Come On' remained in the charts and the Stones found themselves gigging more regularly. If it hadn't exactly set the world on fire, the press stories and photos were starting to cause a stir – as was their hair and non-uniform visual image. As Oldham put it, 'That record filtered in, hung around . . . and had the whole business waiting anxiously to get the next sample of Rolling Stones talent.' At the end of September, the Stones embarked on a 30-date UK tour, supporting the Everly Brothers and their hero Bo Diddley on his UK debut. Little Richard was also later drafted in to hot up ticket sales.

Oldham went into PR overdrive. As *The Rolling Stones Book* said, 'Andrew laid it on pretty thick. He told anecdotes about the boys, about their musical wayoutness, about their determination to wear any old clothes apart from the usual mohair suits, about the theory that the day they started using after-shave lotion they'd be finished. Word got round fast about "those crazy Rolling Stones". They were tagged "rebels", which suited the fans fine. The fans were fed up with the holier-than-thou, well-scrubbed, boy-next-door look of so many popsters. It was obvious that the Stones couldn't care less about the usual pop routine – and that gave them an air of not knowing what was going to happen next.

'Result: the fans were very anxious to get tickets for the boys on tour.'
In August, the *New Musical Express* carried its first ever story about the Stones when 'Come On' entered the charts. Keith is described as 'nineteen, Dartford-born, and a former post office worker [though when Keith lived this temporary

workaday existence is unclear – never having had a fulltime job between art college and the formation of the Stones]. He collects Chuck Berry and Jimmy Reed records and is saving up to buy a houseboat on the Thames.'

September also saw the boys moving out of the rapidly-degenerating Edith Grove flat. Oldham found Mick and Keith a better place in Mapesbury Road, Brondesbury, north London. Brian went off to live with the parents of a girlfriend in Windsor, Berkshire. Soon after, Andrew moved in with Keith and Mick, and the balance of power in the Stones now fell firmly toward Oldham, Jagger and Richard(s). Brian was no longer the leader, while his own original band colleague, Ian Stewart, was no longer in the Stones. With Brian's fragile personality, things could only get worse for him as they got better for everybody else.

It was also around this time that Oldham introduced Keith to his girlfriend Sheila Klein's best friend at a party. Linda Keith was a glamorous seventeen-year-old brunette from West Hampstead. Working as an assistant on *Vogue* magazine, she was just about to start a modelling career. Oldham insists that she was Keith's first girlfriend, and that he'd played matchmaker because, at nineteen, 'I thought it was time that Keith went out with something other than his guitar.'

But it was this quality that endeared the reticent rock 'n' roller to Linda. Many years after their relationship had played out, she'd look back on him as 'shy, introverted, very appealing, lacking in confidence,' explaining, 'I liked the fact that he was so involved with music, that it was such a prevailing part of his and my life.'

There was still the problem of the next single. Keith and Mick were not writing seriously yet, but were very wary of doing another cover version. Ironically, the answer came from the Stones' biggest rivals – the Beatles. Back to Peter Jones:

'So . . . Andrew happened to be walking along Jermyn Street, near London's Piccadilly Circus. Hands in pockets, quick striding, brow furrowed as he tried to recall the melody line of a song which might be the answer. And a taxi pulled up by the traffic lights. Inside, Paul McCartney and John Lennon, no less. They rammed down the window and yelled to their erstwhile publicist. "Get in, Andy!", they roared. "We've got something to tell you." Andrew leapt in. The Beatles had been to a Variety Club of Great Britain lunch and had a bit of time to kill before they had to start work again.

'"We've got some numbers which might be right for the Stones," they said. Andrew brightened up. He knew that the Beatles had heard the Stones work; knew for sure that they were pretty keen on the sounds created by the boys from the South. "What's it called?" he asked. Said the Beatles: "'I Wanna Be Your Man'". They went on to say that they thought it was the right kind of song, but wondered if the Stones would mind using material written by a "rival group". Said Andrew: "If it's right for the boys, I couldn't care less if it was written for Dorothy Squires. Let's have a listen . . ."'

Andrew took John and Paul to Ken Colyer's club, where the Stones were running through likely candidates for the next single. They ran through the new song, quickly whipped up a middle eight, and immediately the grateful Stones knew they were onto a winner. 'Looked as if our problems were over,' reflected a relieved Oldham. He was right. This time the recording session went fine, with the band more relaxed and on a buzz to be doing a Beatles song written just for them.

On 1 November, the Stones released their version of 'I Wanna Be Your Man'. Now this was more like it. A storming R&B sneer. Noisy, raucous and frenetic, with Mick's voice rasping and Keith delivering a first taste of his trademark stinging economy on guitar.

Meanwhile, the flip side's 'Stoned' was a nightclub vamp co-written by the band, nicked from Booker T and the MGs' 'Green Onions' according to Keith. It was completely instrumental, apart from Mick's intoning of the title and cries of 'outta my mind'. (On my copy the label says 'Stones' instead of 'Stoned' – apparently a rare misprint pressing.)

Keith (foreground), Mick and Brian in the studio, with Andrew Loog Oldham wearing his Phil Spector shades.

The track is notable as the first Stones-credited composition to make it to vinyl – even if it was a jam knocked up in half an hour. Although the six group members – including Stu – got an equal share of the songwriting royalties, the tune was credited to 'Nanker-Phelge'. This was the birth of Mick and Keith's famous first pseudonym, which cropped up a few times in the early years. A 'nanker' was the ugly face favoured by the group when they pulled their eyes down and pushed their noses up with outspread fingers, while 'Phelge' was the name of a nerdy acquaintance.

The single became the Stones' first top ten hit, reaching number nine and staying in the chart for thirteen weeks – at around the same time that Chuck Berry was in the top ten with 'Memphis, Tennessee'. So it was *Thank Your Lucky Stars* time again, but ten times better than their rather stilted debut.

They dumped the checked uniforms for leather waistcoats and their hair was longer. Most of all, though, it had the impact and sheer wildness that their live show was reputed to give out. Now I was well and truly a convert. To my nine-year-old mind, this was how to look, how to behave, and how to sound. There was a world of possibility and fun that Keith was already passing on.

In the 27 December issue of *NME*, Richard Green wrote, 'The Rolling Stones create a sound so exciting and gripping that few other groups can come within shouting distance of it.' The Stones were also voted sixth best British Vocal Group in the annual *NME* readers' poll.

Another of Andrew Oldham's major achievements was getting Mick and Keith to sit down and write songs. 'Oh yeah, from the word go,' he later recalled. 'Not only because you could see how self-contained the Beatles were, but because a lot of the things that I'd been following that were coming from America were written by established songwriters like Goffin-King, Sedaka, Pomus and Shuman and Lieber and Stoller. That was reality. The record companies were coming saying things like, "This one's terrific for Cliff Richard." That was "Blue Turns To Grey", which was an English single and a hit for him before the Stones did it. "Heart Of Stone" was the first song Mick and Keith wrote that we figured was too good to give to someone else. Anyway they wanted to write. It didn't take much urging.'

But Keith has always credited Oldham, as he told me. 'It had never occurred to me. I thought that was something else, like being a novelist or a computer operator. It was a completely different field, that I hadn't thought of. I just thought of myself as a guitar player.

'To me, and to Mick at the same time, writing a song was as different as someone who makes a saddle for a horse and someone who puts the shoes on it. It's a different gig. I play 'em, you write 'em. We explained this to Andrew and he just locked us in a kitchen for a day and said, when you come out, make sure you come out with a song. So we sat down and wrote "As Tears Go By", which went on to be a number one when Marianne Faithfull sang it. So we thought, yeah, it can be done. 'Cos at the time that was the sort of song we'd never play. We were trying to write "Hoochie Coochie Man" and you come out with a song that's almost like "Greensleeves"! But, it gives you the confidence to think, well if we can write one, we can write two.'

As the trailblazing year of 1963 drew to a close, the Stones finally found themselves on the ladder – even if there were still a few rungs to climb.

Looking back at the early days spent learning, practising and slogging against hardship, Keith is well aware of the fact that thousands of bedroom hopefuls over the years have learned guitar because they wanted to be him. He's always said that he wants to be remembered as someone who 'passed it on'. While the sixties saw the Stones inspire a spate of blues-influenced groups, the seventies and eighties would see a spate of 'Keef' lookalikes, a lot of whom didn't even learn how to play guitar. They just wanted to be Keef.

'Yeah, but we hear bands trying to copy us and realise that they're trying to copy us at a certain point in our career,' he told me in '83. 'Usually very early on, when what we were trying to do was sound like someone else – equally unsuccessfully! We were trying to emulate somebody. They just took the quick hop around us. If you'd seen the people that we were trying to emulate then we'd be on an equal footing.'

Keith talked about the same thing when interviewed for American fanzine *Raygun* in '94: 'I mean, it's quite flattering really. I keep seeing myself on TV. Everybody starts by imitating their heroes. For me it was Chuck Berry and Muddy Waters. I say good luck to people who want to emulate me, but they better realise what they're getting into. They better know that there's more to this than attitude. It's about music. It's about the blues. That's what sustains me.'

CHAPTER TWO

STONES FEVER 1964-66: A FAN'S EYE VIEW

Back in January 1964, I was a highly pissed-off nine-year-old Stones fan. There was a poster on my local cinema announcing the Rolling Stones as a forthcoming attraction on their first headlining tour. Not only that, but the support act was the Ronettes – the trio of New York goddesses launched by Phil Spector into the hearts of young boys everywhere. There was no way my parents were going to let me go, but it was still the first time my stomach felt the now-familiar sensation of excitement at the close proximity of the Stones. It turned out to be the only gig that Brian Jones missed, as he got lost in a heavy fog. Keith had to wing it all alone . . .

That same January saw the group release their eponymous debut EP, opening with Chuck's 'Bye Bye Johnny' and featuring a first taste of Stones balladry on their cover of Arthur Alexander's 'You Better Move On'. It topped the EP chart for 14 weeks.

21 February saw 'Not Fade Away', the Bo Diddley-fied Crickets cover that gave Keith's acoustic sound its first airing and Mick's maracas a good shake. Their first Top Ten hit, it reached number three. It also inspired me to form a makeshift Stones tribute band and mime to it at the next school Christmas party. (I was Mick, I'm afraid.)

The first album was released on 17 April and went on to top the album chart for eleven weeks. Self-titled, with no lettering on the moody sleeve, it consisted mainly of R&B and rock 'n' roll covers from the Stones' live set. Recorded in only four days over January and February, it was a raw, stunning debut. Loaded with snotty attitude, but obvious passion for the music, its impact was startling.

Covers included Willie Dixon's 'I Just Wanna Make Love To You', Jimmy Reed's 'Honest I Do', Bo Diddley's 'I Need You Baby', and Rufus Thomas's 'Walking The Dog', while Chuck Berry is represented by 'Carol' and his version of Bobby Troup's 'Route 66'. There were two Stones compositions - 'Now I've Got A Witness' – a jam credited to 'Phelge', after an old Edith Grove housemate – and wistful teen ballad 'Tell Me', which was the first Stones song to bear the credit 'Jagger-Richard'.

Between 5 and 20 June the Stones played their first US tour. They had to face empty seats and suffer insults from TV hosts like Dean Martin, as well as the police and public. The highlight was recording a bunch of tracks at Chicago's legendary Chess Studios. This was almost too much for Keith to take in – not only was it the birthplace of so many of his favourite records, but one of the first people he encountered was Muddy Waters.

'I walked in and he was painting the fucking ceiling, man!' he often claims. Other accounts state that Muddy gave them a hand unloading their gear, but it's become one of Keith's favourite stories. The following day, Chuck Berry turned up – his pleasant mood may have been on account of the Stones recording one of his songs.

One of the first tracks they recorded would become the next single. 'It's All Over Now' was a cover of a current hit by the Valentinos, written by band leader Bobby Womack. It was released on 26 June and became the Stones' first UK number one. The track was notable for the developing country slant of Keith's vocal harmonies and his blistering guitar solo.

The Chess sessions also saw the Stones record the *Five By Five* EP, plus tracks for their second album. *Five By Five* was released on 14 August and topped the EP charts for several weeks. The standout track was the controlled dynamite of Chuck's 'Around And Around'.

On their return to the UK, something happened that would cement Keith's now thriving relationship with his girlfriend, Linda Keith. Driving back from the Summer Solstice festival at Stonehenge, Linda had been caught in a crash and thrown through the windscreen.

Lying in a hospital ward, all mirrors banned so as not to distress her with the sight of her facial cuts and bruises, Linda was visited by Keith. '. . . He leant down and kissed me on my face, and – at that moment I will never forget – showed me that I wasn't a monster, and I wasn't revolting. And that was Keith.'

For all the fleshly temptation on tour that he'd occasionally give in to, it seemed these two fledgling free spirits were made for each other.

In 1964, the Stones had also started catering specifically to their teenage fan base. The Rolling Stones Fan Club – which I joined in October as member number 10019 – gave you for a mere five shillings (25p!) a membership card, semi-regular newsletters, badges, photos, biogs and the chance to buy Stones ephemera – as well as a Christmas card from the boys, drawn by Charlie Watts. The fan club kicked off big-style with the scream-agers, but seemed to run down when the age of innocence melted into psychedelia, drug busts and tabloid scandal. You couldn't very well tell a twelve-year-old that Keith had just moved house, and adopted a new dog called Ratbag, when it was all over the front page that he was awaiting trial for possessing illegal substances.

The club also published the monthly *Rolling Stones Book*, which started in June 1964. It followed the style set by the Elvis and Beatles monthlies, packed with photos and fan trivia, and edited by a different member of the group every month.

Underneath the fluffy manner in which the mag presented Keith, there are some insights that present a contrast to the walking chemical laboratory of just a few years later. (Although, as would later emerge, we weren't told everything.) Here's some highlights from Keith's page in the first issue:

Q: *Was there originally an 's' at the end of your name? [He was 'Keith Richard' until the late seventies, when he cleaned up and turned over a new Keith.]*
A: Yes . . . it just kind of got lost in the travelling.
Where were you educated?
I went first to Dartford Technical School, then on to Sidcup Art School. It was late in my schooldays that I really got fascinated by anything artistic.
You mean you'd really like to be an artist?
Well, that was my ambition. I still like to make sketches of the things that I see.

NAME ...*Christopher Neale*...

ADDRESS ...*1.2.8. Churchill Ave.,*
......*Aylesbury,*......
..........*Bucks*..........

NO ....*100.19*......

DATE OF ENROLLMENT *October 1964*

ANNABELLE SMITH,
93-97, REGENT STREET,
LONDON, W. 1.

Passport to heaven: my fan club membership card.

Seems I was quite good at design and that sort of thing, but now I've been with the Stones I'd rather play music than anything else.

Where do you live?

With Mick. We share a flat. It's pretty chaotic, but we can get together there on songwriting in the sort of atmosphere that suits us best. That's to say . . . it's chaos, but our sort of chaos.

If you hadn't joined the Stones, what would you have been?

A lay-about. But a very high-class one.

Obviously you like R&B, but what other kinds of music impress you?

Good-class pop music is fine. I also go for Country 'n' Western stuff. But it's silly to stick all music into categories. I like anything in any mood . . . just so long as it's good.

What is the greatest love in your life?

I'd say: a guitar. Some of my friends have said I'm in love with guitars and they could well be right. I think it's a wonderful instrument and it's specially wonderful because you can never ever learn all there is to know about it.

Any special ambitions?

I'd like to see the Stones stay at the top of the charts. When people ask this question, though, I suppose they want me to answer that I want to make money. In fact, I want to be rich and happy.

Any special off-beat memories about your show-business career?

Perhaps the funniest was when we all went off to a castle down near the east coast and built a brick wall round the front door. 'Course, it was owned by a friend of ours. [Keith told me this one in the early Eighties and was still cracking up. The unlucky recipient turned out to be manager Andrew Loog Oldham, who only found out about it when he roared out of his garage.]

Do you like movies?

Didn't anyone explain that I was in the original *Sheik of Araby*? Sure, I like the more way-out movies and I'm like all the others in being very keen on Sophia Loren. There, as they say, *is* a bird!

Anything you especially dislike?

Not a lot. But two-faced fakes are high on the list. Can't see why people can't be straightforward.

Somebody described you as looking like Oliver Twist. Any comment?

Please, can I have some more?

Keith's first turn as acting editor was in issue three that August. It started with this editorial message:

'Thanks everyone for giving us our first number Number One hit with "It's All Over Now". We got a great kick out of recording it, but it was nothing to the terrific feeling of seeing it top the charts.

'Songwriting has become a very big thing in my life and I seem to spend all my spare time working on new ideas. I have written a special feature for this edition, which I hope you will like, telling you all about it.

'A list of the dates we'll be playing between August 10th and September 9th is on Page 31. Performing on stage is our favourite way of spending an evening. It also gives us – and you – a chance to see each other again.

'Yours,

'Keith Richard.'

It took a while for Keith and Mick to develop their songwriting partnership. At first they were playing all covers – albeit obscure blues/rock 'n' roll gems which most of the fans probably thought were originals anyway. As if they cared – as long as Mick wiggled his hips.

In Stanley Booth's book, Keith says that 'As Tears Go By' – which was donated to Marianne Faithfull – was the first song they wrote. But I'd also heard it was 'Tell Me', the sole Jagger-Richard tune on the first album. I asked Keith about it during our 1980 interview session, and he told me how they first started making what he would later call 'my babies'. Whichever song came first, it seems we have Mr. Oldham to thank for the foreplay:

'I can thank Andrew Oldham for many things, but more than anything forcing me to sit down and write these horrendous songs, 'cos when you start it's always the worst. We'd farm them off to somebody else 'cos we didn't wanna know. Gene Pitney? Marianne Faithfull? Sure, have this one. You've gotta get all that shit outta your system before you can really start writing. At the time you write 'em you're even amazed you can write that. "I'm just the guitar-player." Hats off to Andrew for that one, just for making me find out I could do it.'

As it transpires, 'As Tears Go By' was the first one they turned out, but it was the Phil Spectorish ballad, 'Tell Me', that was the first song the Stones themselves committed to vinyl.

'Yeah, and that was a demo,' he revealed. 'Andrew stuck it on the album because we needed another track. It was cut as a demo and Andrew was going to try and flog it off to somebody. But we bunged it on. In America it was the first thing we did that got pulled out. Then we realised about songwriting. Apart from playing, that's the other thing I enjoy doing more than anything. Trying to hammer out a new song.'

Keith's self-composed article for the *Stones Book* gave a revealing insight into how those cogs started turning:

'Mick and I have been writing songs together for about a year now. We didn't make a lot of fuss about when we started, we just began working at it, because it was something that we both liked doing.

'In fact, very few people realised that we did write songs until Gene Pitney recorded "That Girl Belongs To Yesterday". Gene's a big mate of ours and has helped us terrifically by turning that number into a big hit.

'You never know how things are going to turn out in this business but being a professional songwriter would suit me fine.

'Two other numbers of ours are out now. "As Tears Go By" has been recorded by the new girl singer, Marion [sic] Faithfull, and our version of "Tell Me" has been released as a single in the States, and I understand it's doing very well over there.

'At the moment, we've got about a dozen songs sort of half-finished. Most of them are intended for our next LP, but we've got a lot of work to do on them yet and it gets more and more difficult to find time every week. Sometimes, we can finish a song in ten minutes, but others hang around for months on end.

'I usually write the music with a title in mind, then Mick adds the words. I can't write a note of music, of course, but then neither could most of the best songwriters of the last 50 years. I don't find any difficulty as I've got a very good memory and can easily complete a song after I've been keeping the song in my head for several weeks. If I suddenly get what I think is a good idea, I do sometimes put it on tape but not very often. Mick's just the same – how he remembers words which he thought about a month or so back, I just don't know.

'Every songwriter has a number of songs which he'd wished he'd written. All of Dionne Warwick's stuff – in fact, anything by Burt Bacharach and Hal David. Those two are really brilliant. Their ideas are so original.

'The great thing about songwriting is that despite the thousands and thousands of songs which have been written there are still so many melodies yet to be discovered. But, one thing I have still not been able to do – that's write a number good enough for the Stones to use as an "A" side in England. Most of the numbers that Mick and I write are pretty complicated whilst the Stones need relatively simple ones with very few chord changes in them. But, it does sound crazy saying that we can't write stuff for the Stones when we're part of them.

'Of course, my big ambition is to have lots of hits but, also I would like to have our songs recorded by lots of different artists. I'd love to see what someone like Dionne Warwick would do with some of our numbers. No, that's daft, anything she did with them would please me. I like the music business so much that if I didn't make it with songwriting I think I'd have a bash at being a record producer aiming at selling my discs in both the British and American markets. Trouble in this country is that practically every British artiste is established in his or her own style and it gets more and more difficult to create anything new. In the States, on the other hand, they are forever experimenting and getting new sounds. Often nowadays, the Americans only put a rhythm section on records but it comes out sounding like a full orchestra. It's fantastic.

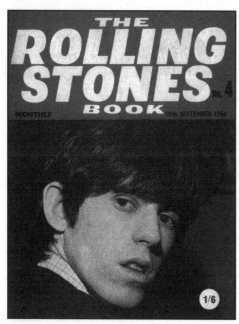

The Stones' personal mouthpiece to their fans.

'Being a record producer is a tough job but I think I could handle it. Andrew Oldham takes our sessions now, but all of the Stones have a say in what goes on and it's terrific experience. Really I wouldn't like to do the whole job on my own, I'd rather have someone working with me, like Mick for example.

'In my opinion, many record producers are in a rut. There are so many new sounds floating around just waiting to be discovered, and only people like Phil Spector and Andrew Oldham are brave enough to experiment with them. I'd like to get a variation on the American group sound, with the singers sounding like part of the orchestra.

'I don't think that there's any other form of recording I'd like to tackle, simply because you can't express yourself if you have to keep a style that's been fixed already. Apart from songwriting and producing, the only other ambition I've got is to buy a huge house on a small tropical island where it's always about a hundred degrees. I'd just sit in the sun all day and have some servants (including Mick Jagger) looking after me! That would be my heaven!'

Not content with his first dab at feature-writing, Keith also edited the letters page – typical fan stuff with some nice replies.

Between '63-'65, the newsagents were stacked with special one-off publications devoted to a particular artist and aimed at teenage girls and punters like me. Some are hilarious, as the words obviously came second to the pictures. *Life with the Rolling Stones*, from August '64, was in tabloid format and presented a profile of each Stone.

Here's Keith: 'Catch him unaware and he'll probably look deep in thought. Keith Richard, aged nineteen, close friend and songwriting pal of Mick Jagger, is one of the furthest-out people that makes up this fantastic group.

'He lives with Mick. When he phones anyone, he announces himself as "Phelge", for a joke, and gets very cross with people who compare the Stones with the Beatles. Then, he's not joking.

'He's not the most organised of characters. He is usually dressed the opposite of carefully. "But not dirty," he says.

'Like every other member of the group he is mad on music, and like all guitarists, he is always plucking away, trying to work out new tunes that the Stones can feature on their next act or their next record.

'What does Keith do when he is not working? "Stay in and sketch, usually," says the ex-art student. "If there's a pen lying around in a dressing room, I'll pick it up and do portraits without thinking about it."

'He wears a leather jacket perhaps more often than the rest, smokes and drinks a little, and hates to be interviewed for long spells. He's restless.'

In the December '64 issue of *The Rolling Stones Book*, edited by Brian Jones, Keith had his stars read by contributor Christine A. Osbourne. She seemed to come strangely close at times: 'Like his fellow-Sagittarians . . . even his closest friends say they've never seen him in a mood.

'Too decisive and outspoken to the extent of making bitter and unforgiving enemies is many a Sagittarian's chief fault. But Keith is lucky in this respect. He does speak his own mind and he will stand up for something he believes is right – but not in such a way as to upset anyone.

'Almost without exception, Sagittarians are fond of music and literature and possess much ability in these fields. Keith, of course, shows this not only in his guitar-playing, but songwriting too . . . . But his prominent characteristic is his generosity. Anyone in need has only to ask and Keith is ready and willing to help. His one fault is his total inability to separate the genuinely needy from the confidence tricksters. Sagittarians fall every day to the hard luck tale of somebody. Constant advantage is being taken of their generosity and Keith's sympathy is the easiest thing in the world to win. He just can't say no!' (Quiet at the back again.)

'Little Red Rooster' was released on 13 November and came in at number one. It was a cover of a Willie Dixon song which had been a hit for Howlin' Wolf in '61, a shockingly bold move that paid off – a dark, slow blues with coruscating slide guitar from Brian, the sort of thing that never got in the charts until the Stones showed how it was done.

Meanwhile, back at *The Rolling Stones Book*, staff writer Tony Webster wrote an in-depth appraisal of each of the Stones as musicians in the November issue. Keith is appraised thus: 'Lead guitarist, Keith, is the Stone who moves about the stage most, with the exception of Mick. He has a very original style but claims he owes it all to his grandfather. "He used to play in a dance band, and when he first started to teach me to play he did it via the 'pops' of the 1930s. He didn't try and make me learn all that classical gear, which usually kills any talent stone dead. He just told me to follow trends and play the kind of music I liked."

'Keith is respected as being a fast, original guitarist. Lead guitarists love making "digs" at each other, but Keith is one person who they very seldom try to "knock".

'He's got a rather weird musical ambition: "I want to play the piano and also the auto-harp," he says. When he is asked what an auto-harp is, he claims it is similar to a zither and most questioners get a feeling that Keith is having them on! All the Stones are great leg-pullers!' There ya go.

The Rolling Stones Number Two was released on 15 January in the UK and immediately made number one. The Chuck-fuelled onslaught of the first album had partly given way to a more R&B-flavoured slant – although there are wicked versions of 'You Can't Catch Me' and 'Down The Road Apiece'.

This time there were three Jagger-Richard compositions – 'Off The Hook', 'What A Shame' and 'Grown Up Wrong'. Muddy had witnessed them recording his 'I Can't Be Satisfied' at Chess, and gave it the thumbs-up, and there was also a version of Dale Hawkins' '57 hit, 'Suzie Q'.

Their more soulful side sneaked in via covers of Solomon Burke's 'Everybody Needs Somebody To Love', the Drifters' 'Under The Boardwalk' and Otis Redding's 'Pain In My Heart'. Another cover, Irma Thomas's 'Time Is On My Side', had already been a top ten hit in America and would remain a Stones favourite right through to when Keith did an amazing version with his X-Pensive Winos in 1992.

The album also featured sleeve-notes by Andrew Loog Oldham in a surreal *Clockwork Orange*-style. Keith later confirmed they were all into the controversial novel at the time – though it wasn't mentioned in the fan club magazine.

In his 1978 *Trouser Press* interview, Oldham explained why many had thought the Stones were lined up to turn *A Clockwork Orange* into a film. Apparently, it was to be their counter to the Beatles' more lightweight screen career:

'*Clockwork Orange* started it. What happened was that [film director Stanley] Kubrick, without having finished *2001*, already had the rights to the movie – he bought it for almost nothing off Anthony Burgess – something like one grand . . .

'We never had the rights. I believe if you lie enough it becomes a reality. In that instance, it didn't, but we had a great four or five months with it. I wouldn't have done all those great sleeve notes without Anthony Burgess.

'The whole thing then was to get in the *NME* and papers like that, because you could just measure your success by how many inches you'd get a week. That was all during the *Clockwork Orange* period. Eventually we had to face the fact that we didn't have the rights to do it. It reached a point where I was reading the newspapers and believing the stories I'd planted in the first place, forgetting that it was me who told it to them.'

Oldham switched to planting stories that the group were going to film a book by a Yorkshire schoolteacher called *Only Lovers Left Alive* instead. *The Stones Book* went with that one for a while, before a short-lived fan club newspaper called *Stone Age* reported they were actually going to start work on a movie called *Back Behind in Front* in early '65, 'filmed in sepia, black and white.'

When I interviewed Keith in '83 we talked at length about movies – or, rather, the fact that he had no desire to make them. He knew what Oldham had been pulling back in '64. 'Yeah, Andrew Oldham taught us the Movie Trick. Andrew wised us up on Fleet Street. A crash course. From the minute we started, there was always a movie. Because that's one of those bits that Fleet Street can't resist. Didn't matter if it was bullshit, we always said, "Yeah, we're in discussions with certain people from Los Angeles. Sorry we can't reveal the details." You'd always get a couple of columns in the *Daily Mirror*. Andrew was like Professor of Public Relations. Amazing.

'We had it down. That's where we learned it all from. That's why we'd turn up at the Savoy dressed in clothes where we knew we weren't gonna get in. You have to have a tie and a suit – 'specially in the early sixties – to get in these places. We'd deliberately turn up and make sure there were a couple of photographers around. That is what it was based on. We played the game of manipulation of the media. I mean, Malcolm McLaren is a half-assed Andrew Oldham.'

And so with the *Clockwork Orange* thing?

'Yeah, and I was into it as he was. We used to go round in his American car with his chauffeur-cum-bruiser and beat up people on the way. It was great fun.

We'd build a brick wall in front of somebody's driveway in the middle of the night. Cement and everything – six foot brick wall ... spend all night doing it. Especially if it was somebody that we'd made a phone call to who had to be in London at six o'clock in the morning. Whizz out of their stately home at five in the morning and bash straight into this brick wall built right across their driveway!'

Nearly twenty years before that conversation, Keith had been back in the editor's chair of *The Rolling Stones Book*. Incoming:

'Hello!

'I want to start off by thanking everybody who remembered my twentieth birthday. I have got their cards and presents all over my flat. In fact, I spent several days during the Christmas and New Year period sorting them all out. I think I've got enough initialled handkerchiefs to last me through all of 1965 at least – even with half a dozen heavy colds!

'By the way it was my twentieth – not my 21st birthday [sic]. A lot of people got my date of birth wrong, because a sheet was printed with the incorrect date about a year ago, and it seems to have gone all over the place. Just to answer all of those who have written to me about it: NO, I am not 21 this year and YES I am the youngest Stone.

'Several of us have been working on new songs during the past few weeks. Apart from Mick and I, both Bill and Brian are starting to take songwriting seriously. [As Keith later said to Victor Bockris, however, 'Brian was utterly impossible to write a song with. He would dominate anything he was into – there was no way you could suggest anything. Then Brian wouldn't make a decision about chord changes, where the changes should go.' Given the general dodginess of Bill's later solo output, too, it's just as well that Jagger-Richard remained the songwriting axis of the Stones.] A lot of people have asked about our releases in 1965. It's impossible to say exactly what we will be doing months in advance. We always seem to leave it until after we have recorded several numbers till we decide whether something is good enough or not to be released as a single or on an LP.'

The same issue revealed that Keith had acquired a seven-inch long puppy while the Stones were in the US and called it Runty.

'The Last Time' was released on 26 February and boasted one of Keith's most distinctive riffs yet, plus a country influence in the harmonies. It was the Stones' first self-composed A-side and their second number one. It was backed with 'Play With Fire', one of the classic moody sixties Stones ballads. The song was actually based on a staple singers song from '55 called 'This May Be The Last Time'. The flip was Jagger-Richards' 'Play With Fire' – a sinister ballad which saw them namechecking London locations like Knightsbridge for the first time. Keith later called it, 'an experiment... Elizabethan blues'.

That month's *Rolling Stones Book* told us that Keith had just bought a 2.4 Jaguar in metallic blue, that he and Mick had 'one of the most comprehensive collections of R&B records ever collected' – and that the support act on their Australian tour was none other than future TV pet doctor Rolf Harris.

A Stones progress report – analysing the way their sound had changed as they travelled the world, working in different studios – quotes a 'top session drummer' as saying, 'Keith Richard is now thoroughly accomplished. Before, I used to think of him as a hit-or-miss guitarist. Now he's built up an instinctive "feel" for what is right or wrong. Sure, you'd expect people like the Stones to improve with experience . . . but there's talent there we didn't really expect.'

(The same issue also includes an amusing, with hindsight, nudge-nudge letter from one Pat Humpage[!] of Birmingham: 'I wondered if it would be possible for me to borrow Keith for a few days – I could collect him when you next appear in Birmingham. I promise I wouldn't mishandle him and I would keep a plentiful supply of Coke just for him . . . Here's hoping you will oblige by lending me Keith.')

The March issue introduced 'The Stones Answer' section, where the band were given one of those quickfire Q&A's. It illustrated Keith's state of mind in the midst of earl '65's snowballing success:

Q: *Marriage?*
A: Don't believe in it.
Future?
Know something? I never even think about it. Today's what counts.
America?
Their way of thinking can be as antiquated as our standard of living.
Touring?
Tiring.
Stones' new LP?
Instrumentally, I think it's much more advanced. Also the range of songs is much greater. And I can promise there's a much wider range to come in the future.
Cars?
I like them comfortable, well-upholstered. But most important, there's got to be a record player installed.
Girls?
Mmm . . . !
Pet current hate?
Some of the neighbours who live near the place I share with Mick. They've got some very funny habits but it's them that stare at us. We have to creep in and out of the place.
Ambitions?
Things are fine now. But I want to keep on writing songs with Mick. It's a good partnership, I think – we never seem short of ideas.
American R&B stars in Britain?
No, they don't make it big over here. I reckon there's three reasons why they don't click with the British teenager fans. One, they're old. Two, they're black. Three, they're ugly. This image bit is very important – though I must say it doesn't matter to us. But the Americans have helped get things going over here . . . their influence is big if their popularity isn't.

The magazine is packed with such fascinating stuff, best read with the benefit of hindsight. Keith was back in the editor's chair for June:

'Hello!

'It's nice to be back. All this tearing around the world is OK, but I still reckon this is the best place to live. Every time we get near the end of one of those long, long 'plane journeys home, it's great to see good old London Airport again with all its muddle of 'planes, buildings and huts at the end of it.

'We spent several whole days in the studios in Chicago and Hollywood working on new tracks. We seem to have taped loads of songs over the past couple of years and then forgotten them. Still, it'll be nice to play them back when we're old – if anyone can remember where they put the tapes, that is!

'Hope you like the new EP. Some of you should, because you're on it. It was completely different making this short album. In the recording studios you know you're making a record; you concentrate on nothing else. On stage the audience is part of the whole thing. There is always far more excitement up there, due to the reaction between us and you, which is very hard to get in the studio. That is one of the reasons why we've always wanted to do a live recording. It's very difficult to get a good balance though. I think we've got to thank Andy for pulling it off. See you all in Scotland.'

Keith is talking about *Got Live If You Want It* – the five-track EP released on 11 June, which again went to number one in the EP charts. It featured versions of 'Everybody Needs Somebody To Love', 'Pain In My Heart' and 'I'm Moving On'. Nanker-Phelge get songwriting credits for 'I'm Alright' – just that one line, repeated over a bluesy, crowd-baiting riff – and the crowd chant of 'We Want the Stones', which was actually listed as a track. The magazine's news page describes how 'tremendous atmosphere is obtained – thanks to the ingenuity of the "men behind the scenes", producer Andrew Oldham and engineer Glyn Johns.' The sleeve says it was 'recorded live in London, Manchester and Liverpool'. Popular legend claims that Johns simply lobbed a mike over the balcony to record both the band and the crowd!

I saw the visual side of the live madness on TV – once at the *NME* Poll Winners Concert and another time on *Ready Steady Go*. It was absolute mayhem.

With 'The Last Time' still fresh in the memory, the mag alludes to a new monster waiting in store: 'On the subject of singles, the Stones' latest in the States is a number called "Satisfaction", written by Mick and Keith.' Back home, we had to wait until August for the riff-of-all-time that popped into Keith's head one night while he was asleep. '(I Can't Get No) Satisfaction' was one of the songs recorded during the Hollywood session that Keith mentions. The ultimate teenage rock 'n' roll anthem, it ran straight to the top of the charts.

It was also at this time that the management partnership of Andrew Oldham and Eric Easton split asunder. Mick, Keith and Oldham were dissatisfied with the new deal Easton had struck with Decca Records, which only guaranteed advance payments on the back of overseas revenues the band had already earned up to eighteen months ago. So Oldham brought in a brash New York music biz accountant named Allen Klein to oust Easton and improve the band's royalties situation.

'In walks this little fat American geezer, smoking a pipe, wearing the most diabolical clothes,' Keith would later recall. 'But we liked him, he made us laugh . . . Andrew knew he didn't know enough about the legal side of it to be able to do it. So we had to get someone who knew how to do it.'

'Allen certainly dazzled me and the Stones,' said Oldham in his autobiography, 'at least in the Mick and Keith department, and that's what was driving the train . . . we had a killer on our side who would handle Easton and Decca.'

Klein's tough negotiation won a deal that guaranteed the Stones $3 million over the next five years – a considerable sum for the mid-sixties. '. . . We came out with the best record contract, so that impresses a guy,' recalls Keith, still basically grateful to Klein despite all the later bad blood. 'He did a good job.'

Klein would continue to make more money for the Stones than was possible under the ludicrously one-sided deals offered by record companies in the early sixties. But his own control-freak tendencies and sharp business practices would store up acrimony. For the time being, though, he was the man for the job – not least because he was able to project an unlikely image as some kind of New York mafioso.

'That was Andrew,' Klein would later acknowledge, 'he just created it, that I was like a gangster. He said they'll love it in England. . . . That's what the British think of all Americans who might be Italians.' (Klein is Jewish.) Whoever came up with the idea, Klein was only too willing to pose in photos with a shotgun, wearing a t-shirt and sneakers – not the standard image for an accountant at the time. And of course Keith, who'd been in love with the outlaw image since he was a little boy fantasising about the Wild West, lapped it up.

But, as journalist and music PR Keith Altham said, 'With Allen Klein it was not so much physical fear as the sense that he was prepared to go into a record company office with an abundant knowledge of contractual law and accountancy and demand to see certain things that nobody had ever asked for. . . . So rather than have Allen Klein come down on them, they'd fork out huge sums.'

In September, the Stones released their third album, *Out Of Our Heads*. This was a classic, with belting covers of Larry Williams' 'She Said Yeah', Martha and the Vandellas' 'Hitch Hike', Don Covay's 'Mercy Mercy', Sam Cooke's 'Good Times' and Chuck's 'Talkin' 'Bout You'. But there were also strong Jagger-Richard compositions like 'Heart Of Stone' and 'I'm Free', which would still be in their live set at the Hyde Park and Altamont free concerts.

And all the time, that Richards guitar-razor was getting sharper and deadlier. The October issue of *The Rolling Stones Book* expressed editor Keith's pleasure at the response to *Out Of Our Heads*, and carried a hilarious feature called 'Stones Clothes' with Knightsbridge boutique owner Jackie Cryer – fashion expert for the *Thank Your Lucky Stars* TV show – voicing her opinions of the Stones' dress sense:

'When I first saw the Stones I thought they were terrible and foul and nasty. Honestly! It was at the Crawdaddy, at Richmond, and I was rather upset. They just wore those awful old sweaters and dirty old jeans and they looked . . . well, rather sinister! . . . But now I think the Stones are very good – no, fabulous. It's no longer a scruffy image. They're clean, well-dressed – even if they are wearing casual gear, you know it's expensive. The main thing about them is they are so thin, all of them. Thin people can get away with wearing anything. So the basic shape is there – and I really do think they're well turned out nowadays.

'There's Keith Richard, wearing those white shoes and the dark jackets. He'd look good in anything . . . I've been asked how I'd dress the Stones if I had the chance . . . Often I've seen Bill wearing all-black gear, with Keith tending towards white, or near white. Just for a change, I'd like to switch them around. They could

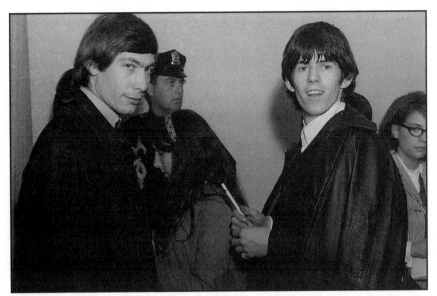

Charlie and Keith arriving in New York for their second American tour, October 1964.

take the variation of colour. Oh yes – tell you something else about them. I'd like to see Keith or Bill wearing a white "gangster" tie, over a jet-black shirt. They look that bit villainous – it would look great. I love this 1930's look for men, it's fantastic. Of all the groups, the Stones would look best in this sort of style. Actually, Keith would look fine in one of those well-cut pinstripe suits, double-breasted. I know they're now considered a bit square, but it's a style that would suit Keith perfectly. Sort of an Al Capone, or George Raft, style of dressing.'

Suits you, sir. They should still publish this magazine – it'd be great to get a commentary on today's immaculately turned-out model.

In early October '65, Keith was knocked unconscious for five minutes during a stage invasion in Manchester. At the end of the month, the Stones swiftly followed through on the success of 'Satisfaction' with 'Get Off Of My Cloud'. Classic sneery Stones pop, it hit number one again. In November, Andrew Loog Oldham started Immediate Records and a production company with Mick and Keith called We Three Productions.

Keith kickstarted the New Year with a brand new car, announced in the January *Stones Book*. A dark blue Bentley Continental, it would become famous as the 'Blue Lena' – named after jazz singer Lena Horne. The magazine also carried a report on the recently completed US tour, including an incident in Sacramento where Keith nearly bought it once again. During 'The Last Time', he went to sing the chorus and found his mike was facing the wrong way. He gave it a knock with his guitar to put it right. Blinding flash. Keith out cold. Crowd going mad, thinking he's been killed. He was rushed to hospital, where he came around twenty minutes later. When he next looked at his guitar, he saw that two of the strings had been burned clean through like fuse wire. The thick rubber soles of his Hush

Puppies saved his life. (Keith also lost his passport early in the tour, but Charlie did present him with his much sought-after autoharp.)

The feature also mentions a recording session at Hollywood's RCA studios with engineer Dave Hassinger which yielded eight tracks, at least some of which must have ended up on the *Aftermath* album. It alludes to a mysterious epic in which, the Stones said, they go 'raving mad' for eleven minutes, which can only be the landmark 'Goin' Home'. The longest track the Stones have ever done, before or since, at that time it was the longest single rock 'n' roll track ever recorded.

The main notable thing about Keith, looking back through these magazines, is how little he's changed in his outlook and approach. Take a report called 'What They'll Be Doing in '66', wherein we hear that he wants to spend more time recording: 'Keith, especially, is the ideal recording "type". He's got the patience of a saint. He'll stay calm, cool and collected even after eight or nine unsuccessful takes. Once he's got his teeth into a session he'll work round the clock – and round again – until he gets the results he wants!'

Sounds familiar? But then, only a couple of years later he'd be making *Beggars Banquet* and embarking on his rigorous five or six days on/two days unconscious regime. (We're also told how, 'Mick and Keith love the discotheque type of clubs and will probably try to see all the artists appearing wherever they may be, especially the coloured "soul" people..')

The next single, '19th Nervous Breakdown', was released in February '66. It showed a harder, darker direction, with Keith's booming riff and elements of paranoia. Bill Wyman's divebomb fretwork near the end is a masterstroke. With all that touring the band had soon discovered the benefits of speed, and the edginess was starting to show. It made number two in both the UK and US.

Keith himself was back again in the March issue of the *Stones Book* – where we learned that he'd failed his driving test that month, and had to continue using his chauffeur, Patrick, to drive his Bentley Continental:

'Hello!

'I'm writing this editorial in Melbourne, where we're doing a three-day stint at the Palace Theatre, near the end of our Australian tour.

'Travelling has made many group members leave showbusiness because it can either ruin your health or become a drag generally. I've been pretty lucky healthwise and I certainly don't consider it a drag. I still get a big kick out of flying and sailing round the world and meeting fans from all different countries.

'One piece of travelling I'm really looking forward to is our next tour of England, playing to the fans who were the first to buy our records. You know it's strange how short a trip from say Slough to Manchester seems to us now, after the thousands of miles we travelled across Australia and America.

'To tell you the truth, I get a bit bored when I'm not working. There's always the songwriting, of course, but as far as I'm concerned you can't actually beat playing to an audience. I never get tired of performing. And when it comes to touring, I like the whole thing – thinking beforehand about the places we're going to visit, the excitement of packing my bags, boarding the plane, and most of all getting on stage performing – which is all I really want to do at the moment.

'I've got no aspirations to be an all-round entertainer, or to write a musical . . . nothing like that for me. I just don't like it. Perhaps I may change later on, but that's how I feel at the present time.'

That's as good an illustration of Keith's personality as ever there was. He's still saying the same things today. The parallels continue in a feature about the 'Stones on Stage', even down to the preferred size of venue: 'It's the greatest of feelings, as far as I'm concerned, to stand up there on stage with a big appreciative audience in front of you and a tremendous powerful sound behind you. I prefer playing the smaller places though, not the clubs, but the theatres. S'funny, when we were doing the tiny clubs, theatres seemed immense. Now that we've done the big auditoriums, we think the theatres are small places. In the really big stadiums it's much more difficult to get yourself across. There's no real contact with the audience.'

The new expansiveness in the Stones sound manifested itself when *Aftermath* was unleashed on 15 April, going straight to number one. For the first time, Mick and Keith had written all the songs, including their first drug ditty in the Eastern-flavoured 'Mother's Little Helper' – about bored housewives hooked on tranquilisers. All sorts of flavours were creeping in, largely because of Brian's growing obsession with mastering exotic instruments, like the dulcimer which appears on the delicate ballads 'Lady Jane' and 'I Am Waiting'. Further classics included 'Stupid Girl' and 'Under My Thumb', a pair that never quite clicked with the feminists' and the album ends with that epic blues jam, 'Goin' Home'.

The album also signalled an onslaught of people covering its original Jagger-Richard songs, with the Searchers recording 'Take It Or Leave It', the Zombies on 'Lady Jane', Chris Farlowe following 'Think' with 'Out Of Time' and Gene Latter tackling 'Mother's Little Helper'.

Most significantly, 7 May saw the release of the classic 'Paint It, Black', the most arrestingly different Stones outing to date. By now, Brian was obsessed with trying out ethnic instruments which he could master in double-quick time. This one uses the sitar to heighten the dramatic effect, and the slamming beat can only be described as pre-dating techno! Naturally, it went to number one.

That month's *Stones Book* carried the news story that Keith had recently bought a fifteenth-century house in Sussex, surrounded by a huge moat. 'I'll have to keep a large stock of bread as the moat has an added attraction – ducks,' he's quoted as saying. Redlands was now on the map, and it was the place that Keith hoped would make a permanent home for him and Linda.

So howzabout a guided tour? In June, Sue Mautner pre-dated *Hello!* magazine by taking you around Keith's stately pile. Some highlights: 'Fortunately it was a beautiful sunny day when I drove down to Keith's fifteenth century house in Sussex, because "Mr. Richard hasn't arrived yet," said the old gardener as I approached the drive . . . I walked round the back of the house to find a horse grazing in the next field, which later on I found out belonged to Keith – not the horse but the field. Lying on the beautifully mowed lawn was a rather old-looking paddle boat – obviously that would also be explained later . . . Much to my surprise I found the porch door open, so I took the liberty of entering.

'The first room I found myself in was the lounge – no furniture, just a massive oak-panelled room with parquet flooring, wooden beams, two enormous stone pillars and a huge stone fireplace with a gigantic flue coming down the chimney. Keith had already moved some of his belongings because there was a white fur rug on the floor, an electric piano, a harpsichord and a guitar plus, his record and book collection and, of course, his hi-fi.

'I was very interested and surprised to learn that his books consisted of *The Great War*, *Dictionary of Slang*, *Guns*, *Great Sea Battles*, *Drawings of Rembrandt* and books on England, and even more surprised with his record collection. Amongst the Beatles, Otis Redding, Dylan, Simon and Garfunkel, the Everlys, the Temptations and Elvis were Chopin's Nineteen Waltzes, Rossini and Segovia . . . . The upstairs consisted of five bedrooms and a bathroom. I knew which was Keith's room because the bed was unmade, and there was a pair of shoes and a Dennis Wheatley book lying on the floor.'

Of Keith himself, the writer noted how he'd eased out of his snappy mod phase – from sharp dogtooth check jackets to the woman's fur coat he was wearing that day, bought for £20 from a broke hippie chick he felt sorry for.

'It was a very big turn-on,' said Linda about Redlands, 'but it was pretty near the end of our relationship and I don't have good memories of having good times at Redlands.' Despite his hopes for their future together, drugs were coming between Keith and Linda.

Not that he had any problem himself, not yet being the mad, bad and dangerous-to-know 'Keef' of legend. It was Linda who led the way – at first, she smoked more grass than him (when she gave him some particularly powerful stuff she claims it made him throw up!) and was the first to experiment with acid. Keith had gradually learned to enjoy a reefer, and had conducted the first of his notorious five-days-awake binges on speed while on tour.

Hard drugs were also creeping in, as he replaced the edginess of amphetamine with the smoother, more potent, shorter-lived (and more expensive) buzz of cocaine. But he hadn't touched heroin, and expressed no interest in it. For Linda, though, the brakes were off. She was diving into smack, and a photograph of her OD'd on downers had recently made the press. Whatever Keith's later lifestyle, back then it was nothing but a cause for concern to him. 'He wasn't happy with the stoned Linda and it all got a bit awkward,' his old girlfriend later explained, understatedly.

And little did Keith know that, just over six months later, drug use would make Redlands the most infamous mansion in England.

In July, news came in that Keith had finally passed his driving test! There was also a double-page spread of 'Keith and his Guitar', with the man in a variety of poses and a black-and-white polka-dot shirt. The accompanying blurb is funny – but also pretty accurate: 'Keith Richard is the tall, tousle-haired tunesmith of the Rolling Stones, the musical power behind the ingenious words of Mick Jagger . . . On stage, his face and body move with the sentiment of the music, twisting and twining with the rhythmic movement of the song. He caresses his guitar with the fondness that a mother would have for her child or a man would have for his dog. Perhaps it's the best friend he'll ever have – it's certainly never let him down yet.'

Right on.

Keith was back as editor for the last time in August, as the magazine would cease to exist by the end of the year. He'd just been to the States again:

'Hello!

'We've come to the end of a very long and successful tour, the result of which is five very exhausted Stones – who at the moment are taking a well-earned rest before returning home.

'Since last month, we have appeared in about twenty cities, so we've been literally living out of a suitcase, which as you can imagine presented a few problems: for example, I'd probably find myself with two right socks [before going on stage] which obviously meant someone was walking around with two left feet – usually Charlie!

'We hardly managed to get a real look at the places we went to, but we thought Houston and Hawaii were quite good. Charlie was in his element in Houston, he went mad for those ten gallon hats and six-shooters – he thought he was back in the wild west! Hawaii was more my scene – all those gorgeous sun-tanned girls with grass skirts and flowers in their hair. When we arrived at the airport they all put garlands around our necks and started kissing us. It was just like an Elvis Presley film!!!'

Keith's letters page contains one from 'a mad, admiring, loving, parasitic, Anne-Marie XXXXXX,' congratulating Keith on the album *Today's Pop Symphony* by the Aranbee ('r'n'b', geddit?) Pop Symphony Orchestra. 'I wish more people could hear how great it is cos I know they'd buy it.'

It was a semi-solo project Keith had produced and played guitar on for Loog Oldham's Immediate label. Probably the first 1960s album to fuse contemporary pop songs with classical orchestration, it featured arrangements of the Stones songs 'Play With Fire', 'Mother's Little Helper', 'Take It Or Leave It', 'Sitting On A Fence' and 'I've Been Loving You Too Long' – alongside some of his favourites by the Beatles, the Four Seasons, the Drifters, Otis Redding, Wilson Pickett, even Sonny and Cher.

Keith is highly flattered by the response. 'I'm pleased you wrote in about my LP, Anne-Marie, cos up til now, no-one had mentioned it, and I was feeling very brought down about the whole thing. But I must say that you've made my month by writing to me about it.'

Predating the orchestral atrocities of early prog rock, the Aranbee album was far more in tune with the epic 'big pop' sounds of Spector or Bacharach and David. That it remained so obscure for so long (it only recently received a CD release) may have been a deciding factor in why Keith didn't make another solo record for twenty years.

The next Stones single, released on 24 September, was the harsh, hallucinogenic psycho-swirl of 'Have You Seen Your Mother, Baby, Standing In The Shadows?' It stalled at number five, breaking the run of number ones. 'It's about the attitude that exists between parents and their children,' said Andrew Oldham. The single also caused controversy because the publicity photo had the group in full drag, with Mick as a maiden aunt, Brian as an air hostess and Keith in a rather fetching RAF number.

The Rolling Stones Book shut up shop in November 1966. The last issue consisted mainly of photographs, and it was interesting to note how – even in the space of three or four issues – the group had started to change. Keith is on the cover in his big black bug-eyed shades, the clothes are becoming more 'way out', as it was called back then, and there are some very large, glazed eyes – notably Brian's. Things (and Keith himself) would never seem quite as innocent again, as 1967 loomed.

CHAPTER THREE

THE ACID REIGN

Undone Buttons

As 1966 ended, the Stones were burnt-out from years of touring and having to trot out an album they weren't 100 per cent committed to.

'We sort of dried up there for a bit,' Keith later admitted in a 1987 *Guitar World* interview. 'Nobody would have known it, but we were knackered, quite honestly. We worked live 350 days a year, making records in between as well. Four years of non-stop grind. Loved every minute of it. But even at that age you can wear yourself out, given the amount of female company we had . . .'

As they began 1967, the Stones were still mixing their new album, recorded at RCA Studios, Hollywood that previous August, then London's Olympic Studios in November and December. In January, they got an early taste of the controversy they would soon become accustomed to. 'Let's Spend The Night Together' was the first Stones single my parents openly disapproved of. As an innocent twelve-year-old, I came up with the same argument Mick used some-where that it was about having a nice time with someone at a club. No wonder it didn't wash.

Meanwhile, the flip's 'Ruby Tuesday' continued the tradition of the Stones baroque ballad. It was the most sublime realisation of Brian's gift for embellish-ment, as he blew a breathy flute through Keith's swansong to Linda Keith, who had flown the coop at the end of the previous summer. Resonating piano, reversed tapes and crashing, orchestral drums add to the emotional drama.

'It was probably written about Linda Keith not being there,' Keith told *Mojo* in 2003, with wry detachment. 'I dunno, she had pissed off somewhere. It was very mournful, very, very Ruby Tuesday, and it was a Tuesday.' Linda was now one of Jimi Hendrix's more high-profile girlfriends. Keith bore Hendrix no animosity. 'I think he's a nice cat actually,' he told friends.

But he'd called Linda's parents up to tell them their daughter was strung-out and wasted in New York. It resulted in them making her a ward of court, and in compulsory psychiatric treatment. Keith and Linda would never speak again – though she seems to have mellowed toward him in later years, and, as her friend Sheila Oldham (nee Klein) says, 'it was a caring thing for Keith to do. It probably saved her life, actually.'

On 13 January, the Stones appeared on America's hugely-influential *Ed Sullivan Show* and were forced to dampen down the controversy by changing the chorus of 'Let's Spend The Night Together' to, 'Let's spend some time together.' This they did with a reluctant sneer.

Then came the new album. *Between The Buttons* was released on 20 January in the UK, getting to number three, and 11 February in the US, where it reached number two. The cover is a misty dawn shot of the band, taken on London's Primrose Hill by Gered Mankowitz, who smeared Vaseline on his lens to achieve the effect. I remember thinking that they shouldn't have got the group up so early – Brian looks strangely tired, although quite content.

This is probably my least favourite Stones album, marking Andrew Oldham's last full production for the group. He goes out with a muddy burp, swathing everything in reverb, drowning the rhythm section and diminishing the impact of a good bunch of songs. Probably their most poppy record, it's frustratingly studded with tunes that could have been classics with a decent mix. Keith just thinks of *Between The Buttons* as the last album the Stones made before they hopped off the album-tour treadmill, which had been going on for years.

But it contains 'Connection', Keith's first solo vocal on a Stones record. It's the best track, naturally. The guitars chop and churn, as the lyrics tell of the trauma of all that travelling – although you can read a drug reference into the title, if so inclined. (Keith would later revive this one with his X-Pensive Winos, when the song's thrashing power really hit home.)

Ultimately, *Between The Buttons* was a watershed between the Stones' pop era and the psychedelia that would go supernova on their next album.

Spring Of Hate

'There was a time in '67, when everything just stopped, everything just stopped dead. Everybody was trying to work it out, what was going to go on. So many weird things happening to so many weird people at one time.'

That was Keith in *A Life on the Road*, a late nineties book of interviews with the Stones. The Stones had discovered acid before they even recorded *Between The Buttons*. In fact, the band – and Keith in particular – had been turned on to a wide range of drugs on the first American tours.

'There were two thoughts about [acid] as far as I can remember,' Keith told *Mojo* in 2003. 'Not about acid per se, just about everybody else taking dope. It was like, "Jesus Christ, our secret's out! Who opened their mouth?" . . . . Before that – pot, some amphetamines, uppers, downers, some smoke and nobody knew about it . . . . Acid blew that wide apart. I was never that dedicated to it. If I knew it was good stuff I'd have a few good trips. I never got into an evangelical thing about it, like this is the beginning of a new world. I was like, "Wow, I'll take this if I've got a couple of days off."'

1967 was some year. Some took to it like bees to a bud. Some had a little more trouble. Keith fell into the latter category. He never was a hippie. It just wasn't in him. Sure, he was starting to love drugs, and he'd give any sort of music a whirl. But he left the sitar to Brian, and the Maharishi to Mick. Once the Stones had had their dalliance with psychedelia, he'd stick his snakeskin boot down on the pedal and rev the band forward into the glorious blues mutations of the late sixties. LSD may have opened doors, but the main inner force that Keith Richard discovered in 1967 was the potential of open G-tuning on a five-string guitar – as we shall see.

The hippie era was initially confusing to young Stones fans like myself. But, as the clothes got more 'out there', and the music was constantly evolving, taking in new sounds, then the weirder and scarier our favourite group became, the more we loved it. After 1967, the Stones would never be thought of as just a pop group again.

The Beatles and the Stones were at the vanguard of the sixties' new attitudes. The establishment had had it their own way since time immemorial. They'd thought Elvis was dangerous for a while, but the army took care of him. Before the Beatles and the Stones, all we had in Britain was the other Richard – old Cliff, permanently off on a summer holiday. The Beatles opened the door for a new pop music based on rock 'n' roll roots, but when the Stones came in they really mashed it up. They were seen as a threat from day one – but now, a new movement was burgeoning within the ranks of the young which brought sexual freedom and drugs into the equation. It had to be stopped. The establishment needed a scapegoat, and the Rolling Stones were perfect.

First came the London Palladium. To this day, Andrew Loog Oldham believes it may have been something as trivial as refusing to go on the Palladium's revolving stage that started the establishment clampdown.

While the Beatles had always willingly done the show, and rode the roundabout at the end with the likes of Bruce Forsyth and a troupe of jugglers, the Stones had always turned down the offers. When they succumbed – because the new single needed a push, after the relatively poor showing of 'Have You Seen Your Mother, Baby, Standing In The Shadows?' – they did it on their own terms. No tuxedos; an uncensored 'Let's Spend The Night Together', plus 'Ruby Tuesday' and 'Connection'; Keith and Brian turning up on acid, pissing off the Palladium staff with their moody demeanour.

The young TV audience was used to seeing the Stones regularly blitz their *Ready Steady Go!* home turf, but this was different. They didn't disappoint, even if host Dave Allen – who built a career on being a drunken Irishman – tried to take the piss with some inane banter, which Mick later described as 'pathetic'. Keith looked like a kind of psychedelic yob in t-shirt, scarf and velvet trousers. After the first song, Mick grinned at one of the screamers in the audience and said, 'Hello fruity.' Even that was a shock-horror moment for some, with its very mild sexual connotations of the time, but it was simply an innocent retort to a banner that said, 'Fruity Mick'.

Of course, the Stones on Sunday evening TV were always going to horrify the primetime audience. But the unbelievable furore about the roundabout incident – in the end, comedians Peter Cook and Dudley Moore went on with cardboard cut-outs of the band – brought an eruption of outrage which wouldn't be seen again until the Sex Pistols swore on the *Today* programme, ten years later. My mum and dad were disgusted – by the song, by the Stones' appearance, by their very existence – but the more my parents hated them, the more I loved them. Strangely, Andrew Oldham had tried to persuade the band to go on the roundabout. His tactics of '63-'64 seem to have created a monster that he couldn't handle. Tellingly, he wouldn't see out the rest of this year with the Stones, as the tough-nut Allen Klein increasingly took over the band's affairs.

The following week, Mick was interviewed in *NME* by their Stones correspondent Keith Altham about the fuss. 'The only reason we did this show was because it was a good national plug,' he admitted, 'anyone who thought we were changing our image to suit a family audience was mistaken.'

Years later Keith put it more bluntly, as quoted in Victor Bockris's biog: 'Bollocks to that, we're the Stones. It was Mickey Mouse showbiz. Fuck you, just 'cos everybody else is going to go around waving like they're on the end of a children's hour doesn't mean we will. We bothered them because of the way we looked, the way we'd act. Because we never showed any reverence for them, whatsoever. That riled 'em somewhere.'

And now that an uncompromising Rolling Stones had been thrust into the face of Joe Public, the die was cast. They were Public Enemy Number One, and would have to be cut down to size. So far, there had only been minor events like the Stones urinating on a garage wall in 1964 because the toilets were locked. Sold by a shrewd Oldham to the press as an act of insolence, it projected an attitude of 'We piss anywhere, man!' But now drugs were the big, looming menace, and the combination of drugs and the Stones was potential dynamite to the establishment. So, squash the rich young Stones by busting them. Easy.

There was an excellent book published in '93, one of the few that Keith has contributed to. *The Early Stones* was compiled by photographer Michael Cooper's former assistant Perry Richardson, with text by the author Terry Southern, an old mate of the band, and commentary from Keith, Anita Pallenberg and Marianne Faithfull. It gave Cooper some credit for the remarkable pictures he took of the Stones between '63 and '73. He would later become one of the more tragic Stones casualties, his long-term heroin addiction and accompanying depression leading to suicide. One of the reasons, according to the book, was that he never received his rightful acclaim.

Keith has only written two forewords – one for Muddy Waters, the other for Michael Cooper's photographic collection. He obviously loved the bloke – 'he had the same records I had!' – and described him as 'a catalyst' who introduced new friends and contacts. Cooper seems to have been the guy who brought together the whole 'new young aristocracy' circle, which used the Stones and the Beatles as its epicentre.

'It was impossible to be with Michael for any length of time and not get turned on to his life as he got turned on to yours,' praised Keith with hindsight. 'After a while you'd start seeing things through his eyes . . . I mean, he turned me on to always looking at the odd little scenario in the street, and he devoted that same level of ability, intensity, and skill to capturing the making of the Stones.'

Anita recalled the Stones' early days of hobnobbing with the young and rich in the same book: 'Once with the Stones – it was the Ad Lib, one of those clubs – everyboy was just on these benches, eyeing each other. Keith was going, "What the fucking hell do these guys want?", and they were all going, "chat, chat, chat, chat, chat," all frivolous and everything, and Keith was saying, "Fucking tarts, assholes, cunts!". . . The way I saw it, Mick and Keith quickly realised that those people all had something that the Stones wanted, and the Stones had something that all these kind of decadent aristrocrats wanted . . . '

Nevertheless, looking back, it seems almost like a countdown to disaster.

The ball started rolling with the 5 February issue of the *News of the World*. Here they reported an encounter with 'Mick', where he talked about taking acid, popped speed pills, and asked a girl if she fancied smoking some hash. In actuality, the interview had been conducted with Brian at a London club. Mick himself then went on a popular tea-time chat show and refuted the allegations, branding the press as liars and announcing that he was taking legal action. It didn't help. The Stones were now a major target, and soon realised they were under surveillance.

Those tireless guardians of public morality at the *News of the World* went into overdrive, probably to save face and a hefty cash pay-out. Somehow, they found out that Keith was planning a party at Redlands the following weekend. They considered it their public duty to refrain from embarrassing trouserless vicars for one week, and tip off the police.

Three years earlier, the first of a new series of anti-drug laws that appeared with monotonous regularity throughout the 1960s was passed. The Dangerous Drugs Act 1964 criminalised the cultivation of cannabis (possession was already an offence) and illicit possession of amphetamines. It was an implicit recognition that, as Britain began to swing, more of its young people were using reefers and pills. As of yet, no pop stars had been busted, which made for an even better story for the Sunday tabloid.

A week later, on 12 February, Redlands was raided. The bust sent a seismic shockwave, kicking off a ten-year period when the law continually tried to topple the Stones. Keith was having a house party at the time. Guests included George and Patti Harrison, Mick and new girlfriend Marianne Faithfull, plus other members of their London set – like art dealer and smackhead Robert Fraser, with his Moroccan servant Ali, antique dealer Christopher Gibbs and Michael Cooper. There was also an American drug supplier called David Schneiderman, who called himself the Acid King. (Brian and his girlfriend, Anita Pallenberg, had been having a fight and were absent.)

The Acid King served up a hearty breakfast of top-grade White Lightning LSD, which gave the revellers a pleasant day-trip as they strolled around the surrounding countryside. Harrison and his missus left early, and the rest of the party settled into post-trip chill-out mode by watching TV with the sound off and listening to Bob Dylan's *Blonde On Blonde* album.

With the MBE-honoured Beatle safely out of the way, a squad of police officers from the Sussex force swooped at eight o'clock, warrant in hand. Obviously inexperienced country coppers, they were pruriently enthralled by the fact that a young woman – known to the papers as 'Miss X' – was clad only in a fur rug. In their after-work pub chat, the police blew the incident up into the apochryhal story of how they stumbled in on Mick retrieving a Mars bar from the girl's most intimate regions.

Nobody was arrested that day, but eventually the officers took away anything their untrained eyes suspected might be drugs. Overlooking heroin stuffed down the couch, they seized some incense sticks, which had been causing the sweet smell they thought must be hash, and some sachets of mustard Keith had collected on tour. They did find four amphetamine tablets, which were in

Marianne's coat pocket and which Mick gallantly said were his, having been obtained legally in Italy with the knowledge of his London doctor. Robert Fraser had a bottle of heroin tablets, which he said were pills for his diabetes. They confiscated one of those for analysis, but replaced a lump of hash they found in Mick's jacket, thinking it was dirt. Meanwhile, the Acid King was sitting there with a case of drugs, which he said was film stock that would be ruined if they opened it. Keith asked the police to refrain from treading on his Moroccan tapestries.

Confused, fascinated and shocked by the totally alien scene they'd barged into, the best that Chichester's finest could come up with at the time was that Keith could be held responsible for allowing drugs to be used on his premises.

As the bemused police left, someone put on Dylan's 'Rainy Day Women', turning up the volume at the 'Everybody must get stoned' refrain.

The reason for the bust has been the subject of much discussion for over 35 years. The involvement of the *News of the World*, and the abrupt disappearance of the Acid King the next day, has often led to the conclusion that it was a set-up designed to bring down the Stones.

After the bust, the Stones vacated London to avoid the press. Keith, Brian, his driver Tom Keylock, Anita Pallenberg and the film director Donald Cammell's girlfriend, Deborah Dixon, took the road to Morocco through Southern France, but Brian was hospitalised after a severe asthma attack. Keith later said this might have been brought on by the strong acid they'd partaken of, coupled with the sense that something was stirring between himself and Anita. She was then nineteen, a blonde German-Italian model hailing from Rome, as charismatic, cultured and intelligent as she was gorgeous.

After a couple of days, it became obvious that Brian would be in hospital for a week. Keith and Anita continued the trip, and an affair began that would develop into an infamous, lengthy and tempestuous relationship. As Sheila Oldham later remarked, 'I think Keith was really hurt by Linda [Keith] and it took him quite a long time to get over it. It may have made him realise that he needed a strong woman as a lifeline.' In Anita, who describes Keith as 'a shy little guy who couldn't come out of himself' when she first met him, he found what the unstable Brian may also have recognised in her: the perfect woman for a Rolling Stone.

Keith and Anita were joined in Marrakesh by Mick, Marianne and Robert Fraser, before Anita and Marianne flew back to France to pick up Brian from the Toulon hospital. By the time they returned to Marrakesh, Brian had realised what was going on and got drunkenly violent with Anita – especially when she refused to participate in an orgy with two Moroccan hookers he'd picked up.

While Jones was off recording the ethnic Moroccan music that would make up his *Joujouka* album, the others did a runner to London via Madrid. It was officially the end of Brian and Anita's relationship.

On their return, Keith and Anita holed up in a little flat he kept in St John's Wood. They learned that the newspapers had been spattered with stories about the Redlands bust, and that Mick, Keith and Fraser would have to appear in court in May to answer drugs charges. The furore had started and, even though the Stones didn't think they'd done anything too serious, they hired top lawyers. The case was

Brian, Keith and Mick photographed in Morocco by Cecil Beaton.

rapidly becoming a luridly high-profile embodiment of the us-against-them mood of the time. Even a £7,000-bribe paid to the police by Keith's personal minder, 'Spanish Tony' Sanchez, had sunk without trace or effect.

Meanwhile, the Stones had a European tour booked for March and April. The jaunt started in Sweden, where they were strip-searched down to their Y-fronts at customs. The gig at Helsingborg saw fans throwing fireworks and bottles, while police used dogs and truncheons in retaliation. There was another riot on 2 April in Vienna, when someone threw a smoke bomb. There were more strip-searches in France, before the band went on their first ever visit to Eastern Europe. In Warsaw, police used tear gas and batons on 3,000 fans trying to storm the Palace of Culture, where the Stones were performing.

And so it went on until 17 April, in Athens. It would be the last Stones tour for over two years, and certainly went out with a bang. By the time they returned, its anarchic atmophere would be prevalent across the western world, especially in America.

The tour was obviously fraught with tension between Brian and Keith, whose tactic was to hang back. Brian and Anita attended the Cannes Film Festival, where *A Degree of Murder* – in which Anita appeared and for which Brian had contributed the soundtrack – was the German entry in competition. Keith laid low at the hotel, while Brian blew it once and for all by flying into a rage and beating Anita up. End of story.

Anita went to film Roger Vadim's *Barbarella*, playing a wicked witch-type character, while Keith had the next Stones album to think about – plus another pressing problem at home.

On 10 May, Keith, Mick and Robert Fraser appeared in Chichester Crown Court, and were remanded on bail of £100 each to appear at West Sussex Quarter Sessions on 27 June.

By a remarkable coincidence, Brian was busted the same day at his flat in South Kensington, charged with possessing cannabis. 'They timed it to the minute,' said Keith. The papers had a field day. By now, there was a growing feeling of total war between the generations.

The Stones began their new album at Olympic Studios the following week. The sessions for *Their Satanic Majesties Request* reflected the tensions within the Stones at the time. It marked the first conflict between the band in the studio –over the same basic arguments that still rage today. 'I can remember virtually nothing of those sessions,' says Keith in *According to the Rolling Stones*. 'It's a total blank. We were pretty much the way we look on the cover! So really it was a very stoned time.'

Fired up by the success of *Sergeant Pepper*, Mick wanted to out-psychedelicise the Beatles. Keith wanted to ahere to the Stones' rock 'n' roll roots. Brian, who'd ceded so much musical ground to Mick and Keith that his main contributions now consisted of little embellishments, wanted to go back to a purist blues style. The different stratum ran parallel on that album, occasionally merging but often fighting within the same track. As an aural representation of the differences building within the group, it's an interesting piece – but, not for the last time, Mick's instincts would be proven wrong. The next album, *Beggars Banquet*, would be Keith's retort.

Satanic Majesties had to be constructed amidst the drug busts, pressure from the media, and Mick's wholehearted but short-lived immersion in the LSD experience. Even though they were following different conceptions of where the Stones should go, *Satanic Majesties* was still the first Stones album to be totally dominated by Mick and Keith, with the alienated Brian playing a greatly diminished role. Neither was Andrew Oldham the all-powerful Svengali producer of before – in fact, feeling marginalised by Allen Klein as manager, and with pill problems that paralleled Brian's, he walked after completing only two tracks and left the production to engineer Glyn Johns. Meanwhile, Charlie and Bill, as frustrated as ever in his songwriting ambitions, followed the leaders – although Wyman did get his first and only solo credit on this album, as a result of Keith and Mick not turning up at the studio one night.

On 15 June, Keith and Mick were part of the large crowd filmed singing backing vocals to the Beatles' 'All You Need Is Love', during the global *Our World* TV broadcast hosted by David Frost. But the big day was the 27th, when the three-day Redlands trial began in Chichester. Keith was charged under Section 5 [A] of the 1964 Dangerous Drugs Act. This read: 'If a person, being the occu-

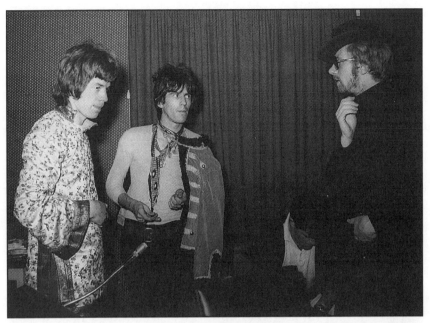

Mick and Keith at their final recording sessions with Andrew Oldham, at Olympic Studios, London, May 1967.

pier of any premises, permits those premises to be used for the purpose of smoking cannabis or cannabis resin or of dealing in cannabis or cannabis resin (whether by sale or otherwise) he shall be guilty of an offence against this act.' The stipulated sentence, on conviction, could range from a fine of up to £1,000 to ten years in prison.

This was the biggest gig of Keith's life so far. The eyes of the world were on this first rock-star drug bust. Up until now, Keith had been the quiet, dark horse with a guitar, while Brian and Mick soaked up the glamour and attention. From the moment he appeared outside Redlands, fag in mouth, sporting a dark frock coat and lacy shirt, he was thrust to the forefront. By now, Keith's face and demeanour were starting to reflect his decadent style of living. His hair was the classic spiketop, eyes darkly contemptuous of bourgeois propriety and complexion white as a sheet.

The prosecution and the media homed in on the fact that Marianne Faithfull – now revealed as 'Miss X' – was covered only by a fur rug. The prosecution continually harped on about it while presenting their case. It prompted Keith's most memorable quote of all time, elevating him to the hero status he would enjoy from that moment onwards.

Prosecutor: 'There was, as we know, a young lady sitting on a settee wearing only a rug. Would you agree, in the ordinary course of events, you would expect a young woman to be embarrassed if she had nothing on but a rug in the presence of eight men, two of whom were hangers-on and the third a Moroccan servant?'

Keith: 'Not at all.'

Prosecutor: 'You regard that, do you, as quite normal?'

Keith: 'We are not old men. We are not concerned about petty morals.'

The jury must have been suitably horrified. They were only out for a few minutes before finding Keith, Mick and Fraser guilty of the charges. The stern and stiff-lipped Judge Block sentenced Mick to three months for possession of the amphetamines, plus £100 costs, while Keith got a year in Wormwood Scrubs, plus £500 court costs. Fraser got six months for the smack, plus £200 costs.

As Mick was taken to Lewes prison, Keith was carted off to the Scrubs, where he was instantly plunged into the humiliating prison routine. Keith was deloused, walked the exercise yard in a circle with the other inmates, and was shown his job in the factory, making little Christmas tree decorations for cakes. But he also received a hero's reception from his fellow inmates. Making light of it all, he later quipped, 'The food's awful, the wine list is terribly limited, and the library is abysmal.' But then, he knew that Allen Klein and the legal team would soon have him out on appeal – which they duly did the following day.

The volcanic public outcry, the spewings of triumph, discontent and outrage, made a whole generation decide that they too would like a life of fun, drugs and naked girls in

TIMES PAST   THE TIMES   FUTURE

PRINTING HOUSE SQUARE, LONDON, E.C.4.   TELEPHONE: 01-236 2000

WHO BREAKS A BUTTERFLY ON A WHEEL?

Mr. Jagger has been sentenced to imprisonment for three months. He is appealing against conviction and sentence, and has been granted bail until the hearing of the appeal later in the year. In the meantime, the sentence of imprisonment is bound to be widely discussed by the public. And the circumstances are sufficiently unusual to warrant such discussion in the public interest.

Mr. Jagger was charged with being in possession of four tablets containing amphetamine sulphate and methyl amphetamine hydrochloride; these tablets had been bought, perfectly legally, in Italy, and brought back to this country. They were not a highly

They were separate cases, and no evidence was produced to suggest that he knew that Mr. Fraser had heroin tablets or that the vanishing Mr. Sneidermann had cannabis resin. It is indeed no offence to be in the same building or the same company as people possessing or even using drugs, nor could it reasonably be made an offence. The drugs which Mr. Jagger had in his possession must therefore be treated on their own, as a separate issue from the other drugs that other people may have had in their possession at the same time. It may be difficult for lay opinion to make this distinction clearly, but obviously justice cannot be done if one man is to be punished for a purely contingent associ-

that Judge Block should have decided to sentence Mr. Jagger to imprisonment, and particularly surprising as Mr. Jagger's is about as mild a drug case as can ever have been brought before the Courts.

It would be wrong to speculate on the Judge's reasons, which we do not know. It is, however, possible to consider the public reaction. There are many people who take a primitive view of the matter, what one might call a pre-legal view of the matter. They consider that Mr. Jagger has "got what was coming to him". They resent the anarchic quality of the Rolling Stones' performances, dislike their songs, dislike their

'I was seeing more of cops and lawyers than anyone else.' Keith and counsel arrive at West Sussex Quarter Sessions, Chichester, 29 June 1967.

the living room. (Well, they did in my case, anyway.) You got what you paid for, Judge Block. Two years later, one of the main movers in the Redlands bust was arrested himself, when the rampant corruption in the Drugs Squad finally came to light.

NME's Brendon Fitzgerald asked Keith in '95 if it really was a case of 'Leave the moptops alone and nail the Rolling Stones.'

'No,' he responded. 'Because then they went for them. They did John. They thought we were the easier target, I think, but they didn't stop at us.'

In other words, it was all-out war, and if they couldn't stop the Stones . . .

The case brought a flurry of outrage at the injustice – from *The Times* to underground publications like Oz, who devoted a whole issue to the case. If the Stones went down, so did their generation. It was a showcase stitch-up. *The Times*' pro-leniency 'Who Breaks A Butterfly On A Wheel?' editorial was the best press release the Stones ever had. The Who garnered themselves some great press too, covering the 'The Last Time' and 'Under My Thumb' as an overnight show of solidarity. It was widely agreed that the Stones had only have received such stiff sentences because of who they were.

On 31 July, the bust went to appeal. Lord Chief Justice Parker amended Mick's sentence to a conditional discharge and quashed Keith's conviction as unsafe on the basis of inadmissible evidence. Keith and Mick must have shared the instant feeling of uplift that ran through the nation's youth – even if Keith was partitioned-off in the court with chicken pox. Thanks to expensive, high-powered lawyers, the establishment's victims came out triumphant, stronger than ever. Thank you to Judge Block and the ham-fisted constabulary – from me and a few million other 1960s teenagers.

On 15 August, the authorities did manage to achieve one goal – to squash the pirate radio stations that had been livening up the UK's airwaves since 1963. Before Radio London had closed down, they'd been plugging the Who's 'Under My Thumb' cover and 'We Love You' – a track the Stones had knocked out to thank the fans for their support during the trial. It was a double-edged gesture, as behind the declaration of love to their fans lurked a two-finger salute to their persecutors. It was released on 18 August and reached eight in the UK.

The track was backed with 'Dandelion', a glorious psychedelic pop song that dated from the 'Ruby Tuesday'-'Let's Spend The Night Together' sessions. (So good that Keith named his daughter after it.) But 'We Love You' was the killer. It was wired drama from the start, opening to weird noises, the clang of a prison door, and the mother of all piano riffs from Nicky Hopkins – a young keyboard player who'd supplant Stu on record when something other than down-the-line blues was called for – before all hell broke loose: crashing drums, Eastern-tinged mellotron, and the soaring refrain of the title.

Obviously aimed at the law, the word 'love' had a sardonic undertow that could have been substituted by 'hate'. Play it next to the Beatles' 'All You Need Is Love', and it's an embodiment of the nice boys/bad boys polarity that existed between the two groups – as was the fact that members of both groups sang backing vocals on both records.

'I'm free to do what I want, any old time.' Keith and Mick get out of court.

The Stones made their own promotional film, a proto-video, for 'We Love You', but it was instantly banned. (It wouldn't be seen again until it was found in a shed years later.) Based on the 1960 film *The Trials of Oscar Wilde*, it was a piss-take of courtroom pomposity. Mick played the persecuted Wilde with Marianne as his gay lover, Lord Alfred 'Bosie' Douglas, while Keith was Bosie's dad, the vengeful Marquis of Queensberry. It came out in August and reached number eight in the charts, though it should have gone higher.

In September, Keith, who was spending much of his time in Rome, obtained planning permission to build a nine-foot wall around Redlands.

Open Plan

After all the furore, Keith finally found himself off the rollercoaster he'd been on since '63. Four years of one-nighters all over the world, twenty-minute sets to screaming crowds, had robbed him of some of his musical creativity. At one point, Keith and Brian were lobbing in snatches of 'Popeye The Sailor Man' during 'Satisfaction' and nobody noticed. By the time touring ground to a halt in '67, Keith was already looking for a new musical impetus. Once again, he found it through the blues.

Open G tuning with a five-string guitar was the discovery that defined the classic Keef tone we know and love. It provided the coruscating razor-slash of groin-level groove power that would be the motor of all the Stones' future classics.

Keith explained it in an epic interview with Alan di Perna for his favourite publication, *Guitar World*, in October '87: 'A whole lot of blues had become available that we just couldn't get in England back in '61 or '62 . . . I started studying the liner notes and listening to cats play and I realised, "The guy plays in a different tuning. Ah!" . . . I came across the five string G tuning on slide guitar records first. Then we did a session with Ry Cooder and he turned me on to other cats, all slide players. I played around with it a bit and realised you could do chordal stuff with these slide tunings . . . And I felt, "Hey, this is like learning again. You gotta put your fingers in new places!" . . . I started working things out in five string tuning, and that got me back into studying and transferring ideas to and from six string tuning . . . Suddenly I was back into the guitar like a motherfucker!'

Keith also spoke about his open tunings to Jas Obrecht in the October '92 issue of *Guitar Player*, citing Cooder, Taj Mahal and the late Gram Parsons, 'who are all students too,' and open G as a life-changing experience that strikes 'a resonant chord within you':

'It's just that vibe. And I realised that one of the best rhythm guitars in the world ever is Don Everly, who always used open tuning . . . . It's the weirdest thing, right, because it's country shit, basically. That was why the Everly stuff was so hard, because it was all on acoustic. So then I had to ask, "Can I translate this five-string thing onto electric, or will it just rumble and not make it?" . . . So it's more working on the sound. Five strings, three notes, two fingers and an asshole, and you've got it! You can play the damned thing. That's all it takes. What to do with it is another thing. It was like a rebirth. Suddenly I got enthusiastic about playing again.'

And so the classic Keef sound was hatched through '67, going public in '68 with 'Jumpin' Jack Flash'. Ironically, Keith was forging the fiercest tones of the darkening late sixties while his group were immersed in a lysergic stew, surrounded by petals and gurus. Before they could move on, the Stones had to get that acid out of their heads, along with the last vestiges of sixties pop. *Their Satanic Majesties Request* was a necessary exorcism of all things overblown and excessive.

There would only be tantalising flashes of Keith's bluesy new guitar sound on the next Stones album. *Their Satanic Majesties Request* was the first record to be made in times of trouble, at their leisure, and off their bollocks. The working title had been *Cosmic Christmas* before *Her Satanic Majesty Requests And Requires* was chosen – a parody of the 'Her Britannic Majesty . . . ' request on the old-style British passports Keith and Mick had to surrender when they came to trial – and then changed after Decca's objections.

Michael Cooper had designed the cover, bettering the Beatles' *Sergeant Pepper* with the Stones dressed up as warlocks and pixies in 3-D. The most widely ridiculed Stones album, it was either dismissed as a ropy answer to *Sergeant Pepper* or acclaimed as a work of vision, even genius. It's neither, though it does beat the Beatles into a peaked military cap. In 2003, *Sergeant Pepper* only has three or four tracks that haven't badly dated, but it's still *Satanic Majesties* that evokes scorn and derision.

Bear in mind that, at the time, even tough-nut mod groups like the Who were coming out with the amphetamine-meets-acid thrash of 'I Can See For Miles', while the Small Faces were moving into 'Itchycoo Park'. Even fellow R&B heavyweights like Graham Bond and Zoot Money were fronting psychedelic outfits and slipping kaftans over their rotund frames. Acid was loosening everybody up, taking them into realms they might later be ashamed of – just like ecstasy, twenty years later.

So, in the light of the new invasion from the States, which was inspiring UK groups like the Pink Floyd to leap out of art school into a sonic lava lamp, how did original inspirations like the Stones fit in?

It was a similar situation to the one they'd be in with punk rock ten years later. The Stones had originated a new rock 'n' roll sound which was adapted first by acid freaks, booting that classic sound into the cosmos, and later by punky speed-freaks trying to rip away those colours and get back to black-and-white energy. Under siege from the psychedelic movement, the Stones momentarily capitulated with *Satanic Majesties*.

The stroboscopic guitar solo does not suit you, sir. Neither does the aural blancmange and words about lilies in lakes. (Do pixies get hard-ons?)

Keith summed it all up in an '81 *Rolling Stone* interview, when he said, 'It's a fractured album. There are some good bits, and it's weird, and there's some real crap on there as well.' There's a mid-seventies bootleg, billed as *The Beatles And The Stones – Sing This All Together*, which is mainly out-takes, instrumental and demo versions. It's immediately noticeable how Keith's guitar riffs got toned down on the final release.

Their Satanic Majesties Request was released in the UK and US at the end of the first week of December, reaching number three and number two respectively. On the whole, the British music press of the time gave the Stones' new direction the thumbs-up. *Record Mirror*'s Norman Jopling was one of the first to pick up on the R&B renegades at the Station Hotel, and you might have expected him to dismiss its trippy experimentalism.

But no. He reckoned the new album launched them 'into a higher, better, and altogether more satisfying musical level . . . . The best album by far that the Rolling Stones have ever recorded.'

It seems like all the derision – both from critics and the band themselves – came only with hindsight. As of yet, there had been no 'Jumpin' Jack Flash', or *Beggars Banquet*. And the classic Stones template had yet to be laid down.

Keith, Brian, Charlie and Bill at Heathrow, London, en route to New York, 13 September 1967. Keith and Mick (who arrived on a later flight from Paris) were both refused entry because of their drugs trials, but were allowed to stop overnight in a New York Hotel.

CHAPTER FOUR
THE DEVIL RIDES OUT

Energy Flash

As 1968 rose on the horizon, the Stones started to feel like they could breathe again. There were no tours planned. Love was in the air for Keith and Anita, as well as Mick and Marianne. And the love generation had started to turn militant. The oppression they had experienced fostered righteous anger, sparking protests. Acid had already had its day, making way for pharmaceuticals of a harder and less soppily utopian nature.

The mood of the day was still freewheeling hippiedom, but there was a steelier undertone, a political awareness and a general feeling that it was time to fight back. After the Technicolor honeymoon, a lot of music was stripped back down. The Beatles went back to basics on 'The White Album', while Dylan went back to his folk and country roots on *John Wesley Harding*. The Stones simply deconstructed themselves, returning with the monumental triumph of *Beggars Banquet*.

Keith, in particular, had never felt comfortable with a flower in his hair, and came back with a vengeance almost scary to behold. He'd been re-immersing himself in the blues, bumping into decades-old masterworks by the likes of Skip James, Blind Blake or Reverend Robert Wilkins. With his new open tunings ready to be put to the test, there was no way the next album was going to be a hallucinogenic concept epic.

Keith started working up his ideas in the Fifth Dimension – a primitive studio he'd had built in the garden cottage at Redlands. The Stones' engineer of the time, George Chkiantz, had installed big speakers, and Keith would stick his ideas down on a basic Philips tape recorder. Sometimes, his raw, distorted sounds would make it through to finished tracks like 'Parachute Woman' and 'Street Fighting Man' (which was initially called 'Primo Grande').

Keith was fired up with enthusiasm and ideas, but the Stones needed a new producer to replace the departed Andrew Loog Oldham, who was eventually paid off by Allen Klein for his formative endeavours with the band. They found someone to steer them to primeval glory in 24-year-old New Yorker Jimmy Miller, who'd made a name through his work with the Spencer Davis Group (he co-wrote their huge hit 'Gimme Some Lovin"), Traffic and Spooky Tooth.

The unsung Spooky Tooth were a classic example of a UK blues outfit delving into psychedelia before returning to what they did best. If you listen to their second album, the Miller-produced *Spooky Two*, the sound and vibe that would soak the Stones' classic albums through to *Exile On Main Street* is already there: the gospelly choruses, gouging blues guitars, robust keyboards and a no-frills approach which still managed to sound epic. (When Primal Scream recorded 'Movin' On Up', twenty years after Jimmy Miller ground to a halt with the

Stones, they were accused of hijacking the late-sixties *Beggars Banquet* sound. Not so. Miller was simply at the controls for that one too.)

Keith's much-quoted appraisal of Jimmy Miller appeared in *Crawdaddy* in '75: 'We were just coming out of *Satanic Majesties*, acid, everything was on the point of dispersal. I had nicked Brian's old lady, it was a mess, and Jimmy pulled *Beggars Banquet* out of all that. It was really a gas to work with him. We tried to do it ourselves, but it's really a drag not having someone to bounce off, someone who knows what you want and what he wants. You get someone like Jimmy Miller, who can turn the whole band on, make a non-descript number into something, which is what happened on *Beggars Banquet*.'

'Most of all I wanted the Stones to be themselves, not my idea of what they should be,' said Jimmy in *Rave* magazine. First he did it with 'Jumpin' Jack Flash', the Stones' two-fisted, guns-ablazing return to form. One of the most invincible Keef riffs of all time – which he later said was his favourite out of the whole canon – chopped and snarled up a dense maelstrom of sound. By the time Mick came in, it sounded like a thousand guitars going over that same riff, both acoustic and electric, all distorted over the fattest drum sound Charlie ever produced.

While Keith also supplied the malevolent bass runs, Bill claims it was him who came up with the riff on a keyboard one day at rehearsal – on 12 March 1968, to be exact, when Keith and Mick came in to find himself, Brian and Charlie jamming on it, and the track simply grew. Keith took it back to the Fifth Dimension and pummelled it into his single-mike Philips reel-to-reel recorder. Then Mick gave the first of his new style of rivetingly demonic showstoppers, with Bill's sinister organ creeping in halfway just to add to the atmosphere of menace. By the quasi-psychedelic ending, the Stones had given new meaning to the term Wall of Sound.

I used to wonder why Stones mate Phil Spector, who they admired so much, had never produced the band. Later, I realised that Andrew felt it wasn't necessary as they had England's answer to Spector in himself. But, if that speculative collaboration had ever happened, it would have sounded something like 'Jumpin' Jack Flash'.

Keith later attributed the song's chorus and title to his old gardener at the time, Jack Dyer. Mick and Keith had been up all night working on the song. A storm was starting to break outside as dawn broke, and Jack walked past the window. When Mick asked who it was, Keith replied, 'Jumpin' Jack.' Mick flashed on that and, with their best riff since 'Satisfaction', a monster was born. (Keith would later claim that it *is* the 'Satisfaction' riff – played backwards.)

'Jumpin' Jack Flash' was the first result of the Miller sessions which started in earnest on 15 March at Olympic and went on for over a month, with engineers Eddie Kramer (Jimi Hendrix's favourite), George Chkiantz and Glyn Johns. Sessions reconvened in May. At the same time, the group were working on other songs which had been sparked up at Fifth Dimension, a studio in Surrey, or a rehearsal studio they'd bought in Bermondsey Street, south London. These included a Robert Johnson-inspired ballad called 'Meet Me At The Station', born from a session where the band sat around the mike and played pure raw blues, later retitled 'No Expectations', 'Factory Girl', 'Dear Doctor', 'Stray Cat Blues', and versions of Howlin' Wolf's 'Rock Me Baby', Robert Johnson's 'Love In Vain' and Robert Wilkins' 'That's No Way To Get Along' (retitled by the Stones 'Prodigal Son').

In true Stones style some of these tracks would take an album or two's time to mature sufficiently – as Keith says, songs are like wine. For example, a cover of Muddy's 'Still A Fool' would grow into 'Two Trains Running', and eventually became 'Midnight Rambler', while 'Stuck Out All Alone' would grow into the epic 'You Can't Always Get What You Want' by the end of the year.

With cylinders now firing at such a high level, the decision was made to rush out 'Jumpin' Jack Flash' without putting it on the album. 'The best thing we did with Jimmy was "Jumpin' Jack Flash",' said Keith in a lavish booklet put out in '93 as part of a 25th anniversary edition of *Beggars Banquet*. 'Originally we cut it as an early track for *Beggars*. But we released it straight away because we wanted to have something out while we were working on the album, as we'd left such a long gap between singles.'

When asked by Terry Southern, in Michael Cooper's *The Early Stones*, how he felt to have written the theme song of his generation, Keith replied, 'What I can say is that when I play that first riff in "Jumpin' Jack Flash", something happens in my stomach – a feeling of tremendous exhilaration, an amazing superhuman feeling. An explosion is the best way to describe it. You just jump on that riff and it plays you. It's the one feeling I would say approaches the state of nirvana.' In 1968, the Stones gave 'Jumpin' Jack Flash' the best launch possible, by playing their first live show in the UK in over two years.

The First Time

My first ever Rolling Stones gig came as one of the most fortunate surprises I've ever had.

One day at school, our chemistry teacher, Mr. Pike, announced that on 12 May he was running a coach trip from the school to the annual *NME* Pollwinners Concert at the Empire Pool, Wembley. I was still only thirteen and I'd never been to a pop concert before, but wanted to lose my gig-going virginity – especially as *NME* had announced that Jimi Hendrix was one of the headliners. The rest of the bill either shone or was shite – the teeny groups and novelty acts who were dominating the charts, plus Cliff Richard.

A few weeks later, I was mortified to read that Hendrix had cancelled, due to US commitments. We still made the trip on a Sunday afternoon, and sat through the bill amidst a horde of screaming girls. The line-up included Status Quo, Peter Frampton and the Herd, Lulu, the Tremeloes, the great Dusty Springfield, Scott Walker and Dave Dee, Dozy, Beaky, Mick and Tich. I was particularly impressed by the Show Stoppers, and their 'Ain't Nothing But A Houseparty' (it was the first time I'd encountered an American soul band) and the Move's blistering take on Spooky Tooth's 'Sunshine Help Me' (originally produced by Jimmy Miller).

Two of the most vociferous screamers in our crowd were a saucy pair of miniskirted girls from the local high school. They couldn't have been more than fifteen, but these two stray cats managed to wheedle their way into the backstage area – and returned smiling, with some hot news. Another band had been added to the bill at the last minute. I didn't pay much attention at first, being too busy sulking during Cliff's featherweight showbiz routine. But finally, the news reached our row. The Stones were gonna play. In about ten minutes time, I'd be seeing the other Mr. Richard. I couldn't have catapulted further into the air than if someone had thrust a red-hot poker 'twixt my aching cheeks.

After what seemed about two hours, 'zany' compere Jimmy Saville introduced the Stones.

Boom. What followed eclipsed any of the previous reactions. I swear the foundations were shaking. It was the first – and only – time I've been in the middle of full-throttled screaming mayhem. There they were, tearing into the first ever performance of 'Jumpin' Jack Flash'. I'd never be the same again – even if they could have been playing 'Popeye The Sailor Man', given the noise of the crowd.

It was hard to think that, only a few months earlier, this group had been bowling about in kaftans. Keith swaggered on in black leather jacket, white drainpipes, fag in mouth, draped in a scarf. It was the first time I'd clapped eyes on him in the flesh, and he was already resembling the exotic rock 'n' roll hoodlum persona which would emerge over the next few years. Mick did his thing in blue velvet strides, throwing his shoes into the crowd, while Marianne – in a razor-blade patterned blouse – threw tulips from the front row. Sadly, this would be the first and last time I'd see Brian in action, courting the adulation in a green-fringed jacket. But it was a classic moment that will live with me for the rest of my life. In fact, it's a gas.

When the Stones were done, I remember how Keith took off his jacket and was whirling his scarf around his head as he bounded off.

The Devil Rides Out

On 21 May 1968, Brian got busted again for possessing cannabis at his flat in Kings Road, Chelsea. It was the morning after a Stones outing to see Stanley Kubrick's groundbreaking new film, *2001: A Space Odyssey*, where the group had dropped acid. Brian had recently hitched up with Linda Keith, Keith's ex, for a short time, as if in retaliation for Keith taking Anita. (She'd distinguished herself by overdosing on downers at Brian's previous flat in Belgravia, getting him evicted.) Now, in his fucked-up state, he was confronted by the cops with a lump of hash they found in a ball of wool. As Brian had only recently started renting the place, he maintained that he knew nothing about the gear, and broke down. He pleaded not guilty, and was remanded for three weeks on £2,000 bail. In early June, he was committed for trial at the Inner London Sessions.

On 24 May, 'Jumpin' Jack Flash' was released. It debuted on TV with a dark and stunning video featuring Mick in war-paint, and Keith and Brian in enormous insect shades. The impact was enormous. NME called it 'vintage Stones', adding, '[they] have a unique flair for taking a basically simple formula and turning it into a miniature epic.' 'Jumpin' Jack Flash' was the first UK number one single the Stones had enjoyed since 'Paint It, Black' in '66, and went to number three in the US. The Stones took out an ad in the *NME* of 22 June: 'Dear readers of

NME. Jumpin' Jack Flash is really gassed that he made Number One. So are the Rolling Stones. Thank you. We are slaving over a hot album which is coming out next month. Until then . . .'

Meanwhile, Brian was becoming a problem. He'd suffered a nervous breakdown after his first bust and was sure that his second arrest was a set-up. He couldn't handle seeing Anita and Keith together every night, and was plunging further into self-destruction.

Many nights at the studio, Brian was incapable of playing. It left Keith to overdub the greasy meshes of viciously sensual guitar throughout most of the album. When Brian chose to shine, he could still be transcendental – as in the beautiful 'No Expectations – but the core instrumental sound of *Beggars Banquet* is Keith's multi-tiered guitars, the brilliant piano of Nicky Hopkins, Mick's distinctive harmonica and that newly upfront rhythm section. Frequent visitors to the studio, who may also be in the mix somewhere, included Traffic's Dave Mason and Eric Clapton, who'd been fancied as a likely Stone ever since they first had problems with Brian.

In June, controversial French film director Jean-Luc Godard had moved his crew into the studio to film the Stones as they recorded. He was making his first English-speaking film, called *One Plus One*, which the press release said was based on two themes: construction and destruction. The Stones were supposed to represent the former, while the latter was depicted by Black Power activists reciting political poetry before killing some white girls against a wrecking yard backdrop. (Another section had some bloke reading Hitler's *Mein Kampf* aloud in a pornographic bookshop – intended to be 'swinging sixties' star Terence Stamp, who bowed out when he was busted for drugs.)

In briefings to the Stones, Godard was wilfully enigmatic and impenetrable. But this apparently was the point. All the band really knew was that this legend of the art-house wanted to capture them on screen.

And he picked exactly the right time. It wasn't planned that way, but *One Plus One* ended up chronicling the entire evolution of 'Sympathy For The Devil', one of the last tracks to be recorded for the album. (The film was retitled *Sympathy for the Devil* in the States.) After all the press hoaxes about the *Clockwork Orange* film, and other semi-mythical projects, the first Rolling Stones film would be a baffling series of violent images woven around the band simply working in the studio for a few days.

The film records endless run-throughs as the song slowly unfolds and is sculpted into its breathtaking final form. On 5 June, Bobby Kennedy was assassinated, so Mick's line, 'Who killed Kennedy?' got changed into the plural.

I finally saw *One Plus One* at a one-off showing at London's Electric Cinema in Portobello Road in the early eighties. It's the only visual document of the Stones creating a song out of nothing over a few days (and one of their all-time classics at that), and for that reason it's fascinating. As for the rest of the film, it was dated even twenty years ago.

The film was also shown at '68's San Francisco Film Festival. *Rolling Stone's* Marjorie Heins was there, and loved the way the whole convoluted affair built towards to the triumph of the finished tune: 'As it stands, the song is so fine, so insistent, that it carries not only the voice of the Devil, but that of historical necessity, sexual drive and wishful thinking. It keeps playing and playing, coming and coming. When at the end it finally comes, the tension of the film is released and there is a sense of achievement, as if all the groping and provoking and sloganeering do reach some goal.'

The Stones have basically constructed their songs by the same gradual process ever since. 'Sympathy' started life as a Dylan-style folk vehicle called 'The Devil Is My Name'. By the time Keith had finished pumping up the groove and sitting in on high-tensile bass, Charlie added a fierce tribal samba beat and was joined by conga player Rocky Dijon. The guitars became slashing machetes, Hopkins went into keyboard overdrive and Mick eventually delivered one of the most impassioned vocals of his life. The icing on the cake was when Jimmy Miller started up that contagious 'whoo whoo' chant with a choir consisting of Keith, Anita, Brian, his new girlfriend Suki Poitier, Bill, Charlie, Glyn Johns and Nicky Hopkins. But the saddest part of *One Plus One* was when the camera lingered on Brian, looking totally out of it in the wake of his bust, with his guitar not even plugged in.

These disparate elements would become even more apparent in 2003, when dance music titan Norman 'Fatboy Slim' Cook remixed the track, even using the 'whoo whoo's all the way through. Breaking from the usual remix tradition, he actually highlighted the original elements and gave the Stones their first American chart-topper for years.

The words were inspired by Mikhail Bulgakov's *The Master and Margarita*, which Marianne had given to Mick to read. The book is set in 1930s Russia, where Satan pays a visit to St Petersburg accompanied by naked female vampires. The song's lyrics use this as a jumping-off point to present the Devil as an unseen force in crucial events throughout history, with Mick introducing him as 'a man of wealth and taste'. It was very clever, and would open a can of worms in the light of ensuing events – such as Altamont, where, amidst the carnage, Mick would claim, 'Something funny always happens when we do that song.'

With such a blatant title, the Stones were obviously now going to have black magic added to their list of war crimes. For years, rumours would appear about Keith and Anita being particularly fond of a dabble, although Keith would later dismiss it as just a casual interest of the time. Although he admitted, in *Top Pops*, to reading about alchemy, magic and UFOs, he played down his interest by saying, 'I didn't have a heavy education so I can't manage heavy books.'

In David Dalton's book, *The First Twenty Years*, there's an interview with notorious occultist Kenneth Anger, for whom Mick supplied synth-noodling for his film *Invocation of My Demon Brother*. Anger was a fringe member of the Stones' 1960s Chelsea set, and saw the band as 'dilettantes' when it came to magic – although he also believed Anita, with her powerful, sexy personality, was 'a witch'.

In Robert Greenfield's '71 interview in *Rolling Stone*, Keith says, 'Kenneth Anger calls me [his] Lucifer's right-hand man.' When asked about this, Anger explained, 'I was going to film a version of *Lucifer Rising* [the most notorious of his cinematic 'magic spells'] with the Stones. All the roles were to be carefully cast, with Mick as Lucifer and Keith as Beelzebub. Beelzebub is really the Lord of the

Flies, and is like the Crown Prince next to the King in the complicated hierachy of demons. Beelzebub is like a henchman for Lucifer . . . The occult unit within the Stones was Keith and Anita, and Brian. You see, Brian was a witch too. I'm convinced. He showed me his witch's tit. He had a supernumary tit in a very sexy place on his inner thigh. He said: "In another time they would've burned me." He was very happy about that. Mick backed away from being Lucifer. He thought that it was too heavy.'

So what was the active magical element in the Stones' music?

'It has such strong sexual connotations. It's basically music to fuck to.'

The psycho-sexual ambience surrounding the Stones in the late sixties and early seventies could be overwhelming. There were definitely forces at play which probably started with Brian Jones – the most worldly, unpredictable Stone – in the band's early days. Sex had previously been swept under the mat. Now the Stones were celebrating it in its darker forms, exploring former taboos like underage sex and displaying a sexual ambiguity in the way they dressed.

As '68 progressed, the drugs crept from acid to cocaine and, for some, hero-in. Sexual tension was rife within the Keith-Anita-Brian triangle, and the law were not yet off their back. But in the middle of all this, the Stones were whip-ping out luminous epics like 'Sympathy For The Devil'.

By sheer coincidence, the studio caught fire during the filming. ('Something funny always happens when we do this song,' indeed.) Around four in the morn-ing, one of the film crew's arc lights bent over and set light to the ceiling. The Stones and the crew were evacuated and three fire engines arrived to put it out, drenching the equipment. Although the damage to the studio wasn't too bad, if Bill Wyman and Jimmy Miller hadn't saved the tapes, *Beggars Banquet* might have turned into the Great Lost Stones Album.

At the end of June, the Stones regrouped at the Fifth Dimension and started to rehearse a chilling song called 'Sister Morphine', for which Marianne wrote the words. With Brian out of action much of the time, Marianne and Anita were exer-cising influence over their boyfriends' music by suggestion, or simply vibes and reactions. Marianne gave Mick books to read, and drew his attention to the Robert Johnson song 'Love In Vain'. Anita's influence became especially pervasive. On one occasion she told Mick that 'Stray Cat Blues' needed an aural rejig, call-ing it 'crap' – so he went off and did it, probably because nobody else, except Keith, would have had the nerve to be so forthright. As she allegedly told her and Keith's dealer, 'I feel rather like I'm the sixth Rolling Stone. Mick and Keith and Brian need me to guide them, to criticise them and give them ideas.'

Keith, who has always favoured another guitar to spar with, found himself a potential partner in the midst of Brian's deterioration. Young American slide gui-tar exponent Ry Cooder proved to be a big influence and a productive musical catalyst. He'd started his career playing on *Safe As Milk*, the startling first album by Captain Beefheart and his Magic Band – psychedelic blues at its finest. Phil Spector's former arranger, Jack Nitzsche, brought him over to see the Stones, but it begat a long-running controversy that would lead to Cooder becoming quite bitter about Keith in later years. At these sessions, Cooder played on 'Love In Vain'

Keith and Anita, pictured with a friend at the premiere of Yellow Submarine *at the London Pavilion Cinema, 17 July 1968.*

and supplied the frazzled slide on 'Sister Morphine', initially recorded as a single by Marianne Faithfull and eventually seeing the light of day on *Sticky Fingers*.

The way Ry Cooder tells it, Keith nicked all his licks. From Keith's point of view, they struck up the kind of musical relationship that he adores: two guys and two guitars, trading, learning and inspiring each other with their respective styles. Keith had been getting into open tuning since the previous year, teaching himself via old blues records. Ry had this down pat, and showed Keith some more handy hints. Naturally, there were also rumours that Cooder was going to join the Stones. Nitzsche also asked Cooder to contribute to the soundtrack he was composing for Mick's upcoming movie, *The Performers*.

But, whatever way you look at it, Mr. Cooder, as good he is, has never churned up such an inimitable racket as Mr. Richards. He is simply too academic. Ultimately though, he became another influence for Keith to chuck into his bucket, joining Chuck, Muddy and the rest of the gang in a rock 'n' roll-blues cocktail.

After completing recording, Mick, Marianne and Jimmy Miller joined Glyn Johns at Sunset Sound in LA, where he was mixing the album. They were followed by Charlie Watts and his new wife Shirley, before another party arrived, consisting of Michael Cooper, Anita, Keith and his new mate Gram Parsons. This was the visit where Cooper took his famous photos of the posse when they visited the Joshua Tree National Park, on mescaline.

Keith recalled the trip in Cooper's book, *The Early Stones*, providing the caption to a set of photos showing the blasted group loitering on the rocks, wrapped in blankets. 'Ah Gram Parsons – when we were all up in Joshua Tree looking for UFO's . . . . Some loon had managed to put a working barber chair on top of the mountain, so you could goof on sunsets and sunrises and UFO's from the comfort of this adjustable, revolving chair, which I think Gram put us on to.'

G.P.

Gram Parsons was a crucial, life-changing acquaintance for Keith, and an undeniably huge influence on the Stones. From their first meeting in '68, Gram would remain Keith's close friend until his tragic death in September '73. In Gram, Keith found a gentle kindred spirit who shared a likeminded passion for music and drugs.

'Gram probably did more than anybody to sort of put a new face on country music,' said Keith in *The Early Stones*. 'I mean, the reason now you've got your Waylons and Willie Nelsons, and why their music got accepted is probably more because of Gram than anybody. Country music up until that time – around the end of the sixties – was like just its own little backwater; he brought it into the mainstream of, you know, "Don't forget about this shit . . ."'

At first, the arrival in '68 of full-blown country music in the post-psychedelic fall-out seemed curiously corny. The Byrds had been pursuing 'space country' on *The Notorious Byrd Brothers* in '67, but Gram's arrival in their ranks for *Sweetheart Of The Rodeo* took it the whole way, even being recorded in Nashville. The same summer saw *John Wesley Harding* – Dylan's first album since *Blonde On Blonde*. It came as a total shock, with several tracks featuring a rural, pedal-steeled strum, and granted Dylan a whole new voice. And then the classic American sound turned sepia, rustic but totally hip, as Dylan's old backing group, the Band, released *Music From Big Pink*, American roots music gone electric.

Beggars Banquet was obviously influenced by the fact that it was cool to unashamely explore the roots again. When Gram Parsons sauntered into the Stones' orbit, he was seen as the real deal. And he did, indeed, pass it on, as Keith loves to say.

Gram was raised in Waycross, Georgia, charming all and sundry with his laidback brand of Southern courtesy. He'd cut his teeth on country artists like the Louvin Brothers and Hank Williams, but also liked the rock 'n' roll of early Elvis and the Everlys. Years later, he'd still talk of the Southern jukeboxes which sat James Brown, Otis Redding, Jerry Lee Lewis, Merle Haggard and James Cleveland together in the same selection.

Although he was a gifted musician who could play like a dream, Gram would ruffle the rednecks because he looked like a rock star. He saw it as only natural when he formed the International Submarine Band in '65, regarded by most as the first group to fuse country and rock 'n' roll, but met with perplexed indifference when they released their one and only album, *Safe At Home*. By late '67, Gram fronted a loose ensemble called the Flying Burrito Brothers, but had started hanging out with the Byrds. In March '68, he joined up – initially as a piano player – and helped steer the space rockers beak-first into the upfront country sound of *Sweetheart Of The Rodeo*. Unfortunately, for legal reasons many of his vocal contributions were mixed out. But songs like his spectacularly emotional 'Hickory Wind' were enough to earn him a reputation as the ultimate cosmic cowboy.

Keith first met Gram when the Byrds toured the UK in May. The Stones checked out their gig at the London underground club Middle Earth, where Gram became immediately smitten with the Stones' lifestyle and attitude. He and Keith kicked off with a pissed-up night visit to Stonehenge, and thus began a beautiful friendship. Before the Byrds took off for the South African leg of their tour, however, Keith and Anita filled Gram in on the nastiness of apartheid. He promptly quit the group and started hanging out with Keith.

It's been said that the Stones enticed Gram away from the Byrds, whom he'd only been with for five months, to sprinkle some country flavour over their pie. But all that Keith did was open Gram's eyes to a whole wide world beyond country. Gram's wealthy family and his generous trust fund also explained, according to Keith, how he 'could get better coke than the Mafia'.

Apart from the coke, Gram did Keith more of a service by teaching him the rudiments of country music. He showed him it went much deeper than the glossy Nashville stuff, with the grittier strands hailing from Bakersfield, California. And it didn't end there, because he was into all kinds of music from gospel to rockabilly. Keith, in turn, turned Gram on to his beloved blues. The pair hung out together, got wasted together, and, as later habits took hold, would even try to kick junk together. Most of all, they played music together. It was a two-way musical appreciation society. Gram's passion and imparted knowledge was an indefinable force which imbued the Stones from *Let It Bleed* through to *Goats Head Soup*, and also after he'd passed. Keith might never have turned out a wracked country ballad like 'The Worst', on '93's *Voodoo Lounge*, if he hadn't been touched by Gram Parsons. Gram probably did more to guide Keith to his current status as the ultimate purveyor of rootsy, emotional ballads than anyone.

Talking about the influence of country music in the February '86 issue of *Guitar World*, Keith said, 'I grew up listening to really good music, a lot of it too sophisticated for a kid, like Sarah Vaughan, Billy Eckstine, Ella Fitzgerald and Count Basie. At the same time we had George Jones, Ernest Tubb, Jimmie Rogers, Hank Williams; I grew up with them as well. To me country music comes quite naturally – after all, those melodies basically originate in England, Wales, Scotland, Ireland. The playing is not that difficult, it's just that the studs and rhinestones are hard to find in England!'

When Gram finally returned to Los Angeles, he found that fellow Byrd Chris Hillman had also left after the nightmare of the South African trip, so the pair set about reviving the Flying Burrito Brothers. Their early '69 debut album, *The Gilded Palace Of Sin*, upped the ante for country rock.

When the Stones visited LA in October of that year, to finish *Let It Bleed*, Gram and Keith got even closer. It started to piss Mick off, as he seems to have felt threatened not only by their friendship but by Parsons' sheer talent and coolness. Gram became besotted with Keith and his lifestyle – although he had the usual trouble in keeping up with him. Some have said that getting sucked into the Stones' vortex was what led to his death. It definitely didn't help his own band. But, from Jason Walker's detailed biography, *God's Own Singer*, Gram comes over as a naturally sensitive person with excessive tendencies – Keith or no Keith.

As former super-groupie Pamela Des Barres describes in her book, *Rock Bottom*, 'Gram Parsons' short, tangled life was like one of George Jones's weepy songs – full of Southern madness, backstabbing, cheating, suicide, liquor, lawsuits, more drugs than should be allowed, too much family money, and too little love.' In fact, the person who probably loved Gram the most was Keith, whom Pamela quotes: 'Gram was special. If he was in a room, everyone else became sweet. Anything Gram was involved in had a touch of magic to it.'

Gram would accompany Keith and his friend and biographer Stanley Booth to Altamont, where the Burritos were supporting. The Stones let the Burritos put 'Wild Horses' on their second album, *Burrito Deluxe*, before *Sticky Fingers* was even released. Gram was present during much of the recording of *Exile On Main Street*, and is a highly recognisable spiritual influence on that amazing record, even if he didn't play on it.

After increasing drug abuse and the demise of the Burritos, Gram Parsons embarked on an overdue solo career which was sadly short-lived. He only made two albums, *G.P.* and the posthumously-released *Grievous Angel*, before, in September '73, aged 26, he died of a drug overdose as he celebrated completing the latter at the Joshua Tree Inn. A massive legend grew around his funeral rites, when his body was hijacked from the airport by road manager Phil Kaufman and cremated at his beloved Joshua Tree – as per Gram's wishes.

As Keith has said, 'You know, the person who I'm most pissed off about not still being around is Gram – with Michael [Cooper] running him a close second. I think that I probably learned more from Gram than anybody else.'

Just A Shot Away

With the new album finished, the Stones returned to London and threw a party for Mick's 25th birthday at a new West End club called Vesuvio's. Crammed with friends and contemporaries, the place was treated to the first ever playing of *Beggars Banquet* from Mick's acetate.

While they were mixing the album in California, Mick and Keith took a fancy to a toilet wall they encountered in a Mexican garage. Instead of pissing over it, they asked photographer Barry Feinstein to photograph it as a potential album cover. It was scrawled with an intriguing selection of graffiti, most of which had a certain young Stones fan scratching his head at the time.

The offending artwork resulted in a stalemate that would delay the album's release for months. It was originally scheduled to come out in August, but Decca said the cover was offensive. The big boss, Sir Edward Lewis, informed the band that the album could not be adorned with a seedy toilet wall, as they'd be prosecuted for obscenity. They wouldn't even put it out in a brown paper bag, marked 'Unfit For Children', as per the Stones' suggestion.

'The job of a record company is to distribute,' said Keith in *NME*. 'All they've got to do is put it in the shops, not dictate to people what they should or should not have.'

For now, the Stones had to be content with the US only release of an incendiary single from the album called 'Street Fighting Man'. It sparked a fair amount of uproar, perfectly mirroring the swelling unrest of the times as the Vietnam war and civil rights issues turned America into a hotbed of demonstrations, riots and heavy-handed attempts at control by the authorities.

On 27 May, Mick and Marianne had attended the huge anti-Vietnam demo at the American Embassy in London's Grosvenor Square. Not wishing to be embroiled in the battle with riot squad police, Mick went home after chucking a few rocks and wrote the words to 'Street Fighting Man'.

It was hardly the same group who'd been singing about lakes, ladies and lilies a few months before. The track had started life at Keith's Fifth Dimension on his trusty tape recorder, before the band rehearsed it under the title 'Primo Grande'. The finished track is dominated by massed banks of acoustic guitars, thrashing against Charlie's cliffhanger beat to create a simmering tension which undulates like a police siren.

'Street Fighting Man' also sparked instant controversy because the picture sleeve depicted a violent demonstration. It was instantly withdrawn, making it among the most valuable of all Stones collectables. The song was released at the time of the Democratic Convention in Chicago, which was hit by riots, many radio stations refused to play it, and it only made number 48 in the charts. But with its no-nonsense attack, the Stones were now mirroring their times much more effectively.

As Keith commented to *NME*'s Keith Altham, 'They [Decca] told me that "Street Fighting Man" was subversive. Of course it's subversive. [But] It's stupid to think you can start a revolution with a record. I wish you could.'

He expanded on the theme during Robert Greenfield's '71 *Rolling Stone* interview: 'Before, America was a real fantasy land. It was still Walt Disney and hamburger dates and when you came back in 1969 it wasn't anymore. Kids were really into what was going on in their country . . . . But by the time it came Nixon's turn in 1968, people were concerned in a real different way.' With songs like 'Street Fighting Man' and 'Sympathy For The Devil', the Stones were now lobbing aural grenades of their own. What else could a poor boy do?

Brian had a temporary respite from his problems when he took George Chkiantz to Morocco to record the music of Joujouka, hypnotic ritual rhythms beat out on primitive percussion and punctuated with basic wind instruments. According to Chkiantz, he was totally straight while he was making his field recordings. But when he returned to London, Brian plunged straight back into the abyss, and the intended album wouldn't see the light of day until October '71. *Brian Jones Presents The Pipes Of Pan In Joujouka* would be released on Rolling Stones Records as a posthumous tribute, now regarded as a pioneering piece of world music.

With *Beggars Banquet* gathering dust while the war over the cover dragged on, Mick started filming his movie debut – now entitled *Performance* – in early September. This would take up the next two months, and it threw Keith into limbo. He could no longer fill in the time with his girlfriend, because Anita was playing his best mate's love interest in the film. Added to his boredom were the frustration and depression that resulted from Mick and Anita getting very intimate on an almost daily basis.

Keith responded by snorting heroin for the first time. The mother of all numbing agents started creeping into his coke to make speedballs. He also plunged himself into the only thing he could really rely on – music – and wrote much of what would comprise the Stones' next album, *Let It Bleed*.

The world might not have had 'Gimme Shelter', which Keith thrashed out on his cassette player in twenty minutes of emotional darkness, if Mick hadn't shagged Anita. But then, Keith may not have got into smack either – although, given his lifestyle of the time, it would probably have become inevitable at some point.

Originally, writer/co-director Donald Cammell offered the part of Pherber – girlfriend of Turner, Mick's reclusive former pop-star character – to Marianne Faithfull, but she fell pregnant. Her original replacement, Tuesday Weld, then suffered an ankle injury. In stepped Anita. She'd become pregnant by Keith, but explained that, as she'd already signed the contract to appear in the film, she'd had to have an abortion. Ironically, Marianne had suggested that Mick base his doped-out, vulnerable character on a combination of Brian's stoned torment and Keith's outlaw cool.

Warner Brothers had been hoping for another whoopee-doo Beatles-style pop movie, when Mick was brought in as the star. But, instead of teenage fun, they got the blackest, most provocative, mind-twisting celebration of sex, drugs and violence ever produced by the British cinema.

The film loosely concerns an East End gang enforcer – a 'performer' – called Chas, played by James Fox with cold-eyed relish. He crosses his boss, Harry Flowers (played by Johnny Shannon, a boxing trainer from London's Old Kent Road), and gets out of hand by letting his 'performance' turn into the murder of a former mate, thus breaking the gangster code. Chas has to go on the run, and takes a spare room at the rundown but exotic residence of Turner, a fey, faded rock-star archetype, and his two female co-habitants – Pherber and Lucy, played by Michelle Breton. He feels uneasy amidst the free and easy decadence he strolls into, but tries to fit in so he can lay low before fleeing to the States. Chas ends up imbibing magic mushrooms and becoming a fourth corner of the love triangle, while his sense of identity is lost and transposed in the scary, hallucinogenic chaos. Eventually Chas is tracked down. He shoots Turner point-blank through the head before he's dragged away. The closing shot shows his face looking out of a car window – except that now it's Turner's.

The film was co-directed by Cammell with cinematographer Nicolas Roeg, who went on to make *Walkabout, Don't Look Now* and *The Man Who Fell To Earth*. Much of the filming, between September and November, took place in a house at Lowndes Square, Chelsea, although Turner's abode was supposed to be in Notting Hill's Powys Square where the exteriors were shot. (I've stood on the spot where Chas rings the doorbell and Anita shouts, 'Push!' through the intercom.) The décor's combination of Moroccan artefacts and arty flourishes was supplied by a mate of the Stones, Christopher Gibbs, and his exotic antiques business. To add to the atmosphere of decadence, most of the Redlands bust crew were present – Anita and Keith renting a room at Robert Fraser's nearby flat for the duration of the filming.

For many, Anita is the real star of *Performance*, with her translucent foxiness and stoned cool. Suddenly, Keith seemed like the luckiest man alive – but was he? Call it method acting, but Mick and Anita took their screen roles as lovers very seriously. James Fox walked in on them in a dressing room, and found a full-scale 'rehearsal' under way. The sex scenes were not faked, although they were carefully edited and soft-focused on the released print. Keith certainly didn't appreciate the short film of out-takes, which won first prize at an Amsterdam porno festival.

As he waited outside in his Bentley for filming to end at seven every night, or sat in Fraser's flat laying down new songs, Keith was tormented by knowledge of what was going on. With Fraser a long-term heroin user, it was only natural that Keith would try and dispel the feeling of gloom and the knotted turmoil in his stomach, getting comfortably numb during those long, agonised waits.

Anita was at the centre of her second inter-Stones love triangle. It was potentially even more sensitive, as Keith had been friends with Mick for a lot longer than they'd known Brian. If he'd chosen to confront Jagger, it could have been the end of the Stones. When Brian lost Anita to Keith, he'd responded by getting even more fucked up. Now Keith was doing the same thing. Luckily, he'd prove that he was made from 'good stock'.

The moment Mick Jagger set foot on the set of *Performance* is the moment the short-lived age of peace and love drew towards its end. As Cammell would later reflect, 'The movie was finished before Altamont and Alatamont actualised it.' Some have even speculated that black magic was thrown into the cauldron of sex, violence and drugs – Cammell's father was a friend of Aleister Crowley, the 'Great Beast' who inspired Kenneth Anger – and that *Performance* cursed the lives of those involved in it.

In her autobiography, Marianne Faithfull says that those involved 'began to fall apart almost the moment it was finished. It was like a virus infecting everything.' James Fox was certainly never the same again. He'd plunged himself into the role of Chas by living and mixing with gang-related characters around London's East End. He even found Johnny Shannon at the infamous Thomas A. Beckett pub, and insisted he took the part of Harry Flowers. Fox became the gangster Chas for a while, but the switch to rock-star debauchery halfway through the film threw him off-balance. There's a story that he was slipped some acid for the mushroom trip scene, and it certainly looks like it. Fox wasn't seen on a screen again for years, turning to religion and handing out evangelical leaflets from door to door.

Michelle Breton later got heavily into heroin and ended up in a sanitarium. Mick's acting career would never get much further than the derided *Ned Kelly* –

although his Stones career obviously went from strength to strength. Anita followed Keith in plunging into heroin, their mutual addiction eventually destroying their relationship. Most tragically, Donald Cammell only made another three films, before shooting himself in the head in '97 – the way Chas killed Turner. Only Nicolas Roeg came out of it fully intact.

Performance marked the first real conflict between Keith and Mick, who had previously bonded together while Brian declined in parallel to the Stones' rise. Anita had been by far the biggest thing in his personal life so far, so it hit hard to see her in the porno out-takes with his best mate. As Keith is oft quoted as saying, '1968 was a funny year. It had a hole in it somewhere.' And it wasn't in Keith's arm – just yet.

Performance left its mark on me too, in a strange way. I had the hottest date of my life one night in early 1971. By then I'd been thrown out of school for my wholehearted immersion in the Rolling Stones lifestyle: long hair, disregard of uniform, 'Jumpin' Jack Flash' Keef-shades, hash. At my hometown's college of further education there was a stunning fellow student, a girl from California called Jacqueline. I asked her to the movies and the film was *Performance*.

As we sat there in the back row, I realised this was no ordinary movie. The images of sex, violence and drugs flashed through a shocked cinema, turning my date into a wide-eyed wreck. As we walked out, she made an excuse and said she was going home. I went to the pub, where I then spied her huddled in a corner with a local skinhead – who promptly lumbered over and socked me in the chops.

Many years later, in 1997, I was running a dance music label called Eruption, an offshoot of the late Creation Records. An American post-punk singer called Patti Palladin got in touch and played me her version of 'Memo From Turner', from the *Performance* soundtrack. She'd got its sardonic sneer spot on. I thought the track was good enough to release if I took it into the studio and beefed up the groove. Patti was also close friends with Anita Pallenberg, and had some samples from the film, like Anita shouting, 'Push!' as Chas tries the door. We utilised those, and turned the track into a heaving, ten-minute monster.

Our timing was good. London's Institute of Contemporary Arts held an exhibition on *Performance* in late '97, plus screenings and an afternoon seminar with original cast members. I walked into the ICA, straight into a blast of the 'Memo' remix I'd done for Patti. Then she turned up with Anita Pallenberg, who I met for the first time. Obviously mellowed with age, I found Anita charming, very funny, and still devilishly attractive. I was made up that she loved my remix, and she scrawled, 'Push! Love Anita' on the sleeve.

But the single never came out, as Creation got cold feet about the movie samples. Maybe it was the curse of *Performance* again.

Beast Of A Feast

Brian's case came up in court on 26 September 1968. He was accused of possessing cannabis, and gave his address as Redlands, where he'd occasionally been staying with Keith and Anita. Brian's defence was that the gear had been left in the rented flat by the previous tenants. He said that he didn't touch cannabis because

'Sorry I'm late!' – Keith turns up after the Beggars Banquet *party pie-fight.*

it made him paranoid, and the whole affair had severely upset him as the band were just climbing back to their former heights. But it only took the jury 45 minutes to find Brian guilty, much to his shock. However, the chairman of the court, Mr. Reginald Seaton, obviously wasn't convinced by the decision and responded by fining Brian £50 plus costs, accompanied by the obligatory stern warning. There were sighs of relief all round, not least from Keith and Mick in the public gallery.

From October through November, the Stones started rehearsing at their studio in Bermondsey with a view to playing live. *Beggars Banquet* was crying out to be taken to the stage. But it wasn't until early December when they popped up on *The David Frost Show*, performing 'Sympathy For The Devil'. They were obviously miming, with Brian sat at the piano, but the new song came over very strong.

Beggars Banquet was finally released in the first week of December, making number three in the UK and number two in the US. In holding back the release, Decca had pitted the Stones against the Beatles, and the whole saturated Christmas market.

The battle over the cover had been resolved when the Stones were forced to capitulate. They did so in the blandest possible terms, by simply printing a white party invitation on the front emblazoned with the title. It looked unfortunately like the sleeve of the Beatles' 'White Album', which had come out on 22 November. More impressive was the inner-sleeve photo, shot at a Hampstead mansion, depicting a roistering feast. It shows Keith, the stoned court jester, feeding beggar Mick an apple off of a dagger, while Brian plays with a large dog. The shot was set up by the ubiquitous Christopher Gibbs, who also came up with the album title. Ironically, the offending crapper would appear on the sleeve when Decca put out the remastered version in '93.

In keeping with the epicurean theme, the launch party for the press was held at the New Elizabethan Rooms at London's Kensington Gore Hotel. It was the feast scenario again, with straw on the floor, candles, wooden benches and serving wenches. Top-hatted Mick welcomed the assembled media, then dished out the albums and some gold boxes. Inside the boxes were custard pies, and the event swiftly degenerated into a slapstick free-for-all, in which Brian seemed to come out the worst. 'An arctic pie blizzard,' was how *Record Mirror's* Lon Godard described it. Perhaps wisely, Keith only turned up when it was all over, amidst rumours that he was either ill or his chauffeur couldn't find the venue.

The album itself was a crossfire hurricane of sex, magic and attitude. It made the Stones' earlier forays into the blues sound innocent, tinny and dated, and obliterated the psychedelic muddle of '67 into a distant memory. Strutting with a dark soul, the Stones had seemingly emerged from their turmoil. This band wasn't following anybody now, and for the next few years would seem to be above the rest of the music scene – indeed, above the law – as they became not the only the greatest but the most dangerous rock 'n' roll band in the world.

Beggars Banquet was almost frightening, too much to take in at the time. Even 35 years later, the record sounds mercilessly brilliant. As timeless and gripping as those blues records that first inspired the Stones, it starts with 'Sympathy For The Devil'. Mick's 'Ow!' in the intro is the most effective single-syllable exclamation in rock history.

The final track, 'Salt Of The Earth', started life as a song called 'Silver Blanket'. The first verse marks Keith's first solo vocal performance on a Stones song, a slurred call to 'drink to the hard-working people'. It's a tribute to the working classes, which swells from its balladic start to full-blown gospel by the accelerating finale. George Chkiantz recalled Keith's tentative first steps to the mike in Steve Appleford's song-by-song analysis, *It's Only Rock 'n' Roll*: 'He didn't really know to do vocals. He'd watched Mick do a million of them, but when it came to himself he seemed charmingly diffident.' But, like his future vocal performances, it didn't come from anywhere else but the heart.

The press fell over themselves to praise the new album. *Rolling Stone's* Jon Landau wrote a review that echoes with eerie prescience: 'Violence. The Rolling Stones are violence. Their music penetrates the raw nerve endings of their listeners and finds its way into the groove marked "release of frustration". Their violence has always been a surrogate for the violence their audience is so obviously capable of. On *Beggars Banquet* the Rolling Stones try to come to terms with violence more explicitly than before and in so doing are forced to take up the sub-

'We're hoping to see this magician. . . ' Mick, Anita and Keith at Heathrow, en route to Rio.

ject of politics. The result is the most sophisticated and meaningful statement we can expect to hear concerning the two themes – violence and politics – that will probably dominate the rock of 1969.'

The Stones rounded off the year with another event which added to their mythos: *The Rock 'n' Roll Circus*. While the Beatles had their *Magical Mystery Tour* TV special, which would meet a favourable if puzzled reception that Christmas, the Stones wanted to follow the impetus set by their proto-video for 'Jumpin' Jack Flash', and create a big event centred around them playing live. They decided to add the extra dimension of a circus big-top, inviting special guests to play amidst the jugglers and acrobats. It sounded like a good idea at the time, especially as it would get the group back to playing live again.

The original projected bill included the Who, the Flying Burrito Brothers, Dr John, Marianne Faithfull, Traffic, the Isley Brothers and Taj Mahal. Keith suggested Johnny Cash, who declined. Mick said no to the fledgling Led Zeppelin. In the end, Taj Mahal, the Who and Marianne appeared, plus the unknown Jethro Tull. John Lennon also came in at the last moment, fronting a supergroup consisting of Eric Clapton, Keith on bass, Mitch Mitchell from the Jimi Hendrix Experience, and Brian's choice of French violinist Ivry Gitlis, plus Yoko Ono in a bag. Allen Klein was continuing to be tight with the Stones' cash, and ignored their request to book the Burritos and Dr John. So the event was chaos before it began, but between 10 and 11 December the extravaganza was shot at Intertel Studios in Wembley.

On the first day, the Stones and the supporting cast rehearsed in the ring, while filming took place over the next two days. Mick was the ringmaster, while the rest of the Stones dressed as clowns except Keith. He went for a satanic man-in-black look, with black top hat, eye-patch and suit, smoking a big cigar. At one point he found himself introducing a fire-eater.

The audience had all received invitations after sending in a coupon to the NME. The Stones didn't go on until after one in the morning, by which time the audience had been there for fourteen hours. Their set consisted of 'Jumpin' Jack Flash', 'Parachute Woman', 'No Expectations', the new song 'You Can't Always Get What You Want', and a manic 'Sympathy For The Devil', which saw Mick stripping off his t-shirt to reveal a sorry-looking Lucifer painted on his chest. The only trouble was that they had to do each song over and over again, to get the recording right. The whole shebang wound up with a spirited swayalong to the recorded version of 'Salt Of the Earth' at around five in the morning, with every-one looking quite 'loose'.

The Rock 'n' Roll Circus was never shown. The band, especially Mick, hated their set when they saw the footage in comparison to the Who. Plans were made to reshoot, but it never happened. Then it became instantly dated, after Brian died. It would finally see the light of day on video, over twenty years later.

At Christmas, Keith, Anita, Mick and Marianne went to Rio de Janeiro for a holiday. According to the popular press, however, they were going to consult a magician on the occult. 'We have become very interested in magic, and we're very serious about this trip,' said Keith, spoofing the *Sunday Express* and playing up to the media's image of them as satanic occultists. 'We're hoping to see this magician practice both white and black magic. He has a long and difficult name which we cannot pronounce. We just call him "Banana" for short.'

In October, Marianne had announced that she was four months pregnant with Mick's baby, but miscarried the following month. Now Anita was pregnant, but haemorrhaged on the journey. Thankfully, she didn't miscarry hers and Keith's child – who would be born alive and healthy at the end of the following summer.

CHAPTER FIVE

BLEED ON ME

Sister Morphine

1969 was a year of death.

Keith, Anita, Mick and Marianne had seen in the new year in Rio de Janeiro. Marianne described the jaunt in her autobiography, *Faithfull*, claiming the vibes were 'weird. It was a short time after *Performance* . . . . Keith and I were still feeling very jangled from Mick and Anita's affair on the set. There was no residual effect on Anita. Like all her affairs it was a fling, and when it was over – that was it. But Mick obviously did not feel the same way, and the shadow of *Performance* cast a pall over the whole trip. Mick was continually whispering come-ons into Anita's ear, but for Anita it was over.'

Even though Anita had no wish to become Mick Jagger's new girlfriend, she liked the edge that the situation lent her, the position of power it placed her in. While Marianne and Keith diverted themselves by smoking the industrial-strength local weed, or, 'guzzling cough mixture, anything we could get our hands on,' Mick wrote the lyrics for what would become 'You Can't Always Get What You Want' – inspired by the mounting drug habits of his girlfriend and their Chelsea set acquaintances.

Keith was working on the ideas that had started to take shape during the tortured *Performance* period: 'You Got The Silver', his love song to Anita, the slow burning 'Gimme Shelter', and 'Let It Bleed'. While they were staying at an isolated ranch in Brazil, Keith also came up with a country romp called 'Honky Tonk Women', its early versions obviously inspired by his newfound friendship with Gram Parsons.

Marianne wrote, 'the situation between [Keith, Mick and Anita] seemed to boil up into a lethal brew.' She herself left early, which Anita attributed to the Brazilian climate. Now Anita was in a truly pivotal role between Keith and Mick. As she has said, she was like a sixth Rolling Stone by this point.

As 1969 got underway, Keith was also succumbing to heroin's seductive lure. Having started snorting it with Robert Fraser when Anita was filming *Performance*, he now got his first taste of withdrawal symptoms and the instant curing properties of the poppy. It's the classic pattern. When you're shivering, sweating, shitting and shaking, instant relief really is just a shot away. But in the early stages, the benefits of the drug can be quite profound creatively. Before the internal rot, and the bad consequences of full-blown addiction start to kick in, you are on a roll. If you don't do too much, you see the world as a wonderful place that's brightened up by your sparkling presence – at least until it really starts biting back. Nothing can touch you. You don't get colds and – with a little cocaine tickle on the top – you are the life and soul of the party.

It's only when it dries up, you get arrested, or the body doesn't take kindly to the street vendor's additives, that it becomes a problem. Keith, who had easy access to the best pharmaceutical heroin from registered junkies, came up with three of the best albums of all time when he was on it.

But it still isn't wise to operate heavy machinery or drive – especially when you consider that Keith's favoured cruising speed was around 100mph. After Anita persuaded him to buy a huge Mercedes, which used to be a staff car for the Third Reich, he promptly wrote it off after nodding out at the wheel. Anita broke her collarbone in the crash. (It was a foretaste of Keith's 1976 motorway crash, when he would get busted after zoning out while driving his Bentley.)

The first Stones-related record of the year was Marianne's new single, 'Something Better', released in late February. It's a delicate ballad which she unveiled at the Rock 'n' Roll Circus. But it was the flip's 'Sister Morphine' which caught the attention, a song she'd started working on with the Stones at the *Beggars Banquet* sessions. She received a co-writing credit with Mick and Keith for this terrifyingly graphic lost gem, which the Stones would later adapt for '71's *Sticky Fingers*.

I met Marianne for the first time at the end of '79, when she was about to make a comeback with the brilliant *Broken English* album. I was interviewing her for *Zigzag*, the magazine I was editing. It was her first major interview for a few years, and there were some initial nerves as we sat nursing vodka and orange in a cosy bar on London's Jermyn Street. These soon evaporated though, and I found her to be warm, engaging company. We talked about the new album, before steering into the drug years, and finally the Stones.

Marianne's artistic assertiveness had really begun back in '69 with the icy blanket of 'Sister Morphine'. It's a heart-rending death-bed plea for medication in a hospital, with Marianne's voice, having dropped a full octave since her mid-sixties debut, sending shivers down the spine with its desperate intensity. She sounds like the angel of death.

'I was,' agreed Marianne, whose heroin habit was just starting when it was recorded. The sound is suitably desolate, like a bluesy take on Lou Reed's *Berlin* album, and features Mick (who also produced the track) on acoustic guitar, Charlie on drums, Bill on bass, Jack Nitzsche on piano, and Ry Cooder on sinister slide guitar. But it's the words which cut like a razor to the heart.

'Yeah, I was very pleased with those,' said Marianne, amazed to meet somebody who actually possessed a copy. 'A lot of it's imaginary, some of it's experience, and some of it's what you're imagining in your highly paranoid state, that you would like to happen. You just take it out to the furthest limit. I was very paranoid at that time . . . . I wrote the words in Rome, and it was recorded in America when they were mixing *Let It Bleed*.'

At the risk of being pedantic, at that time the Stones were actually mixing *Beggars Banquet* and didn't start recording *Let It Bleed* until March '69. In her autobiography, Marianne writes that, when she extracted 'Sister Morphine' from the

Keith and Anita in Rome, where she was working, partly in order to escape the British immigration authorities.

depths of her soul, she'd only tried heroin once – which would place it in early '68.

'People tend to assume that "Sister Morphine" comes from an incident in my life, that it is a parable of a junkie's last hours . . . "Sister Morphine" was in my head – a story of what it might be like to be an addict. "Sister Morphine" is about a man who has had a terrible car accident. He's dying and he's in tremendous pain and in the lyrics he is talking to the nurse.'

She continued, 'I do believe in inspired bursts. These things come through you . . . A vivid series of pictures began forming in my head, and I wrote a story about a morphine addict. It had something to do with Keith and Anita, although they were no more addicts than I at this time. They were just beginning to dabble in smack. But I think one of the reasons that I wrote those lyrics was I knew Keith would like them. I might have cast Anita in one of the roles. Say Keith was the man in the car and Anita was the nurse, what would happen?'

Marianne also revealed that the line about 'the clean white sheets stained red' was inspired by the pregnant Anita's haemorrhage during the boat trip to Brazil. A doctor gave her a shot of morphine – making her the envy of Marianne and Keith, according to Ms. Faithfull.

By the time the Stones' version surfaced on '71's *Sticky Fingers*, 'I was the character in the song. You have to be very careful what you write because a song is a gateway, and whatever it is you've summoned up may come through. It happened to Mick and Keith with that whole satanic business. I became a victim of my own song.'

Whereas Marianne received a composing credit on the single, the Stones' release (which used the same backing track apart from some slide guitar from Keith) credited the track to Jagger-Richard. It wasn't until the '93 re-release of *Sticky Fingers* that Marianne got her joint composing credit. However, while it was always intended that she'd get paid, her contract with Decca prevented her receiving a credit, as the Stones had left the label by then, and almost stopped her getting any money.

She told me how she eventually got paid: 'Mick is mean. He'll always be a student of the London School of Economics. We had split up. Very bad blood and all that. This story I heard from Allen Klein. It might not be true. Keith Richards wrote to Allen Klein and told him that I did write the words and I needed the money. So now and again, I get a royalty cheque for "Sister Morphine". I've been living off "Sister Morphine" for years. I just got one today. $485!'

Marianne was off heroin when we met, although – as with most addicts – the battle wasn't over yet. When I visited her in New York ten years later – by which time I was addicted myself – she saw right through me, and hesitated to do the interview. But she talked from the perspective of one who knew, and recommended ways of coming off. Her words became a factor in my own battle – Marianne Faithfull helped me to *get off* smack. Her final words in '79 would also stay with me. We were talking about Anita, who at that time was splitting-up with Keith. He was trying to stay away from smack by now, but she still had a terrible problem with it – along with booze and other drugs. Going by photographs, Anita had lost her wicked beauty and had bloated considerably. Marianne said, 'It's very frightening. That's what would have happened . . . no, that's *not* what would have happened to me. If I'd have stayed on it, I'd be dead. I'm not as strong as her.'

In March 1969, Keith and Mick stepped up a gear on the songs that would form the new Stones album. They took a short break in Italy, working on 'Monkey Man' and an epic called 'Midnight Rambler', suffused with raw acoustic guitar and harmonica, which they'd started during the *Beggars Banquet* sessions.

Recording sessions for the album would take place at Olympic studios, culminating in July, with producer Jimmy Miller back to sprinkle some of his magic. Despite Keith's huge contribution to *Beggars Banquet*, Miller felt that *Let It Bleed* was the album where he really took musical control of the Stones. Part of it was due to necessity, as Brian had now entered his terminal decline. His musical contributions were non-existent, as he was actively discouraged from attending the sessions.

'The important thing about *Let It Bleed* is the amount of work Keith did,' said Miller in *Rave* magazine. 'When Brian died, Keith took over the musical leadership of the Stones, and did it brilliantly ... he'd suddenly just play something that would knock me out, some guitar figure I'd never imagined, which made the whole thing work.'

In May, it was Mick's turn to get busted again after cannabis resin was unearthed during a raid on his Cheyne Walk house. That same month, Keith bought a house a few hundred feet away. He'd also play bass on gospel-soul musician/Beatles sessioneer Billy Preston's new single, 'That's The Way God Planned It', a rousing gospel knees-up which hit the top ten in the UK, before the band worked on 'Honky Tonk Women' – the song Keith had started writing in Brazil at Christmas.

It had grown from down-home country picking into the rousing sleaze-anthem that became one of the Stones' biggest ever singles. In addition to Keith and Mick on heat, the track boasted a brass section and a girl chorus. Jimmy Miller kickstarted Charlie on the distinctive beat with a cowbell, and Brian wasn't present at all. For the last recording session, on 1 June, the Stones brought in a young guitarist called Mick Taylor who added some of the country licks between the verses. While Ian Stewart would claim the distinctive guitars were Keith over-dubbed five times, in a 1975 issue of *Crawdaddy* the man himself credited Taylor with much more – saying the song was all country until, 'it got turned around to this other thing by Mick Taylor, who got into a completely different feel, throwing it off the wall another way.' Taylor himself is quoted in Bill Wyman's *Rolling with the Stones* as saying, 'I added something to "Honky Tonk Women", but it was more or less complete when I arrived. I played the country kind of influence on the rock licks between the verses.' Just to confuse matters, Ry Cooder later claimed Keith nicked the riff from him. Whatever, the track turned out to be a monster, the perfect showcase for Keith's new trademark raunch.

On 5 June, Blind Faith – the first 'supergroup', featuring Eric Clapton, Stevie Winwood, violinist Rick Grech and ex-Cream drummer Ginger Baker – played a huge free concert in London's Hyde Park. Jagger went along, was impressed by the crowd of 150,000, and promptly agreed that the Stones would play one the following month, on 5 July. With a projected US tour and the prestigious Hyde Park gig, it was time for the Stones to do something about Brian.

Exile On Pooh Corner

It was fairly obvious that, although his ghostly presence would still be included in photo sessions, Brian Jones had progressively faded as a Rolling Stone since his troubled year of 1967. If his contributions to *Beggars Banquet* had been minimal but effective, Brian was hardly anywhere to be heard on *Let It Bleed*. Besides making the odd contribution on Moroccan percussion or autoharp, sometimes he'd be propped up in a corner with his guitar slung around his neck – but unplugged. Brian's drug convictions meant that he couldn't get a US entry visa, which would affect the Stones' plans to tour America. He wasn't well enough to tour anyway, as the barbiturate, booze and (occasionally) smack-addled path to self-destruction he'd set out on showed no sign of turning around.

The rest of the band knew he would have to leave, and so did Brian. Keith, Charlie and Mick drove down to Brian's new house, which he'd bought the previous November. Cotchford Farm, near Hartfield, Sussex, had belonged to A. A. Milne, author of Winnie the Pooh. It had a statue of Milne's son, Christopher Robin (as immortalised in the book), in the garden, as well as a big, heated swimming pool.

'Mick, Charlie and I drove down there together to see him at his house,' recalls Keith in *According to the Rolling Stones*. 'It was a bit like going to a funeral, really . . . . We were saying to him, "How do you feel about this? We're going to go back out on the road and you're in no condition to join us, man . . . ." We offered him the chance to stay, but it was an offer we knew was going to be refused. He wasn't going to come back; it was already a foregone conclusion. It was just a matter of how he took it. It was kind of sad because Brian kept talking about the plans that he'd got.'

Mick's statement of the time read: 'Brian wants to play music which is more to his taste rather than always playing ours. So we decided that it's best that he's free to follow his own inclinations. We've parted on the best of terms. Obviously friendships like ours don't break up just like that.'

The following day, Stones press officer Les Perrin issued a statement – supposedly from Brian: 'I no longer see eye to eye with the others over the discs we are cutting. The Rolling Stones' music is not to my taste any more . . . I have a desire to play my own brand of music, rather than that of the others. We had a friendly meeting. I love those fellows.'

Brian put on a brave face, but when the Stones left, he sat alone and cried. After all, they had started off as *his* band.

Brian was apparently in the process of forming a supergroup, citing names like Jimi Hendrix, John Lennon and Bob Dylan. He was already starting to get his appallingly abused body back into shape, loved his new house, and seemed to regard the inevitable news as a weight lifted and a fresh start. A photo taken in his garden, shortly before he died, shows a smiling Brian looking just like he did in 1964 – even down to his striped sweater.

Mick Taylor was waiting in the wings. The twenty-year-old blues virtuoso had cut his teeth with John Mayall's Bluesbreakers. Mayall was an Alexis Korner-type godfather figure, whose band also acted as a kind of school for dynamic young blues musicians. Eric Clapton joined Mayall after leaving the Yardbirds, to be followed by Peter Green. When Green left to form Fleetwood Mac with another Bluesbreaker, John McVie, Mick Taylor came in as his replacement. He played on three of Mayall's great sixties albums: *Crusade*, *Bare Wires* and *Blues From Laurel Canyon*. In early '69, Taylor parted company with Mayall, who was embarking on an acoustic blues project. Mayall recommended him to Jagger, who invited him down to a session. Taylor had seen the Stones back in '63, and was a fan, so he decided to give it a whirl.

His trial by fire consisted of overdubbing those licks to 'Honky Tonk Women', plus playing along to 'Gimme Shelter', 'Live With Me' and an early version of 'Lovin' Cup', which would finally appear on *Exile On Main Street*. Much to his surprise, he was asked to join the band. 'I just assumed I was the best guitarist available at the time,' he later commented. He was probably right, as the first choices had been Eric Clapton – who was too busy with Blind Faith at the time – and Ronnie Wood of the Faces, who Mick had actually called, but, as Faces bassist Ronnie Lane took the call and never passed it on, wouldn't get the message for five years!

Taylor was another innocent-looking blonde. Quiet, with a studious manner and lightning fingers on the guitar, he'd already established his own tone – a sweet, clean dazzle which could be tempered by a sky-scraping slide. For years, Keith had been carrying the guitar duties alone, as Brian first moved on to other instruments and then became too fucked-up to play anything at all. The addition of Mick Taylor would leave Keith free to concentrate on his fearsome driving rhythm.

'Mick Taylor turns up and plays like an angel,' said Keith in *According to the Rolling Stones*, 'and I wasn't going to say no. I thought I'd let the guy develop, because by then I thought I was an old hand – I was all of 25 years old! That's what four years on the road would do to you. You came out at the other end and you were already 50; you'd seen a lot of things.'

Mick Taylor was introduced on 10 June at a photo session at Hyde Park, where the Stones announced that they would playing their free concert on 5 July. 'He doesn't play like Brian,' said Jagger. 'He's a blues player.' Sadly, Brian had claimed he was leaving the Stones to return to his blues roots.

Even if he ended up a shadow of that fresh-faced kid in Hyde Park, Mick Taylor would go on to survive five years in the Stones. He was something that they'd never had before – a flashy guitarist. The records show that Keith was more than able to deliver lethal solos – his stinging salvos on 'Sympathy For The Devil' are worth more than a thousand fluid notes per second. But Keith's forte has always been as the band's relentless engine. Taylor would allow the Stones to explore new avenues, and be a part of some of their finest musical moments.

Although understanding of the situation, Brian was choked. He'd get people to drive him to Olympic, where the Stones were working on *Let It Bleed*, park outside for a few minutes, then drive off to nurse his private grief. Cotchford Farm was his sanctuary, as he oversaw the place's renovation. Brian brought in a team of builders, led by a character called Frank Thorogood – who moved in semi-permanently with his friend Janet Lawson, a nurse. Thorogood was a schoolfriend of

Mick Taylor (second from left) is unveiled to the press at Hyde Park, 1969.

Stones chauffeur Tom Keylock, and had also worked at Redlands.

I remember well the morning of 3 July, 1969. It was my fifteenth birthday. I bounded downstairs, full of whoopee, and there was the front page of the newspaper: Brian had died in the swimming pool at Cotchford Farm.

The only time I'd felt so sad was when Otis Redding had been killed in a plane crash a couple of years earlier. But this was one of the Stones, for God's sake.

The bare facts seemed to be that there was some kind of party going on that night at Cotchford Farm. Brian had taken some drugs, and gone for a swim in his pool around midnight. He was left unattended for a few minutes, after which he was discovered floating lifeless in the bottom of the pool, by Janet Lawson.

The coroner returned a verdict of death by misadventure, with drowning as the cause of death. The post-mortem revealed that Brian's heart and liver were enlarged as a result of alcohol abuse but, while his blood contained traces of Mandrax and amphetamine, his system carried no traces of hard drugs. One theory is that he suffered an asthma attack in the pool, as an inhaler was found nearby. But a more sinister and enduring theory concerns Thorogood and the builders, who had been relentlessly abusing Brian's hospitality, leeching off him and throwing parties, while resenting the pop star's wealth and fame. Consequently, on 2 July Thorogood had gone to the Stones' office to pick up wages for his gang, and found that Brian had halted them.

The prevailing theory about this tragic turn of events has inspired many books. A. E. Hotchner's *Blown Away: The Rolling Stones and the Death of the Sixties* carries an account from Brian's boyhood friend, Richard Hattrell. He recalls meeting a member of the Walker Brothers pop trio, who had been at a party that fateful night at Cotchford Farm. The Brother told him he saw a couple of the builders holding Brian down in the pool. Hotchner tracked down one of the builders, who told him some of the men had got a little drunk and worked up that night, trying to scare Brian in the pool and going too far. Terry Rawlings' *Who Killed Christopher Robin?* says that Frank Thorogood confessed on his deathbed to Tom Keylock in '93.

Keith has been persistently asked about Brian's death ever since it happened. At our first interview, in 1980, it was the only time during the whole three-hour conversation that he looked a little agitated. The question arose when we were talking about 'Spanish Tony' Sanchez's grab-and-tell sleaze expose, *Up and Down with the Rolling Stones*, in which he depicts Brian as a drugged-up shell, beaten into the ground by police oppression and his heartless colleagues.

At the mention of Brian, Keith looked down and seemed to cloud over.

'He was getting in a real state towards the end. That was the main reason he eventually left the band. He was just no longer in touch with anything. Although he was real strong in lots of ways, he just found his weakness that night, whatever happened. I still take all the stories from that night with a pinch of salt.

'I've no doubt it's the same with anybody when those things happen. There's a crowd of people, then suddenly there's nobody there. Instead of trying to help the guy, they think of their own skins and run. It's the same as what happened to Gram Parsons – someone gave him a turn-on, he passed out and they all got chicken and ran without even calling the ambulance or anything.'

Keith didn't seem comfortable talking about something that had obviously bothered him for a long while, so I suggested changing the subject.

'Industrial accidents,' was how he summed it up, shaking his head. 'In my own head I think about it and reach the same conclusion as last time, or I start to think about it again and get another idea on it. If you're not actually there when those things go down you can never say . . . I don't know what really went on that night at Brian's place. I know there was a lot of people there and suddenly there wasn't and that's about it. Yeah, off that subject, right?'

But Keith has given a variety of opinions on Brian over the years, both as a person and on his death.

'I've seen Brian swim in terrible conditions, in the sea with breakers up to here,' he told Robert Greenfield in his 1971 *Rolling Stone* interview. 'I've been underwater with Brian in Fiji. He was a goddamn good swimmer.' Back then, Keith also reckoned, 'Brian could be so beautiful in one way, and such an asshole in another.'

When Keith first encountered Brian, he'd been blown away by his slide-guitar skills. They went on to conquer the world together. As one of Keith's well-known personality traits is his loyalty, we have to assume he was driven to absolute exasperation by the time he wanted Brian out of the group. As he said, 23 years later, in *According to the Rolling Stones*, 'Did he have an asthma attack in the pool, or was he shoved under? It wouldn't surprise me. Brian could really piss people off. What really killed Brian though was not getting the mixture right between the music and the fame.'

Aftermath

The day after the news of Brian's death, the Stones unleashed their new single – the magnificent 'Honky Tonk Women'. It screamed 'instant classic' on first hearing.

Keith's open-G intro set up one of the dirtiest, sexiest grooves to grace a Stones record. It's a whiplash synthesis of Keith's groin-level pump and Charlie's deftly accented beat. It's been sampled everywhere, from hip-hop records like Ultra-Magnetic MCs' 'Travelling At The Speed Of Thought' to house music DJs, like Roy Davis Jr. Keith would be horrified to see his band's work plundered, but it's also a kind of tribute if you can build a killer five-minute club track on just one drum fill.

As the track gains steam, more guitars enter the fray, clanging with sharp metallic interaction. Mick's lyrics are the perfect topping – 'She blew my nose, and then she blew my mind.' It's never been out of the Stones' live set since.

The day after the single was released, the Stones played their mammoth, free concert in Hyde Park. At first, they were going to pull the gig out of respect to Brian, but the 'show must go on' ethos kicked in, and they decided to do it as a tribute to him.

The Stones began rehearsing at the Beatles' Apple building in Savile Row, London. It was around this time that Keith received one of his distinctive image modifications when members of avant-garde troupe the Living Theatre pierced his ear. He was the first rock star to boast a bone earring, swinging boldly in the breeze. (I later took the plunge in '74, before realising it was fine for a rock star but not so clever for a cub reporter.) 1969 can be considered the year that the trademark 'Keef' look was patented, before spawning a horde of lookalikes.

Granada TV captured the Hyde Park event for the *Stones in the Park* documentary. An estimated 300,000 fans flocked to the park, sitting through sets by Family, King Crimson and Alexis Korner's New Church before Stones-time. MC and stage manager Sam Cutler got about 50 Hell's Angels in to handle security – although they came over as impersonators of their American forebears, trying to look moody in their studded leather jackets. Holed up at the Londonderry House hotel, the Stones were conveyed to the site in an old army ambulance.

Cutler strolled on in a cool, calm and collected manner, which would be sorely tested later that year at the Altamont speedway concert. 'This is an historic occasion,' he announced, 'and the press of the world are here. This is the crucial concert for the whole pop scene in London.' Then came the Stones. Mick walked up to the mike, sporting what can only be described as a white frilly mini-dress, and pleaded for quiet. 'Now listen, cool it for a minute. I really would like to say something about Brian, about how we feel about him just going when we didn't expect it.' He read two stanzas from Shelley's 'Adonis', before Brian's minder Tom Keylock released several thousand white butterflies – most of which had died, as they'd been boxed up in the heat all day. It may have been an allusion to The Times' 'Who Breaks A Butterfly On A Wheel?' editorial, and to the fact that one of the butterflies had now been broken

Keith kicked off the music on his Flying V guitar. If anything, his appearance was more shocking than Mick's. His hair was longer than it had ever been, or ever would be. He looked white-faced and wasted, having been up for days. Stoned immaculate. There was thick black kohl around his eyes. He may not have been the first rock star to wear make-up, as Little Richard had been doing it for years, but the difference in Keith's demeanour from the bouncy, fresh-faced kid of five years earlier was startling. *Record Mirror* described him as 'steadfast and zombie-like with heavily madeup eyes'.

The set stumbled into life with a version of Johnny Winter's 'I'm Yours, She's Mine', before moving up a gear with 'Jumpin' Jack Flash', through 'Mercy Mercy', 'Stray Cat Blues', 'No Expectations', 'I'm Free', 'Down Home Girl' and the debut of the as-yet-unreleased 'Love In Vain' (a highlight) and 'Lovin' Cup', then known as 'Gimme A Little Drink'. 'Honky Tonk Women' proved its show-stopping potential before another first, 'Midnight Rambler' – the best of the lot, as they moved through the song's various episodes with grim relish, with Mick on his knees, smacking the stage with his big, studded belt, as Keith stabbed out the death-chords built around Muddy Waters' 'Still A Fool'. By the time of 'Satisfaction' and 'Street Fighting Man', the well-behaved crowd were really moving. The set wound up with the Stones joined by a troupe of African drummers for 'Sympathy For The Devil', which broke down into an interminable, ragged jam that emphasised the bad sound quality.

'Hyde Park?' said Keith later in *NME*. 'Yeah, I can't stop dreaming about it. It had to be the biggest crowd I've ever seen. They were the stars of the show, like some massive religious gathering on the shores of the Ganges. I was a bit shaky at first but then I started enjoying myself and it was just like it was two years ago.' But there were no screaming fans in the era of post-psychedelica.

'I've always dug them,' defended Keith. 'If people want to listen and they're all sitting there quietly I will concentrate on playing and give them something for their ears. But if they're screaming I will forget about solos and just hit it. An artist feeds off an audience, and vice versa.'

Keith would reflect on the day, more than 30 years later, in *According to . . . :* 'The gig at Hyde Park was so bizarre . . . . There was a very volatile audience and on top of everything we were having to deal with the fact that Brian had not just left the band, but left the planet . . . not only was it "here come the new, improved Rolling Stones", it was also a funeral . . . it was one of the largest gatherings ever held in London. There was a powerful feeling that there were a lot of us, that things were changing, that we had something to give. By then we were being leant on aggressively by the authorities, so to us it was a great show of solidarity. It must have made them tremble a bit down the road in Whitehall.'

Most of the press's reservations were overshadowed by the sheer significance of the event. *Disc's* Hugh Nolan wrote, 'the nice thing was that nearly 99 per cent of the audience came to listen and not (as they might have done five years ago) to scream,' but added, 'To be brutally frank, not all of the Stones' very long set was the best music they have ever played: understandable since they haven't played anywhere in such a long time and since Brian Jones' replacement Mick Taylor has only been with them for a few weeks.' But *NME's* review, by Nick Logan, may have been the one that first coined the Stones' 'best rock 'n' roll band in the world' tag.

After Hyde Park, Mick went to Australia with Marianne to film *Ned Kelly*.

But a massive overdose of barbiturates caused Marianne to collapse into a coma at their hotel, remaining unconscious for six days.

With Mick away, Keith was left to hold the fort. He conducted his first interview for two years, with Nick Logan of *NME*. It was the point at which his popular image was cemented. First of all, he was late. Then, 'in roared a beaming figure in a wide-brimmed black hat, purple vest and green trousers. "I'm all bombed out," announced the unshaven Keith a little breathlessly, after descending forcefully on a chair.'

When Logan remarked about the two-year period since Keith last communicated with the press, he replied, 'There were so many things that happened in between that stopped us getting into things again. I even wanted to get away from my guitar in 1967. I love it again now. Music is with me all the time. I listen as much as I can . . . Taj Mahal, Dr John, Led Zeppelin, Blind Faith. Everything is becoming more and more mixed, barriers are falling away . . . The divisions in music get less and less every year.'

And with Mick away, how did he feel about having to deal with all the shit that appeared in the papers?

'In a way, if it happens to Mick it happens to me anyway. I don't give a ?*!@. When you think about it there is nothing you can do. And to bother to fight about every little detail . . . well. They know they are making you appear an even more glamorous person to a certain public no matter what they write.'

As Keith warmed to his theme, he saw the potential fun he could have with the monster the press were creating. '. . . I suppose I am in a more peaceful frame of mind than I was two or three years ago. But I don't know how I will be when we get back to touring – probably biffing photographers on the nose again, with people holding me back. Everything was violence then.'

Then the subject of the police came up. 'I don't like the way police attitudes have changed. They are getting new power and it is growing at an alarming rate because once something is that big it wants to get bigger. It is becoming a social police, more and more concerned with how you live. Clashes have happened already in America and the police are really loading themselves up with hardware. We are just up there shouting with everybody else.'

What for?

'Who knows; nobody can really say. Just, not this. People cannot afford to be intolerant any more.'

NME ran the headline, 'Today's "more peaceful" Keith Richard looks ahead to touring . . . "I'LL PROBABLY BE BIFFING PHOTOGRAPHERS ON THE NOSE AGAIN."'

Prodigal Return

On 10 August 1969, Anita gave birth to hers and Keith's first son, Marlon (after Marlon Brando), at King's College Hospital, London, weighing in at a healthy seven pounds, four ounces. The proud father turned up in his Bentley, and took them to his new house at Cheyne Walk. Marlon's godfather was Robert Fraser, who organised a Tantric Indian baptism. It was Keith's first taste of fatherhood, and he took to it like a duck to water. He doted on Marlon, the happy event bringing him closer to Anita. But the familial bliss would only be permitted to last for a couple of months, as the Stones had an album to finish and the first American tour with their new lineup.

In the middle of August '69, the milestone Woodstock music festival took place in upstate New York. It's now held up as the embodiment of the love generation and communal harmony, but Mick turned it down for the Stones. He probably wished that he hadn't, as the Who took the spot and enjoyed a massive career boost. Two weeks later, the UK experienced its first mega-festival, at the Isle of Wight. Keith took time out from Marlon and Anita to hire a yacht, which ferried himself and some mates over to watch Bob Dylan play to 200,000 punters.

On 17 October, the Stones flew to Los Angeles. Marlon, then only two months old, was left behind with Anita. But Keith hated to leave him, and the phrase 'wild horses couldn't drag me away' swam around in his head. Anita would later tell Victor Bockris that the time after Marlon's birth was 'a very heavy period and I suffered for about three months. There were so many creeps [dealers and hangers-on] in the house. Then when Keith went on the American tour that was very hard for me because this is the time when the father should be with the child and I felt completely forgotten. So I just started taking drugs again, and then I smothered all my feelings with drugs.' Anita found herself hanging out most of the time with Marianne, who was by then an addict.

On arrival in LA, Keith immediately hooked up with Gram Parsons, who'd be his soulmate for the duration. They dove into Old Charter bourbon, good weed and music. Also along for the ride was Stanley Booth, researching a book that was officially approved by the Stones. He hailed from Gram's hometown of Waycross, Georgia, fitting into the cool little circle that Keith needed for good times and moral support. Booth recalls one night when the party went to a hip Japanese restaurant and met some local hostility. As Keith returned from the toilet, a woman of mature years remarked, 'You'd look good if you put a rinse on your hair.' To which Keith shot back, 'You'd look good if you put a rinse on your cunt.'

The Stones were working at Elektra Studios, and the band HQ was a large rented house on Oriole Drive, in the hills above Sunset Strip. During the mixing, Keith played close attention to the levels on his guitar parts. But when the album was mastered, it was swiftly rejected because the sound had been 'limited' – the recording technology had sanded off the rough edges for that smooth American radio sound. The Stones sent it back for 'unlimiting'.

While away from his new family, Keith eschewed the patrolling groupies in favour of hanging out with Gram Parsons and Stanley Booth, listening to old blues and gospel records. 'Keith and Gram delighted in turning each other on, as we said then, to things they hadn't heard,' wrote Booth. The impact of those late-night sessions still lives on with Keith today. He also reported that Mick was getting jealous of Gram, the start of a resentment that would often boil over during the rest of Parsons' short life.

Keith was on overdrive during this period. As well as finishing the new album, he had to work Mick Taylor into the band and direct a new live set consisting mostly of tracks from *Beggars Banquet* and the as-yet unreleased *Let It Bleed*.

Keith, just a spectator at the 1969 Isle of Wight festival.

The Stones' first American tour since '66 kicked off at Colorado State University on 7 November. Blues veteran Bukka White visited backstage, clocked Keith's National steel guitar – his own favoured instrument – and asked him to play something. When he did, the venerable Bukka held his hand over Keith's head and proclaimed, 'This a star, here. This a Hollywood star. If I'm lyin', I'm dyin'.'

Tickets for the tour sold out within hours of going on sale. 23 shows in seventeen cities would gross the Stones over $2 million. It led influential journalist Ralph Gleason – one of the founders of *Rolling Stone* – to slam the high ticket prices. Smarting from the criticism, with the memories of Woodstock and Hyde Park still fresh, the Stones started hatching plans for a huge free concert to thank their fans.

Meanwhile, they chose their own support acts for the tour, picking from a back-line of B. B. King, Chuck Berry, Ike and Tina Turner and Terry Reid every night. The two shows at LA's Forum on 8 November broke the record set by the Beatles in '66, attracting 18,000 fans and grossing $260,000. Bill Graham, the San Francisco promoter who made his name with the Fillmore Auditorium and would promote the Stones' northern California gigs for many years, recorded and broadcast the next night's Oakland concert on San Francisco's KSAN radio station.

Within a few days, the broadcast was pressed and in the shops as the Stones' first live bootleg album, *Live-R Than You'll Ever Be*. The Stones themselves would record their triumphant shows at Madison Square Gardens later in the tour, for a live album called *Get Yer Ya-Yas Out*. Both this and *Live R* are blistering illustrations of what the Stones Mark 2, as Keith called them, were serving up on their comeback tour.

Sam Cutler was spot-on when he introduced 'The Greatest Rock 'n' Roll Band in the World' every night. This tour was the first time the Stones were able to hear themselves on stage, playing to a stoned crowd who were actually listening to those cathartic renditions of 'Jumpin' Jack Flash' and 'Street Fighting Man'. Jagger had moved into his lasciviously satanic ringmaster mode, and Keith was driving the groove with supernatural intensity over Charlie's metronomic swing. Bill and Stu fleshed it out, while new boy Taylor brought another dimension with his bluesy embellishments on outings like 'Love In Vain'.

The footage of the Madison Square Gardens shows featured in David and Albert Maysle's movie *Gimme Shelter*, a record of the '69 US tour, is glorious, showing how the Stones had come into their own on stage. Keith, in his favourite sequinned red jacket of the time, had cut his long hair after Hyde Park into the proto-spiketop which would launch a thousand haircuts.

In 1969, the Stones really seemed like leaders of a generation. The heavy-handed approach of the cops at some of the gigs only strengthened the mood of defiance and celebration. And, as the tour progressed, the plans mushroomed for that grand finale to finish it off and kiss goodbye to the sixties.

'This band has been like a phoenix,' said Keith in *According to* . . . . 'And the 1969 tour of the States was our first resurrection. We felt we were a new band; we were starting again . . . . The '69 tour was essentially a continuation of the Hyde Park gig – we knew that we really had to tighten up and get our stage chops together, but at least we had a working unit again.'

After the tour wound up at the huge West Palm Beach Pop Festival in Florida, the Stones recorded three new tracks at the renowned Muscle Shoals Studios in Alabama. Muscle Shoals had built a hefty reputation on the great Atlantic soul classics like Aretha Franklin's 'Respect' and Percy Sledge's 'When A Man Loves A Woman'. The Stones went there to soak up some of the vibe, and build on the sound which Keith had started with *Beggars Banquet*. To warm up, they tackled two country songs which Keith had been taught by Gram Parsons: 'Your Angel Steps Out Of Heaven' and George Jones's 'Say It's Not You'.

The Stones came out with 'Wild Horses', 'You Got To Move' (their version of the Mississippi Fred McDowell song they'd been playing on tour), and 'Brown Sugar', which would all surface on the album after *Let It Bleed*, *Sticky Fingers*. Also at the studio was Ahmet Ertegun, boss of Atlantic Records, who the Stones were talking to about distributing a new record label they planned to launch when their contract with Decca expired in 1970.

The Muscle Shoals sessions resulted in two of the best things the Stones have ever done. With moves afoot to disengage from Allen Klein, they were on the brink of both a musical and career renaissance. 'Brown Sugar' was some way to start a new label. Mick had started writing it as a song called 'Black Pussy', while in Australia filming *Ned Kelly*. Keith then took his riff onslaught into its sleaziest pastures yet.

'Wild Horses' was the song Keith started writing when he had to leave Anita and Marlon to go on tour. Then, while Mick was away on the tour, Marianne discovered that he'd made singer Marsha Hunt pregnant, and left him for Italian film director Mario Schifano. Mick needed to vent his hurt, and asked Keith to delve into his grab-bag of gestating tunes. He came up with 'Wild Horses', which Mick added new verses to.

'Wild Horses' is just beautiful. The studio playback sequence in *Gimme Shelter* is one of my favourite film moments – as Keith lies back on the studio couch, eyes closed and snakeskin boot tapping. The shot of him passed out on the studio floor later emerged as a nifty badge.

The track also features the eloquently soulful piano-playing of Jim Dickinson, who was one of the top Memphis soul studio players. (Jim got called in because Stu refused to play any song with minor chords!)

This was a time when the Stones didn't enjoy lengthy breaks between albums. Keith was on a roll the whole time, recording songs for the next album before the new one was out. It was a situation that only extended from *Beggars Banquet* to *Exile On Main Street* – but which happens to be the Stones' musical and creative peak. Even when they were mixing *Let It Bleed*, Keith and Mick wrote the basic tracks for 'All Down The Line' and 'Shine A Light' which would eventually appear on *Exile*.

On 26 November, the Stones called a press conference at the Rainbow Room on top of the RCA building in New York, and announced they would be playing a free concert in San Francisco on 6 December. Mick said he wanted to create an alternative society for the day 'which sets an example to the rest of America as to how one can behave in large gatherings.' In the *Gimme Shelter* movie, which also documented the concert at the Altamont speedway track, Mick is resplendent in white suit, flashing an aura of total confidence, even arrogance. Next to him sits Keith in black, his earring dangling, his complexion the colour of parchment. He looks like he's been on the road for a few weeks and hasn't seen many beds. It's a startling contrast which sums up the way the world would view the pair over the next ten years.

Blood On The Track

The new Stones album had been recorded under the working titles *Automatic Changer* and *Sticky Fingers* – although Keith had wanted to call it *Hard Knox And Durty Sox* at one point. It was a tad confusing when, in an interview the previous June, Mick had said the Stones were going to release a new album called *Sticky*

Fingers in September, closely followed by another one before Christmas, as they already had seventeen tracks in the can.

Whatever, the album was titled *Let It Bleed* by the time it was released on 29 November in the UK and 5 December in the US, going to number one in Britain and number three across the Atlantic. Not bad, considering the Beatles had recently released *Abbey Road* and *Led Zeppelin II* was slaughtering everybody. (The Beatles' final album, *Let It Be*, was already finished but not yet released. 'Coincidence,' said Keith, who thought up the Stones' album title.) The cover may have been shit – a cake with little models of the band, baked by celebrity cook Delia Smith – considering that the Stones' original choices were surrealist artists W. C. Escher and Man Ray, who both declined. But the instruction on the inner sleeve, 'THIS RECORD SHOULD BE PLAYED LOUD,' just had to be taken seriously.

Let It Bleed is the twin brother of *Beggars Banquet*. The structure is identical: kicking off with a formidable scene-setter, in the form of 'Gimme Shelter', then placing its outings into blues, country and nasty rock 'n' roll in the same running order. Finally, both albums go out on epics which speed up at the end into no-nonsense, balls-out gospel.

Where *Beggars Banquet* had pointed to a stripped-down, politicised new direction, *Let it Bleed* took it all the way with iron saddlebags. In the two years since *Satanic Majesties*, the Vietnam war had dragged on, Martin Luther King and Bobby Kennedy had been assassinated, and Charles Manson had showed what hippies could do if they turned lysergically evil. The Stones had never sounded more astute at mirroring the vibe of the times. At the same time, the prolonged influences of Gram Parsons, the Band and Dylan's new country-inflected direction strengthened the Americana element in the music.

'I think it's the best stuff we've done so far,' said Keith in *NME*. 'It's like a progression from *Beggars Banquet*, only heavier.' As Nick Kent and Roy Carr wrote four years later, the album saw the Stones acting out 'their now standardised roles of vandals, outlaws and satyrs'.

It all starts with 'Gimme Shelter', my all-time favourite Rolling Stones track. It's the only possible theme song to *Let It Bleed*'s soundtrack to the death of the sixties, oozing ominous dread and apocalyptic warnings. It's also a total realisation of what made the Stones so unique at this time: a controlled, omnipotent tension, deliriously performed and embellished.

Keith starts proceedings with a deathly shimmer of guitar, before the whole dark beast comes lumbering in on lunging riffs and slashing chords. Mick rants about armageddon, while soul singer Merry Clayton (who used to sing backing vocals for Ray Charles) supplies the haunted, panic-stricken counterpoint. The atmosphere conjures images of rolling black clouds, lightning bolts and revving Harley Davidsons. The fact that the music was born in twenty minutes out of Keith's fevered, speedball-fuelled brain, as he waited for Anita to come home from a hard day of shagging Jagger, could explain its sheer ferocity. And his words, too, which were read back in the day as widescreen universal, were also very personal: 'Oh, a storm is threatening, my very life today / If I don't get some shelter, oh yeah I'm gonna fade away.' Keith recorded the track using an Australian copy of

Chuck Berry's semi-acoustic Gibson, the neck of which broke off as he hit the last note. (He was probably imagining it was Jagger's.)

'Country Honk' was exactly that – a down-home country version of 'Honky Tonk Women', in the style of which Keith wrote it. Byron Berline added some suitable fiddle in the LA studio car park, with Jimmy Miller marking time on a car horn. 'That's how the song was originally written, as a real Hank Williams/Jimmie Rogers/1930s country song,' said Keith in *Crawdaddy*.

Let It Bleed contains the best Jagger vocals on any Stones album. He's got it all – arrogance, sexual aggression, tenderness and realistic character-play, before all the hollering self-parody set in. Charlie and Keith have never lost the fearsome groove they display on 'Live With Me' and so many others – it's just that some of the songwriting started to go askew.

Another highlight was Keith's live tour-de force 'Midnight Rambler' in its original, more subdued studio form. The episodic masterpiece was the Stones' fullest assimilation of the blues into their own vision, oozing malevolence.

Amidst the riot that is 'Live With Me' comes a filthy, rasping saxophone from rock 'n' roll heaven. Say hello to Mr. Bobby Keys. This man's worth a book all to himself. Apart from sharing the same birthday as Keith, the sax man would become the nearest thing to a sixth Rolling Stone – apart from Stu.

The genial and dangerous Mr. Keys, born on 18 December 1943, had instant credibility with Keith, hailing from the same town of Lubbock, Texas as Buddy Holly and playing with him early in his career. Keith had first met him in '63 when he was backing US pop idol Bobby Vee, of 'Rubber Ball' fame.

In Steve Appleford's *It's Only Rock 'N' Roll*, engineer George Chkiantz tells a story about Keith's obsession with getting the acoustic guitars right during the *Let It Bleed* sessions. Keith was sitting in the sound booth, playing the same chords over and over again, while Mick and Jimmy Miller disputed a minor point about the drum sound up in the control room. When the engineer came down to fix some microphones, Keith asked what was going on. Chkiantz told him about the ongoing discussion. 'Look,' said Keith, 'my hands are beginning to bleed. I've been playing the acoustic now for several hours. I won't be able to play it for much longer, and I really want to get this track down tonight. So you tell them to get their finger out of it.' It was Keith's first utterance of protest all night. Chkiantz conveyed the message to Mick and Jimmy, who went back to where Keith had been sitting and spotted his guitar. 'It was just covered in blood,' Chkiantz recalled. 'He must have been in considerable pain.' Keith did, indeed, let it bleed, and maybe that's where his title came from.

'You Got The Silver' had been in the works since the *Beggars Banquet* sessions, and marks Keith's first full vocal on a Stones album. He'd started it in his Fifth Dimension studio as a love song to Anita, before honing it endlessly during the *Performance*-era limbo, and taking it to Olympic Studios. Bootlegs from that period have Mick singing the early Olympic versions, but on vinyl Keith stepped out on this hallucinatory acid-country ballad, full of whizzing slide guitars and wafting textures over the strident acoustic riff. It was the final showing from Brian, playing autoharp, and would pop up in Michelangelo Antonioni's hippie road movie, *Zabriskie Point*, the following February.

*Keith watching the Flying Burrito Brothers performing at the fateful 1969
Altamont Speedway concert.*

Let It Bleed proved that *Beggars Banquet* was no one-off. It carved their new
sound into the mass psyche with a sonic machete. Reviews were suitably ecstatic.
Greil Marcus wrote in *Rolling Stone*, 'The Stones have never done anything better. This era and the collapse of its flimsy and bright liberation are what the Stones
leave behind on the last song of *Let It Bleed* . . . the rules have changed with the
death of the sixties.'

Let It Bleed was released in the US on 5 December. The following day the Stones
played their free concert at Altamont. It has become one of the most infamous
landmarks in rock 'n' roll history, fraught with sinister vibes, darkness and, ultimately, death. So much has been said about this blood-soaked kiss-off to the sixties, but Stanley Booth's eyewitness account remains the most authoritative version.

Keith would later shrug Altamont off, but there were warning signs from the
outset. The original choice of venue – San Francisco's Golden Gate Park – fell
through after City Hall wouldn't grant permission. The next venue, Sears Point
Raceway, was nixed as it was owned by a film studio who demanded film rights,
which would have clashed with the Stones' and Maysle brothers' own movie plans.
At the last minute they settled on a bare demolition derby track, in a place 30 miles
South of Oakland called Altamont. It was in the middle of nowhere, bleak and
devoid of facilities. A crew organised by support band the Grateful Dead's office
put up a stage that was only four feet high. The Dead also called in their friends

the Hell's Angels to handle security, apparently in return for free beer. *Rolling Stone's* Michael Lydon later wrote that a girl had told him that the sun, Venus and Mercury were all conjoined in Keith's sign of Sagittarius that day – not a good omen.

Keith, Mick, Stanley Booth and Gram Parsons – whose Flying Burrito Brothers were also on the bill – visited the site the night before. Keith liked it so much he stayed overnight, partaking of acid, cocaine, weed and opium. Taking into account that he'd been on tour for the previous four weeks, he could well have been on Venus or Mercury. At that point, the earliest arrivals were building fires and getting ready for the good times the following day.

Eventually, 300,000 people flocked to the remote location, many fuelled by an unpromising combination of bad acid and cheap wine. Tensions simply escalated throughout the day. Everyone had to train their eyes on a four-foot stage, while straining to hear the inadequate amplification. Biting cold set in as darkness fell. And then there were the Angels. As if the event wasn't badly organised enough, having a gang of loaded, violently inclined bikers as security was the final ingredient in a recipe for disaster.

The music started with Santana, and there were already stabbings and scuffles breaking out. The Flying Burrito Brothers' 'Six Days On The Road' provides the only light relief in the *Gimme Shelter* film's Altamont footage, but their set was blighted by the continual violence in front of the stage. The Jefferson Airplane fared even worse, with singer Marty Balin knocked unconscious when he tried to stop an Angel beating someone up. The Grateful Dead arrived, heard what was going on, and promptly left. Crosby, Stills and Nash were the last band on before the Stones, who took their customary eternity to take the stage. By this time it was cold and dark. The Angels had ridden their Harleys through the crowd and parked up in front of the stage, daring anyone to lay a finger on them. The atmosphere was a mixture of terror, tension and anticipation.

Finally, the Stones appeared, and launched into 'Jumpin' Jack Flash'. Mick was in his tour attire of black hoop-top and black-and-orange cloak, while Keith sported the red spangled jacket he'd favoured for most of the tour. The audience could hardly make out the band for Angels. After 'Carol', the Stones played 'Sympathy For The Devil' and the violence started again. The group stopped playing, restarted, and Mick appealed for calm.

It's often been observed that Mick seemed ineffectual and slightly silly at Altamont, amidst the scowling sea of black leather. Meanwhile, Keith stood his ground and came up with an equally menacing stare, grabbing the mike: 'Either those cats cool it, or we don't play. I mean, there's not that many of them. That guy there . . . If he don't stop it . . .'

Sam Cutler looked out over the mayhem and appealed for a doctor, as Keith tried to cool things down by taking the band into Jimmy Reed's 'The Sun Is Shining', 'Stray Cat Blues' and 'Love In Vain'. As they started 'Under My Thumb', the violence seemed to be ebbing until a black kid at the side of the stage was seen to flash a gun. At that point, eighteen-year-old Meredith Hunter was stabbed and stomped to death. The band stopped again, with Keith coming back to the mike: 'OK, man. Look, we're splitting, if those people don't stop beating everybody up in sight. I want 'em out of the way, man.' (I sampled that off a bootleg once, for a dance track protesting the Criminal Justice Bill that criminalised unlicensed raves in the UK.)

Keith later told Stanley Booth, 'I don't think I could keep my mouth shut in a situation like that. What Mick was saying wasn't having much effect. Mick pleading for brotherhood. So I just pretended that there was somebody there to say, "Stop that motherfucker." Because if there's nobody else willing . . . I jeopardised everybody there at Altamont with that thing, but it was something to me that just had to be said or all control was gonna be lost . . .'

At the time, the Stones didn't know the murder had happened and carried on with their set. They gave 'Brown Sugar' its first ever airing, followed through with 'Midnight Rambler', and closed with 'Street Fighting Man'. Then they piled into the last helicopter and swerved unsteadily out of the jaws of hell. In the movie, it looks like a scene from *Apocalypse Now*. As they sat there shivering, the group had little idea of the repercussions, and the general comedown, which would be generated by their second free concert of 1969. But according to Keith, so he later claimed, 'It was just another gig that I had to get out of fast.'

Goodbye, sweet sixties.

CHAPTER SIX

The Guitar Player Gets Restless . . .

. . . And the Guitar Player Looks Damaged

After spending most of the sixties as the Stones' quiet musical bedrock, by the end of that decade Keith was carving out his own formidable legend. He was also taking over the musical reins of the Stones more than ever. But he would spend most of the seventies feeding, fighting, and ultimately trying to stupefy the demon that he says lives inside of him – and inside all of us.

But until '72 Keith was still at the peak of his powers, if sliding inexorably into the numbed-out haze of heroin. *Beggars Banquet* and *Let It Bleed* had booted the band into a whole new stratosphere of creativity, and the next two albums would complete arguably the most formidable quartet of albums in rock 'n' roll history. Between '68 and '72, the drugs and the chaos came together in a kind of strange alchemical honeymoon which would peak with *Exile On Main Street*. But Altamont had thrown the ultimate curve.

By the time the Stones had clambered aboard the last helicopter out of there, and adjourned to Keith's hotel suite back in San Francisco, it was 7 December – Pearl Harbor Day. In the stunned aftermath, Keith played Gram Parsons the spanking new 'Wild Horses' for the first time. Gram was so bowled over that he asked if his Flying Burrito Brothers could cover the song for their next album. The Stones agreed, as long as it wasn't released as a single.

The mood that night was a mixture of anger at the Angels, and severe depression. Mick didn't like the Angels' suggestion that Meredith Hunter was trying to kill him, and harboured a fear of being shot on stage for years after. And then there were the recriminations and accusations. (In the words of Kris Kristofferson's hip country song, everyone was keen to 'Blame It On The Stones'.) Four people had died at the concert: Hunter, two more who were run over by a hit-and-run driver, and a guy on acid who drowned in an irrigation canal. In January '71, a Hell's Angel was tried for the murder of Meredith Hunter, but claimed self-defence and was found not guilty.

It took some time for the full horror of what transpired at Altamont to emerge. In the light-hearted manner of the British music press at that time, *NME* initially called the event 'the world's most fantastic pop concert ever' – before conceding that 'four people died and scores of unfortunates had to be treated by doctors and psychiatrists for all manner of ills . . .'

Keith compared the free gig at Altamont with its predecessor at Hyde Park, telling Bill Wyman, 'You can put half a million young English people together and they won't start killing each other.' *Rolling Stone* called it 'perhaps rock 'n' roll's all-time worst day'. But you can't simply blame the Stones for single-handedly killing off the sixties dream. By the end of '69, San Francisco's Haight Street – the former hub of the hippie 'be-in' movement – was awash with acid casualties and heroin addicts. Many now called it 'Hate Street'.

Keith's effective last word on the subject came in his '71 *Rolling Stone* interview. He maintained that the Angels were psychotic bastards, but added, 'Who do you want to lay it on? Do you want to blame somebody or do you want to learn from it? I don't really think anyone is to blame. Altamont, it could only happen to the Stones, man. Let's face it, it wouldn't happen to the BeeGees.'

After Altamont, the Stones high-tailed it out of town as fast as possible. Keith flew into Heathrow – straight into Anita, Marlon and a herd of pressmen. Anita had told them that she was being threatened with deportation if Keith didn't marry her. Quizzed about it, the battle-weary Keith replied, 'It's a drag that you are forced into marriage by bureaucracy. I refuse to get married because some bureaucrat says we must. Rather than do that, I would leave Britain and live abroad. But if I want to continue to live in England, and that's the only way Anita can stay, we'll get married. I have nothing against marriage – I'd just as soon be married as not. We'll get it straightened out sooner or later, but first I've got to get some rest.'

Kenneth Anger's suggested solution was a pagan wedding – but Keith didn't like the black magic connotations, and passed on it. To him, the occult had only ever been interesting for its sinister pantomime, and the symbolism that Anita got off on far more than him.

What he didn't pass on was heroin. Having already become attached to the drug over the previous year, the fact that Anita had become hooked provided a temptation that Keith couldn't refuse. After the propulsive highs of *Let It Bleed*, the US tour, even Altamont, Keith was still buzzing but had to come back to everyday reality. It was a post-tour comedown with nothing to do. For some, becoming a dad would have been enough – but, even though he adored Marlon, Keith simply found it too hard to plunge into domesticity.

As he said when I interviewed him in 1980, 'I used to clean up to do a tour, because I just didn't want to be on the road and have to be hassled. But, physically having to readjust when a tour just stops [snaps fingers] – "Now what can I do?" I'm physically readjusting to then going home and living a quiet family life for two months. That'd do me in. Ba-boom, I'd go back on it. It was only when I had nothing to do that I got into heroin. I still had all this adrenaline, with my body saying, "What time's the gig?" That's when I'd go back on it. If I had to work I'd clean up. But what a hassle!'

The Stones did play some London shows in the final days of the 1960s. The first – the Saville Theatre, in Shaftesbury Avenue – came just a week after Altamont, on 14 December. There were two shows, and my chemistry teacher, Robin Pike, attended both. He describes the first as 'one of the worst Stones gigs I've ever seen. The band was shell-shocked, like they hadn't got over Altamont, and people were just sat there.' The press made much of the reserved reaction from the seated audience, drawing comparisons between the mid-sixties mayhem and the polite applause greeting each new song in '69. *Disc*'s Mike Ledgerwood slated the audience as 'pathetically apathetic . . . all that effort and energy . . . and so little enthusiasm in return.'

It was a sign of the times. After the hippie explosion, and before the fresh mania of glam rock, musicianship substituted for excitement. People just sat and listened. As 1970 loomed, the Stones were no longer teen pin-ups. The new-look 'Keef' was not suited to cavorting about in front of a few thousand screaming teenyboppers. Within a year though, the Stones would be taking the stage to a crowd that was now growing up with them – a new breed of rock fan that paid homage to the rock icons who'd exploded out of the 1960s.

After the gigs, Mick and Marianne made a court appearance to plead not guilty to possessing cannabis. When the case came up at the end of the month, Marianne was acquitted but Mick was fined £200 with costs. By now, the couple's relationship was history, although they did make one last vain attempt to keep it together.

Meawhile, 'Spanish Tony' Sanchez had moved in with Keith and Anita, as a kind of minder-cum-drug supplier. The man hailed from the Soho dope underbelly, and was retained to keep the couple happy.

It's near impossible for a couple to be together with only one partner doing smack. If they can't stay clean, both have to be on the stuff in order to inhabit the same zone. Sex certainly isn't a unifying factor when you're on it. And when one partner is injecting, it's unavoidable that the other will start doing it too. At first it's for economic reasons, but then you get hooked on the actual ritual of cooking up, tying off, and injecting the drug straight into the bloodstream.

In the States, Keith had just been taking the odd snort of smack to take the edge off his four-day coke cycles. Anita was now injecting it. Keith soon joined her – by skinpopping, as opposed to mainlining into the vein. Early 1970 can be seen as the start of Keith's slide into near-total numbness. Luckily, he still had enough internal momentum left to swagger through the Stones' next two monumental albums. But this period also saw Keith get into his off-duty lifestyle of the seventies – holed up with Anita and Marlon, smacked-out or wired-up on coke, with side orders of weed and bourbon, and still playing his guitar. And all because, when he's not on stage or in a studio, 'the guitar player gets restless,' to quote from 'Torn And Frayed'.

Liver Than You'll Ever Be

Despite their success, the Stones' financial affairs were distinctly unhealthy. Huge tax bills had come in relating to a lot of money that had gone to Allen Klein. As Andrew Oldham retrospectively explained the financial situation, 'in 1965 Allen had formed a company in New York called Nanker Phelge Music Ltd and ... told us we'd all own it and it would own the rights to our North American recordings ... The shares were never issued to the Rolling Stones and myself. Allen had issued them to himself ...'

Under the terms of the deal he'd created for himself, Klein didn't have to pay the Stones a penny of their royalties for years. He kept them solvent and helped them maintain a luxurious lifestyle, but by issuing loans from what he regarded as his money. When Keith was buying his house at Cheyne Walk, he had to dispatch Tom Keylock to New York to sit on Klein's desk until he obtained the £20,000 he needed for a down payment.

A massive shake-up was needed. On 4 February 1970, there was a meeting between Mick's friend Prince Rupert Loewenstein, who they were bringing in to manage their financial affairs, and the Stones' accountants, lawyers and tax advisers. The outcome was that it would be far more economic for the band to move out of the UK to France to avoid the high tax rates – which, back then, were 89 per cent of earnings above £15,000 a year. The Stones agreed that they would relocate for 21 months in April '71, in order to take care of the tax situation and disengage from Klein. The prospect did not thrill Keith, who felt all at sea in foreign cultures where people spoke another language, liked English food too much, and was quite happy in the homes he had.

Andrew Oldham had not only handed over the Stones' business management to Klein in '67, it seemed he'd sold the band lock, stock and barrel. Mick and Keith spent the ensuing months of 1970 trying to get their rights and royalties back, eventually resorting to a £20 million lawsuit. The compromised outcome would be that Klein ended up owning the Stones' recordings and publishing rights up to 1969.

At the end of July, the Stones' contract with Decca expired too. Determined not to be taken for mugs ever again, the Stones started setting up their own record label. The group wrote to Decca, saying that they were going elsewhere and Klein would no longer be representing them. It pissed Klein off, as he'd been talking about a new deal with Decca – but the Stones had grown to hate their old label, and Keith had found out the company was investing money in the American bomber planes that were going to Vietnam. Despite his fetish for weapons and bad guys, he shared his generation's distaste for a war that dropped napalm on innocent civilians.

The Stones' new label would be distributed in America by Atlantic Records, whose Ahmet Ertegun had a formidable pedigree in soul and blues. Marshall Chess – son of Leonard Chess, founder of Chess Records – was brought in as general manager.

The Stones seized control of their own financial destiny. Keith may not have trusted anybody else any more than he trusted Klein, but the Stones went on to become the biggest-earning band in the world. In 1970-71, they transformed into the money-making behemoth they are today, enabling Keith to maintain his often outrageous lifestyle.

In the first half of 1970, the Stones continued work on the album they started the previous year. At Olympic Studios, they worked on tracks like 'Sweet Virginia', 'Stop Breaking Down', 'Hey Mama', and 'Can't You Hear Me Knockin'?'. There were also bootleg staples like 'Leather Jacket', 'Hamburger To Go', and a rollicking belter called 'I'm Going Down'.

The sessions also saw Mr. Richards establish the recording process which Charlie Watts dubbed 'Keith Time'. As the smack began to take hold, Keith would sometimes miss sessions. He might turn up very out of it, or very late, though he was still capable of firing out brilliance.

It seemed to recall the behaviour patterns of Brian Jones. But, when Brian messed up, Keith was always there to cover for him. Keith, on the other hand, had called the shots musically on the sessions for *Beggars Banquet* and *Let It Bleed*, and still held the reins on the new album – ultimately entitled *Sticky Fingers*. But the other people involved now had to fit in around Keith's bodily schedule for the day.

At this time, he also had his reinforcements around. Bobby Keys continued to spice up the sound with Jim Price, and Gram Parsons was also present at a lot of the sessions. Both Gram and Bobby appreciated pharmaceutical refreshments, commencing a period when Keith and his closest buddies were permamently higher than the sun. Mick wasn't over-enthusiastic about any of this, especially the ongoing Gram situation. He and Keith were reported inseparable, and had even started to dress similarly. What pissed Mick off, apart from Keith's spiralling smack habit, was how much musical input he was getting from Gram. But then, the Stones had never been stronger in terms of their own musical output.

Apart from their first live album, *Get Yer Ya-Yas Out*, Decca were owed one more single to fulfill the contract. So the Stones promptly presented them with a little ditty called 'Cocksucker Blues'. Previously, Decca's Dick Rowe – 'the man who turned down the Beatles' – had turned down the Muscle Shoals tracks, and the unreleaseable song seemed about the best way to spite him.

On 30 August 1970, the Stones set out on a month-long European tour with a secret warm-up gig in Malmo, Sweden. The set was similar to the '69 US tour, except that 'Jumpin' Jack Flash' was now the oldest song in the set list. It was the first time that the Stones had played live with additional musicians, featuring the horn section of Bobby Keys and Jim Price, as well as Nicky Hopkins. Supporting were blues troupers Buddy Guy and Junior Wells, plus a new r&b singer called Bonnie Raitt.

For its time, the Stones' travelling stage was as groundbreaking as that of the *Steel Wheels* tour in '89. A huge proscenium arch housed the sophisticated lighting system and several rows of curtains, and cost so much that the group made little or no money on the tour. But they were setting an extravagant precedent, as well as putting a recurring bee in Keith's bonnet. It would take him until the 21st century's mega-tour to admit these exaggerated presentations were necessary to reach the masses who wanted to see the Stones.

But Keith's dominant concern of this time was procuring enough smack and coke to get through the gigs. Despite his crafty, custom-built shaving-cream container and fountain pen – designed to foil the enthusiastic efforts of customs officers – Keith and his partners-in-crime, Anita, Bobby and Gram, often had to rely on the local promoters to come up with the goods. If they didn't, there simply wouldn't be a show. But the Stones didn't cancel one concert.

When the tour hit Paris, Mick went to a party and met his future wife – Bianca Perez Morena De Macias, from Nicaragua. The pair soon became inseparable. Keith was dubious, as she epitomised the jet-set elite he despised. Anita was even more hostile at this stunning new addition to the Stones' female circle, flirting with Mick, and treating Bianca with disdain.

Poor Bianca's name was soon accompanied by a rhyming alternative beginning with 'W'. But nobody could miss the fact that she looked like a beautiful female version of Mick. Some, including Bianca herself, observed how he could now feel like he was fucking himself.

After the tour, November saw more recording in a big front room at Stargroves, Mick's newly-acquired country pile. They used the new Rolling Stones Mighty Mobile, a state-of-the-art studio built into an articulated truck, used by other bands recording on location for years to come. It was here they cut the underrated diamond that became 'Sway', and spent a fruitless night hammering away at a new Jagger song called 'Bitch' – without Keith. Finally, the guitarist turned up around breakfast time, and, with a cry of 'Give me that fuckin' guitar!', knocked the song into shape with its nasty, prowling riff. There were also early versions of songs that would pop up on *Exile On Main Street*, like Robert Johnson's 'Stop Breaking Down', 'Sweet Virginia', 'Bent Green Needles' – later to become 'Sweet Black Angel' – and 'Good Time Woman', which would evolve into 'Tumbling Dice'. They eventually finished the album at Olympic in December.

The previous year, Keith had been jamming a pretty, Eastern-flavoured acoustic guitar riff he called 'Japanese Thing'. The band took it and turned it into the epic 'Moonlight Mile' – without Keith, who was getting ever deeper into smack, although snatches of his original guitar were retained from the demo. Haunting strings were then added by Paul Buckmaster, who started out with medievalists the Third Ear Band before making his name as an arranger with Elton John.

September finally saw the release of the live album, *Get Yer Ya-Ya's Out*, which went to number one in the UK and six in the US. Hailed as one of the greatest live albums of all time, it perfectly captures the sleazy, grinding majesty of the Stones at this time. Nearly every song eclipses the original, especially 'Midnight Rambler'. The album goes down as a quintessential showcase for Keith, who seems to be ignoring everything else to lock grooves with Charlie Watts.

On 18 December, Keith celebrated his 27th birthday with a big party at Olympic Studios. Guests included Eric Clapton and Al Kooper, who joined Keith and the band for an impromptu jam through 'Brown Sugar', which later appeared on the flip of the 'Cocksucker Blues' bootleg. It's firing, and for a while Keith wanted it to be the next single, instead of the scheduled Muscle Shoals original.

Gimme Shelter, the film of the '69 US tour and that fateful day at Altamont, appeared at the end of the year. It made compulsive viewing. Another hangover from the end of the sixties made itself felt when *Performance* finally premiered in London, on 4 January 1971. Mick didn't attend, being fogbound in Paris, but Keith and Anita did.

Enter The Tongue

According to Bill Wyman, all the band had their own suggestions for the name of the Stones' new record company – including Panic, Ruby, Snake and Red Lights. Keith particularly liked Low Down, Meanwhile and Juke. But UK label boss Trevor Churchill favoured the high-concept Rolling Stones Records. Its logo was the internationally recognisable mouth and tongue, seen on all Stones-related product ever since. It was designed by John Pasche, a Royal College of Art student who was shown a picture of the Indian goddess Kali by Mick, and homed in on the Jagger-like mouth.

But it was all nearly irrelevant to Keith, who by now was firmly entrapped in a heroin haze. He finally decided it would be a good idea to clean up before he moved to France in April '71. He spoke to Mick about it, who, in turn, consulted renowned ex-junkie William Burroughs. The infamous author had been cured of a 30-year habit by British doctor John Dent and his reputedly painless apomorphine cure. Dent had died, but his mode of treatment was being continued by his former nurse.

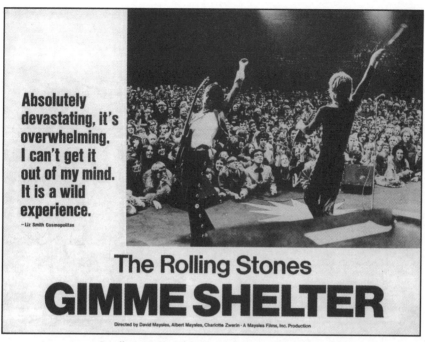

Goodbye 1960s. The Gimme Shelter *film poster.*

In February, Keith holed himself up in Redlands and took the cure. He promptly underwent four days of withdrawal hell – all the worse for the fact that he was addicted to top-quality gear. Technically cured, he lasted a couple of days before Michael Cooper turned up with some smack. Later that month, Gram Parsons arrived with more of the same, so any hopes of being cured were out of the window. The pair did at least try to kick together at Redlands, lasting for about five days of mutual cold-turkey agony. During this time they'd huddle together, and try to work out songs at the piano to take their minds off it.

It was also around this time that Keith had another car crash – this time in the pink-sprayed Blue Lena. After stashing his gear, he hopped over the nearest garden fence to escape the police – and found himself in Nicky Hopkins' back garden! The piano man invited Keith in for a cup of tea.

In March, the departing Stones undertook a short farewell tour of the UK, starting in Newcastle on 4 March and winding up at London's Roundhouse ten days later. The set consisted of the highlights from the previous year's jaunts, with additions from the new album like 'Wild Horses', 'Dead Flowers', 'Bitch' and 'Can't You Hear Me Knockin'?'. The brass section and Hopkins were present and correct, with Stu joining in occasionally.

But, by some accounts, they were not always that hot. Keith had always been the Stones' motor, but now he was running on half-cylinders. Having failed to clean up, his music was starting to suffer. Travelling separately with an entourage consisting of Anita, Marlon and his nanny, Bobby Keys, Gram Parsons and his dog

The infamous Redlands, Keith's life-time home.

Boogie, from whom he was inseperable at this point, Keith missed trains and planes, and got into a conflict with airline staff and police in Glasgow when Boogie was forced to travel in the hold. Gigs often started late. Sometimes the wait wasn't worth it. It was the first time Keith's smack problem had actually affected the band, and would set the tone for the rest of the decade.

Robin Pike, my old teacher, was one of the diehards who charged into the free-for-all at the Roundouse to get a ticket. At that time, the Sunday all-dayers at this old engine shed were a celebration of hippie culture. Robin, who initially got thrown out because he was wearing a camel overcoat and was suspected of being an undercover cop, reports that the Stones were 'fabulous' compared to the Saville Theatre gigs, especially Mick. But Keith was 'totally gone. He wouldn't remember a thing.'

On 26 March, the Stones were due to film a TV special at the Marquee Club in Wardour Street. Keith arrived late, in a bit of a state. Still bearing a grudge against the club's owner, Harold Pendleton, for dissing him in the Stones' early days, he took a swing at him with his guitar for a second time!

Never broadcast in the UK, but available as a pirate video, the show didn't feature them at their best – in fact they were sluggish. (In later years, Primal Scream thought it sufficiently entertaining to include in their tour bus viewing, constantly re-running the part where Keith not-so-discreetly rubs his nose.)

On 30 March, the Stones threw a farewell party at Skindles night-club in Maidenhead, Kent. It was attended by John and Yoko, Clapton, William Burroughs and assorted mates. When the hotel cut the power at two in the morning, disabling the ongoing jam session, Jagger hurled a table through the French window. Within days, the whole Stones camp would be relocated in the South of France.

The Stones announced the launch of Rolling Stones Records on 6 April 1971 – from a chartered yacht in Cannes harbour. In a corporate deal that foreshadowed how they'd conduct business in future, they'd signed with American car-park corporation the Kinney Group, who would distribute everywhere except Atlantic's territory in the US. Mick announced that the Stones would guarantee six albums over the next four years, including their next, *Sticky Fingers*.

For the first time, the Stones trailered a new album with a single that would actually appear on it. 'Brown Sugar' was released on 16 April, hitting number one in the US and two in the UK. The song is a salivating sex-beast which Keith locks into like a Doberman on a human leg. *Shake it, baby* – but it won't quit. By the end section, he's simply chord-abusing for the sheer hell of it. It's dirty, sweaty, brassed-up, and captures Jagger in his prime of explosive hedonism. Bobby Keys supplied the perfect finishing touch when he hooted a sax solo that made his name for life.

It's those subtle embellishments that give 'Brown Sugar' its amazing edge. 'We use acoustic guitars a lot to shadow the electric, always have done,' said Keith on the press release. 'It gives another atmosphere to this track, makes it less dry. It's cheap, too.'

Sticky Fingers itself popped out on 23 April in the UK, one week later in the US. It had taken nearly two years to make, from basic ideas to finished product, though a lot had been recorded before *Let It Bleed* was released. It was also the most successful Stones album to date. The sleeve credits thanked 'everyone else who had the patience to sit through this for two million hours'.

The sleeve boasted a photo of a man's denim-clad crotch, complete with unzippable fly. Pull it down and there's a pair of bulging Y-fronts, to prevent the zip scratching the record contained within. The cover illustrated Mick's desire to steer the band away from lyrics about blood and Satan, returning the focus to the ever-present sexual element. By bringing in ultra-hip jet-set figurehead Andy Warhol to design it, it also showed the circles that Mick was hanging out in since he'd met his new girlfriend.

Once you've unzipped the sleeve, the record within is a multi-faceted delight – from Keith's first chord-chop on 'Brown Sugar' to the oriental closing drift of 'Moonlight Mile'. The mood has shifted from *Beggars Banquet* and the crashing armageddon of *Let It Bleed*. Matured and polished, although still capable of unmitigated sleaze, the music also shows an extra dimension via the input of Mick Taylor. In the laconic junk-country of 'Dead Flowers', the country influence inherited by Gram had become more apparent, with lyrics that contained the most overt drug imagery in any Stones song: 'I'll be in my basement room with a needle and a spoon.'

In *NME*, Nick Kent and Roy Carr would call the album, 'The Stones' grand celebration of jet-set debauchery captured to perfection in their now chic demonic posture.'

When *Sticky Fingers* hit the stores, the Stones were settling into a life of tax exile in France. So opened another chapter in Keith's life. It would be riddled with chaotic incident and bodily abuse, alongside the great music.

CHAPTER SEVEN

TORN AND FRAYED

The French Connection

So now the Rolling Stones were the first rock 'n' roll tax exiles. Their intention was to stay at villas in the South of France for the requisite time to satisfy their tax problems, while also recording the next album. They would be allowed to stay in the UK for 90 days a year.

Since April '71, Keith has never come back to the UK as a permanent resident. In this time he has been based anywhere from New York or Jamaica to Switzerland or France. Having to leave his home country rankles with Keith to this day. When we spoke in 1980, it was still a bone of contention. Never mind the impossible wealth, the fame, and all the excessive perks they brought with them – for Keith, it was a combination of extortionate tax rates and the police that had driven him out. I asked about the Stones' seventies image of being cut-off and aloof:

'Remember who cut us off. It weren't us. We were kicked out. It was that or they tried to put us in the can. They couldn't do that so they tried to force us out economically, which they did. They just taxed the arse off us so we couldn't afford to keep the operation going unless we got out. Nobody's out through their own choice. I mean, we can live with it. By now, after travelling all these years, it doesn't really bother me where I am as long as I can come back occasionally. If we hadn't all been kicked out no doubt we'd still all be here. It wasn't a matter of choice, it was a matter of no choice. Get out. That was it.

'I mean, it's understandable, y'know, the Stones are rich tax exiles, blah blah blah, but it's only alright if you can live like that. Charlie came back to live in England – has for a year or two. If we hadn't been used to being on the road all the time I don't s'pose any of us would have wanted to go. Wouldn't have gone. But we wouldn't have been able to keep the Stones together and stay in England, so it was a matter of having to get out. No point in moaning. The only thing I wouldn't do is what they've tended to do over the last few years – bugger off to Los Angeles and live in that weird, cut-off climate out there. That Rod Stewart syndrome. I probably could have got like that if they hadn't rubbed my nose in the shit so many times that I never forgot the smell of it! [laughs]'

On 12 May 1971, Mick got married to Bianca in a civil ceremony at the seventeenth-century St Anne Chapel in St Tropez. It was the predictable carnival for the world's media: star-studded guest list flown in by chartered plane; extravagant party afterwards; one pissed-off Keith.

Anita now hated Bianca with a passion, and the feeling was mutual. Bianca had as much emotional power over Mick as a woman can have over a man who's besotted with her, but the band didn't like her for her aloof manner. She didn't approve of their general debauchery. Keith couldn't handle her circle of jet-setters, and feared that Mick – ever the social climber – would get sucked in. Apart from the bad implications for the Stones, it was alienating him from his oldest friend, after all.

Although he was playing the role of best man, Keith reacted to the circus by punching a photographer, smashing a camera and hurling an ashtray. At the reception he passed out under a table. After a short while, with Keith and Anita growing increasingly hostile, Bianca would hole up in Paris.

Keith, Anita and Marlon started their own exile by moving into the opulent grandeur of the Villa Nellcote, which looked over the fishing village of Villefranche-sur-Mer. Also in tow were Tony Sanchez and Boogie the dog. The place was already swathed in legend. It had been built by an English admiral at the end of the nineteenth century (who topped himself by jumping off the roof), with Roman-style pillars and huge fireplaces. In World War Two, it was the local Nazi heaquarters, complete with swastikas engraved on the air vents. The wine cellars were where the Nazis carried out their interrogations. The palatial villa overlooked the harbour, which used to be a pirates' cove. Here Keith moored the yacht he'd christened Mandrax – which, cocking a snook at the French police, was the patent name of a British sleeping pill that served a similar role in the drugs culture to the American Quaalude. He sailed it like he drove his cars, often with similarly damaging consequences.

The Stones were just about to start recording the next album when Keith did an epic *Rolling Stone* interview with Robert Greenfield. It was a milestone that revealed him to the press for the first time as a sharp raconteur. Greenfield, who'd later go on to write a graphic account of the Stones' excessive '72 US tour, described the scene at the villa as like a cross between F. Scott Fitzgerald's *Tender is the Night* and *The Shirelles' Greatest Hits*.

Asked about the chosen location, Keith replied, 'People say, "Why the South of France?" It's just the closest place where we can relax a little and then record. That's why we're all living in the same place . . . I hope it's worthwhile.'

It undoubtedly was, but at a cost. *Exile On Main Street* saw Keith working at home. Rather than hitch the Rolling Stones Mobile up to another location, he suggested they use the cellars below Nellcote. It had the theoretical avantage of not waiting for Keith to turn up as he'd already be there.

It looked good on paper, before reality gave it a twist. From the moment Keith moved into the salubrious villa, he was surrounded by a gaggle of dealers, junkies, hangers-on and variously shady characters. Apart from $5-$10,000 a month rent – estimates vary – Keith was footing the bill for an endless supply of quality food, rivers of booze, and the purest smack and coke. After all, nearby Marseilles is known as the heroin capital of Europe. *Exile* was made amidst a party in junkie heaven, in a basement where the hot, cramped conditions were apparently hellish. And that's a major reason why it's such a damn fine record!

But at the time, the whole scenario was bliss for Keith. He wouldn't have to worry about getting to and from the studio, and could record any time he felt the urge – as long as there was an engineer awake. Apart from a steady stream of drugs, he was surrounded by like-minded musicians and best buddies Gram Parsons and Bobby Keys. A young guitar-maker from Texas, called Ted Newman Jones, made a pilgrimage to Nellcote to give Keith a guitar, and ended up being his personal roadie for years. There was much jamming, trading of knowledge and ideas, and plenty of time taken out for partying, or even trips to the nearby casinos for a spot of gambling.

The first few weeks in Villefranche were spent settling in. Keith partied and played music, sailed in his yacht, and got into trouble in late May when his red E-type Jaguar was in a scrape with a car containing Italian tourists. He lost his rag, demanding on-the-spot compensation, which resulted in the harbour master intervening. When he and Keith started threatening each other with knives and pistols, the harbour master decked Keith, who then got a smack from Keith's minder, Spanish Tony. After the police were called, possible assault charges against Keith were dropped when he claimed self defence and Spanish Tony fled the country for a while.

In early June, Keith stayed true to form when he went go-karting and managed to fall off, hurting his back.

Tropical Disease

Once Keith was properly settled in, the 'Tropical Disease' sessions, as he called them, started at the beginning of July. Getting all the Stones in the basement – christened 'Keith's Coffee House' – at the same time was quite an achievement. 'Keith Time' was firmly established, as the lengthy, nocturnal waits for him and his visits to the bathroom were complemented by trips upstairs to put Marlon to bed – which could take hours.

Charlie and Mick Taylor were around a lot of the time, as were Stu and Bobby, but the disapproving Bill Wyman hardly seems to have been there at all, playing on eight tracks out of the eighteen that saw release – most of which were started at Olympic. Meanwhile, Jagger was interrupting the sessions to see his new bride, who wouldn't go near Nellcote, in Paris. He later said he hated the debauched chaos of the sessions, and also probably resented Keith having so much control. All of Keith's friends were turning up and having one enormous party. Stones gigs and albums had already adjusted to running on Keith Time. Now he was constructing a whole album in Keith World.

In the ramshackle making of the album, the necessary electricity was hooked up from the power supply for the local railway system. People would get electrocuted, or the power would cut out altogether. The old cellars were 'like a labyrinth of concrete and brick cubicles,' Keith told *Mojo*. 'Not so much separate rooms, more like tables, stalls. Charlie's round the corner in the second cubicle on the left . . . I could see Charlie's left hand flicking away. I would never rely on headphones; as long as I could see that I knew that we were in time.'

'It was such a dump,' Mick Taylor told *Mojo*, 'Dilapidated, dingy, mouldy, musty, there was always damp running down the walls . . . it was just crazy.'

But Keith liked the sonic possibilities and experiments that the situation would germinate. 'Just because of the peculiar qualities of the room. You'd simply jam an acoustic guitar into the corner of one of these cubicles and just start playing and you'd hear it back and you'd think, That doesn't sound anything like what I was playing, but it sounds great. So you started to play around with the basement itself, aiming your amplifier up at the ceiling instead of like normal . . . connected, umbilically, to machines somewhere else . . . down in the basement you weren't particularly aware of the fact that you were recording. Things are looser.'

Because of all the business of relocation, Keith and Mick had not really sat down and consciously written any songs, apart from a few held over from *Sticky Fingers*. *Exile* saw the start of Keith's 'Incoming!' theory, his belief that songs are already floating about in the ether and only have to be picked up by his antenna. Jagger preferred the more worked-out approach, which is why he thinks *Exile* doesn't have many Proper Songs on it. Keith saw it as a natural extension of *Sticky Fingers*, 'all flying out of the same kind of energy,' already underway before its predecessor had even been released.

Goings on at the Villa Nellcote became the stuff of legend: The extravagant daily banquets for the masses, often with 30 guests at one sitting, which Keith often turned down in favour of bacon and eggs. The Corsican drug dealers and small-time pushers from St Tropez. Anita shooting up the chef's teenage daughter with smack. Jagger moaning that he couldn't use a microphone because somebody was tying off with the lead. John Lennon throwing up on the stairs after partying too hard with Keith. Local dealer Fat Jack starting a fire in the kitchen while doubling as a cook. Bodies and post-party garbage everywhere. It was excess on a Fall-of-the-Roman-Empire scale, with Keith playing Nero. Bill Wyman says that it 'made *Satanic Majesties* look organised'.

But meanwhile, down in Keith's Coffee House, the music was cooking. No wonder it came out so scrambled, clammy and magnificent . . . eventually.

Jimmy Miller's contribution cannot be underestimated. As Keith has said many times, he was at the peak of his powers, and it was him, Glyn and Andy Johns who had to control the chaos that gave birth to *Exile*. Band members were coming and going, doing their parts and splitting, but Miller had to keep track of proceedings, not to mention augmenting the sound on percussion. As Mick Taylor observed in *Mojo*, 'Nobody has really stated how important Jimmy Miller's contribution was. If it hadn't been for Jimmy, *Exile* could not have been made.'

Maybe Keith summed it up when he said, 'It sounded like making a record under bombardment.'

Gram Parsons was another crucial figure in the creation of *Exile*. Not in terms of appearing on the tracks – he was simply there for Keith as 'another musician, a writer, just to bounce ideas off, without any sense of intrusion.' Gram came for two months in July, with his young girlfriend Gretchen. After bonding further with Keith in England on the Stones' farewell tour, Keith had agreed, in a drunken conversation, to produce an album for him for release on Rolling Stones Records – but only if the Stones' hectic timetable permitted.

In the absence of Mick, Keith often needed a sounding board and someone to hang with. Gram's influence hovers over *Exile*, although he apparently never played on it. Keith told Stanley Booth that he believed Gram played with him when he was working out some of the songs, but isn't on the album – 'No, Gram was just

Marlon, Anita and Keith attend a screening of the Rolling Stones film
Gimme Shelter *in Cannes, 1970.*

too much of a gent to impose himself that much.' But he was there during the crucial weeks, his spark and his musical taste working as an unconscious force.

'I miss him, man,' said Keith in *Mojo*. 'When guys who play guitars and write songs hang around, that's what they do – you get up in the morning, have a bit of breakfast, pick up a guitar and before you know it you're swapping ideas of all kinds – musical, lyrical, spiritual and criminal! Gram is on *Exile* in spirit, but playing? Not that I can remember. Though I can't swear he's not on there because a lot of things were done when I was alseep.'

As Gram told *Melody Maker* at the time, 'Mick and Keith liked a few of my songs and we gotta lotta kicks outta just sitting around playing together. All I did was sing and pick with the Stones.'

But Keith was forced to expel Gram from Nellcote when his heroin problem got out of hand. He started passing out due to excess and exhaustion, and it had got to the point where he was spending all his time totally wasted on large amounts of Keith's gear. Keith tried to tell Gram to take it easy, but eventually had to get someone else to tell him his time at Nellcote was up. Gram was deeply hurt and returned to the UK. He would hitch up with the Stones again on the '72 US tour, but was thrown out of Keith's room for the same reason. Once he was out of the Stones' satellite, Gram ploughed into his own sadly short-lived career.

Back at Nellcote, Bill now refused to attend the sessions at all. Mick was fed up, and spent much of his time with Bianca. Marshall Chess was starting to ask questions about a likely release date.

As September wore on into October, things continued to cloud over. By now, Miller, Andy Johns, Bobby Keys, and even Mick Taylor were using smack regularly – top-of-the-range pink 'cotton candy' from the Marseilles connection. The fact that these four, plus Keith, were the team who laid down many of the basic tracks on *Exile* could explain its sloppy, drug-sodden ambience.

The sessions trickled on. One day, Keith and Anita nodded out in their room and set the bed on fire. By this time, their relationship was feeling the strain of mutual addiction, although Keith still found time to pay attention to Marlon. Anita was getting increasingly fed up with the constant influx of unwanted guests, and ploughed further into a mound of heroin. It wasn't a great idea, as she was now several months pregnant.

On another night, all eleven of Keith's guitars were stolen while he was in the house, including the Flying V he'd used at Hyde Park. He blamed it on 'the Cowboys' – lowlife local drug dealers. 'There was a robbery and we got some of it back later and there's been a few burials throughout the seventies,' Keith told *Mojo*'s Sylvie Simmons, hamming up the outlaw-chic. 'Justice prevailed. We'll leave it at that.'

Meanwhile, back in London, the four original Stones plus Brian Jones' father had filed a High Court writ against Andrew Oldham and Eric Easton, charging that they'd deprived them of record royalties. They also sued Allen Klein for $29 million, alleging that he failed to represent their best financial interests. On 21 October, Bianca gave birth to a baby girl in Paris, who she and Mick named Jade. Jagger announced he was taking a month off to savour the joys of fatherhood, further putting the brakes on the Nellcote sessions.

Down at the ranch, it looked like time to shut up shop and get out of town. The police had had their eye on Nellcote and its array of shady visitors. Disgruntled former employees, like the chef whose daughter Anita had turned on to heroin, had made official complaints. The police knew all about the Stones, and didn't like them. The band decided to relocate their recording sessions to Los Angeles before something bad came down. They were allowed to leave – except for Keith, who was required to stay in France while investigations proceeded. After some legal manoeuvres from the Stones' lawyers, Keith and his family were allowed to leave Nellcote as long as they kept paying the rent as an act of good faith. They left behind a hefty stash of smack, coke and hash – which was duly discovered when the big bust finally happened on 14 December. By that time, Keith had been out of the country for two weeks, but the problems would linger on.

The group spent three months at Sunset Sound in LA, putting the finishing touches on the album. Keith took a detour via Nashville to replace his stolen guitars. Arriving in LA, Keith and the pregnant Anita had landed themselves with a gigantic addiction hangover from the six-month Nellcote party. As Bill wrote in *Rolling with the Stones*, 'Keith knew he had to get things under control.'

'LA was a huge contrast,' Keith later told *Mojo*. 'It was weird taking the tapes from that basement and playing it in real studios. Just trying to adjust and, What have we got here? Is it going to sound terrible? But guys would come dropping in just to listen from other sessions and we started to feel real good about it.'

According to Bill, the Stone Canyon house Keith rented during the sessions was another contrast to the craziness of Nellcote. He describes how a girl called Jane Villiers, who was a cook for Keith's neighbours Mick Taylor, his wife Rose and one-year-old daughter Chloe, started popping over to the Richards' with meals. 'She was shocked at first, later saying, "He answered the door, wild-eyed, his hair tousled and trousers halfway down his bottom. 'Who are you?' he asked, eyeing me suspiciously . . . . I thought at first he was exactly like his image – the scruffy, wild Rolling Stone who took drugs and didn't care a hoot about appearances. Keith, to my astonishment, turned out to be the warmest and kindest Stone of them all."' She described his rented house as 'a cosy warm home full of laughter and strewn with three-year-old Marlon's toys'.

Keith stayed in LA until the end of March, finishing up the album with the two Micks. Jagger recorded his vocals over the subterranean Nellcote grooves and the tracks that originated at the *Sticky Fingers* sessions, while backing vocals and extra instrumentation were added.

One night at the end of January, Mick, Keith and Dr John, the renowned New Orleans musician who'd come to sing backing vocals on *Exile*, went to see Chuck Berry at the Hollywood Palladium. The trio ended up jamming on three songs – before Chuck threw them off because he thought Keith was too loud. He was later reported as saying, 'I really didn't recognise him because he had a hat right down over his face. If I'd known it was them I might have suffered it through, 'cos I love them. They've even recorded some of my numbers.' It wasn't the last time Keith would cross swords with his hero . . .

At the end of March, with the album nearly finished and an enormous American tour booked to start in June, Keith decided it was time to clean up. He couldn't return to France because, apart from the December bust, the police were compiling a big dossier of complaints from former Nellcote employees, and had smashed a Marseilles heroin ring who pointed a finger at one of their best customers. If he set foot there, they'd throw the book at him. So Keith, Anita and Marlon relocated to Switzerland. On 26 March, Keith entered a clinic near Geneva and sweated it out again. He was followed a few days later by Anita. Having failed to kick by cold turkey, she was prescribed the minimum amount of methadone she needed to fight off withdrawal and minimise damage to their unborn child. On 17 April, gave birth to a daughter who they named Dandelion (later to be changed to Angela).

Her birth was followed by the completion of one of the greatest albums of all time.

To quote the man himself, 'what have we got here?' *Exile On Main Street* (recorded under the working title *Eat It*) boasts a ragged spirit which owes everything to feel and nothing to precision. It has a luminous, decayed majesty; the band tackling everything from country to gospel to blues to stripped-down rock 'n' roll with wild abandon. As Keith has also said, it was like the Stones' personal realisation of their adolescent dream, when the closest they thought they'd ever get to the USA was the obscure blues albums ordered through the Chess Records mail order catalogue. Keith celebrated with a six-month party and captured its peaks for posterity.

Exile On Main Street cannot be summed up in broad terms. It is definitely the sum of its parts – but what parts . . .

It starts with 'Rocks Off'. After they'd recorded the basic track through until the early morning, engineer Andy Johns went home after Keith passed out – only to get an 'Incoming!' distress call to return and capture what was now escaping out of his guitar. The track's humping swagger stokes the feel of an erupting party.

'Rip This Joint' is a rampant roadhouse blowout, with a ripsnorting Bobby Keys solo. 'Hip Shake' is the blues cover, taking James Moore's original via Slim Harpo on a dark, driving shuffle. 'Casino Boogie' epitomises *Exile's* claustrophobic funk with two guitars meshing and mating, carnival horns and Keith's wasted howl. Jim Price attributed the oppressive sound to the type of distortion Keith was putting on his guitar, effectively conjuring a picture of the hazy basement and its lolling, strumming occupants. The lyrics were inspired by the nearby casinos, where Keith liked to hang out.

The gambling dens also inspired 'Tumbling Dice', which started life as 'Good Time Women' during the *Sticky Fingers* sessions. Rock *with* the roll – its slow-motion lurch embroidered with Keith's delirious guitar. He's always insisted on playing it slow – 'That's the perfect tempo. Try to hot that one up and you lose the flow.' The song has become a live highlight. Every time I've seen it, Keith finishes up stroking that endless, heavenly coda with a massive grin. Then he drops to one knee, kisses his plectrum and flicks it into the crowd.

'Sweet Virginia' sets side two's acoustic mood with an all-out country singa-long. The most notable embodiment of Gram Parsons' presence – he's got to be in there on backing vocals. 'Torn And Frayed' is another landmark in Keith's Parsons-influenced immersion in country music. It doesn't resort to pastiche, the feeling is simply there in the haunting, soaring harmonies, the tune's loping strum and Al Perkins' rippling steel guitar. This song has matured like a fine wine. Its full merits could even have escaped Keith, as he nearly admitted in a 2003 edition of *Uncut* when asked about his favourite Jagger vocal: 'There's one like "Torn And Frayed" on which he brings out this country thing. We should do it more often on the road. When I hear that song I think, "Shit, did I write that?"'

'Sweet Black Angel' began life at Stargroves, where Keith jokingly named it 'Bent Green Needles'. It took on a more serious hue when Mick turned it into a tribute to black activist Angela Davis, who at the time was awaiting trial for murder. It was a rare political statement from the man who a few years later reckoned, 'black girls just wanna get fucked all night.' (When The Clash recorded a song called 'Stay Free' in '78, guitarist Mick Jones dropped in Keith's acoustic riff from 'Sweet Black Angel' near the end.)

'Loving Cup' is a soaring, cut-and-thrust ballad with beautiful piano from Nicky Hopkins. Few records have sounded so damn sexy. 'Happy' is Keith's vocal, and probably his theme song. By now, he'd found that Jack Daniel's sour mash whiskey came in handy to loosen up his throat when parched from the heat. It has to be autobiographical, as he shouts, 'Always took candy from strangers / Didn't wanna get me no trade / Never want to be like papa / Working for the boss every night and day.' The original version was knocked up one afternoon while waiting for the others, with just Keith on guitar and vocals, Bobby Keys on baritone sax and percussion, and Jimmy Miller on drums. Keith is at play on the classic open-G riff and his own brand of high-strung bass action. On tour, he's always returned to 'Happy'. How can he not?

'I did "Happy" just because I happened to have that together, and it would have taken another four or five hours for Mick to have learned it. Mick said, "Well, you do it because you know it,"' he told *NME*.

'Turd On The Run' takes the Stones' original blues model and pumps it full of amphetamines. 'Ventilator Blues' is Mick Taylor's only Stones songwriting credit, awarded for his taut, nasty riff. The title refers to the impossibly hot and airless conditions, while the track stinks of evil funk.

'On "Ventilator Blues" we got a weird sound of something that had gone wrong – some valve or tube,' said Keith to Sylvie Simmons. 'If something had gone you forgot about it . . . You had to bodge it as you went along.'

'Just Wanna See His Face' is the most unusual track on the album. One night in the basement, Keith was noodling at a nagging riff on the electric piano. Jimmy Miller tapped a bit of percussion, while Mick Taylor played bass. As Mick joined in with some scat-singing about Jesus, they captured the jam for posterity. Misty, religious, ceremonial, it's unlike anything the Stones have done before or after. Asked about the religious overtones, Keith, who, though his flirtation with the occult was long over, remained immune to the piety of religion, simply said that it was cut on a Sunday.

'Let It Loose' dates from the Olympic sessions – a yearning gospel ballad, which saw Mac 'Dr John' Rebennack organising the backing choir when it was finished off in Los Angeles. 'All Down The Line' is one of the few full-on rockers, spawned during the *Let it Bleed* sessions. Keith's on turbo-charged form – as he is on 'Stop Breaking Down', which was derived from a Robert Johnson song and boasts the toughest sheet-metal blues riff, sparking and blasting on lethal open-tuned chords. 'Shine A Light' is a gorgeous gospel ballad, before 'Soul Survivor' tops it all off with one of Keith's mightiest riffs of all time.

No wonder that, out of all the Stones albums, *Exile* remains closest to Keith's heart. He might have wavered on naming his personal favourite before but, when I asked him in '83, he replied, 'Ah, *Exile* . . . Definitely *Exile*.'

There was a substantial press build-up towards the release of *Exile*. For the first time, Keith handled the main interviews with *NME* and *Melody Maker*. Phoning in from 'somewhere in Europe', he understatedly explained, 'making this album was a much more relaxed affair than usual . . . . I might do the bass part or Mick Taylor might pick it up and play. Then Bill Wyman would turn up three hours later, but we'd laid down what we wanted so it wasn't worth doing it all over again. A lot of the tracks were cut with just three of the Stones there.'

Asked about his disinclination to masturbate his ego with long solos, Keith explained, 'I don't think in terms of lead guitar or rhythm guitar. I just think in terms of guitar players. I mean, on some of the tracks on the album we've got four or five guitars going and they're all playing different licks and counter figures. We're not into that trip of "you're the lead guitarist and I am the rhythm guitarist".'

In his *MM* interview, Michael Watts asked Keith how he felt about the successful glam-rock groups of the time like T.Rex and Slade. 'We all know where those riffs come from,' came the reply, inferring that the Stones were the true godfathers of glam. Watts then popped the question which would haunt the Stones forever more: could this be the last time? Keith debuted the reply he'd refine over the next 30 years.

'Oh come on! We're not exactly old! Muddy Waters, Howlin' Wolf are still getting it on. It doesn't figure. Just because we got a few kids these days! It's been ten years and I'm still not touching 30.'

Everyone was waiting for *Exile On Main Street* – from the teeny mags to the hippie underground. For the first time, it was almost like the critics were getting into their machine-gun turrets to shoot down the Stones. 'The trouble is that people expect too much from bands like us,' Keith had told Roy Carr. In retrospect though, it was the same thing that happened to the Beatles and Hendrix when they unleashed four sides of vinyl. It's a lot to take in when you're a reviewer on a deadline, and *Exile* was not an easy album to get into. It would take a while for its dark power to weave its spell.

The first single off the album, 'Tumbling Dice', was released on 21 April 1972 in the UK and made number five, scraping into the Top Ten in the States. It was a different story for the album. In the last week of May, *Exile On Main Street* went straight to number one on both sides of the Atlantic. The cover was a mash-up of photos of the band, strange handbills, scrawled lyric fragments and handwritten credits. It suited the music perfectly, predating the cut-and-paste visual assault of punk rock by five years. The finishing touch was a string of postcards depicting the band messing around in gangsterwear. The photos of the group were taken by Swiss movie-maker Robert Frank, who the Stones had commissioned to film their upcoming American tour in June.

The attitude of the press was generally positive. *Melody Maker* were on the button, with Richard Williams appraising it as the best album the Stones had made. Dismissing the previous albums as fillers, he wrote, 'the goodies were always spinning at 45 rpm. But, unbelievably, as they approach their thirties they're just getting better and better, losing none of the arrogance and adding a musical maturity which doesn't prejudice the inherent raunch.' Williams was one of the first reviewers to give Keith some big props, in the style to which he's since become accustomed: 'All these tracks are witness to the immensely gifted and curiously underrated Keith Richards whose rhythm guitar is the spark which ignites the fire. Richards has adapted and coarsened the Chuck Berry approach, and is capable of swinging the band on his own – it's the function of a rhythm guitarist,' he acclaimed.

But Keith remains convinced to this day that the record was roundly panned. The main culprit may have been Lenny Kaye in *Rolling Stone*, who went on to play guitar in Patti Smith's group. Kaye, whose opinions were usually noteworthy, explained that he came away from the album feeling 'vaguely unsatisfied' and that the Stones needed some 'horizon-expanding'. This would have left an impression on Keith, as the distinctly lukewarm review appeared in the issue of *Rolling Stone* with him on the cover during the US tour.

When I spoke to him over eight years later, he claimed, 'I remember *Exile On Main Street* being slagged all over the place when it came out and then the same guys six years later holding it up and saying, "Oh, this new album's not as good as *Exile On Main Street*." Now I read about two or three reviews when they come out, and that's it . . . . We've done what we intended to do – put out a record. After all, it's popular music. *Un*popular music is about the worst thing you can make. I'd rather it be popular. So I'd rather use that criteria than two or three writers slagging it off.

'If music just stayed the same as the three or four reviewers people read wanted it to stay, or just because it isn't like their pet favourite of the moment . . . People say the public's fickle but critics are ten times more fickle than the public!'

When I encountered Keith another decade on, in '92, I'd just written an enthusiastic review of his solo album *Main Offender* for *NME* and wondered if he'd seen it. 'Cheers, but I don't read any of 'em!' he thanked me.

He was asked about the press response to *Exile* by Barney Hoskyns in a 1997 issue of *Mojo*: '. . . it was quite understandable, being that double albums have a lot going against them. You know there's gonna be a certain amount of confusion, with so much material. At the same time, what *Exile* did was it just kept growing until it made its mark over a period of time. It slowly seeped in. I mean, you don't wanna do that kind of thing too often. In the beginning we didn't mean to make a double album, but it all just poured out.'

In the 21st century, most music mags now cite *Exile* as the greatest Stones album of all. In the January 2003 issue of *Q*'s 'Hundred Greatest Albums Of All Time' list, *Exile* was voted number 26 by the readers, acclaimed as 'an edgy masterpiece', with *Let It Bleed* at 64. (In acknowledgement of the later impact of Nirvana, who made number one on the list, Keith would claim *Exile* was 'the first grunge record'.)

When *Mojo* devoted a whole issue to the Stones in mid-2003, it seemed that only now could Keith really appreciate the magnitude of what he was getting up to in that basement. 'I don't often play Stones stuff but if I see a copy of *Exile* hanging about, I nick it and play it. I still love that record very much. I would say that there is the best of the Stones in there – up till now. It was a very prolific period. I've no doubt that one day we'll put out an *Exile* outtakes album.'

Rip This Joint

When *Exile* hit the streets, the Stones had already started rehearsing at the Rialto Cinema in Montreux, Switzerland. Their business issues had also been resolved when their lawyers and accountants worked out that Allen Klein did indeed owe the group millions, but that a lawsuit could tie up all their money for at least two years. To get Klein out of the picture, they settled on $2 million. Klein also got the back catalogue up until 1969. It was a clean break, but Klein was probably right when he told *Melody Maker*, 'I have the ability to think like a thief.' Along with the Beatles, the Stones had one of the most lucrative back catalogues of the sixties, and then lost it.

Out of the business mire, the Stones were ready to hit the road. On 20 May, they flew to Los Angeles to prepare for what would become known as the most infamous tour in rock'n' roll history.

Asked by *Melody Maker* if he wasn't going into the tour with some trepidation after Altamont, Keith replied, 'It's rare that we do an American tour when someone doesn't die. That thing on film just made it more obvious. I mean, on the '64-'65 tour we had a cop getting squashed. It's nothing new in our experience. We're just gonna try and make sure it doesn't happen this time.' Just in case, Keith and Mick carried .38 revolvers and hired extra security, as word had been received of possible repercussions from the Hell's Angels.

The tour started on 3 June at Vancouver's Pacific Coliseum and traversed North America in the Stones' chartered Lockheed Electra plane, boldly emblazoned with the tongue logo. It climaxed in New York at the end of July, with three nights at Madison Square Gardens. The tour would end up playing to nearly three quarters of a million people, and become the biggest-earning tour in rock history so far, grossing $4 million.

The staging also became a symbol of seventies excess, hanging a huge Stones tongue banner and 40-foot wide mirror above the group, which designer Chip Monck used to wreak visual havoc with his powerful lighting system. The support act was Stevie Wonder. Keeping the whole show on the road was ex-public schoolboy Peter Rudge, who compared it to a military operation. Also keeping the show on the road, as resident pharmacist, was Keith's mate Fred Sessler, who, as an ex-employee of Merck & Co who manufactured pharmaceutical cocaine, had all the best connections for supplying top-quality coke.

This was the STP – as in 'Stones Touring Party', or 'Stop Tripping Please', or possibly even named after a lethal hallucinogenic of the time – tour, where the Stones wrote the rule book for excessive on-the-road behaviour. It's also the point at which Keith exploded into full-blown icon status.

But all the tales of orgiastic gross-out, and heroic pharmaceutical intake with the jet-set elite, have overshadowed how the tour cemented the Stones' place as premier live titans. The UK farewell tour had not lived up to its full potential, due to the state of Keith at the time. Over a year later, he was starting with a clean slate. But still, fuelled by bugle and hard liquor, Keith partied harder than ever on the '72 outing. According to Stanley Booth, he was still snorting smack if he fancied it, but was pretty much out of the junk swamp. It's reflected in the live recordings from the tour, where Keith, as the band's epicentre, is wired and spot-on. Mick, too, had shifted his stage persona from '69's Satanic Majesty to a glittered-up consummate showman.

They started the tour with a warm-up before 17,000 in Vancouver. Mini-riots erupted outside among ticketless fans and Keith blew two guitars. The set now featured *Exile* tracks 'Rocks Off', 'Tumbling Dice', 'All Down The Line', 'Rip This Joint' and 'Happy' – which saw Keith take a solo singing spot for the first time. Some nights they'd add more *Exile* tunes, or 'Johnny B Goode'.

Stanley Booth was on this tour too, the best writer to capture the insanity of the Stones on the road. Booth could easily have written an account of the '72 extravaganza to equal his *True Confessions of the Rolling Stones*, but he left that to *Rolling Stone*'s Robert Greenfield, who reported the gory details in *Stones Touring Party*. Booth later explained why he passed on it in his biography *Keith*, and brilliantly summed up the antics on the Stones' 'big, ugly 1972 tour' in the process: 'Featured sideshows on the tour involved a travelling physician, hordes of dealers and groupies and big sex-and-dope scenes. I could describe for you in intimate detail the public desecrations and orgies I witnessed and participated in on this tour, but once you've seen sufficient fettucine on flocked velvet, hot urine pooling on deep carpets and tidal waves of spewing sex organs, they seem to run together. So to speak. Seen one, you seen 'em all. The variations are trivial.'

Blimey. Booth mentions being backstage at the LA Forum with Keith, Gram Parsons, piano player Jim Dickinson and a film assistant boy carrying a stash of Mexican brown heroin, but adds, 'This was the cocaine-and-tequila-sunrise tour. People have written much rot concerning Keith's heroin addiction at this time – he was still doing odd toots; granted the toots were of a size to sedate a Kentucky Derby winner, but it wasn't as bad as it was going to get.' And it would get pretty bad.

Greenfield got a whole book out of this tour and its events. Some are verified by Robert Frank's banned *Cocksucker Blues* movie, but the book was essentially damned by Keith when it appeared in '74 for factual inaccuracies, mainly concerning female acquaintances. But there can be no doubt about one of the film's most famous images – Keith and Bobby Keys giggling like schoolboys while lobbing a TV set out of a hotel-room window. It has almost reached dictionary status for describing rock 'n' roll stars behaving badly. 'It provided the most satisfying crash,' said Keith in *Uncut*. 'But the only reason we did it was because the damn thing refused to work. It took a while to do because they used to bolt them to the floor in those days.'

Then there was the three-day stay at Hugh Hefner's impossibly opulent Playboy Mansion, where the band stayed when they played Chicago, for 'security reasons'. A full-on three-day orgy with Hef and the bunnies, with the odd break for gigs. The Stu-Watts-Wyman axis found other ways to entertain themselves, like backgammon and pinball.

Frank's cameras were – probably wisely – denied access, but Greenfield wrote about the non-stop party in *Rolling Stone*: 'Keith Richards is lying flat on his ass in a deep plush sofa. Keith's scarecrow frame is sporting brass studded jeans, leopardskin boots, mixmaster avocado hair, and red sunglasses. Five years ago he would have been stopped outside the front door and never even allowed to state his name or stand in front of the camera. Today he is lying flat on his ass digging Hugh Hefner.'

But Greenfield also gave this description of Keith performing during the tour: 'Keith on stage seems always to be at the brink of disaster, about to fall into the crowd or off the back steps, about to knock over an amp or tear his voice to shreds once and forever while singing "Happy" . . . . Some nights it was as though they brought Keith to the hall in a cage and his hour and a half on stage was the only freedom he was going to get . . . . The energy he generated when he was absolutely on was scary.'

'What never changes is how wired you get after a concert,' Keith told Greenfield. Two concerts and you're twice as wired. Didn't get to sleep until ten this morning.' You surprise me, sir!

On 18 July, the Stones were supposed to kick off two nights at Boston Gardens. Fog meant the plane had to be diverted to Rhode Island. As they emerged from customs, a local photographer muscled in. Security blocked the lensman, who carried on being persistent until Keith gave him a slap. The situation mushroomed and ended up with Keith, Mick, security man Stan Moore, Robert Frank and Marshall Chess being hauled off to jail. The Stones were due on stage in an hour, and the Mayor of Boston was worried that a riot would break out at the venue. Stevie Wonder played

Stoking the Cult of Keef Part One: on the cover of Rolling Stone (6 July 1972).

on, while the Mayor called the Governor of Rhode Island. The Stones posse were released on bail, and the show went on – by all accounts, a stormer.

The following night, Keith checked out Bobby Womack – former singer of the Valentinos, and the man who wrote 'It's All Over Now' – at the Sugar Shack club. Their paths would cross again soon.

On 22 July, Keith's vocals appeared on a Stones single for the first time when 'Happy' was released in the US only. It made number 22 and was the last *Exile* track to be plucked out as a 45. On the same day, the Stones' plane was en route to Pittsburgh. Frank felt that his movie needed spicing up – hence various blowjob scenes, and a couple of groupies stripping off as assembled STP members clapped along and enthusiastic roadies steamed in. It was mostly play-acting according to Keith, who, despite Stanley Booth's claim that he was putting a wider berth on smack, was filmed being shot up by groupie Cynthia Sagittarius in the Pittsburgh gig locker room, before nodding out. Frank's hotting-up segments were what resulted in the film never seeing the light of day, except on bootleg and as a little-seen concert film called *Ladies and Gentlemen: The Rolling Stones*.

The New York shows (where Keith checked into the Carlisle Hotel as Count Ziggenpuss) were the expected grand finale. Despite the fact that much of the STP were now addled shadows of their former selves, they were triumphant.

Melody Maker's Roy Hollingworth turned in an exhilarating account, writing, 'Two months of solid gigging had created the perfect Rolling Stones . . . No chinks, no bluffing, no living on reputations, they really were a steaming beast, getting higher, and randier, and bitchy as tarts down a dark alley.' Turning his attention to the guitar man – 'spraying chords about and losing his balance' – he observed, 'Keith looks like [cartoon hedgehog] Spiney Norman, his hair sticking straight up like somebody had just tossed a grenade down the back of his neck. His face all wasted, his teeth black and broken, his guitar at a low, loose angle, and his music plain beautiful.'

The last night of the tour, 26 July, was Mick's 29th birthday. There was a birthday cake, a food fight and a party at the St Regis Hotel. Muddy Waters and the Count Basie Orchestra provided the music, while a naked Warhol 'superstar', of the female variety, burst out of another cake.

The tour's two most famous images are photos of Keith which both appeared on the cover of *Rolling Stone*. The 6 July issue had an Ethan Russell shot of him leaning against a wall at Seattle airport, under a sign saying, 'PATIENCE PLEASE . . . A DRUG FREE AMERICA COMES FIRST!' Under his shades, Keith sports a look of total stoned defiance. His jacket boasts a patch saying 'Coke', with the Stones tongue on the other side. Then there's the 3 August issue with Annie Liebowitz's classic shot of Keith in the dressing room, absolutely zonked out. He's sporting his favoured stage gear for the tour of white silk shirt, Levis sewn with a mushroom over the crotch, and his much-loved Tibetan prayer flag. It's since popped up everywhere from bootleg covers to T-shirts in the Japanese Stones shop bearing the legend, 'On The Nod'.

Stoking the Cult of Keef Part Two: on the cover of Rolling Stone *(3 August 1972).*

All of this elevated Keith to another plateau of fan worship. But he doggedly kept the Stones' essential rock 'n' roll flag flying during this period. He was spurred on by what Stanley Booth diagnosed as Mick's 'incipient exhibitionistic elephantitis' turning the Stones into 'a costume party'. If Mick was hanging out with 'hardcore beautiful people', then Keith was going to set himself on stun. He hated the hangers-on, like author Truman Capote – 'that old queen' – and his companion Princess Lee 'Radish' Radziwell, sister of Jackie Onassis. One night after the gig, Keith could be found banging on their hotel room doors, howling abuse and eventually daubing Capote's door with tomato ketchup. His attitude in most of the tour photos screamed, 'Fuck you!' to all the jet-set hobknobbing and arse-slobbering going on around him. As long as he had his doctor's bag, mates like Keys, Booth and Sessler and a rabid crowd to play to, Keith could stay relatively sane. But it required hedonism of a previously unheard of degree.

Or as Mr. Booth so succinctly put it, 'You can see how a sensitive person like Keith might need medication, but none of this stuff cheered me up. I hoped for better things.'

At the end of '73, Lester Bangs reflected on the state of the Stones in *Creem*, especially Keith. He clearly approved. 'Keith was obviously one of those people (like Dylan circa '66) who look the absolute best of their entire lives when they're clearly on the verge of death. It seemed to lend him a whole new profundity and eloquence, even though he was barely playing at all! . . . . He looked everything dark and tragic that the Stones trip had ever threatened: soul flattened, skin sallow, bone scraped, and behind the reflector-shaded eyes the suggestion of a diseased intelligence too cancerous to even spit imprecations anymore. Fucked up. It was beautiful.'

Armagideon Time

On 9 August, Keith, Anita and the two kids adjourned to Montreux, Switzerland, where Keith had to battle with his usual post-tour comedown. He combated it by having his Bentley shipped over, continuing the heroin use which had built up throughout the tour – and skiing. In later years, Keith would proudly boast that, even when he was a complete junkie, he managed to make *Exile On Main Street* and learn how to ski.

Keith and his family stayed in Montreux for the next four months. Their times in Switzerland were probably the nearest they got to experiencing a happy and secure family life. There were still drug dealers coming and going, but compared to Nellcote it was a desert island.

It was just as well. After the Nellcote experience, followed by the madness of the tour, Keith was feeling fucked. The musical climate had also changed since the Stones came back in '68. They were no longer competing against post-hippie somnambulism, but new heroes like Bowie and the behemoth Led Zeppelin. Glamour, spectacle and excess were translating into massive record sales.

Jagger knew this, and didn't hold *Exile* in high esteem. Keith, on the other hand, knew that the record was a one-off, unique to its time and circumstances. It was his masterpiece, conjuring a spirit which would be impossible to repeat.
So where would he fit into glam rock? Keith's one condescension to the glittery mode of '72 was a bleached streak down the side of his hair, although he'd been wearing makeup since '67.

Living in different countries meant that Keith and Mick no longer got together to kick around ideas. Keith also hated Bianca, and Mick hated Keith's lifestyle. Their next album would be germinated by the Jagger-Richard partnership working on song ideas separately.

In November, Jagger came to visit Keith to try to kickstart the process, to little end. They just weren't as close anymore, either in terms of geographical distance or friendship. When Mick was around, Keith would spend much of the time in the toilet, feeding his habit. Then he might emerge and hurl a gem at Mick, like bawling, 'Angie!', and letting Mick take it home.

Keith needed new musical impetus to get his juices flowing again. He found it in reggae music. He saw the film *The Harder They Come*, and it gripped him in the same way as Muddy or Chuck had in the sixties. With Gram Parsons out of the picture, reggae joined country music in Keith's musical melting pot.

From Keith's point of view, *The Harder They Come* had it all: brilliantly vibrant music, exotic surroundings, ganja and guns. Ever since his childhood cowboy fantasies, Keith had always bought into his conception of outlaw chic. He'd developed a bit of a weapons fetish over the years, too, and by now wasn't averse to packing a piece, just like the Jamaican rude boys.

The Harder They Come centred on a young man trying to make it through the Jamaican ghetto, and the trials and tribulations he faced as part of day-to-day life. It made a star out of young singer Jimmy Cliff in the lead role, and had a truly explosive soundtrack. Cliff's tunes, such as 'You Can Get It If You Really Want It', the stirringly emotional 'Many Rivers To Cross' and the classic title track, showed how much the island's music had progressed since ska was so popular with UK skinheads a few years earlier. There was a new depth and maturity in the message and the musical construction. Production techniques were audacious, often stunning. With this music, the sky was the limit.

As with any music that he becomes intoxicated by, Keith played the movie soundtrack over and over, and would later be moved to cover the title track. He discovered other reggae maestros like Toots and the Maytals, madcap producer Lee Perry, and the Wailers axis which was about to explode onto the world stage. It was a whole new world for Keith, and he had to know more.

Hence the Stones booking a month at Kingston's Dynamic Studios, to record their next album. The place was owned by veteran producer Byron Lee of the Dragonaires, and was where Jimmy Cliff had recorded some of his hits. It also offered new surroundings, far away from Keith's legal problems in France.

In the last week of November, the Stones' entourage docked in Kingston, Jamaica. Keith was very much a travelling man at this time, having started the year in the South of France, spent time in the US, and then Switzerland. Now the band were staying at the Terra Nova Hotel, which had been the home of Chris Blackwell, who has done more to further the cause of reggae music than any other white man. His Island Records label had released *The Harder They Come*, and would also galvanise the meteoric rise of Bob Marley with the seminal *Catch A Fire*.

Keith had caught a bug and was soon tapping straight into its source. He'd hung with the originators of rock and blues, Chuck and Muddy, and embraced the essence of country music with Gram Parsons. If there was no discernible reggae influence on *Goats Head Soup*, the album the Stones recorded in Kingston, it was probably because Keith hadn't yet learned the intricacies of reggae and its hallucinogenic big brother, dub. It wouldn't start to filter through for another year or so, but, since 1974, there hasn't been a Stones album which hasn't been touched by the hand of Jah in some way. Even now, you can walk into any room containing Keith and his mighty portable sound system and be assailed by prime dub or reggae, past and present. Reading about Keith's newfound obsession 30 years ago turned me on to reggae, reflecting his old passing-it-on ethos.

'Basically, I'm Jamaican,' Keith told me in '83, during a tirade about why he couldn't live in the country of his birth. He then launched into a convincing stream of patois. 'Yeah, mon! Lion! Bloodclaat, mon! I'm a Jamaican. I'm a resident of Jamaica. That's where I live. That's where I'm based for eleven years, as much as I can be based anywhere.'

Keith would eventually settle in the US, but Jamaica has kept calling him back throughout his life. Which isn't to say that his clan glided smoothly into a new life in paradise. Keith knew he couldn't stay at the Terra Nova because of the ongoing tension between Anita and Bianca. Anyway, he loved the island so much that he wanted to buy his own place there. He settled on a villa two hours north in Ocho Rios, overlooking Cutlass Bay. Idyllic, beautiful, and surrounded by dreads with pockets full of top weed, it came close to making a new life for Keith. The place belonged to former pop star Tommy Steele, a jolly cockney who first scored big with 'Rock With The Caveman' in the fifties. Keith promptly bought the place for £75,000 cash. It was called Point of View.

Goats Head Soup was slow to hot up. Apart from Keith's shaky condition, the personal addictions of Jimmy Miller and engineer Andy Johns were starting to catch up with them. The Stones had even left the similarly incapacitated Bobby Keys behind, to overdub his sax later, thus removing one of Keith's best playmates. Circumstances dictated that *Goats Head Soup* would be Mick's album this time around.

Lester Bangs recalled the stories filtering back from Jamaica in December's *Creem*: 'Like Keith ... according to a friend, wiped so far off the map that he picked up a bass and began trying to play a lead guitar line through it for a take. And was so gone, supposedly, that he kept on for thirteen minutes before he realised he had the wrong instrument.' A far cry from the possessed musician duelling with himself on the previous album.

No sooner had the Kingston sessions started twitching into life than the Nellcote legal situation finally came to a head. The papers were having a field day, reporting that the whole band were now facing heroin charges. The French police demanded to speak to them, so the Stones – minus Keith, of course – flew to Nice to meet the presiding judge in the case. It worked out fine for everyone, except Keith, as the police witnesses said that they had been made to sign false statements, so the other Stones' drug charges were dropped. However, arrest warrants were drawn up for Keith and Anita on charges of drug trafficking. There were echoes of Redlands, as Keith once again took shit for turning his home into party central.

Publicist Les Perrin put out a statement, quoting Keith: 'The first I heard of the warrant for my arrest was when I read it in the newspapers here [Jamaica] this morning.'

Michael Watts from *Melody Maker* came out to the island, quoting Keith on the arrest: 'At the moment I know they've got a warrant out for questioning but I don't know if I'm going to go back and be questioned. It's all a bunch of political bullshit. It's always somebody trying to be promoted. I have a feeling that the French are trying to show the Americans that they are doing something about the drug problem. But rather than actually doing something about it they bust a big name. The only thing I resent is when they drag my old lady into it. I find that particularly distasteful.'

'Talking 'bout the Midnight Rambler . . .' 1973 tour.

The rest of the band had returned to the island to continue work on the album. Watts reported that they had laid down a dozen tracks, including obscure and unheard titles like 'You Should Have Seen Her Ass' and 'Four And In'. The 'Angie' idea started to blossom into a haunting ballad, while a Keef rocker about death emerged called 'Dancing With Mr D' which turned into a pantomime horror-rocker after Mick put his words on it. Keith worked on the ballad 'Coming Down Again', which would turn into one of his finest moments, and got to vent his Chuck spleen on a risqué little ditty called 'Starfucker'. They also worked on a lush instrumental which would turn into 'Waiting On A Friend' on '81's *Tattoo You*, and 'Tops' from that album started during these sessions too. Recording continued until 13 December, when they broke for Christmas.

Just before Christmas, there was a major earthquake in Nicaragua, with Bianca's hometown wiped out. On Boxing Day, Mick and Bianca flew out to check on her mother's welfare and take some supplies. Mick and Keith agreed the Stones should play a benefit concert. Bill Graham duly set it up for the LA Forum on 18 January. Keith, who spent Christmas in Jamaica, joined the band in LA in mid-January.

The Stones had slotted in a tour of the Far East and Australia for the New Year, but, because of the arrest warrants for Keith and Anita, the Australian government refused to grant work permits, closely followed by Japan and Hong Kong. After playing the benefit, raising $350,000 for the earthquake fund, the Stones flew to Honolulu, Hawaii, for two dates. They then filled in the gap left by Japan by going to LA's Village Sounds studio to work some more on the album. They resumed touring in New Zealand on 11 February, before finally gaining entry to Australia and hopping around there until 27 February. 'Keith Richards, even more evil than before, is still the prancing gypsy,' said the *Adelaide News*.

After the tour, Keith returned to Jamaica to find that Anita had passed her time at home with an ever-growing posse of Rastafarians – much to the chagrin of their rich, white neighbours. Keith was pissed-off enough with the situation to fly back to London in March, embarking on a homecoming bender with Spanish Tony Sanchez. Over in JA, Anita's behaviour resulted in cops raiding the house and a bust for possession of ganja. She was put in a cell, where she was raped and beaten by both guards and prisoners. Keith paid a $12,000 bribe to get her out – arranged, it turned out, by the same slimy, double-dealing local white businessman who got her busted – and Anita was returned to London, along with Marlon and Dandelion. Another country had gone sour on Keith – for the time being, anyway.

The Stones recommenced work on *Goats Head Soup* – named after the goat patties they'd lived on at the Jamaican studio – in early May at Olympic. They cut three new album tracks – 'Hide Your Love', 'Heartbreaker' and 'Silver Train' – as well as 'Through The Lonely Nights', a yearning country ballad which would end up as a future B-side.

Andy Johns became the latest Stones casualty when he was too smacked up to complete the sessions. He was replaced by Led Zep man Keith Harwood, while Jimmy Miller had regressed to carving swastikas in the studio desk and saw his role diminished to playing a little percussion. It would be the last Stones album he worked on, but the band had learned a lot from him. Just as he'd been vital to the success of *Exile*, Jimmy's permo-nodded demeanour helped deflate the impact of *Goats Head Soup*. '... Went in a lion and came out a lamb. We wore him out completely,' said Keith in *Crawdaddy*. With both Miller and Keith on auto-pilot, it's no wonder the resulting album fell a little short. After they finished 'Starfucker', which Atlantic made them change to 'Star Star', mixing took place at Island Studios in Notting Hill, London.

On 26 June, Keith and Anita got busted again. As ever, the junkie hotbed of Cheyne Walk had attracted the attention of the law. Also present that particular evening were Marshall Chess and Prince Stash de Rola. Keith, Anita and Stash were taken in after the cops found heroin, cannabis, Mandrax and two of Keith's guns.

They were later released on bail, but the bust marked the latest step down the ladder. It had been around four years since Keith started descending deeply into heroin. He'd managed *Exile* by the skin of his teeth, but things were starting to go badly wrong. Anita later told Victor Bockris she felt responsible for getting Keith further into smack, 'and I was a bad influence on him and it was all a mistake.'

Keith and Anita adjourned to Redlands when the album was finished. To add to their misery, the old place caught fire on 31 July. The family all got out and managed to save some valuable antiques, but the thatched roof went up, requiring extensive renovations. Keith also lost some of his favourite guitars, like Newman Jones' custom-built skull 'n' dagger model.

That month, the Stones had announced plans to tour Europe in September through October. They wouldn't be taking in France because of Keith's ongoing legal problems. In mid-August the group started rehearsing in Rotterdam, Holland. It was time to start whetting the public appetite, so they filmed themselves performing the new single, 'Angie', plus album tracks 'Silver Train' and 'Dancin' With

Mr D', for BBC TV's *The Old Grey Whistle Test*. Mick now looked like one of Gary Glitter's band, while the guitar player looked wasted.

In August 'Angie' was released, reaching number five in the UK and number one in the US. Nick Kent later reckoned that when Keith inspired Mick's lyric with his cry of 'An-gie,' it actually meant, 'Anita-I-need-ya.' Keith later said it was inspired by his new daughter, Angela nee Dandelion (though many have tried to claim Mick wrote it about Mrs. Bowie).

The phrase 'follow that' seems inadequate. *Exile* had been Keith's album, but now he was disempowered. Just listen to the levels on the vocals. *Goats Head Soup* sounds polished and clean. Guitars are put through the popular effects of the day, like mushy Leslie speakers, the whole thing sounding buffed up and compressed for American radio. Exactly what the Stones fought against on *Let It Bleed*.

The album's stand-out track is Keith's 'Coming Down Again'. This deathly slow ballad sounds like the morning after the six-month Nellcote party, and sees Keith in reflective mood. Giving his most sensitive, broken vocal performance to date, he asks, 'where are all my friends?', before touching on infidelity with the great line, 'slipped my tongue in someone else's pie.' The music is suitably funereal and desolate, boosted by another strident Bobby Keys solo. (Primal Scream would mine a similar seam in 1990 with a track called 'Damaged' on their *Screamadelica* album – the last thing that Jimmy Miller ever produced.) Nick Kent summed it up in his *NME* review when he said, 'it stands out in its own wasted way as the only really honest track on the whole album.'

Kent, despite panning 'Angie', loved the album, writing, 'half this record is uniquely good and that's much more than we could really expect in these desperate days, particularly from a bonafide superstar institution. This album is truly great.' He was more accurate when he said that 'on *Goats Head Soup* the Stones have really nothing to say, but somehow say it so well that the results transcend the redundancy of the project in the first place.' He seemed resigned to the fact that it contains nothing on a par with 'Gimme Shelter'. As a Stones obsessive myself, I was worried.

All My Time's Been Spent

The European tour opened in Vienna on 1 September 1973. It included the Stones' first UK jaunt since the farewell tour, and a massive press party amidst the splendour of Blenheim Palace, birthplace of Winston Churchill. Keith really was in walking-dead mode at this time. He went into the party and immediately adjourned to the toilet to shoot up with Bobby Keys. Apart from that, it was all rather sedate and un-Stones-like.

Nick Kent was there, of course, and gushed, 'The only truly exciting moment for yours devotedly was the appearance of his hero Keith Richard, who sprinted around restlessly with his kid Marlon and a suspicious-looking grey-haired stranger [Spanish Tony?] in tow. Decked out in beat-up "Granny Takes A Trip" clothes, his hair still appearing to have been cut by someone under the influence of at least five Mandrax and washed in sheep-dip, he looked like the only person present that night who might conceivably have something to do with rock 'n' roll.'

Above left: Keith and Anita, having escaped from the fire at Redlands. Above right: Anita salvages a chair from the smouldering house, 1 August 1973.

Later he added, 'Anita Pallenberg appeared momentarily to whisk away her ever-more restless husband.' The scruffy Anita had been waiting outside in the car, too out of it to get dolled up. Finally, she got fed up waiting for Keith and stormed in. A furious row broke out and the couple were driven off, fighting all the way.

The following day, the Stones started a three-night stint at London's Wembley Empire Pool. I had a ticket for the afternoon matinee on Saturday, my first bona fide Rolling Stones concert. I was now nineteen, more able to appreciate what the Stones had been singing about all this time. I'd got into the peripheries of the music business by running fan clubs for David Bowie and Mott the Hoople, whose singer, Ian Hunter, had said, 'Keith Richards is what rock 'n' roll's all about.' I'd also stuck a toe into the world of drugs.

The pre-gig excitement I felt that day has never left my being. I bought the special Stones issue of the *Evening Standard*, then the tour t-shirt, sat through the support band – routine Rolling Stones Records signing Kracker – and did a good impersonation of a kettle about to explode.

The first time can never leave anyone cold, unless they're already dead. I didn't come down from the buzz of actually seeing the Stones for days. No matter that Keith barely moved and looked 'wasted and unsure', as *NME* put it. Even playing at smacked-out half-cock, he was a mesmerising stage presence. Sporting his favoured black velvet jacket of the tour, he lurked next to Charlie for most of the set, chopping out those riffs and only soloing once, on 'Starfucker'. This was in the days before video screens, so the group were ant-like in dimension, but the sum of the lights, music and sense of occasion made for the most compulsive gig I'd seen in my life so far.

The highlight was 'Midnight Rambler', nearly fifteen minutes of psychodramatic depravity. I sat there practically gibbering with disbelief as Jagger crawled along the stage during the slow blues segment, Keith stalking over him like a glamorous Frankenstein monster, sparking those sheet-metal stun-chords with grim relish. It seemed to consummate those ten years I'd spent immersed in the Rolling Stones. Everybody's allowed a life-defining experience, and this was probably mine.

After London, the tour headed northwards. It was backstage at the Birmingham Odeon, on 19 September, that Keith was given the news that Gram Parsons had died the previous night. He had returned to the Joshua Tree Inn with some friends to celebrate completing his beautiful new album, *Grievous Angel*. They'd been drinking all day, and Gram took some of the Phenabarbitol he was prescribed to combat seizures he'd suffered since a 1970 motorcycle crash. Gram simply slipped away. Traces of other drugs were found in his system, but it was not the full-blown heroin or morphine overdose that has been reported. When Phil Kaufman took Gram's body and drove out to the Joshua Tree Park, toasting his friend in a pre-arranged cremation rite, he realised later he'd chosen almost the same spot as where he, Gram, Keith, Anita and Michael Cooper had taken acid and watched for UFO's a few years earlier.

Even in his numbed-out condition at this time, Keith was deeply affected, and would sit for hours at the bar with an equally upset Bobby Keys. He hadn't been so close to Gram since Nellcote, but knew that his star was definitely on the ascendant. *Grievous Angel* was to be the crowning point of Gram's career when it was released posthumously. Sadly, he'd had a lot to live for. Pete Frame was right when he wrote in *Zigzag*, 'it seems we only heard the tip of the iceberg.' 'Coming Down Again', on *Goats Head Soup*, plays like the perfect epitaph to Gram, and an apt tribute to his colossal impact on Keith.

Keith ploughed on through the tour. He was further rocked when his beloved grandfather, Gus Dupree, passed away. Michael Cooper, hopelessly addicted to heroin, died around this time too. Two weeks after Gram died, it all got too much for Bobby Keys, who was also seriously addicted to smack. As fucked-up as Keith was at this time, he never committed the cardinal sin that Bobby did in failing to turn up for a gig. Keys was sent back to the States, and wouldn't rejoin the Stones camp for years.

The tour ended in Berlin on 19 October, with a debauched party. Keith wasn't really in celebratory mood. There had been some consolation on 17 October, when a French court gave him a one-year suspended sentence, a $1,000 fine and a two-year ban from entering France, for the Nellcote drug offences, but he was still facing a court appearance in London. On 24 October, Keith admitted possessing Chinese heroin, cannabis and Mandrax, plus a revolver, shotgun and ammunition, at Cheyne Walk. His lawyer claimed the drugs been left at the house by guests who'd stayed there when Keith was abroad. He was fined £205, while Anita was given a one-year conditional discharge for possessing Mandrax.

With his legal problems behind him, Keith's attention focused on recording the next album, which would start in Munich the following month. He also found himself hanging out a lot with a certain Mr. Ronald Wood.

CHAPTER EIGHT

ENTER THE WOOD

Glimmer Twin Meets Soul Brother

'Everyone takes things so seriously, y'know? But rock 'n' roll – if it ain't fun, it's nothing. Thank God for Ronnie Wood, I say. They could be burying him and he'd be laughing. Last thing you'd hear out of his coffin would be "Ahahaha!" It's the right attitude. Same attitude as I've got. It's reminded the rest of the Stones too that it's always been our basic attitude.'

That was Keith talking to me in '83. As primarily a rhythm guitarist, he's always thrived on having a sympathetic guitar to bounce off. And with Ron Wood he certainly could – sometimes literally! Ronnie – who joined in 1975 and became an official Rolling Stones junior partner in '93 – is the third man to play lead guitar for the band. Keith had finally found his perfect match.

Brian Jones was initially an awesome fountain of inspiration for the young Keith – both with his musical skills, and a lifestyle that Mr. Richards would not only emulate but eventually surpass in terms of excess. However, the pair often didn't get on. In fact, Keith later described him as 'a right cunt at times'. Then came Mick Taylor, probably the most advanced virtuoso the group has ever boasted. But he didn't click personally with Keith, and musically the two roles of lead and rhythm guitar sometimes seemed too separate.

When Keith hitched up with Ronnie – who can both look and sound very similar to himself – he finally found his soul mate. As a guitarist, Ronnie has a dextrous sensitivity, especially in the slide department. But he can also rock out and – most importantly – he can spark off and mesh with Keith. They have spent countless hours jamming together, anywhere from hotel rooms to studios to private gardens. There's a telepathic sense of interplay and complimentary riff-slicing between them that's still awesome to behold.

As well as being a truly nice bloke, Ronnie is also a professional nutter who thrives on mischief on the road. He became Keith's perfect partner-in-crime, sharing a similar taste in hedonism and refreshments. And he could even knock out a dynamite sketch as a memento afterwards . . .

On a *Top of the Pops* Stones special in September 2003, Keith's face lit up when Ronnie was mentioned, patting his heart and saying the man's name four times with a big grin. Keith observed how people say they can't tell which one is which when they're playing – 'but you're not supposed to, that's the whole point!' When he first appeared with the Stones in the UK at Earls Court, London, Ronnie's role seemed more like that of new court jester – running about, jostling and gooning with the others. But he was always there in the sound, lending his sweet, soaring tones and blues-power sensitivity to Keith and Charlie's locked-in roll. Just the man for the job.

Ronald Wood was born in Hillingdon, Middlesex, on 1 June 1947. His father, Archie, had a 24-piece harmonica band that toured the racetracks of England, in which he played hand piano and told jokes – which could explain Ronnie's sense of humour.

The younger Wood started off playing drums for a local outfit called the Thunderbirds – who later knocked off the 'Thunder' part and became the Birds – while attending Ealing Art College, switching over to guitar. The band built up a live following, playing mainly Chuck Berry, Motown or even Beach Boys covers. They made three singles for Decca between 1964-65.

Their style was jagged, stomping British R&B, with Ronnie shining through on his stun-guitar starburst solos even then. The Birds never quite cracked it, but might have done if allowed to develop a bit more. So Ronnie went off to join the Creation, who'd scored a massive hit with 'Painter Man' and were having a reshuffle, passing the guitar duites to Mr. Wood. They'd been pioneers in using feedback and violin-bowed guitar, which Ronnie duly continued with until they split in the summer of '67. He then hitched up with ex-Yardbird Jeff Beck in the Jeff Beck Group, replacing ex-Shadow Jet Harris on bass. The group also featured a singer called Rod Stewart.

The band made a couple of landmark albums in *Truth* and *Beck-Ola*, bludgeoning, proto-Zep, bluesy rifferama with plenty of ego-exercising from Beck's frets. *Truth*, in particular, was considered a milestone in British rock.

Ronnie and drummer Micky Waller formed the powerhouse rhythmic juggernaut. By the second album, a young piano sessioneer called Nicky Hopkins was also on board. However, Beck's notorious moodiness resulted in the band splitting up – two weeks before they were booked to play Woodstock. It gave Rod Stewart the tilt to start a solo career, but also cemented his relationship with Ronnie.

Ronnie had been playing with the remaining members of the Small Faces – Ian McLagan, Ronnie Lane and Kenny Jones – following Steve Marriott's departure in '69. When they decided to form a new group, Ronnie ended up bringing Rod with him. The Faces were born – although at first they also featured Ronnie's brother Art, and were called Quiet Melon!

The Faces were one of the classic British bands, even though they only made four studio albums between '69 and '75 – *First Step*, *Long Player*, *A Nod's As Good As A Wink* and *Ooh La La*. The debut was somewhat tentative – a first step indeed. But the next two are classics of bar-room mayhem, with tracks like 'Stay With Me' defining their raunched-up good-time soundtrack. The Faces were also great musicians – as heard on their cover of the Temptations' 'I'm Losing You', or soulful ballads like 'Sweet Lady Mary' – but their specialty was their live show, a non-stop party with a sky-high whoopee quotient.

I was lucky enough to see the Faces at their peak several times between 1970-71. Their set usually started with the aptly-titled 'Hard Me A Real Good Time', which set the tone for an evening of fun, frolics, and, occasionally, football, as Rod led terrace chants and kicked balls into the audience. No wonder their crowd consisted largely of beered-up lads, apart from the teenies who came to scream at Rod.

Ronnie commanded the right-hand side of the stage. I was often reminded of Keith as he strutted and staggered about, peeling off bluesy licks and hot-wiring the rhythm section, usually with cigarette in mouth. He played a mean slide guitar, could beautifully embellish a ballad with his sighing tones, and was a cavorting, larger-than-life presence, flamboyant to the max. And the Faces liked to party. For one tour they even had a bar on stage!

At the same time as the Faces, Rod was conducting his own solo career. Ronnie also appeared on his classic solo albums between 1969-74: *An Old Raincoat Won't Ever Let You Down*, featuring Ronnie on a version of 'Street Fighting Man', *Gasoline Alley*, *Every Picture Tells A Story*, *Never A Dull Moment* and *Smiler*. These were more sensitive affairs, with Ron handling most of the guitars and his subtler acoustic shades shining through. Rod's personal success escalated after the massive hit that was 'Maggie May' in '71. Then the rest of the band started getting itchy feet.

The Degenerate Everly Brothers

If the Beatles were the Stones' good-natured rivals in the sixties, it was the Faces in the seventies. There was much ribald banter between the two camps, but Ronnie was hanging out a lot with Mick. There were also rumours that Mick had asked Ronnie to fill in on an American tour if Keith couldn't get a visa. The pair worked on a track called 'I Can Feel The Fire', which would eventually appear on Ronnie's first solo album. They also knocked up the original demo of 'It's Only Rock 'N' Roll (But I Like It)', of which Kenny Jones' drums and some of Ronnie's guitar were retained on the end product – along with David Bowie's handclaps! 'The basic track remained pretty much the same so there I was, contributing to a Stones album before I was a Stone,' Ronnie said later. The sleeve of *It's Only Rock 'N' Roll* credited him with 'Inspiration'.

During '73, Ronnie had started recording his own album in his home studio at the Wick in Richmond. Enter Keith in April and the beginning of Ronnie's passage into the Stones. Ronnie describes the birth of his strong friendship with Keith in *The Works*, his autobiography published in '87: 'It was sheer luck, really. My ex-wife, Krissie, was down at a club and saw Keith at another table. She could tell he wanted to get away from the people he was with, so she went up to him and said, "Hey, wanna come back and hear what Woody's done for his solo album?" . . . [Next spring] He came over to my house, expecting to stay a few hours. He wound up staying four months. Then we did a concert together.'

'Ronnie's cutting an album down in his house,' recalled Keith in *A Life on the Road*, a weighty tome put together by the Stones in '98 with interviews by Jools Holland and Dora Loewenstein. 'I said, "Lucky sod, studio in his house." I mean, me, I'm one of the Rolling Stones and I didn't even have a tape recorder . . . I think we went on for 48 hours the first session before anybody thought of leaving. So it was, "Have you got a spare room? I'll send out for a bag of new clothes." We stayed there, working and playing snooker, and worked non-stop for three or four months putting Ronnie's album together. That was my first extended period of working with somebody else outside the Stones, because up until that time it was the Stones or nothing.'

Hooking up with Ronnie in April '74 was a good thing for Keith. The rest of the Stones had refused to do a summer tour, with one major reason being the state that Keith was in. So he would have been at a loose end once the Stones album was finished, which was always a dangerous situation for him. (Not that he wasn't in trouble already!)

Things weren't going too well with Anita either, and his Cheyne Walk abode was under constant watch from the cops. Working with Ronnie gave him both an escape and a lifeline. Keith is all over *I've Got My Own Album To Do*. It was as if, after the laborious sessions in Munich, he was let off the leash, finding a new soulmate and having the time of his life.

Band relationships with Mick Taylor had soured to the point where the 'junior guitarist' was contemplating leaving. But with Ronnie, Keith was free to have some fun, claiming he hadn't felt so good about working with another person since he first got together with Mick. When the Stones were putting the final overdubs and mixes together for their new album, Keith was sometimes too wrapped up in Ronnie's record to make it. In 1974, he made the first small steps toward his solo career of the late eighties and early nineties. But in the process he'd also found the Stones their perfect second guitarist, and was breaking him in.

On 13 and 14 July 1974, Keith appeared with Ronnie at Kilburn State Cinema, north-west London, for gigs billed as 'Ron Wood: If You Gave Him Half A Chance'. The pair fronted a band consisting of Ian McLagan and the rhythm section of Andy Newmark and Willie Weeks. I couldn't get a ticket for love nor money, but friends who did go said it was amazing. Keith was upfront for the first time, with the perfect sparring partner next to him. Nick Kent in *NME* said it was 'a grand meshing together of sublime musicianship and the archetypal dishevelled get down,' describing Keith and Ron as 'not unlike a degenerate Everly Brothers.'

In the following issue, Kent would call Keith 'the World's Most Elegantly Wasted Human Being'. The phrase stuck. If any one journalist can be said to have promoted the 'Keef' outlaw image of the time – indeed, the image he still has for many people – then it's Nick Kent: the stories, the disreputable anecdotes, the parallel descent into drug hell by Kent himself, the enthusiasm for music and, above all, a definitive way with words. I still consider him one of the greatest music writers of all time – he lived it, and lived to tell the tale.

Another Kent story concerned a May 1974 shopping expedition to Kings Road, during which Keith attempted to procure some rhinestone-encrusted jeans: 'He struggles manfully first to locate and then to undo the button on his own trousers. Several minutes of this frustrating activity pass without success. Even the transcendental time sense of the World's Most Elegantly Wasted Human Being becomes acquainted with the realisation that little is being accomplished here. "Oh, lissen, man, I'll take the things on spec." And with that, our hero rides, lolling meditatively, into the sunset. From this, living legends are made.' As Bill Wyman commented in his book, 'I had witnessed many such scenes myself, although none involved trousers.'

Ronnie's album was trailered by a single, 'I Can Feel The Fire', which featured Keith on rhythm guitar. It was a real upper, the most buoyant thing Keith had been involved with in years.

The album was released on 27 September 1974. The self-designed back sleeve was the first ever showcase for Ronnie's own artwork, while the front depicts the bleary culprits in his front room. It could have been an all-pals-together jammed-up wankathon, but it's a fine record that's just a Stones throw away from the balls-out whoopee of the Faces. The music is injected with a weighty dose of funk, the ballads are soulful, and the shadow of Keith looms large. He even wrote two songs, the delicate 'Act Together' and the power-surging 'Sure The One You Need', on which he takes lead vocals.

Nick Kent said of *I've Got My Own Album To Do*, 'Richards' presence has given what so easily could have been thought of as yet another super-session masquerading as a solo album the edge of notoriety it's currently gaining for itself.' A cover headline on the July '73 issue of *Creem* had already asked, for the first time, 'Ron Wood To Join Stones?'

It's Only Rock 'N' Roll

Stones-wise, things were tottering along rather more shakily. Keith had sunk deeper into heroin addiction and was now at the top of the Ten Most Likely To Die list. Rumour had got around that doctors had given him six months to live if he carried on as he was. It was a period when he swaggered around all summer in the same gun-metal silver jacket, with a bone earring swinging and his dental bombsite flashing. Nils Lofgren would later write a silly but well-meaning song called 'Keith Don't Go', about the period when Keith nodded out during an interview with 'Whispering' Bob Harris on *The Old Grey Whistle Test* and passed out in his food at a restaurant. These stories are now the stuff of legend. Suffice to say, by 1974 Keith Richard(s) was the number one exotic gunslinger junkie – or whatever new phrase the *NME* dreamt up that week to mythologise him.

It sounds great – but, underneath it all, Keith wasn't happy. He supposedly epitomised the rock 'n' roll lifestyle, but just wanted the chance to play the music. 'I find it a bit of a drag that people feel the need to project their death wishes on me,' he said later. 'I've got no preoccupation with death whatsoever . . . I was nineteen when it started to take off, right, and just a very ordinary guy. Chucked out of night clubs, birds poke their tongues out at me, that kind of scene. And then suddenly, Adonis! And, you know, it's so ridiculous, so totally insane. It makes you very cynical. But it's a hell of a thing to deal with.'

But of course, back then, I and many others loved the way Keith had turned into a combination of dark-angel junkie and the raunch-hoodlum of the five-string guitar. Since his emergence as the prime mover and the coolest looking Stone during *Beggars Banquet*, his fan cult had been increasingly sucked in. By '77 even Keith would realise he'd pushed it too far, but around '74 fascination with his image was at a peak. I was personally fixated, but couldn't quite get away with the Keef look. That wouldn't come until I got on smack myself . . . it's been said that people actually got hooked on heroin because they were copying the Keef lifestyle. You got the hair sticking up right; adorned yourself with bangles and scarves; a smudge of eyeliner; finishing touch: a wrap of China white.

And it's certainly true in some cases. Nick Kent, who became one of Keith's drug buddies, succeeded in gaining himself a colossal habit he wouldn't shake for years. Pete Erskine, a young journalist who interviewed Keith, took some gear and ended up battling smack until he died several years ago. It can happen to anyone.

Sid Vicious, who died from a heroin overdose, was fond of saying, 'I wouldn't piss on Keith Richard if he was on fire.' But Sid's drug buddy, Johnny Thunders, was the classic Keef fan, the guitarist who made his name in the New York Dolls as a glam-rock cartoon version of Keith Richard. He exaggerated 'the Look' and personified the heroin chic that Keith lived through in the early seventies. Unlike Keith, Johnny never shook his addiction and died in squalid, mysterious circumstances in New Orleans.

I can't deny that it crossed my mind too on the first occasions I dabbled with heroin: so *this* is what Keith is into? I was so besotted with the Stones that I looked upon it as being as fundamental in the quest for their essence as a copy of *Muddy Waters' Greatest Hits*.

But that's not the reason why I first tried it. Back in '72, when I first gave it a shot as an eighteen-year-old, I didn't know that Keith was a junkie. The press never stated it blatantly, and I didn't know the signs. When he nodded out during the TV interview, I just thought he was worn out from all that studio work! It was only around '74-'75 it became common knowledge that Keith was not a well man. And I actually made up my mind not to take heroin again – until a few years later, that is, when I got ambushed. Ironically, when Keith was cleaning up, I was dirtying down. But I couldn't afford the top stuff, the best treatment or the big cure. I'd finally knock it on the head in '89, and haven't looked back. When I last saw Keith, in September 2003, we shook hands on the fact that we'd both come out the other side relatively intact.

The Stones released 'It's Only Rock 'N' Roll (But I Like It)' as a single on 26 July 1974, reaching number ten in the UK charts, sixteen in the US.

On the same day as the infamous *Whistle Test* interview, Nick Kent had a lengthy conversation with Keith. Some of it was published in the November '74 issue of *Zigzag*, the fan-based monthly I wound up editing a couple of years later. Nick kicked off his 'very wrecked little chat' by asking about the single.

'. . . The track itself was originally recorded at Ronnie Wood's place with Mick, Ronnie and Kenny Jones,' confirmed Keith. 'I just felt that it said what it had to say very well, what with everybody running around trying to write the definitive rock 'n' roll song . . . So we immediately set about re-recording it, but the problem was that Kenny Jones, in fact, had done a great take-off of Charlie's drumming which, for that number, even surpassed Charlie himself. So Charlie had to do a take-off of Kenny Jones doing a take-off of him and ended up so paranoid about it that I decided to leave the original track on.'

On the September 2003 *Top of the Pops* Stones special, Ronnie recalled that Keith wiped all his original guitar parts off 'apart from a twelve-string'. Keith told Kent at the time that he added about four guitar overdubs 'at least. Mick T's not on it at all. Mick J's playing one guitar and I think Ronnie's playing an acoustic.' The video is a classic, which still gets regularly re-shown. The band play dressed in US Navy sailor suits, before being deluged by bubble-bath foam which ends up completely swallowing Charlie. It appears the Stones had grafted on a new backing track, as some marvellously stinging Keith lines emerge from the mix. Keith himself has got peroxide slashes in his hair, a grey complexion and smack-dead pupils. Seems to be enjoying himself, though.

In August, Keith retaliated in the press against the legendary rumours about having his blood changed in Switzerland. His oblique way with words only succeeded in upping the ante on his reputation another notch. 'That's beautiful. I love that. I've heard about that thing and I'd love to do it just because I'm sure that eating motorway food for ten years has done my blood no good at all. The only times I've been to Switzerland is to ski . . .' Cue the most famous Keef quote of all time: 'I gave up drugs when the doctor told me I had six months to live. If you're gonna get wasted, get wasted elegantly.' Most tellingly, he claimed to another writer, 'I only get ill when I give up drugs,' and announced plans to have his teeth rebuilt.

It's Only Rock 'N' Roll, the album, was released on 18 October, accompanied by a publicity campaign around London in the style of graffiti. It was based on Dutch artist Guy Peellaert's sleeve painting, which depicted the band in ancient Rome. Peellaert's book *Rock Dreams* had made quite an impact that year, in which he took famous photographs of classic rock, soul and country icons and repainted them, exaggerating their images and reputations in surrealistic dreamscapes. The Stones were respectively depicted as feasting with topless women, dolled up in female fetishwear, dressed as Nazis with naked pre-pubescent girls, or drugged up in a seedy hotel room with a sheet-clad Anita. There were also paintings of Mick as his decadent character in *Performance* and Keith and Mick strutting around in pirate costume. Nik Cohn's text to the book read like a sleazy fairy story.

The album reached number two in the UK charts – kept from the top only by Rod Stewart – while reaching number one in America. While it might have seemed the Stones were retreading old ground, the press was positive: 'I doubt whether you'll find another album more eminently rewarding this year,' said *NME*, while *Melody Maker's* Michael Watts enthused, 'This is the album I've been waiting for since *Exile On Main Street*.'

As usual, it would be some years before the record's hidden gems were acknowleged. Keith talked about his reggae-influenced 'Luxury' to Nick Kent in the *Zigzag* interview: 'It all came about when I was driving from the Munich Hilton to the studios, fucked right out of my head and the radio was playing this soul number, which I still don't know the title of, but it had this chord sequence . . . and it turned out later as "Luxury" . . . It's a process of slow assimilation, not like everyone expected when we went to Jamaica to record *Goats Head Soup* that we'd suddenly leap into doing reggae. I actually got into playing West Indian guitar with the Rastafarians when I was out there though. I used to play for hours and hours.'

It was the first time I'd become aware of Keith's passion for Jamaican music. I had to know more, and read up all I could, then went to Daddy Kool, the West End reggae emporium, and snarfed up some hot pre-releases. Obviously I was aware of Bob Marley, but this stuff was the real deal. From there on I made regular visits, and knew what was going on when Keith started assimilating the music further into the Stones. It was his passing-it-on ethic – in action!

Will He Or Won't He?

In December '74, Mick Taylor announced he was quitting the Rolling Stones to go solo. It had been brewing throughout the *It's Only Rock 'N' Roll* sessions. In *It's Only Rock 'N' Roll*, his song-by-song Stones analysis, Steve Appleford quotes Andy

Johns, who engineered the Munich sessions but wasn't asked back because of his own escalating heroin problem. He recalls the Stones playing at a session and Keith suddenly turning to Taylor, saying, 'Fuck you! You play too loud. You're really good live, but you're no good in the studio. So you can play later.'

'I don't know that Mick Taylor really fit in,' said George Chkiantz, the guy who engineered the overdubs in London. After being dismissed from the Stones, Johns went to work with former Cream bassist Jack Bruce's new band. He called up Taylor and suggested he come and join – just as the Stones were about to start work on *Black And Blue*. 'He would have left anyway,' said Johns. 'But the timing of it was obviously that my phone call instigated it. It was the worst thing I ever did. It wasn't a smart move . . . they were jolly surprised when he quit.' This might have been the final push, but Taylor was under pressure from his wife, unhappy about not receiving songwriting credits, and getting deeper into smack. In 1995 Mick Jagger would admit, 'I think he found it difficult to get on with Keith.' Or, as Keith later put it in *Uncut*, 'The fact that Mick didn't know any Max Miller jokes would definitely have counted against him!'

Taylor's statement to the press read as follows: 'The last five and a half years with the Stones have been very exciting, and proved to be a most inspiring period. And as far as my attitude to the other four members is concerned, it is one of respect for them, both as musicians and as people. I have nothing but admiration for the group, but I feel now is the time to move on and do something new.' Keith sent him a telegram, saying, 'Really enjoyed playing with you the last five years. Thanks for all the turn-ons. Best wishes and love.'

Meanwhile, in *Sounds*, Taylor denied that personality problems or financial considerations had anything to do with his departure. 'There was no personal animosity in the split, nothing personal at all. There was no row, or quibbling or squabbling. I'm very disturbed by the stories going around that it was all to do with credits and royalties, things like that. It had nothing whatever to do with those things. I'm very upset by those rumours because I really like all the guys in the Stones. I've really loved working with them these past five years.' Many years later, however, with little success after the Stones, Taylor negated all of the above with a bitter, 'Frankly, I was ripped off.'

The same feature also carried an interview with Taylor's wife, Rosie, who seems to have been the one carrying a grudge. She implied that Mick was so wrapped up in making music that he didn't think of the credit, financial or otherwise. Both mentioned Keith's 'lovely, sweet telegram' – probably unaware at the time that he was really pissed off, coming out with stuff like, 'No one leaves this band except in a fucking pine box.' Taylor had been a brilliant lead guitarist and embellisher. Ronnie Wood would get far more involved in the creative process – and receive several songwriting credits for it.

Mick Taylor's solo career never really took off. He had his own heroin problem, and Jack Bruce, who he briefly worked with, was on the stuff too. Their partnership fizzled out after a promising start, and Taylor went on to make a string of low-key solo albums over the years. In '88, however, he'd pop up on Keith's *Talk Is Cheap* solo album, and joined the band in '89 when they were inducted into the Rock and Roll Hall of Fame.

All change! Mick Taylor walked just three days before the Stones went into Munich's Musicland Studios on 7 December. These sessions were followed by more in Rotterdam in March, and would continue sporadically until the end of the year, eventually spawning the *Black And Blue* album. They saw a string of guitarists come in to 'jam', which really meant audition. Apart from Wayne Perkins and Harvey Mandel, who made it as far as the finished album, the Stones' 'shopping list' – according to *Melody Maker* – also included Jeff Beck, Bowie's old sideman Mick Ronson, Rory Gallagher, Ry Cooder, Peter Frampton, Chris Spedding, Ollie Halsall, Jefferson Airplane's Jorma Kaukonen and Steve Hillage. Also mentioned elsewhere were Free's Paul Kossof, Dr Feelgood's Wilco Johnson, even Hank Marvin of the Shadows.

The *Black And Blue* sessions developed Keith's increasing penchant for sculpting songs out of long jam sessions. Grooves set up and exercised for hours had new colouring added, then, finally, words and an arrangement. Some might not surface until a few albums' time. Keith's reggae fixation continued also, with a cover version of Eric Donaldson's 'Cherry Oh Baby'.

In January '75, Keith played and sang on a version of 'Get Off Of My Cloud' for Alexis Korner's album of the same name, following it up by more recording with Alexis in Rotterdam. Afterwards, Keith spent much of February rehearsing with Wayne Perkins at The Wick. Perkins was a top session guitarist who played on Bob Marley's *Catch A Fire*. He probably came closest out of the legion of hopefuls to landing the job, but Keith thought he sounded too much like Mick Taylor. And so he did, although his playing on the tracks that eventually got released – 'Hand Of Fate', 'Fool To Cry' and 'Memory Motel' – was sublime. His nearest rival of the time was American blues veteran Harvey Mandel, who popped up on 'Hot Stuff' and 'Memory Motel'.

It was never going to work out with the temperamental Jeff Beck, who contributed to several tracks that never got used. There was some sweet irony when Ronnie – who Beck had sacked a few years earlier – eventually landed the post. But there's still a whole bootleg devoted to the Beck sessions, called *Reggae 'N' Roll* after one of the instrumentals. His harsh virtuosity might have worked with Keith's style to make the Stones a lot harder, but he was into jazz rock at the time and there would have been a lot of noodling – not to mention ructions between the two guitarists.

'I was in Rotterdam with no guitar player,' recalled Keith. 'To me . . . it was really important that it [the band] had to be all English . . . . And Ronnie walked in and played and it was just the atmosphere between the two of us. We burn. I knew what he was capable of and what we could get out of him.'

In March the Stones commenced more recording at Musicland, which wound up in early April. Ronnie went over on 30 March and never looked back. He sprinkled his distinctive tones over 'Hey Negrita' and 'Crazy Mama', as well as joining in with backing vocals on half the tracks. It was formally announced on 14 April 1975 that Ronnie Wood would be joining the Rolling Stones for their US tour, while remaining a member of the Faces.

Sounds announced, 'WOOD JOINS STONES', but quoted Mick as saying, 'This is in no way permament.' The Faces' spokesman said that Ron was simply

Bobby Womack, Ronnie and Keith jamming in New York.

helping out his mates. The story also said that the Stones' prime candidates for the vacant post were now Steve Marriott, Wayne Perkins and Chris Spedding.

The rumours continued to spread, but it still looked inevitable that Ronnie would remain in the Stones after the first shot had been fired. He was too perfectly suited, and the Stones, as a unit, didn't have to contend with their lead singer taking off on a solo career (yet). But still, the Stones didn't want to be responsible for imploding the Faces. After fitting in rehearsals at the Long Island estate of Paul Morrissey (who directed Andy Warhol's *Flesh*, *Trash* and *Heat*), and finding time to complete his next solo album in Amsterdam with Bobby Womack in tow, Ronnie would tour the US with the Stones from June to August. Two weeks later, he'd do the same again with the Faces.

The Last Soul Man

In the midst of all this activity, Ronnie had managed to knock out his second solo album, *Now Look*, which was released in June. Keith was still in there, although he hadn't lived through the making of this album as he'd done with its predecessor. This time around, his place in the songwriting and singing department was taken by Bobby Womack . . .

So please welcome another essential figure in the life of Keith Richards and the Rolling Stones. Bobby Womack is a soul legend, who has crossed paths many times with the Stones since 1964, when they achieved their first number one hit by covering his 'It's All Over Now'. Since then he's dueted with Mick Jagger, sang backing vocals, and jammed endlessly with Ronnie and Keith, as well as being plastered all over *Now Look*, which features a lovely cover of his 'If You Don't Want My Love'.

Once again, Keith (and Ronnie) had passed it on: after being bowled over by *Now Look*, I hunted down every Bobby Womack album I could find, including *Lookin' For A Love Again*, *Understanding*, *Facts Of Life* and the then-current *Safety Zone*. When the singer announced a gig at Hammersmith Odeon in '76, rumours abounded that Keith and Ron were going to make a guest appearance. I promptly got tickets and, of course, they didn't show. But, even though Womack's show was brief and patchy, I'd still come to rate him as the finest soul singer alive.

'I met him in Detroit when I was on tour with the Faces,' said Ronnie when I interviewed him in '92. 'He had gone to meet Rod Stewart and because Rod's so highly strung, he was too nervous of meeting Bobby, because he was his favourite vocalist. So he slammed the door in his face and ran off because he was so nervous . . . Bobby came up to me and said, "I just got blown out, will you be Rod Stewart?" I said, "Sure, come with me."' The pair would go on to record a number of tracks after *Now Look*, which still haven't seen the light of day.

Bobby Womack started playing guitar for a gospel group, the Five Blind Boys of Mississippi, before becoming a session man at American Studios in Memphis. He then went on to play guitar for the late soul giant Sam Cooke. (When Cooke was gunned down at the age of 33 in 1964, Womack married his widow Barbara three months later.) In '62, Bobby recorded a song he'd written called 'It's All Over Now', with his group the Valentinos. It reached the ears of the Rolling Stones, who covered it barnstormingly in July '64, their first British number one. 'Man, I was mad as hell!', Bobby told *Blues and Soul* magazine. 'I said, "Let them go get their own damned song!" I had this whole thing about being ripped off, you know, like black musicians always get the bad deal . . . . I wanted the Valentinos to be on the radio, not these guys from England. Of course, I kept on about this stuff until I got my first royalty cheque for the song!'

In October '85 I got to interview the man for *Zigzag*, when he was promoting his *So Many Rivers* album. He'd been through the mill in the ten years since hooking up with Ronnie – his brother murdered by a jealous girlfriend, his baby son lost to cot death, plus the usual music biz rip-offs. It had driven him to hard drugs, but the 1980s saw Womack claw his way back with brilliantly matured soul masterpieces like *The Poet* and *Poet Two*. When I saw him at Hammersmith this time, he played all of his milestones. It was one of the few gigs where one minute I'd be on my seat, bellowing along, the next unashamedly in tears as he performed a ballad. It wasn't hard to see the mutual attraction between Bobby and the Stones.

'Yeah, it reminds me of when I used to perform in gospel. That's what gospel was – one minute people would be jumping up and laughing, next thing there'd be a ballad and they'd be crying. Then you take 'em back laughing and leaving. I just want to reach the depths of their souls. The more they turn on to me, the more I turn on to them. Now let me tell you something. It's a shame how God's children been mistreated. For so many years they thought they didn't have soul. It took England to say, "Hey, we're not followers, we're pacesetters, we're not imitators, we're innovators." That's what it boils down to. It's always been that way since the days of the Rolling Stones. First time I ever heard the Rolling Stones, they said, "We're about funk."'

Bobby would duet with Mick on the troubled *Dirty Work*, on 'Harlem Shuffle', and pop up again on *Voodoo Lounge*, singing backing vocals on 'Moon Is Up'. A vastly underrated singer, and another member of the Rolling Stones' extended family.

An Ancient Form Of Weaving

The end of May 1975 had seen the Stones convene in New York for the most audacious publicity stunt of their career – with Keith booked into the Pierre Hotel as 'Keith Bentley'. They duly unveiled Ronnie, and announced their upcoming '1975 Tour of the Americas' by playing 'Brown Sugar' from the back of a flatbed truck crawling down Fifth Avenue towards Washington Square. Right in the middle of an astonished – and in some cases agitated – rush hour crowd! 'They probably think someone slipped acid in their coffee this morning,' said Ronnie to Keith. The line-up also included musical director Billy Preston and percussionist Ollie Brown, on loan from Stevie Wonder's band. 'It was the best the band has sounded in years,' wrote Alan Betrock for *Disc*, while Chris Charlesworth of *Melody Maker* called it 'the publicity stunt of the decade'.

At the corner of 45th Street and Broadway, the world's largest billboard listed all of the tour dates. When the blasting truck arrived at the Fifth Avenue Hotel, the shocked pressmen, who were expecting just a couple of Stones to turn up, were handed leaflets detailing how the tour would start in Baton Rouge, Louisiana on 1 June, winding up in Venezuela on 21 August – 42 dates in the US and Canada, plus sixteen dates in South America. It made for the longest, most lucrative Stones tour ever, and one of the most excessive. A million and a half tickets went on went on sale at the same time – 85 per cent had sold out by the evening. The whole lot had gone in a couple of days.

The jaunt heralded the first Rolling Stones superstage, a giant lotus-flower shape designed by Robin Wagner, with lights by Broadway designer Jules Fisher. The high-tech version – used in New York, Chicago, LA and later London – could raise and lower its petals hydraulically. The lotus also featured a twenty-foot long inflatable penis, which would become a veritable beast of burden for the band when it reared up during 'Starfucker'.

The tour also ushered in a new dimension in rock-star luxury, as the Stones hired a whole Boeing 707 – nicknamed the 'Starship' – to ferry them from gig to gig. It boasted bedrooms, a bar, TV and all mod cons, with the Stones' mid-seventes eagle logo adorning the sides.

On the day of the first show, at Louisiana State University, Baton Rouge, Ronnie celebrated his 28th birthday. 'Not a bad birthday gift for a kid who's always dreamed of bein' in the Stones,' he said.

After a blast of Aaron Copland's 'Fanfare For The Common Man', the Stones would kick off with Keith standing on one of the petals, thrashing out the opening chords of 'Honky Tonk Women'. They'd go on to play for over two hours, mixing the new and the old, from 'All Down The Line' and 'If You Can't Rock Me' into 'Get Off Of My Cloud'. 'Keith's 'Happy' was a highlight, in all its ragged glory.

Moving versions of 'Angie' and 'Wild Horses' were played back to back, while 'You Gotta Move' was performed with Mick, Keith, Ron and Billy Preston howling around a centre mike, approaching 'the compact power of a backwoods church chorus' according to *Rolling Stone*. In the spectacle-hungry seventies, the Stones rose to the occasion (quite literally) with the twenty-foot dick, a confetti-spewing dragon and a high-wire trapeze for Mick.

Keith, who considered the penis to be 'a millstone around our neck,' tended to stay slumped over his guitar, cranking out the rhythm next to Charlie, while Ronnie cavorted like a kid in a candy store. The man was everywhere and no band member was safe – he'd creep up behind Mick, mugging away, or crash into Keith or Bill. But Keith gelled with him like he had no other guitarist since Brian Jones. They revelled in breaking down the roles of rhythm and lead. Despite being out of his gourd at many of the shows, Keith was still the backbone to each song. He described his new twin-guitar partnership as 'a lot funkier, dirtier, rougher and a lot more exciting.'

'This interplay between Wood and Richard has been the highpoint of the tour, bringing to mind the Stones' earliest incarnation as a straight-ahead, power-fully moving, rhythmic and funky outfit,' wrote *Disc*'s Alan Betrock. 'The excitement generated by Wood's presence in the band has worked so well on a musical and personal basis, that it seems obvious that the Stones want him as a permanent member ... Offstage, Keith and Ronnie have been hanging out together the most intensely, staying up all hours in small music clubs, or just in their hotel rooms listening to records or jamming on guitars ... on the whole the tour has been very professional, very wholesome [!] and almost uneventful.'

Rolling Stone was covering almost the whole tour, including the 17-18 June stint at Toronto's Maple Leaf Gardens: 'Keith Richard seemed as inspired as he has ever been. It's possible that the chief musical news of this tour is Richard's return to onstage prominence. Working with Ron Wood hasn't necessarily improved his style so much as awakened his competitive instinct, but Richard will never play better than he did that night in Toronto. His licks on "Rip This Joint", "You Can't Always Get What You Want" and especially "Tumbling Dice" were searing, simple, supple and effective. When he stepped out to sing "Happy" with a little boy cock of his head, you understood once more just how important he is to this group. And how important Ron Wood has quickly become. Bill Wyman summed it up a few days later in New York: "Woody's a bit like Keith: he takes us back. He's not such a fantastic musician [as Taylor] perhaps, but he's more fun – got more personality."'

'Where it changed,' commented Wood himself, 'they were looking around and looking around and finally said, "Look, we aren't gonna do the tour unless you do it." So I said, well it's serious then, is it? I'd known all along that I'd like to do it, but I hadn't dared to think about it too long. Same as they hadn't, because they like our band as much as we like theirs. And I always think of the Faces before I do anything. But I thought, well, they can't blame me, really.'

We also learned in the article that each original Stone would go home with $450,000 – about £300,000 – apiece, while Woody would get around 225,000 bucks.

At the end of June the Stones played a record-breaking six nights at New York's 20,000-capacity Madison Square Gardens, which sold out within 24 hours. It was the first time out for the full lotus stage, with 200 steel band members, plus Eric Clapton, getting into the closing 'Sympathy For The Devil'. Lenny Kaye –

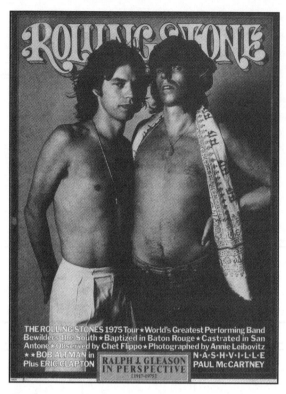

THE ROLLING STONES 1975 Tour ★ World's Greatest Performing Band
Bewilders the South ★ Baptized in Baton Rouge ★ Castrated in San
Antone ★ Observed by Chet Flippo ★ Photographed by Annie Leibovitz
★ ★ BOB ALTMAN in — N·A·S·H·V·I·L·L·E
Plus ERIC CLAPTON — RALPH J. GLEASON IN PERSPECTIVE [1917-1975] — PAUL McCARTNEY

On the cover of Rolling Stone *again as the '75 US tour prepares to kick off.*

the man who'd been impressed by *Exile* – wrote in *Disc*, 'it was clear they were in little danger of relinquishing the crown they have held for the last decade or more . . . Ron Wood seemed considerably more subdued than in his usual roll as Stewart's foil . . . and Keith hardly exhibited himself at all, preferring to stand near Charlie and concentrate on his guitar playing. Unlike his teaming with Mick Taylor's cool dignity, the combination of he and Woody serves to open his instrumental virtuosity. He performed brilliantly and with aplomb . . . Keith sang "Happy", a proud, sullied angel.' *Rolling Stone* magazine reported several teething problems during the opening night. The guitar monitors were picking up local radio and TV stations, while the sound sucked. Afterwards there was a bash at Atlantic Records executive Earl McGrath's apartment, which saw an all-night jam session with Clapton. The following day, Keith and Mick went in to check out the Garden's sound system, and the next show was much better – even if Keith was so wasted that he declined to sing 'Happy' and pissed off back to the hotel before 'Sympathy'. 'All of a sudden Keith was gone,' said Ronnie afterwards. 'Charlie leaned over and said, "Set the beat" – and I couldn't even remember the fuckin' thing! But I just tried to remember the record, and it went all right.'

On 4 July, the Stones played Memphis Memorial Stadium to a crowd of 50,000. It was an eventful night: first of all, the Starship had landed the previous night to find blues veteran Furry Lewis, 83, parked on a whiskey box on the runway with his guitar, singing 'Let Me Call You Sweetheart'. Keith promptly plonked himself down on the tarmac and was taken enough to insist, with the rest of the band, that Furry do the same again at the gig before they came on. Meanwhile, the local police had threatened to arrest the Stones if they played 'Starfucker' or used the blow-up dick. The band's in-house super-lawyer Bill Carter eventually managed to negotiate a proceed-at-your-own-risk scenario. The band didn't use the appendage at outdoor gigs anyway – it might have blown away! They simply sang 'Starfucker' with extra gusto. After the show, Ollie Brown came back out to read from political texts to celebrate the bicentennial of American independence.

Rolling Stone described the backstage scenario after the gig: 'Keith Richards wandered up. "Woody and me, we're driving to Dallas," he stage-whispered to Watts. "See the country, get off the plane for a bit. Come on with us." Watts looked at him incredulously, as if he knew what was coming. "Now? Think I'll take the plane." Twelve hours later, four pm Arkansas time, Richard, Wood, security man James Callaghan and Fred Sessler were pulled over by city police in Fordyce, pop. 5,000.'

It turns out Keith was driving the party through the state in a rented Chevrolet. They had stopped at the Fordyce Restaurant and Station for lunch around three. Keith signed autographs for the waitress, while the colourful ensemble turned the sort of rednecked heads you usually see in road movies. The car soon attracted a crowd of teenagers, so they sped off. 'I bent down to change the waveband on the radio and the car swerved slightly,' said Keith. They were immediately stopped by the local cops, who searched the car and found Keith's knife, complete with a tin-opener and a 'device for removing stones from horse's hooves'.

They also turned up some coke in Fred's luggage. The group were hauled off to City Hall, where Keith paid 160 bucks in bail for two misdemeanour charges – carrying a concealed weapon and reckless driving. Freddie posted $5,000 bond and they promptly got out of town in the chartered plane that Bill Carter had flown down in. The judge told the local paper that Fordyce was 'already famous' because Paul W. 'Bear' Bryant, the University of Alabama football coach, was from the area, and they didn't need to be associated with a Stones bust.

The charges were later dropped on a technicality. During the tour, Keith also found out that Anita had been fined and deported from Jamaica on drugs charges. Keith's mate Freddie Sessler was along for the tour as a kind of partner-in-crime, he never did smack, and didn't approve of Keith doing it, according to Victor Bockris. He did once work for Merck & Co, who manufactured pharmaceutical cocaine for medical purposes, however. The pair stayed close until Fred – who was twenty years older than Keith – passed away around Christmas 2002.

In '95, after the Stones' Brixton Academy gig, I had the pleasure of spending a highly-enjoyable night in Freddie's room at London's Landmark Hotel. Bobby Keys was there too, and both spent most of the night reminiscing about the great times they'd had with Keith over the years. It wasn't hard to see why Keith liked Freddie so much – he was funny, very knowledgeable about music and the Second World War, and discreetly cool. Before I left at ten in the morning, I scrawled Keith a message on a hotel napkin for him to pass on, saying how I'd been blown away by the gig. A true gent.

On the 1975 Tour of the Americas, Keef anecdotes continued to proliferate, such as this one in *Melody Maker*: 'At one point Keith Richard lost his guitar cable twice in the space of five minutes. First, he got distracted from the piece, walked over to his amps, fiddled around for a bit, decided to have a smoke, tuned up, walked up front, lost the guitar cable, went back, plugged in, fiddled with the amp dials some more, walked out, lost the cable again, plugged it back in, was ready to play, but the song had just come to a close. He smiled, slightly embarassed.'

'I know it may not be right for our sinister image, but this tour is really a lot of fun,' said Keith.

It was plain to see the boost that Ronnie was giving the Stones on this tour. Keith was describing it as 'a brand new band for us. It's got a lot more fire.' Rock journalist Barbara Charone was hanging close to the Stones at this time, and brought dispatches from the front. At the end of July, she joined them in Washington DC, and attempted to get some sense out of a still-partying Ronnie at around five in the morning. At this time, the guitarist's future was still the stuff of heavy rumour.

'I don't feel torn between loyalties,' he said. 'I just take it as it comes . . . I don't feel like I have to make a decision because I'm avoiding the issue.' Ronnie confirmed he'd play Europe with the Stones, then Japan and Australia with the Faces, before South America, Japan and Australia with the Stones. Phew. 'After that it's decision time.'

But he foretold that decision as he mused, 'You get spoiled in a way playing with the Stones, they're sorta history . . . I think I've helped change the band. I didn't plan it but it is looser. It's just that you shouldn't take rock so seriously. Mick Taylor and I are two different kettles of fish. I tend to open up the nonsense side combined with getting down to good music, whereas Mick was good music and seriousness. And they've realised that they didn't dig that when I came around.' Ronnie also claimed he wanted to get Keith on the road with the Faces.

'Playing with Keith is a great experience simply because I'm used to shouting all the cues in the Faces; with the Stones, Keith does most of the shouting. Charlie takes all his cues from Keith, so therefore I do.'

On 18 December 1975, while Ronnie was helping out on *Black And Blue*, Rod Stewart announced he was quitting the Faces due to 'the permanent loan' of the guitarist to the Stones. But speculation still ran rife. There was another interview with Barbara Charone in the 24 January issue of *Sounds*. Even though Rod had made his announcement, Ronnie was still being evasive.

'The job is there if I want it. None of the Stones wanted to press too hard about me leaving the Faces so they didn't mention it much. Then Rod came out with that amazing statement. So they've eased up a bit and thought, "Oh well, looks like you'll be in a vacant position." So it's up to me to decide in the next few months.' It was obvious what was going to happen, and Ronnie became an official Rolling Stone on 28 February 1976.

It had been almost a lifelong ambition. 'I always kept a close eye on the Stones. First off, I was a real fan. But, more importantly, I knew I was destined to become one of them. I knew it from the start. Honest . . . I've always been such a believer in fate that I just counted on it happening. I figured I'd be patient with it, go about my business for a few years, and that it would certainly fall into my lap someday. I just had to wait it out. And I did. Over ten years.'

'Ron seems a natural, in the respect that both he and Keith are brilliant rhythm guitarists,' praised Mick. 'It allows a certain cross-trading of riffs not previously possible.' Charlie Watts simply said that Ronnie had brought the Stones back together as a band.

One afternoon in '92, I was walking down a street in Wandsworth, South London, on my way to interview Ronnie Wood. As I approached the door to his management's office, a familiar figure tiptoed into view, a furtive look on his face. He clocked me and looked disturbed. 'You're my interview, aren't you?'

'Erm, yes,' I replied, looking slightly crestfallen. But then he boomed, 'I'm going up the pub, are you coming?'

'Erm, yeah!'

We duly strode down to Wandsworth High Street, Ronnie coming across more like a naughty schoolboy bunking classes. 'They won't find us here,' he said, as we strode into a big old pub. Ronnie was immediately surrounded by autograph hunters, well-wishers and barflies craning their necks. Within minutes he was treating me like an old mate.

Ronnie Wood is one of nature's nice geezers. Hilarious with the one-liners, he constantly buzzes with a kind of excited energy. He'd been firmly ensconced in the band he'd wanted to join since he was a kid for sixteen years now, and in another couple of years he'd be made a 'junior partner'.

We talked about the Stones, who were all working on solo projects at that time, and Ronnie's exposure to the dance scene the previous week: 'I went to a rave in the West of Ireland last Saturday night. It was great because all there was was smoke and strobes and one beat going "boom boom boom". I found it quite interesting – for about twenty minutes! I just hope that some real music can still get by.'

With that, Ronnie had to go to Broadcasting House for an interview, so I cadged a lift to the West End in his Roller – vodka aloft, both of us waving at the Chancellor of the Exchequer as he got out of his car.

No wonder he's Keith's best mate, I thought to myself, as we said warm goodbyes.

It would be another eleven years before I saw Ronnie Wood again – backstage at Wembley with Keith. And he hadn't changed a bit, except for his new sobriety. He didn't remember my interview either

Fifteen minutes after we left Keith and Ronnie in the dressing room – hopping up and down into their stage trousers while grinning like loons – they were at it again onstage. They are now deadlier than ever – the sounds tear and swoon out of their instruments, curling like lovers, spatting like brothers. Keith has realised his ambition to make the Rolling Stones' two guitars sound like one – although there's no mistaking Ronnie's keening high notes, or Richards' own coruscating metronome rhythms.

'It's just about playing with somebody, and every time you get down to playing you're testing each other more,' said Keith to *Guitar World* in October '94. 'Ronnie Wood is an amazingly sympathetic player; he'll get to the root of what you're on almost straight away.'

Not bad for a new boy!

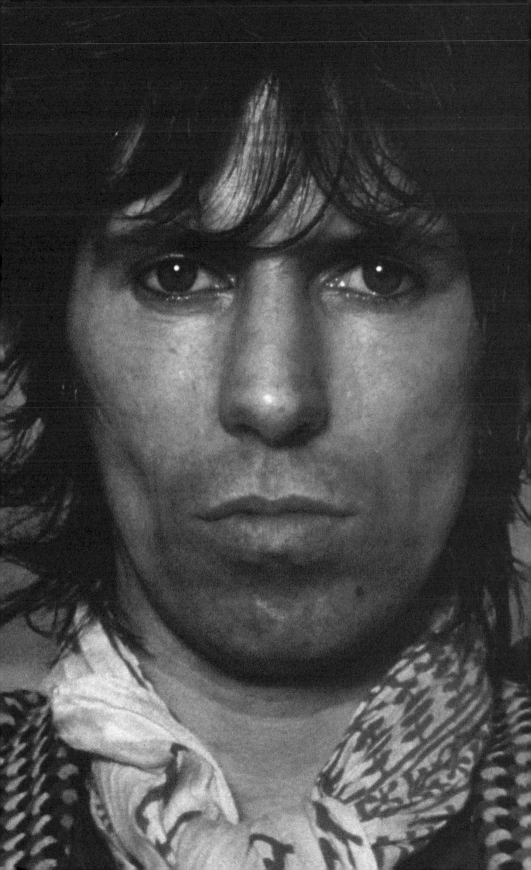

CHAPTER NINE

MAIN OFFENDER

Black And Blue In The UK

The US gigs wound up in Buffalo on 8 August, 1975. The Stones had played 45 shows in 27 cities in ten weeks, netting nearly £10 million. Afterwards, Keith went to Los Angeles to hook up with Anita, who, it was soon confirmed, had fallen pregnant. In October, he hitched up with the rest of the band at Montreux's Mountain Studios for more work on *Black And Blue*, which continued at Munich's Musicland in December.

By now, Ronnie was firmly ensconced in the Stones, and joined them in Munich. While he was away, he got his first welcome-to-the-Stones present – a police raid back at his house. The victims were Ronnie's wife Krissie and her friend Audrey Burgon. The cops found cocaine and hash, but were apparently more delighted to find the girls naked in bed together. So were the papers, who dubbed them 'the sleeping beauties'. When the case came to court, the jury cleared them of the cannabis charge and failed to reach a verdict on the coke. They were finally cleared of that charge in April, but still had to stump up £12,000 in costs. Interestingly, the police admitted they'd raided The Wick looking for another couple – who went by the names of Keith and Anita. They'd even homed in first on the cottage where Keith normally stayed.

'I think it was me and Anita the police were after,' acknowledged Keith. 'I was out of the country at the time but it looks as though they were hoping to pin something on Woody and me in one go.'

In January, Keith took Anita to Geneva, Switzerland, to await the birth of their third child. The boy was eventually born on 26 March , and was called Tara Jo Jo Gunne – his first name after a late friend of Brian Jones, his second two names after the Chuck Berry song. As ever, Keith doted on the baby. Stories even appeared in the UK papers that Keith and Anita were planning a spectacular wedding. One front page hinted that it would take place on stage, though Keith later admitted he'd just said that for a laugh.

Black And Blue was finally released on 20 April 1976, reaching number two in the UK album charts and number one in the US. ('Fool To Cry' was also released as a single, and went to number four in the UK, number nine in the US.)

The sleeve featured a striking close-up shot of the band, taken at sundown on a beach in Florida and notable for the inclusion of Ronnie Wood. It said it all. He was only credited on a few tracks, but by now the man was a fully fledged Rolling Stone.

Black And Blue turned out to be one of those critically dismissed Stones albums, getting a similar, if not worse, reception to *Goats Head Soup* and *It's Only Rock 'N' Roll*. Okay, so it was the 'audition album' but, considering that *Beggars Banquet* featured virtually only Keith in the guitar department too, it shouldn't have mattered.

'Memory Motel' is the standout track, one of the finest Stones songs of all time. Epic, ambitious and capable, in the right circumstances, of moving the listener to tears. I've got bootlegs of early versions, where it was just an instrumental run-through built on Keith's poignant electric piano riff, Billy Preston's haunting string-synth and subtle guitar interplay between Wayne Perkins and Harvey Mandel. It was lovely as an instrumental, but it's one of those rare tracks where Mick and Keith match their distinctive vocal styles and fly.

It's a road song, conjuring images of lonesome nights in far-flung dives and metaphorical ships that pass in the night. Mick starts on about how, 'Hannah honey was a peachy kind of girl,' while Keith's cracked vocal enters on a longingly poignant chord carpet for his cracked vocal: 'She's got a mind of her own / And she uses it well / Ye-ah, well she's one of a kind.' Harvey Mandel lends an almost Tayloresque flourish to this ballad, which strokes the pure essence of country music.

Ultimately, the album continued to bolster the cult of Keef the guitarist on tracks like 'Crazy Mama' and 'Hand of Fate'. People realised he wasn't trying to show off how many notes he could cram into a middle eight, he was simply the rhythm's driver. 'It doesn't matter about the B. B. Kings, Eric Claptons and Mick Taylors 'cause they do what they do,' he said. 'But I know they can't do what I do. They can play as many notes under the sun but they just can't hold that rhythm down, baby. Everything I do is strongly based on rhythm 'cause that's what I'm best at. I've tried being a great guitar player, and – like Chuck Berry – I have failed.'

(I somehow doubt if even the self-critical Mr. Richards would have said that if he'd caught himself on the *Licks* tour seventeen years later . . .)

The reviews were variable, but by now you were expecting the Stones to get slagged off. It happened every time after *Exile* from up until *Some Girls*. But, while *Black And Blue* might have been dismissed by former Stones allies like Lester Bangs and *NME*'s Charles Shaar Murray, it was the one that Keith singled out when I asked what his favourite Stones album was, three and a half years later (although by 2002 it would be *Exile*): 'More and more now I've been listening to *Black And Blue*. Quite like some of that, considering especially that I know the ins 'n' outs of how it was made. That album was put together while auditioning guitar players, trying to find a new guy. It's interesting for me to listen to because there's a different guitar player on virtually every track. Wayne Perkins, Harvey Mandel, other people came round and played with us – even Jeff Beck – who I get on with now, but at that time we were sort of glowering over the guitars.'

There was some controversy over the promotional poster, which depicted a cackling, bruised woman in ripped underwear, hands bound above her head, accompanied by the caption, 'I'm black and blue from the Rolling Stones and I love it.' It invited a furore, and it got one, falling foul of groups like Women Against Violence Against Women who had homed in on rock music and its often misogynistic pre-PC imagery. Keith just thought it was funny.

There had also been a more positive welter of publicity in the UK, arising from the US jaunt. The hordes of Stones fans couldn't wait to see the band with their lunatic new axeman, especially on the much-vaunted lotus stage. There were over one million applications for their Earls Court show – enough for 67 shows in all – so the band added another three dates.

The European tour took place between April and June '76. Just before it started, the *Sunday Times* sent along one James Fox – Mick's co-star in *Performance*, semi-retired from acting since that traumatic, hallucinogenic experience – to interview the Stones at rehearsal in Cannes. The extent of his opinion as a rock critic was that the sound in Frankfurt was 'bad' while the audience were 'quiet'.

But he also notes little details like Marlon and his herd of guinea pigs, and elicits some fascinating Keef quotes, like the story of how Keith and Mick got to be called the Glimmer Twins: 'Back in '68, Mick, Marianne Faithfull, Anita Pallenberg and me took a boat to Rio, which was full of all these upper class English people . . . I was dressed at the time in a diaphanous djellaba, Mexican shoes and a tropical army hat. After a while they discovered who we were and became very perturbed. They started asking us questions: "What are you really trying to do?" and "Do try to explain to us what this whole thing is about!" . . . one woman stepped forward from the group and said: "We've been asking you for days and you just won't say. Can you give us just a glimmer?" Mick turned to me and said, "We're the Glimmer Twins." That one has stuck.'

When they get around to the subject of chemical indulgence, Keith's comments are surprisingly candid for the period: 'Any time I'm not touring or making a record I feel redundant. I turn to all kinds of weird chemicals to make up for it . . . People are always saying about me, they can't understand how I've survived so long . . . People's idea about junk is equivalent to what people think about meths drinkers and winos . . . You should take the trouble to know what the stuff does, how it works, and decide physically and mentally whether you're capable of handling it.'

On the opening night of the European tour, in Frankfurt, Keith fell over onstage – or slipped on a frankfurter, he'd later claim. A few rock writers were allowed into his room. David Hancock of *Sounds* said he looked 'very wasted'. David Widgery, of the short-lived *Street Life*, reported, 'he looks glad to be touring again and extremely unwasted,' describing how he 'stares piercingly through his charred eye makeup and talks rapidly and precisely.' Waste or no waste, Keith was taking no shit.

When Widgery insisted on talking about the political situation in the UK, an extremely animated Keith snapped, 'Don't talk to me about politics. I only want to talk about music. I hate politicians. Politicians are boring. Listen, I haven't really lived in Britain since 1964 when I went to America, the home of all my great musical influences. And I've certainly got no intention of coming back to live in Britain. And don't ask how long the Rolling Stones are going to stay together because you know about as much as we do,' he snarled, adding that the guy was behaving 'like a neurotic provincial queen'.

As usual, the writer answered back from behind the safety of his typewriter, safe from the wrath that has reduced some journalists to jelly. Keith just doesn't suffer hacks gladly, and sees them as easy targets.

Afterwards, Mick walked in, spotted Charles Shaar Murray, who'd panned *Black And Blue*, and had the room cleared. Murray gave his own account in *NME*, in their 1970s style of hipper-than-hip jive-ranting meets Lester Bangs. Like Nick Kent, Murray was bending the Warhol rules of instant fame towards the unbelievable notion that rock writers could become rock stars without making a record. He reported the press gathering in Keith's room. Wasted or unwasted? 'Let's just say "tired".' Murray asks him if he's heard any of the new British groups, like Eddie and the Hot Rods and the Sex Pistols.'I only listen to black music these days,' says Keith.'I ain't too interested in white bands who rip off white bands who ripped off black bands.'

Ronnie passes Keith a note alerting him as to who he's talking to.'I read your review Charles,' he accuses, 'and I thought it was rubbish.' That's the point where Mick twigs who he is too. But, as he's leaving, Murray is stopped at the door by Keith, who kind of apologises for Mick and says he'll call him later to hook up. Charles has just rolled a spliff and hands it to Keith – who promptly disappears. 'I assimilate the fact that Keith Richard, quintessential rock star, cool personified and the idol of millions, has just ripped me off for my last smoke.'

Whatever, it was features by Nick Kent, Barbara Charone and Charles Shaar Murray that most tickled the fancy of this junior cub reporter on Aylesbury's *Bucks Advertiser*, who was just dying to encounter the man called Keith Richard one day.

The Stones kicked off the long-awaited UK leg of their European tour on 10 May at Glasgow's Apollo Theatre for two nights, before going on to Leicester and Stafford's New Bingley Hall. It was after the latter that the first of the doom-clouds that would hang over Keith's head for most of the next three years started to form.

Around five o'clock on the morning of 19 May, Keith was pelting down the M1 in his Bentley – the Blue Lena – after a fairly ropey gig at the cavernous New Bingley Hall. Despite a torrential storm, he'd elected to drive back to London rather than stay in the hotel. Also in the car were Anita, their seven-year-old son Marlon, and a couple of American friends. I know from later experience that Keith threw himself into driving with the same attitude he had toward most things in his life – fast and loose.

When he nodded off at the wheel and shot off the motorway, the car ploughed through the central barrier and ended up in a field. Keith tried to dispose of his drug stash, but the police officers who arrived at the scene searched the car and found a silver chain with a snort-tube attachment, plus some LSD-impregnated blotting paper. Never mind the fact that someone may have been injured.

After being booked at the Newport Pagnell services police station, Keith was taken to the town station for the full monty. The rubber-gloves man was a Detective Sergeant Bull. (There has to be a joke in there somewhere.) Keith was released next day pending the outcome of tests on the tube and paper.

The first of the six Earls Court gigs took place on 21 May. It looked good, but sounded like a distant fart in a bucket. Princess Margaret was one of the backstage visitors, while out front the support band for the whole tour – New Orleans' fabulously tight Meters – braved the terrible acoustics to little avail. This band were the proverbial swamp-funk maestros – taut, lean and sexy as hell – but totally fuddled by the billowing sonic black hole of the exhibition centre.

Even Ronnie Wood's specially made cassette, played between bands, could barely be heard. In the seventies, you normally got the roadie's Lynyrd Skynyrd tape during the interminable wait for the main act. This was one of the first times I'd encountered a group trying to set a mood from within their own ranks. (Of course, tour DJs later became the norm, after bands like The Clash and Primal Scream realised that going to see a group should take in the whole evening, from the moment you walked in.) Ronnie's cassette was Stones influences central – mostly black music, with old blues icons like Robert Johnson rubbing shoulders with the dub reggae that normally emanated from the hotel rooms where him and Keith were chilling. But it was just so faint, with only tantalising suggestions of its content coming up for air.

But whatever, we were all still vibed-up for the Stones and waiting for lift-off. And, after the expected long wait, punctuated by steel drummers swaying through the arena, we had the band.

But we didn't have lift-off. As the tent flew up and the lotus cranked down, it was as if the gods had suddenly emptied a bucket of goat shit over my head. I'd been led to believe the Stones would be unleashing an onslaught of seismic proportions, but these shows would be widely regarded as some of the worst of their career. I have to concur. Apart from the fact that I was sitting at the back of an aircraft hangar-sized venue – in the days before they had video screens – the sound was appalling. Sure, the stage looked great, a massive lotus flower that unfolded to reveal Keith hacking out 'Honky Tonk Women'. But, after the initial impact, the bee-in-a-bog sound quality was simply frustrating: no drums; a sludge of guitars sometimes jacked up to ear-slicing cacophony; muffled vocals. It's the only time in my life that I've been moved to say that the Rolling Stones were crap. In fact, it was so bad that I scored a ticket for one of the other nights and went again. (This time I was much closer, the sound was better, and I was prompted to spring onto my seat and holler along like a twat.)

But there was still something wrong here. As expected, Ronnie was a welcome injection of good vibes. Jagger had moved away from his Satanic Majesty image into the realms of pantomime, as he swung on his Tarzan rope, wrestled a dragon and straddled the infamous rubber prick. Billy Preston seemed hellbent on upping his hired-hand status to that of a Rolling Stone, getting a longer solo spot than Keith.

But Keith, ahh Keith . . . There is a fine line between being 'elegantly wasted' and just completely fucked. At times, the great man seemed semi-conscious, and his playing was sluggish too. Operating on smack-addled autopilot, he moved very little, nodding and swaying over by Charlie. He still had moments of flashing brilliance, as the licks flowed naturally from his fingers, but this was obviously not a well man. Never did his solo-spot choice of 'Happy' sound so ironic.

The fact that the Earls Court gigs were huge, overblown and musically wretched added fuel to a gathering fire for some members of the audience. They had their own bands, called the Sex Pistols and The Clash.

There was something new and scary germinating amongst London's young people. The band of disenchanted teenagers who called themselves the Sex Pistols had already played their first gigs, and were boasting of how their guitarist, an amateur burglar, had stolen some of his gear from the Stones' rehearsal space. True or not, it remains the stuff of punk legend. The Pistols, with their ripped-up visual image and energised thrash, laid out a manifesto which was the opposite to luxury jets, lotus stages and albums that took over a year to record.

Most of London's burgeoning punk community attended Earls Court, and were

The Rolling Stones 1976 European tour programme.

incensed by the theatrical pantomime aspects of the show. By the summer of '76, the movement was spreading like a virus as kids started forming their own bands. The Clash had a song called '1977', which declared, 'No Elvis, Beatles or the Rolling Stones in 1977' – despite the fact that their guitarist, Mick Jones, was one of London's most effective Keef-a-likes. And yes, I was a punk, but I never wavered from the Stones either. They were the original punks. The we-piss-anywhere-man attitude was aped by every punk rocker under the sun, but it was a lot more shocking back in 1964.

The parallels between the early Stones and the punks were too strong for the Stones to remain *persona non grata*. A few years later, Keith would be jamming in Jamaica with Mick Jones, and The Clash's lead singer, Joe Strummer, would cite the Stones as his first musical influence. The Pistols' late bass player, Sid Vicious, while contemptuous of Keith, would become fatally addicted to heroin. 'No Stones in '77, no Sex Pistols in '78,' Keith chuckled to me a couple of years later. But anyway, the punks – apart from Johnny Rotten – were never totally serious about their hatred for the Stones, who'd been the first to incur befuddled opposition from the establishment. Keef would always be the ultimate punk rocker.

In fact, when the Stones entered the studio to record their next album, some of punk's raw energy would rub off as they came up with the door-kicking assault of *Some Girls*. But, in mid-1976, the Stones had brought to Europe their most extravagant stage show ever, amidst a pall of excess, drugs and hobnobbing with royalty. With the country's youth in the throes of a musical and cultural revolution, it was the wrong time to unveil a twenty-foot inflatable cock in a sea of sonic mud.

The concerts also brought some expected flak from the music press. *NME* trailered a double-page review from Nick Kent with a news story that said, 'Finally – was London too ready for the Rolling Stones?', and had a go at the band for the extensive coverage in the national papers that accompanied the tour.

Kent's floridly incisive review homed in on the acoustics, complaining he literally couldn't hear one note that Ronnie played, but found time to praise the only hero of the night: 'for one shameless period, I firmly believed that Keith's strict rhythm slant policy was due to his much-touted "wasted" continence shutting down his more supple finger excursions. IE He was too stoned to play anything beyond slick block chord pastiches through an assortment of specially open-tuned guitars. A pox on the thought! . . . . It was Keith, with his bizarre gravital bearings, who paced the thing, who damn near called all the heavy guitar shots while Ron Wood chunked away merrily on rhythm.'

One of the tabloid stories cited by NME was an 'exclusive interview' in the Evening News by Keith's least favourite journalist, John Blake, under the headline, 'Sleepless Nights With Big Bad Keith'. It was sheer tabloid paradise, the Keef archetype of the time personified, consisting entirely of the following passage: 'Of all the Stones, he is the biggest, baddest and most anti-establishment. For me, he epitomises the doomed, wickedly-magical appeal of the Stones. I had a taste of Keith's life-style when I was in Germany – and it took me two days to recover. His day begins at about 7pm with a couple of drinks and some plastic hotel food. He is a spectacular figure – ugly, with smashed teeth, ragged hair and gaunt, haunted eyes. But dazzling as well, with clothes of scarlet, yellow and sapphire blue.

'After the concert, Jagger goes to his room; Keith goes to the bar with his closest friend, Ronnie Wood, to drink huge shots of 90 proof Jack Daniel's whiskey.'

Blake, who collaborated with Tony Sanchez on his notorious Up and Down with the Rolling Stones, goes on to describe how Keith invited him up to his room at around three in the morning. Here, 'Keith sits quietly in a corner singing an old blues number to his acoustic guitar. The song is called "Cocaine".' NME actually ran Blake's interview in full, starting with him trying to get some dirt on Jagger: 'The trouble is there is always this divide between the singer and the musicians,' says Keith. 'Jagger tries to bridge it by playing instruments and – to me – is a great musician. But he doesn't see it quite like that. He thinks that other musicians, whom he respects, see him as just a lead vocalist and nothing more.'

And then there's Ronnie's reflections on Keith: 'I've learned not to try to keep up with Keith any more. When we're on the road, he reckons on sleeping about one night in four. The trouble is that he's such an interesting guy. You can sit down to talk with him and, by the time the conversation has finished, thirteen hours have gone by . . . But, of all the playing I've ever done, I enjoy working with Keith best. Together, we can produce one solid sound.'

It was good, incisive stuff, despite NME's sniffy stance toward the mainstream papers. But they had a point about the feeding frenzy when Keith got busted during the week of the Earls Court gigs: 'KEITH'S M1 WRECK 'N' ROLL', the Daily Express gleefully announced – though The Observer said the news was 'as comforting as the Queen opening the Chelsea Flower Show.'

In early June the tour hit Paris. By now some members of the band and crew were running rampant. According to Nick Kent, quoted in Victor Bockris's book, 'It was heroin city,' with a special dealers' room backstage. Even he was shocked – and this was a man who claimed to have walked a blue-faced Keith back to life after a particularly potent shot.

While the Stones were in Paris, the terrible news came through on 6 June that Keith and Anita's ten-week-old son, Tara, had suffocated in his cot. Keith was absolutely distraught, but still played that night at the city's Les Abattoirs. (The results were captured on the *Love You Live* album.) Used to channelling emotions through his faithful guitar, Keith gave one of the most gut-wrenchingly emotional performances of his life. Afterwards, when he met Anita backstage, he dissolved into tears. Kent wrote that they 'looked like some tragic, shell-shocked couple leading each other out of a concentration camp,' adding that he feared they were soon going to die. But Keith insisted that the show go on.

On 9 June, police reports confirmed that Keith's confiscated silver tube had cocaine encrusted on it, and that the blotting paper was indeed impregnated with acid. On 6 September, he was charged with possession of these substances. On 6 October, he appeared before Newport Pagnell magistrates again, turning up two and a half hours late. He blamed this on the fact that his strides hadn't got back from the dry cleaners in time, prompting the chairman to comment, 'It strikes me as extraordinary that any gentleman of his stature can only afford one pair of trousers.'

Next weekend they were selling badges depicting Keith asking, 'Where's Me Trousers?' He had to forfeit his £100 bail money and was remanded on bail at a further five grand when he pleaded not guilty and elected to go for trial by jury. This was originally scheduled for November, but had to be postponed when a vital witness went missing. Now the trial would be held at Aylesbury Crown Court on 10 January 1977.

The front page of the Daily Mirror on 10 June carried the headline, 'DRUG SMUGGLING SHOCK FOR THE STONES', reporting that police believed the group and their entourage had been used as 'unsuspecting couriers' for a drugs syndicate as they toured Europe. It apparently came to light while they were examining Keith's Bentley and found further coke in some beads and a bracelet which were 'nowhere near the pop star's luggage'. The story claimed, 'Richard has let police know from France that the beads and bracelet are a mystery to him. Last night, the hunt was on for the owner.' Apparently, the tabloid found it inconceivable that the infamous Keef could be smuggling quantities of coke for his own use, rather than for some shadowy Mafia figures.

Keith answered his grief and worry by immersing himself even deeper in the numbness of heroin. Speaking from personal experience, that stuff is the top number of everything: emotions, love, normal physical functions . . . but there again, if you have Keith's money and connections, life can be fairly normal. You maintain. It's when you run out, or the police turn up, or you can't score, or you get burnt, that the nightmare of withdrawal begins. But Keith, on the whole, could afford to maintain a massive habit with top-grade stuff. Faced with all his personal woes, he simply banged up enough to fell a small herd of bull elephants.

We would later compare anecdotes. I was pissed off about skulking around in burnt-out New York buildings for two hours, waiting for a bag of talcum powder and a gun in the back. Keith admitted that even he was sometimes reduced to sitting shivering in a tenement cellar, waiting for the man, carrying a gun in case he got ripped off at the exit.

'That's the nature of heroin, man. It'll get you any way it can.'

Tony Sanchez wrote a few credible sentences in his much-despised book, *Up and Down with the Rolling Stones*, which centred around his time working for Keith and blew the guitarist's addiction up to epic scale. But Spanish Tony was probably right when he wrote about Keith in the last half of '76 through to '77: 'There was a deeper depression about him these days – a feeling that the drugs that had blackened and rotted his teeth were blackening and rotting his skeleton, burning him out inside as Brian had been burned out. Death seemed to be shuffling out of the mist towards Keith.'

It was around then that Dandelion – now renamed Angela – was shipped out to be looked after by Keith's mum, Doris, where she would stay for good. Meanwhile, Keith made sure that Marlon was with him all the time, no matter where he was or what state he was in.

The tour had continued through Europe until late June 1976. The band were determined to make up for the roundly panned Earls Court debacle, and slotted in a major all-dayer at Knebworth House in Hertfordshire on 21 August. It was a long day, with estimates of the crowd size reaching 200,000. First we had to sit through Todd Rungren, Hot Tuna, the interminable Lynyrd Skynyrd and 10cc – the ultimate mid-seventies festival bill!

Then, after this endurance test, there was nearly a four-hour wait for the Stones, apparently because someone had pulled out the wrong plug. I remember standing in my prime spot in front of the stage, while a whole day's lager made its unstoppable voyage to my bladder. I wouldn't budge, though, for I'd surely lose my chance to come the closest I'd yet been to the Stones' stage. And even if I did piss in the bloke in front's hat, it was worth it. When the Stones finally came on at 11.30, they were spot on. They played around 30 songs – over two and a half hours' worth – and made a complete departure from the lotus set. It abated the Earls Court nightmare – with the Stones' trademark tongue as the new projectory platform for Mick – and now stands as one of the greatest Stones shows.

The complete set ran like this: 'Satisfaction', 'Ain't Too Proud To Beg', 'If You Can't Rock Me', 'Get Off Of My Cloud', 'Hand Of Fate', 'Around And Around', 'Little Red Rooster', 'Stray Cat Blues', 'Hey Negrita', 'Hot Stuff', 'Fool To Cry', 'Starfucker', 'Let's Spend The Night Together', 'You Got To Move', 'You Can't Always Get What You Want', 'Dead Flowers' – *yes!* – 'Route 66' – *double yes!* – 'Wild Horses' – *thrice yes!* – 'Honky Tonk Women', 'Tumbling Dice', 'Happy', Billy Preston's solo spot – but why him and not Ronnie? – 'Midnight Rambler', 'It's Only Rock 'N' Roll', 'Brown Sugar', 'Rip This Joint', 'Jumpin' Jack Flash', and, finally, 'Street Fighting Man' accompanied by a massive firework display.

At Knebworth, you could make out the finer points of the interplay raging between Keith and Ronnie as they sparred, sprang and bolstered each other, while injecting new life into a flashing succession of Stones nuggets old and new. Keith didn't seem so out of it either – or maybe it was just the later hour. Either way, he set the impersonators off on yet another shopping mission with his red and white polka-dot jacket and black leather strides.

Press-wise, the gig re-established the Stones' reputation. *Melody Maker*'s Geoff Brown said, 'If the third Knebworth Fair last Saturday proved anything at all, it was that the Rolling Stones are far from the musical dinosaurs which many believed them to be after their week-long stint at London's Earl's Court earlier this year.'

When I talked to Keith about the Earls Court debacle a few years later, he summed it up pithily: 'Put an ad in: "Anybody wanna buy a lotus-shaped stage?"' Back in '76, Keith's words to Barbara Charone rang very true: 'We still feel it's getting better for us. Playing is still a turn-on. All the hassles are still not enough, when weighed against the turn-on, to call it quits. And there's not that many things that are still a reliable turn-on. Even dope can get boring.'

Aylesbury Ducked

Aylesbury in Buckinghamshire is your quintessential olde English market town. One of the significant battles of the English Civil War was fought just up the road, and one pub still boasts (the decidedly short-arsed) Oliver Cromwell's chair in the bar. In more recent years, the town boasted one of the best-known rock clubs in the country, Friars Aylesbury, between '69-'85.

Its eighteenth-century courthouse is bang in the midde of the Market Square. The last time it had come in for national attention was when the Great Train Robbers were tried in 1964. But for three days in January 1977, that cobbled square would witness the greatest media circus the little town has ever seen. A Rolling Stones drugs trial – the likes of which were becoming all the rage ...

Keith had visited my hometown before – on 21 January 1964, when the Stones played the Granada Cinema as part of the Group Scene '64 tour, which also featured the incredible Ronettes from New York City. When the band were still playing exhausting one-nighters, Aylesbury was just another screaming stopgap on their schedule. The tour itself was notable for Keith, however, who claims he became Very Good Friends with the Ronettes' exotic Ronnie Spector – as he gleefully informed me, twenty years after the event. Back in 1964, though, I was simply gutted that, being only nine years old, I wasn't allowed to go to the gig.

When Keith made his return visit, I was a junior reporter on the local paper, the *Bucks Advertiser*. I had grown up in Aylesbury and spent most of my life there up until then. My job usually concerned stories about vandalised street lights or Women's Institute meetings, while court reporting usually involved a whole day ploughing through shoplifting or drunk-driving cases. Keith's case had been kept very quiet, but I'd heard on the grapevine that it would take place on the morning of 10 January.

Obviously, I was excited. I had a bona fide excuse to sit in the press box and witness the whole shebang for three days. My accomplices were *NME*'s Tony Parsons (now an established author/newspaper columnist), the *Zigzag* crew and assorted mates. I'd never witnessed the Stones circus at close quarters before.

It was a very chilly winter's day, and our tiny gaggle were still the only ones on the steps by ten o'clock. Finally, there was some sign of action as a gold Rolls Royce entered the Square at the top end. This can only be Keith, we thought, as *NME* photographer Chalkie Davies got into position. The car stopped, a legal-looking bloke got out, and then emerged the man himself.

Of course, I'd seen countless photographs of Keith Richard, but nothing quite prepared me for this. He looked like a ghost: parchment-coloured skin stretched tight across gaunt features; dead eyes half-closed; the normally spiky coiffure hanging flat and lank. He'd made the effort to wear a suit, though – black velvet with a white silk shirt and scarf. 1977 was the height of Keith's heroin addiction, and it showed. He scuttled down to the cells, head bowed. I couldn't forget that this was the guy responsible for my favourite records of all time. Breaking with tradition, I said a little prayer . . .

By now Keith was used to court appearances, and just sat quietly and somewhat nervously through this one. Slouching in the prisoners' pit, he looked alone and unwell. Before it started, he'd told Barabara Charone, 'What's on trial is the same thing that's always been on trial. Dear old them and us. I find this a bit weary. I've done my stint in the fucking dock. Why don't they pick on the Sex Pistols?' Business got under way fairly quickly as word got around. The press started arriving, the public gallery rapidly filling up with fans and passing shoppers who came in to gawp. As I headed back to the nearby office they'd ask, 'Is it anybody famous?'

How could normal people, going about their everyday routines, even dream of what Keith had seen, done and been through? That was the problem with the jury too: nine men and three women, all looking at this alien being in the dock. In situations like this, all those years of tabloid propaganda, 'Would You Let Your Daughter Marry A Rolling Stone?', previous drug cases and Mars bar rumours were embedded in the consciousness of Mr. and Mrs. Average. The presiding judge wasn't much better. Judge Laurence Verney was your archetypal bigwig from a family of enough local repute to have a street named after them. He also had a severe reputation for showing zero tolerance to long-haired druggies. It didn't bode well.

Prosecuting was a self-important little man called Bruce Laughland, who reminded me of Kenneth Connor in the *Carry On* films when he was playing a stuck-up local dignitary. He didn't smile much. Much more commanding was Keith's defence lawyer, ex-Attorney General Sir Peter Rawlinson QC. Basically, if Keith went down – and that was quite possible – the Stones were going to be in big trouble. The charismatically imposing Sir Peter, with his Shakespearean flourishes and eloquent manner, made a big play of this. He might have cost a fortune, but he was the only man for the job.

Laughland was brisk and to the point, probably believing he'd have no trouble breaking this particular butterfly on a wheel. Six witnesses were all grilled by lunchtime, including the three policemen who'd arrived at the scene – and probably couldn't believe their luck. Their all-round bumbling would soon become apparent.

Whereas Laughland had been business-like and dull, Sir Peter came in blasting like it was the opening night of *King Lear*. He enquired about the weak grounds for the initial investigation, claiming that Keith was 'singled out, stripped and searched.' He asked insistently why no blood or urine samples had been taken, and also questioned why they only zeroed in on Keith. The copper who made the first search was fairly stiff-lipped and unshakeable – until he blew it by saying that Keith couldn't do anything else but deny ownership of the chain and acid.

Oops. A presumption of guilt before the jury had even gone out to consider their verdict.

Sir Peter was off like a rocket. He literally bounded across the court and demanded the red-faced officer repeat that statement. PC Sibbert – the PC, in my mind, now standing for Poor Cunt – stuttered and eventually complied, but by now he'd completely blotted his little black notebook. Sergeant Rubber Gloves didn't come off any better. Not carrying out tests and focusing solely on Keith provided the fuel to Sir Peter's Oscar-winning fire. Old Rubber Gloves protested that he didn't think all that was necessary.

'And you're a detective sergeant?' asked Sir Peter, incredulously. Another point to the defence. The most damning evidence was some photos which became the subject of much discussion. It couldn't really be denied that these shots, taken at a Leicester gig, showed the chain held up in evidence in court being worn around Keith's neck. In a novel piece of evidence, the Thames Valley Police Force Antiques Officer evaluated the chain and tube as pretty cheap, while a vinaigrette that also hung on the chain was Victorian silver and worth about 150 quid, apparently dating from 1872 – the implication being that it wasn't the sort of thing you'd chuck on the floor of the car.

Then it was lunchtime, with Keith and entourage nipping next door to the Bell Hotel bar. There was a noticeable air of excitement now and the Square was buzzing. Mick Jagger had turned up from Los Angeles to support his old mate – and to see whether or not the Rolling Stones still had a career. Compared to Keith, the briefcase-toting Jagger looked a picture of health in his pale green suit and tie. He watched from the public gallery, sitting next to Robin Pike, the schoolteacher who'd taken me to my first Stones gigs. Sitting in that little courtroom was weird, for somebody who'd only ever seen the Stones as tiny dots on a distant stage. *Holy horseshit! The Glimmer Twins are just a shot away!* I had to keep pinching myself.

Sir Peter began the afternoon session with a long speech about dismissing any preconceived ideas about the accused. This was the bit we'd all been waiting for. Keith was up next, for about two and a half hours, swaying a tad and holding onto the dock for dear life. Anyone who's heard Keith in conversation will be familiar with that vaguely slurry drawl born out of hundreds of all-nighters, fuelled by fags, bourbon and pharmaceuticals. To the jury he must have looked and sounded totally out of it. An alien drug fiend, responsible for corrupting a vast proportion of the nation's youth. He was certainly playing at low volume though, and Judge Verney had to tell him to turn it up on a few occasions.

Keith and Sir Peter's argument was that anyone could have dropped the chain in the general mess in the car. After gigs, the group just grabbed the first jacket to hand. Keith's choice just happened to have the acid in it. But he did have a bit of a problem when the judge asked him to measure the length of the chain against his little finger, so they could compare it with the one in the photographs.

It broke the tension a little when Keith was asked what being a lead guitarist entailed. 'It means I make the most noise,' came the reply, and the courtroom sniggered. When Laughland asked what the other passengers did after the car came to the end of its bumpy ride into the field, Keith simply replied, 'They woke up.' Another good one was when the prosecution were pressuring Keith to ascertain who else might have used the Bentley on the tour, for example, who drove it up to Stafford? 'Jim Callaghan,' replied Keith, truthfully, as it was the name of his long-serving driver. The fact that it was also the name of the British Prime Minister at the time brought more guffaws.

When Judge Verney called time for that day, Keith sneaked out the back door while Mick manfully strode out of the front entrance, through the throng of media and fans. During the trial Keith was staying at the palatial Bell Hotel in the nearby village of Aston Clinton. One of my fellow reporters – also a huge Stones fan – ventured there that evening after Keith and Mick had finally crawled their way out of the scrum outside the court. It came as little surprise when he reported that Keith had propped up the bar most of the night, and was in a bit of a state.

The second morning saw the tabloids blast the story across their front pages, with shock-horror headlines like, 'ROLLING STONE KEITH SNORTED COCAINE'. The scene was a far cry from the previous morning. Most of the music press, more of the national papers, film crews, all greeted Keith as he emerged from the Bentley clutching an empty wine glass. The press box was sardine central. More defence evidence came from the ever-faithful Ian Stewart and transport manager Alan Dunn. Both reiterated that, in the chaos surrounding a Stones gig, Keith could have had anything in the jacket he'd flung on and anyone could have dropped a silver sniffer into his car, as fans were always giving them drug-related gifts. They added that security at Stafford had been a bit of a problem anyway.

Before summing up, the judge asked two questions on behalf of the jury: what else was in Keith's pockets? (There was nothing of any consequence.) And what was the small patch sewn onto the jacket presented to the court? It was overlooked by the straight jury that the patch was actually in red, gold and green Rastafarian colours, while in the Leicester photos Keith's t-shirt displayed 'a fierce-looking man with shaggy hair', to quote the prosecution. Nobody apart from the hipper elements twigged that this was Bob Marley, and that both factors were usually associated with smoking large amounts of weed.

Then the summing up. Laughland went on for an hour in his customary efficient manner. He focused mainly on the photographs, and the fact that, when Keith turned out his pockets at Newport Pagnell services police outpost, there was everything there but the paper containing the acid. He only got heated up near the end, when he tried to shoot down the defence, concluding, 'The implications of this case are such as to stretch credulity beyond the breaking point.'

Mick appeared at lunchtime, this time in the company of veteran Stones press man Les Perrin, who was now very old and not at all well. This may have been his last bout of service for the Stones. Then there was Barbara Charone and a familiar-looking figure who turned out to be their friend John Phillips, former leader of the Mamas and the Papas.

(There was a hook-up between the Stones and Phillips that year, when they recorded an entire album amidst some severe partying. At the time, Phillips was a demonic drug fiend and subsequently lost the tapes, which had been mixed by Mick. However, while spring-cleaning his garage 23 years later, he happened upon the only master.)

By now, I was thoroughly enjoying all of this. Not because I enjoyed seeing Keith suffer – though the quantity of drugs found seemed too small to merit jail – but for the sheer delight of having the Stones in town. Plus the fact that the authorities had once again made themselves look stupid, inefficient and wasteful with taxpayers' money. The trial must have cost a fortune to stage. It was also fascinating to watch the sheer pandemonium that the Stones could spark, and the way that the newspapers could bend facts. (I was still young and naïve back then!)

Most entertaining of all – and the best-paid bloke in the building apart from the Stones – was Sir Peter Rawlinson. He deserved a standing ovation for his summing-up speech. Regarding the omission of the acid when Keith emptied his pockets, he got a little piece of paper, folded it and, with a gay flourish, tossed it over the rail to show how easily you can miss these things. He boomed, whispered, gestured and flung down the incriminating photos in disgust. Though, admittedly, his job of convincing the grey jurors that these minuscule quantities of drugs were not Keith's might have been easier if the guitarist looked like a soap opera star. He wound up with a good line: 'No man must be acquitted because of his name, but neither must he be convicted because of it.'

Around 3.30pm, Judge Verney called it a day. Mick decided to make an early bolt for the door to try and avoid the crowds. Too early, as it happens. He scuttled out of the front door, but got there before his car! It was a hoot as Jagger high-tailed up the Market Square – once immortalised by frequent Aylesbury visitor David Bowie in 'Five Years' – pursued by a baying mob of fans and press. John Phillips had to drag him to the safety of the arriving car, but it provided a diversion for Keith to get out of the back.

Next day, it was far from silent both inside and outside the court. I was very lucky to secure my regular seat in the press gallery. It was amusing to fill in ignorant tabloid reporters about Keith Richard – I just said he was the best rhythm guitarist in the world and he didn't even drink, let alone indulge in what he was accused of. I told another that he was staying at Champneys health farm for the rich and famous, just up the road. They looked at Keith in his black velvet suit, looked back at me, then looked a bit puzzled.

As Judge Verney summed up the evidence to the jury, he homed in on omissions and coincidences in the defence case – like not bringing in the wardrobe man in charge of dishing out jackets, or even the bloke standing next to Keith in the photos. That was Mick Jagger, incidentally, who was sitting right across the courtroom.

At 11.30, the jury went out and so did we. The waiting area was seething with media hounds who crowded around to hear Les Perrin spinning yarns. Mick was bowling about with Phillips, so I unashamedly asked for his autograph and whether he'd like to play at Friars some time. He was very pleasant to everyone who approached him. One girl who'd skipped off from Aylesbury College for the day asked Mick if he'd sign her jeans, so he hoisted up her leg and scrawled.

The wait dragged into lunchtime, so Keith hit the White Swan around the corner. He must have been shitting himself. Apart from the local paper, I was also covering the case for a fanzine called the *Aylesbury Roxette*, which me and my mates had started to encourage the local rock scene. I wrote this observation: 'Despite the crowded court Keith looked lonely sitting there tapping the wood panelling with his fingers. You couldn't help feeling sorry for the bloke going through all this circus. You just wanted to hang by your legs from the gallery and say, "It's okay mate, we're behind you."' Needless to say I didn't, but Robin Pike sent a telegram of support to Keith's hotel 'from friends in Aylesbury.'

The jury were out for around three hours. On their return it was straight to the charges. Possession of the LSD?

'Not guilty,' stated the foreman. Cue mass sighs of relief and a sprinkling of applause. Keith allowed himself a little smile.

The cocaine?

'Guilty.'

You could have chopped the silence with a credit card. A few of the girls burst into tears and Keith visibly stiffened. Jagger seemed surprised and annoyed.

So now it was time for Ol' Rubber Gloves – Detective Sergeant Bull – to trot out the antecedent history. He described Keith as 'a composer of popular music of variable income,' and rattled off the conviction from October 1973, when Keith was found guilty of possessing heroin, Mandrax and cannabis resin, plus firearms. Sir Peter reared up for the last time to make a plea for leniency in the sentence, describing the grave consequences it would have on the guitarist's career if he couldn't play in certain parts of the world. 'You are dealing with an artist who is *non-pareil* in his field,'

AYLESBURY ROXETTE
NUMBER SIX JANUARY 1977 FREE!

SPECIAL KEEF TRIAL ISSUE

photo by Louise Pearson

The Aylesbury Roxette, *our local rock fanzine, for which I covered Keith's drugs trial.*

quoth Sir Peter with a final gesture. Judge Verney then wandered off to decide the sentence and returned after what must have been ten of the worst minutes in Keith's life. This is how he pronounced sentence: 'Keith Richards, while in this country you must obey the laws of this country. The possession of a Class A drug is regarded in this country as a sufficiently serious offence to merit both a substantial period of imprisonment and a fine . . . but in the circumstances of this case, we do not consider that a period of imprisonment is appropriate at all. This is, however, the second conviction for the possession of drugs, and it would be as well for you to bear in mind that should there be a third, a court is not by any means likely to take the same view. In assessing a fine upon you, we had to take into account both the quantity of the drug and the fact that it was, as it appears, intended for personal consumption, and your means. Bearing both matters in mind, we impose upon you the fine of £750, and we shall order you to contribute something towards the cost of the prosecution. We shall order you to contribute £250 towards those costs.'

Phew. Everyone, especially Keith, broke out into huge, relieved grins. There was much hugging and it was obvious that all the case had done was turn him into an even bigger hero.

After the trial, one of the arresting police officers said to Mick, 'If it was you I wouldn't have done it.' That says it all really.

'I got the feeling in the courtroom that there was absolutely no understanding of the kind of life we lead,' said Keith later. 'To them the kind of things we come into contact with would be shocking, but they're as common to us in every-day life as the milkman coming to the door.'

When the two Stones tried to leave, they had to brave the biggest crowd of the whole three days. Keith ducked and charged through all the clamouring and slammed the car door behind him. Mick reached the vehicle but couldn't get in. 'It's me!' he yelled and was swiftly pulled inside. But the Roller couldn't budge more than a few inches at a time, running over Chalkie Davies' foot.

Les Perrin had called a press conference with Keith at the Bell Hotel's pavillion. We hotfooted it to Aston Clinton, only to wait well over an hour for him to appear. Finally he swaggered in with Mick, back in full Keef mode. Pulling on a fag, hair spiked, purple Tibetan prayer scarf replacing the tie, and obviously having partaken of a livener.

Keith described the result as 'a good old British compromise', adding that he'd been touched by the local fans. 'It was great moral support.' After that, most of the questions were inane.

Hack: 'How do you feel about the case?'

Keith: 'I'm just glad it's over. They found me guilty on one charge and acquitted me on the other . . . might get a song out of it.' [He did – 'Before They Make Me Run'.]

Hack: 'Is Anita with you?'

Keith: 'No, she's in Geneva, waiting for me to fly home.'

Hack: 'Does she know the result?'

Keith: 'Yes, I rang her and told her.'

Hack: 'What did she say?'

Keith: 'She was delighted!'

Mick butts in: 'Nah, she said nothing. She was silent throughout the conversation.'

Hack: 'What are you going to do now?'

Keith: 'I'm going to get on with what I'm supposed to be doing . . . get on with rock 'n' roll.'

And so it went on, although Tony Parsons livened things up when he climbed on a table to get closer and bellowed, 'Whatcha gonna do with the chain, Keith?'

Keith looked a bit startled at first, then, after a pause, said, 'Uh, it ain't mine, so they can do what they like with it.'

Another reporter asked if Keith was now going to give up drugs.

'I never take drugs,' came the reply.

The conference wound up. Then came my big chance. As I made my way to the exit, who should be coming out of the gents' toilets? Seizing the moment I'd been waiting for most of my life, I shouted out, 'Keith!' He turned with a start and a glare – expecting either a tabloid hack or another copper. So I just blurted out, 'Congratulations,' and got him to sign my notebook. I burbled some other shit about how glad I was that he didn't go down. 'Thanks,' he grinned. 'Yeah . . . I'm still on the streets, man.'

Both Keith and I were celebrating that night. He was a free man. Me, I'd just met the bloke I'd been following religiously since the age of nine. Three years later, I'd finally get to sit down in a room with Keith and talk, over a bottle of Jack

Daniel's, about how dealers had always thrust their wares upon him just to say they supplied Keith Richards.

'Oh, sure. It was, "Great to see ya, man, I need it and you got it."You've got that to deal with as well, people stuffing it at ya.There's no way I could explain that in Aylesbury court.The things that are given to us. But I knew there was no point in trying to explain it to a straight jury and judge, even to my own lawyer. All the time, they think they're doing you a favour, and probably at the time I thought so too. Some kid sends me an envelope with a quarter of an ounce of smack in it, y'know, "Have a good time, Keith, thumbs up, yeah, right, wheyy!" If you're on it, you'll go, "Yeah, right, wheyy!" back, 'cos you need it and you're not gonna say no. But really, nobody's doing anybody a favour.

'Once I cleaned up and viewed it all from a bit of perspective . . . dealers would still be coming up to me. I'd dig just watching their faces. One thing that got me over that second period of cleaning up the environment was seeing these dealers' faces when they realised there was no sale,' he laughed. 'It was a perverse way of going about it but it got me through the period.'

Police On My Back

After the trial, Keith was still in his drug haze, holed up at Redlands. Meanwhile, Mick was getting things moving for the Stones. In the process of negotiating a huge new record contract for the band, he'd become aware of punk rock, as, in his own way, had Keith.They welcomed the shot of energy, but knew it was simply an update of what they themselves had done 25 years earlier.The problem for Keith was that the punks didn't have the feel, the raunch, the funk – and he thought the music was utter shit. So the Stones thought it would be a wizard idea to devote a side of their upcoming live double album to getting back to their roots, and playing some reggae and R&B classics in a small club – just like the old days, when they were punks.

It was going to be a week at Toronto's El Mocambo, a dark little bar that accomodated just a couple of hundred people.The Stones were trying to rekindle the sparks that flew back in their Crawdaddy days – an art they've now mastered since those first unsteady steps outside of the stadium.

With a big advance and a series of grass-roots gigs, things were looking good. The band duly checked into Toronto's Harbour Castle Hilton on 20 February 1977. But there was no sign of 'Mr. Redlands' – Keith's *nom de l'hotel* for the jaunt. He was still shacked up at Redlands itself, in smacked-out oblivion. It took the much-quoted telegram from the waiting Stones – 'We want to play, you want to play. Where are you?' – to get his arse into gear.

On 24 February, Anita, Marlon and nearly 30 items of luggage flew to Toronto. Keith shot up in the plane's toilet and absent-mindedly dropped the spoon he'd used for cooking into Anita's bag. He was also carrying a gram apiece of smack and coke. Customs swarmed all over them, but only found the spoon – which was sent away for analysis – and a little lump of hash that Anita had forgotten about. They got to the hotel and Keith, who'd been up for five days, decided to go for one of his marathon naps – but not before acquiring an ounce of heroin and five grams of cocaine.

Victor Bockris's book presents evidence that someone within the Stones'

Accompanied by his lawyer, William Carter, Keith arrives at the court in Toronto on 14 March 1977.

organisational machine may have turned traitor and set Keith up for what happened next. Anita had been told there were some people looking for him in the hotel, but didn't pass it on. There was no security posted outside their hotel room. When she heard a knock, Anita answered, and fifteen Mounties stormed in. They found the drugs quite easily, but the big problem was rousing the slumbering Keith. At the time, when he'd finally completed one of his four or five-day stints, he'd be dead to the world for at least the next 24 hours. He'd only just dropped off when the drug squad turned up, and it took them around 45 minutes to wake him.

As he told me five years later, 'I was a bit pissed off that they weren't wearing the proper Mountie gear. They were just normal-looking guys who wanted to grab a bit of publicity for themselves.' No daft pointed hats or red jackets, and the only horse in sight belonged to Keith – who was immediately booked on trafficking charges.

In Canada this could mean a seven-years-to-life sentence. And they wouldn't give him back so much as a solitary hit to ward off the creeping withdrawal. Bill and Ronnie were so shocked by Keith's agonised demeanour when he got back from being charged that they braved everything, including swarming undercover cops, to score him some heroin.

After some rehearsal, the Stones managed to pull off the El Mocambo gigs – even if they had been whittled down to only two – starting on 4 March. The same day, Anita appeared in court to be charged with possessing heroin and cannabis from the airport bust. (She'd get off with a $400 fine later in the month.)

Keith was in a bad state, but lit up when he was stuck out on stage. Chet Flippo described it best in *Rolling Stone*: 'It may have been rooted in desperation, but nonetheless, the Stones pulled out all the stops. And Keith, whose soul had been stained blacker than black many years ago before by the spirit that anointed the legendary Robert Johnson, glowed with internal combustion that no scientist in the western world would want to identify.'

The *New York Times'* John Rockwell praised the Stones' return to their blues roots, but said the idea of them without Keith would be 'inconceivable' and mean the end of the band. Keith was back in court on 7 March – to hear that he was also being charged with cocaine possession – and on the following day, when he was bailed again. When leaving the court, he was accosted by an aggressive photographer and braved hollered insults like 'junkie bastard'. He had to appear again on 12 March, because of a legal technicality involving a *Rolling Stone* journalist being present at the proceedings. At this point he was all but abandoned by the band, who'd been mixing the live tapes at a local studio. The fact that Keith had simply replaced the confiscated smack with another supply convinced Mick that he'd be busted again. They all ran for the hills – even Ronnie Wood, which particularly hurt Keith.

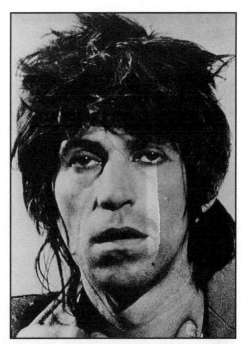

Keith checks he's still alive while facing the press in Toronto, after pleading guilty to the drug charges brought against him in 1977.

But another media furore might have been responsible for their swift departure from Toronto. The *Daily Mirror* of 10 March emblazoned its front page with a story about Mick having an affair with Margaret Trudeau, twenty-year-old wife of the Canadian premier. While road manager Peter Rudge said it was 'like World War Three had started' in Canada, Mick strenuously denied it, but Mrs. Trudeau had checked into the same Harbour Castle hotel and was hanging out with the band. But chiefly with Ronnie, who was also splitting up with his wife. 'She's helping to improve Anglo-Canadian relations,' was Bill Wyman's comment.

It was tabloid heaven. Just the sort of media attention the Stones didn't need at the time. It was the Canadian equivalent of Cherie Blair dating Ozzy Osbourne, and it even brought down the value of the Canadian dollar. When all parties left for New York – fuelling more rumours, althought they left on separate flights – they were never to meet again. Ronnie would later dismiss the affair: 'She just came along and had a boogie with us for two days. She travelled with us and we became good friends. But it was a very short-lived friendship.'

The only member of the Stones camp who stayed on was Ian Stewart. Stu was – and remains still – second to none in Keith's affections. He always brought everything and everybody down to earth, from the days when they rehearsed above strip joints in Soho to the drug-crazed madness of the 1970s US tours. He could cut the Stones down to size with one choice comment, and always played a mean boogie-woogie piano. It was a mark of his own loyalty and love for Keith that he stayed on while others fled. And one of the most legendary unreleased Stones sessions came out of this.

The night before he was due in court, Keith, Anita, Marlon and Stu went into Interchange Studios, where they'd been mixing the El Mocambo tapes. Keith wanted to lay down some tracks. Just in case.

He'd refer to them as 'some songs Gram Parsons taught me, that we used to do together,' from the *Exile* session jams. They are probably the most poignant recordings Keith has ever done. 'I went in the studio and did them myself, overdubbing. I never think of them as finished tapes or anything. I would think of going in and cutting them with a really good country band. It's probably worth a try to do that.'

There's a version of 'Sing Me Back Home' – the Merle Haggard song Gram had recorded about a man going to the electric chair; a stridently spot-on rendition of the classic 'Worried Life Blues'; a pleading 'Say It's Not You'; 'She Still Comes Around', and a spellbinding 'Apartment Number 9' – once recorded by Tammy Wynette, and later a staple of the New Barbarians' stage set. All sad, reflective songs that, as far as Keith was concerned, could have been the last things he was going to record for a few years. And it shows.

This session is now a famous bootleg – the perfect companion to *Booze And Pills And Powders*, which likewise features mostly just Keith and piano, including 'Worried Life Blues'. His broken versions of 'Somewhere Over The Rainbow' and 'Honey Don't Say Don't' come from the same period. Keith unplugged from his electric raunch is another kettle of fish. Bobby Gillespie of Primal Scream says, 'Keith's a great blues singer.' And he's dead right. Alone with just a piano or acoustic guitar for support, he opens his heart and tears out his emotions for a music that can be called 'soul' in the truest sense. It was why he related so well to Gram Parsons – their lives may have been in turmoil, but they sang like wounded angels.

The British cops must have been jealous that their Canadian counterparts were having so much success with Keith. He'd stayed at his Cheyne Walk house until Christmas 1976, so, on 26 March 1977, when they raided it, he was long gone – and they found fuck-all. Meanwhile, Marshall Chess stepped down from running Rolling Stones Records after six years. He'd found himself sinking further into drugs, and had to leave to save his own life.

Keith wouldn't actually go to trial in Canada until February '78. Meanwhile, in early April, after much work from the Stones' legal people, he was granted a medical visa to enter the United States to be cured of his heroin addiction. He attempted to come off smack using Dr. Meg Paterson's 'Black Box' treatment, which had worked for Eric Clapton and would later do the same for Pete Townshend.

Strings were pulled for Keith that would never have worked for anyone with less money. Dr Paterson agreed to take the case, using a friend's seventeenth-century farmhouse, in Paoli near Philadelphia, as an impromptu clinic. She insisted that Anita come too, otherwise it would all be pointless. Keith duly had his medical visa extended, but was confined to a 25-mile radius of the house, and had be kept in check by security guards.

On 1 April, a dubious Keith, who had a backup plan to escape to New York if he smelled a rat, flew out of Toronto with Anita and Marlon. When the pair got to Philly, they had to check out of the lifestyle they had known for several years.

Walking into a world free of junk, they found themselves answerable to other people. They would even have to attend therapy sessions.

Keith and Anita had to wear receptors on their ears, which picked up mild electric signals from a little black box. These stimulated the brain to over-produce endorphins, which have a similar effect to heroin, and thus allow the body to detox without the pain of cold-turkey withdrawal. Over three weeks they'd be detoxed via gradually decreasing doses. It seemed to work okay – while Keith and Anita customised their surroundings with scarves over the lampshades, favourite photos, a block-rocking sound system, incense and empty bottles – but technical hitches like the box messing up didn't help.

The therapy sessions were basically confession time. I underwent something similar when I attended an East Harlem methadone centre in New York. I'd read about Keith's experiences, and would sometimes wonder to myself how he'd have dealt with such personal probing – trying to find out how you got into this mess in the first place, with a view to preventing it happening again.

Keith may have been lucky to have palatial surroundings, but he was a prisoner. At least me and my fellow clinic attendees could walk outside, head up a few blocks to El Barrio and cop, if the going got tough. Sure, it defeats the object, but it's the same constant struggle even when the physical withdrawal has passed. Whether you're in a country farmhouse with a special gadget, or queuing in a Harlem street for a methadone McDonalds, you have to face the world eventually. Keith's task was much harder, because he'd have to face *his* – which, back then, mostly consisted of dealers offering him top-quality gear.

Roy Carr asked Keith about the cure in *Creem*: 'Electro-acupuncture . . . it's so simple it's not true. But as to whether or not they'll ever let people know about is another thing! . . . . I can't even tell you how it works because they don't even know for sure. All they know is that it does work. It's a little metal box with leads that clip on to your ears, and in two or three days . . . which is the worst time for kickin' junk . . . in those 72 hours it leaves your system . . . . Actually, you should be incredibly sick, but you're not.'

What is it with heroin? As I've said, I too fought a battle with it for several years. At first, it's great. Not the turbo-kick of coke, or the euphoria of ecstasy. Nothing so obvious. You just feel cocooned, in cotton wool. Floaty, content, and shot through with a feeling of warmth, which keeps the cold of the outside world at bay.

But then comes the fateful morning when you wake up and something isn't right. You're sweating, retching, going hot and cold while your muscles spasm. Everything seems to ache, every orifice is leaking, and all you can think about is that one shot of the stuff will make the whole world right again. It's like nothing else on earth. If heroin is heaven, withdrawal is the closest you'll ever to get to sheer hell.

And I got like this on the street stuff, which is traditionally cut to fuck. You can bet that the ounce of 'personal' that Keith got busted with wasn't half-comprised of talcum powder. Going cold turkey would probably have killed him – although he did try it a few times, with no success.

As Keith said, 'I never considered myself a junkie because my particular situation was so different and removed from 90 per cent of the people hung up on the stuff.' For most of the eighties, I was on and off smack like a revolving door.

Ironically, during the decade that would see Keith well and truly clean up, on one occasion that we met I was the one who was on the stuff – even though, by then, it simply served to let me function normally.

It's only when you hit rock bottom that your smack-dependent brain becomes inclined to try to tell the body to quit. In my case, it was getting busted and spending three days in a New York jail with the cream of Brooklyn's gang members, while my son waited at home. In Keith's case, it was finally realising that his son and the Stones were the most important things in his life.

Also, if he got busted again – which was a distinct possibility, given all the bad publicity he was getting – he would be going away for a long time. Keith and Anita had already lost their baby, and Anita later admitted her habit may have had something to do with Tara suffocating in his cot. It had reached the point of realisation, the point of 'This can't go on.'

So Keith successfully completed his cure, aged 33. He wouldn't be completely out of the woods for a while, but he was starting to want to quit. As Keith told me in 1980, 'It had to reach that point in Canada where I thought, "I don't wanna be busted any more. I don't wanna go through this shit any more." Knock it on the head, y'know? I wanted to come back and show 'em.'

After coming out of the cure, Keith went to New York to mix the live album with Mick. He was staying in a suite at the Mayflower Hotel, and there were regular jam sessions at Mick's West Side house where some of the seeds were sown for Some Girls. Keith also had a post-junk song called 'Beast Of Burden' in the works. Like many of his songs, its actual target remains ambiguous, but it's been described as being anything from an apology about the smack years to a last gasp for Anita – but then, that's been said about many of his subsequent songs too. But he was musically active, and wading back into the real world the best way he knew how. With a guitar.

But maybe recording an album with John Phillips wasn't the best idea. Phillips was a total junkie at the time. He'd gone the traditional route of rising to fame in the sixties – with the multi-harmonied sunshine and romance of the Mamas and the Papas – before diving into a vat of coke and landing up on smack. He'd been arrested for robbing pharmacies and was considered a dangerous man. So Keith came straight out of rehab to hook up with a man feeding a monstrous smack habit – the old drug buddy who'd offered moral support, and probably something more, at the Aylesbury trial.

So Keith was still not off the junk hook. The thing was, he liked heroin. As he said in *Creem*, at the end of '78: 'The drugs were never really a conscious part of our image. I've never had problems with drugs, only with policemen. OK, drugs were mentioned in a few songs, but nobody in the band went around saying take this or take that. The drugs thing was just an extra side of the image that was forced upon us by political circumstances or whatever.'

While Keith was working on the Phillips album, in August 1977, Elvis Presley died. Then Keith and Anita moved to a house called Frog Hollow, which would host a few incidents of its own. But he knew he had to quit, once and for all. Soon after, he entered the Stevens Clinic in New Jersey and would come out clean again at the end of September.

Lester Bangs had written a piece in *NME*, about how being a rich superstar junkie set Keith apart from the man in the street, who just wanted him to play rock 'n' roll. Bill Wyman put the band's view in his *Rolling with the Stones*: '. . . It was true, Keith didn't have to live by the rules of normal society. Money afforded him that luxury, if indeed it is a luxury . . . . What was irritating for the rest of us was the way his drug-taking was getting in the way of making music. Keith would also say he expects no one to follow his example. But Keith is an icon and people set out to glamorise his life.'

Love You Live was released on 23 September, and launched in the UK with a party at the legendary Marquee Club. I remember attending in my capacity as new editor of punkzine *Zigzag*, and feeling like a traitor as I sat watching the live videos and guzzling free booze. Ronnie, who was sitting at the next table, brought along a life-sized cardboard cutout of the absent Keith, who was still in New Jersey and 'couldn't make it today'. I was unable to suppress a very un-punky grin. Sure, I was into punk rock of the Clash-Pistols variety, but it wouldn't have existed if not for this lot up on the screen – especially the man with the guitar.

And he'd been on nuclear form that sad night at Les Abattoirs, judging by the album. Emotional overload crackled from his limbs through to his guitar, driving the band to rare heights. The slow songs were some of the most heartfelt blues Keith's heart has ever spilled. The El Mocambo tracks were worth the price of admission alone: sleazed-up club versions of Muddy Waters' 'Mannish Boy' and Bo Diddley's 'Crackin' Up', which the Stones hadn't previously committed to vinyl, and new versions of 'Around And Around' and 'Little Red Rooster'. In the mid-seventies, live double albums were synonymous with turgid exercises in ego masturbation. This one effectively blew that preconception out of the water.

Mick and Keith would dutifully promote the live album in the 3 November issue of *Rolling Stone*. With a live album, 'If it's there, it's there,' Keith tells Chet Flippo. 'And if it's not, then there really isn't any point to it.' He also revealed how they'd actually spent hours getting the crowd noises right. 'I'd rather make four studio albums any day,' he grumbled.

The sleeve was a little gross. Andy Warhol had photographed all of the band biting each other, and later complained that Mick had spoiled his shots by drawing over them. There was also an interview with Warhol in his magazine, *Inter/View*, conducted on 29 September in New York with Mick, Ronnie and Keith, who'd just got out of the Stevens Centre. It was an informal chat – though Mick was putting on the ultra-cool for Warhol's crowd, while Keith was almost monosyllabic, pure punk in his reactions.

Warhol asked Keith if he was going away – obviously referring to the court case. 'Am I going away? We all are, yes,' comes the reply. Mick chips in quickly, saying they're going to Paris. Keith shoots back with, 'We're all going to make a record . . . We go where it's available.' They talk about parties, punk rock. Warhol asks Keith if they still sign autographs: 'Oh yeah. It's such a small thing, and it's obviously important to them in some way.' Just as the talk gets on to guitars, Mick steers it over to sex. Warhol is amazed to learn that Keith and Ronnie cut their own hair.

And so it goes on, ending up with Mick talking about Bianca's make-up. It was obvious that the hip New York *demi-monde* was not where the Stones belonged. And Keith knew it. He was more concerned about recording the next album.

CHAPTER TEN

BEFORE THEY MAKE ME RUN

Stone Free?

Keith and Ronnie took Concorde to Paris to start work on the new album. For Mr. Richards, it would be his first Stones album with his best mate Ron, and the first one off of heroin since *Beggars Banquet*. The Stones knew they needed to make a total rip-snorter of an album, as the preceding three hadn't been universally well-received. As Keith put it, 'We were feeling a little under pressure to come out with something a little different.' And the bottom line seemed to lay with Keith, who had to be firing on all cylinders. He'd only finished cleaning up a few days before recording was due to start.

Most people who have kicked junk take at least a couple of years before they feel like they've really done it. And by then they're on the booze! You need something to fill the enormous gap left in your daily timetable – the ritual of scoring, shooting up, having a good time, then nodding out. Keith had never left music, but even that had taken a backseat if he ran out of gear. Now the Rolling Stones were the perfect substitute, the one addiction he'd never want to shake.

So, in October '77, Keith and the boys entered Pathe-Marconi studios in Paris to record what would become the revelatory *Some Girls* album. Conveniently, Keith had bought an apartment in the Faubourg-Saint-Honore back in 1968, which he rarely stayed in – to the extent that he couldn't find it when the Stones arrived.

Unimpressed with the main studios, Keith loved the sound of the rehearsal room, which he customised to his all-important sound requirements. 62 Rue Des Sevres would become one of the Stones' landmark recording locations for the next few albums. It was a great room to play in, every night was a party, and they even installed a bar. Charlie and Bill were over the moon, as the combination of new engineer Chris Kimsey and the room's high-ceilinged acoustics gave the rhythm section a boomy new punch.

The sound was that of a stripped-down guitar band, with Ronnie making his recording debut as a full-fledged Rolling Stone. The chemistry that sparked between Keith and Ronnie during endless jam sessions and rollercoaster gigs was now given free rein in the studio. Mick had also started playing rhythm guitar, under Ronnie's guidance, and wrote his new songs on the instrument.

Whereas *Black And Blue* had been pieced together, *Some Girls* was born out of relentless determination, the fun atmosphere kickstarted by Woody, and the kick up the arse that was punk rock. Here were the Stones back in action without any session-man frills – the album's secret recipe, according to Keith. Even if Bill Wyman claimed it was 'frustrating' that Keith favoured working at different times to the others, the Stones still had the album wrapped up in about six months – which was virtually overnight for them. And it would be the fattest shrimp tossed on the barbie since *Exile*. It was also the album that welcomed Keith back into the Stones, and, indeed, into the world. Things just hadn't been so much fun when he was taking those long lunch breaks.

Some Girls would also bid farewell to Billy Preston, as Keith told France's *Rock & Folk* magazine in July '79. 'After doing two or three albums with Billy there in the studio, we found that, in trying to get a song together, while we were still fumbling around, trying to find the right chords, he'd start playing, and we'd find ourselves following him. I realised, doing *Some Girls*, that there wasn't anybody racing ahead of us, taking the whole thing further and further away from where it would have gone ....When Billy turned up at the start of the '76 tour with his own sound man, that's when it became obvious to me that I couldn't work with Billy and the Stones like that. Billy's great – but the Stones don't need that extra relationship.'

The sessions started on 10 October, and continued until late November when Keith had to break for a Canadian court appearance that saw his case adjourned until February. For the first few weeks they jammed and rehearsed as a live band, before starting the recording process. They gathered again in the second week of December for further recording before a Christmas break, and the final stretch. By which time – according to Victor Bockris – Keith was doing smack again.

Keith had done the initial burst of recording relatively straight, but the pressures of the court case, the possibility of doing hard time which might mean the end of the Stones, his smack-tainted relationship with Anita, plus the drug's indefinable lure must have been all too much of a deadly recipe. But he spent Christmas with Marlon, playing Santa Claus, and sincerely wanted to kick now. It would all be there in 'Before They Make Me Run', Keith's solo song on the album.

It's a rousing shout of defiance and optimism which was the last track to be recorded, in January '78. '"Before They Make Me Run",' recalled Keith during our '83 interview. 'That was with Dave Jordan, who was neither tea boy nor tape op at Island Studios, at Hammersmith. But everybody else had split. So we went over to Paris and spent nine days indulging ourselves, trying to finish this track to get it on the album.' Most sources say the song started life as a track called 'Rotten Roll', but that ten-minute work-out is only vaguely reminiscent in its slow, crawling riffage.

Obviously, the song is inspired by Keith's constant hassles with the law and smack addiction. But he comes over like a defiant free spirit, closely bonded with the ghost of Gram Parsons, surfing a wave of ebullient guitars with a big middle finger pointing at the sky. He still wasn't free of smack when he recorded the song, but it turned out to be junk addiction's swansong. Reflective and rejuvenated (and so good they named a book after them), Keith's lyrics are his resolution to kick the gear: 'I'm gonna walk before they make me run . . . I'm gonna find my way to heaven 'cause I did my time in hell / I wasn't looking too good, but I was feeling real well.' (The song also spawned the phrase 'booze and pills and powders', which surfaced as the title to one of the more indispensable Keef bootlegs.)

Keith talked about 'Before They Make Me Run' to *Trouser Press* in July '79: 'That one is basically all me. There have been others before like that, and there have been lots of others the other way. "You Can't Always Get What You Want" was all Mick's. "Happy" was all mine. Usually, the reason why I end up doing things like "Happy" or "Before They Make Me Run" is that it would take me maybe a week or two to teach Mick the song because it was just a riff that I had put down that I could follow myself but he could find nothing to grasp onto. There comes a point where, instead of spending all that time, it's easier if I do it myself.'

In February, Keith was interviewed by America's foremost drug magazine, *High Times* – inevitably, perhaps. He gave one of his most famous interview responses, when asked if he'd ever been in a sticky situation with drugs: 'No,' replied Keith. 'I don't know if I've been extremely lucky or if it's that subconscious careful, but I've never turned blue in somebody else's bathroom. I consider that the height of bad manners. I've had so many people do it to me and it's really not on, as far as drug etiquette goes, to turn blue in somebody else's john . . .'

Asserting that he felt hopeful about the future, he claimed to find every aspect of his life enjoyable: 'Even being busted . . . it's no pleasure, but it certainly isn't boring. And I think boring is the worst thing of all.'

The following month saw his Canadian court date set for 23 October. But first, *Some Girls* would be released on Rolling Stones Records – no longer the sole domain of the Stones, after the April signing of reggae giant Peter Tosh.

Keith had been on at Mick to sign the former Wailer since the previous year as Tosh was ending an unhappy relationship with his previous record label.

'I was thinking what would be next on my agenda and my telepathy picked up Keith,' said the self-appointed Minister of Herb. 'He got in contact, came over to Jamaica and was interested. You see, when you put your faith in Jah, anything you want can happen.

'That guy's been listening to reggae since '62. He has some tapes and records that even I've never heard yet . . . The Rolling Stones . . . [have] been playing for the same time as me and they've also shared some of the same problems – especially police victimisation.'

After spending ten years as part of the original Wailers trio – along with Bob Marley and Bunny Livingston – Peter Tosh made his own name with albums like *Legalise It* and *Equal Rights*. The man was a rebel, with a sense of danger about him as he sent out tunes like 'Steppin' Razor' in a stoned, lazy drawl. He preached Rastafarian-style revolution, equal rights and smoking weed with an equal missionary zeal.

Keith and Mick had been won over when they attended the now-legendary One Love Peace Concert in April '78. Every important official in Jamaica watched headliner Bob Marley seemingly achieve the impossible by clasping together the hands of the leaders of the island's two opposing political parties. But Tosh appeared earlier with his superlative band Words, Sounds & Power, who included the lethal rhythm section of Sly and Robbie. He sparked up a fat spliff and delivered a fiery rant about police oppression and equal rights. He was later busted for ganja and beaten badly by the cops.

Signing Tosh gave Keith the opportunity to realise a musical and social obsession he'd had for years, and made Mick feel street-cred and cool. The first fruits of the deal were Tosh duetting with Mick on a jaunty rendition of the Temptations' '(You Gotta Walk And) Don't Look Back', which became a massive hit. During spring '78, Keith and Woody also played on Tosh's first album for the label, *Bush Doctor*.

The relationship started out fine, with Tosh supporting the Stones on their next tour. But, as time went on, his behaviour became more erratic as he complained that he hadn't become as big as Marley. Meanwhile, sales of subsequent albums, like *Mystic Man* and *Wanted Dread Or Alive*, were dropping.

When I interviewed Tosh in '81, Marley had recently died and it had hit him hard, to the extent that he talked of little else during our allotted hour. I also got the sense that Tosh now thought the time was right for him to step into Bob's shoes. He praised Keith, for his inital belief and his furthering the cause of reggae ('I told him, "Man, you're dangerous"'), but also moaned about the Stones not giving him enough of a push to send him into the upper echelons. But the bottom line was that his music just wasn't as commercial as Marley's.

In the early eighties, Keith let Tosh stay at Point of View, where he was joined by the inevitable mob of dealers and shady characters. When Keith told Tosh he needed to use his place for a while, Tosh claimed the place was his and threatened Keith. Keith phoned again from Montego Bay airport and said he was coming straight over with a loaded gun. When he got to Point of View, Keith found his house trashed, but no sign of Tosh.

'Tosh is off the label now,' Keith sniffed when I asked him about it the following year. '*Bush Doctor* did real well, but I didn't really like the albums that he gave us after that.'

In 1987, Peter Tosh was murdered during a robbery at his home in Kingston.

The first single from the album, 'Miss You', was released on 26 May, hurtling up to the number one spot in the US and number two in the UK. By now, the rock industry was cottoning on to the twelve-inch single format favoured for club mixes in disco and reggae circles.

Disco might have been invented simply to plant a huge wedge between Keith and Mick. The sound of New York clubland had risen to prominence on the back of *Saturday Night Fever*, conjuring images of men in white suits dancing to the Bee Gees. It was inextricably linked to clubs like Studio 54, which Mick frequented with Bianca. It was also very popular at office parties. But disco also had a raunchy, experimental underbelly, born out of funk and soul. Bobby Womack and Ronnie Wood had been messing with the genre on *Now Look* a couple of years earlier, and Mick had started writing 'Miss You' back on the '76 tour. Fed into the Stones' blender, it showed how they could still take a form of black music and mark it with their own stamp. They'd done it with the blues, rock 'n' roll, reggae, street funk, and disco was just the latest form.

'"Miss You" just happened to be a big disco hit,' said Keith in *Trouser Press*. 'I thank the disco freaks very much, with their flared trousers and slicked back hair. I can't take it very seriously . . . . There have always been clubs where people go where they play records. The problem arose when they started thinking they could make records specifically for that situation. Making it so calculated and insulated. But that's how you can tell a really good disco record. "Miss You" wasn't formularised to be a disco record yet it hit that category. As much as I love to mention names, I can't listen to Rod Stewart's "[Do Ya Think I'm] Sexy[?]" single without cynically grinning. I've known Rod a long time and I think Hollywood just is no good for him.'

But 'Miss You' was the killer hit single that the Stones needed. 'Disco,' admitted *Rolling Stone* with mild distaste, 'but they play it with more aggression than the genuine purveyors.'

However, the flip side's 'Far Away Eyes' played as a novelty tune, as Mick wailed stereotype country lyrics in an Okie-fied country twang. It sounded like an over-the-top redneck impersonation, Benny Hill in a cowboy hat. Gram Parsons must have been turning in his urn, although the balladic backdrop perfectly assimilated the country style via Ronnie's sighing pedal steel guitar.

As Keith revealed later, it could have been different: 'Mick feels the need to get into other caricatures. He's slightly vaudeville in his approach. "Far Away Eyes" is like that. He did it great every time except for the final take. It's good when he does it straight, 'cause it's funny enough doing it without a pantomime. When he sings it as a caricature it sounds like it would be great for a show. You expect Mick to walk out in his cowboy duds on an eighteen-wheeler set. Or sing it into his CB [Citizens' Band radio] as part of his skit.'

Some Girls – originally entitled *More Fast Numbers*, or *Certain Women* – was released on 9 June 1978. Like the previous album, it made number one in the US and number two in the UK, going on to sell eight million copies worldwide.

The album was highly charged and focused compared to its predecessors, with a distinct New York fixation. 'Miss You' opened up, followed by 'When The Whip Comes Down' – the first of the full-tilt punk-energy workouts, set in an NYC fetish club rather than a west London tower block. This punk thing had got to Mick, who insisted, 'Keith is the original punk rocker. You can't out-punk Keith. It's pointless.' The original punk rocker got his wish on this track – to strip down to the bare essentials of Elvis and his original three backing musicians. Mick wasn't so crass as to think he was 'going punk', but there's no denying that both the pace and energy levels were more hot-wired and hedonistic. Another *Black And Blue* might have buried the Stones at this time.

Controversy was stoked by the title track, where Mick lists the supposed preferences of the different women he's encountered while travelling the world. Keith famously remarked that the record was called *Some Girls* 'because we couldn't remember their fucking names!' It was playing into the hands of the angry feminist brigade who railed against the *Black And Blue* sleeve – especially the line, 'black girls just wanna get fucked all night.'

Black civil rights spokesman the Reverend Jesse Jackson cried out for the album to be withdrawn, while black radio stations like New York's WBLS withdrew it from their playlists. Keith was as unapologetic as Mick, when speaking to *Creem*: 'We write our songs from personal experiences. Okay, so over the last fifteen years we've happened to meet extra-horny black chicks – well, I'm sorry, but I don't think I'm wrong and neither does Mick.' Perhaps it was a good job they didn't use the original twenty-minute version.

The album goes out with 'Shattered'. 'That's a classic example of one of the ways Mick and I write songs,' Keith later told me. 'I sit down with a guitar and play that riff, and then at one point I'll go, "It's called 'Shattered'," and from then on the vocal, the way he does it, and what it's about is totally his.' Basically a groove track, 'Shattered' is firmly set in New York City and welds the spirits of punk and disco into a classic Stones hybrid.

The album was universally seen as a return to form. 'It's far from great but it's certainly better than we had any right to expect after all these years,' said Pete Silverton in *Sounds*, which about sums up the general attitude of the time. Having had their previous few albums slagged off, it was time for the Stones to 'prove it' to the press. The fact that they most certainly had wouldn't be fully acknowledged for some time. But still, *Some Girls* went on to become the biggest selling Stones album ever.

Keith summed it up when we talked in 1980: 'Yeah, *Some Girls* . . . just because of the time it came out, etc, etc, and the circumstances, very favourable reaction there, but you know that the next one's gonna get slagged: "Oh, they're just marking time again." But we've just done what we've always done. We'll go in and make a record. We'll go in and make it as good as we can in the period of time that we've got to make it in – which is a long time sometimes, but the bigger a band gets, and the bigger its organisation gets, the longer everything takes. This is one thing I'm always fighting against, saying it shouldn't be like that, but it's just a fact of life. The more that are involved, the bigger the size of the record company, the bigger the importance . . .

'It just takes longer. I mean, we made the first one in ten days, and several of the others too. But now, it's A Rolling Stones Album, and you feel you've got to work and work on it, polish it up . . . and eventually you give in to that pressure a lot of the time, then afterwards you wish you'd just slammed it out, like this rough mix on a cassette. I always try and push it.'

Some Girls was the first Stones album I dealt with as a member of the rock press. I'd been editing the monthly *Zigzag* since the previous May – mainly covering the front line of the punk explosion – and had set out on my mission to get an interview with Keith. But this would take a couple of years, so I did the next best thing and commissioned respected Stones buff Roy Carr's out-takes of a lengthy chat he'd had with the Glimmer Twins for *Creem* and *NME*. It was a rare occasion when Keith and Mick talked into the same tape machine at the same time, almost like a double act.

My review called it, 'very consistent' and mentioned the punk energy. 'I love The Clash but I'll still be keeping an eye on the next Stones eclipse in 1980.' Funnily enough, I honed in on Keith's song, '. . . always the one I look to for more care and raw emotion . . . The song's rough but magic with subtle coursings from the most driving guitar in rock.' In retrospect, I can see I was putting my punk credibility at risk. My magazine had built up such a punk-roots reputation that it was the only organ John Lydon would speak to at the time. Now, in September '78, I surprised everybody by sticking four pages of the Stones between the Buzzcocks and Blondie, with reggae group Culture in the same issue. It was such a silly time, when you had to defend your musical tastes for fear of a flying bottle. Even in 1980, when I did my first interview with Keith, I got some stick when I proudly put him on the cover. Funny how things go – ten years later bands born out of punk, like Primal Scream, would be wearing their Stones influences with pride. (25 years later they'd be supporting them on stage!) But these were volatile times for music, and the Stones were in the thick of it. They'd started punk rock, then become one of its main targets.

Back on the planet: the 'Miss You' photo session.

Keith spoke to Roy about the punks, and the debt they owed to the Stones: 'In America, they kept the line going, whereas in England it seemed that their only objective was to break the line as quickly as possible. Well, there's no way they're gonna achieve that because they've got far too many connections with us. The fact that so many British punk records sound like many of our early records, and that sound is very hard to achieve nowadays, is sufficient evidence in itself. Nevertheless, it seemed to be the particular sound many of them were aiming at. Some went so far as to use some of the old studios we used to use.'

The Harder They Come

With the album at the pressing plant, it was time to prepare for a summer tour. It was also last-orders time for the smack. The Stones went to Todd Rundgren's Bearsville studio, in Woodstock, NY, to rehearse for the tour which was going to feature Ronnie's old mate Ian McLagan on keyboards. Keith was carted in, smacked-out, and recommended black box treatment on his own terms – which didn't rule out other refreshments.

Everyone rallied round as he self-medicated and weaned himself off heroin. Even Mick's new girlfriend, Jerry Hall, who Keith hated, helped to nurse him.

One night, during the rehearsal period, Keith fell for a Swedish model called Lilly Wenglass Green who was a friend of Ronnie's new girlfriend, Jo. The relationship between Keith and Anita was now hopeless, as he couldn't be with her if he wanted to get off smack. So Keith and Lilly hit it off, and would be together for two years. Apparently, her dirty Sid James-style laugh was a major plus.

By the time the tour started, Keith would be able to boast of being clean for longer than a few weeks. When the Stones hit decadent Los Angeles, however, he would start dabbling in smack again. Ronnie and Jo were buying a house in LA, so Keith and Lily rented a place nearby. One close call came when they woke up in bed one morning to find the house was on fire, and had to escape out of the window stark naked. Luckily, as the police and fire brigade were turning up, a cousin of Anita's, who lived up the road, pulled up and whisked them to safety.

But if Keith hadn't been prepared to take serious steps toward becoming smack-free, the tour, and the millions of bucks it entailed, would have been in dire jeopardy. From now on, Keith wouldn't be seen without a Jack Daniel's bottle to hand. *But at least they can't bust me for that,* he seemed to be saying, as he brandished it in nearly every photo.

Cleaning-up also opened the door on the Jagger-Richards wars. As the Stones had risen throughout the sixties, Keith and Mick's respective worlds grew apart. At the start, the former London School of Economics student and the Chuck Berry-loving punk kid were in the same Ford Transit with the same mission.

As they became superstars, Mick followed his business head while relishing the jet-setting lifestyle of his first wife, Bianca. When Keith became addicted, it was all he could do to keep his habit fed and the music together. Mick couldn't control Keith's lifestyle, but he could sure steer the Stones. Big deals, lavish staging, some trendy musical directions, most of the interviews . . . all of which Keith rarely stood in the way of, apart from some of the musical decisions. He might not have approved of the lotus stage, but was probably too out of it to notice until he first set foot on a petal.

The Stones were seen as Mick's band, especially as Keith had always favoured the background anyway. All this was set to change. With Keith back on the ball, he became determined to assert his pivotal role and stop promoters billing the band as 'Mick Jagger and the Rolling Stones'.

The fights would really begin with the next album, which saw Keith easing back into interviews again and playing his arse off, letting them know whose band it really was without saying a word. Mick would start to feel threatened by this, especially when Keith started expressing an occasional interest in business matters. But 1978 was the year that the Keith we know and love today started to show up. It was the year that the heart of the Rolling Stones started beating again.

On Saturday 10 June, the Stones started their first US tour since 1975, with the customary 'secret' gig – this time at Lakeland Civic Centre in Orlando, Florida, where they were billed as 'The Great Southeast Stoned Out Wrestling Champions'. Backstage, Keith bought a stolen .38 revolver from a security guard, which would return to haunt him shortly afterwards.

There wasn't a lotus petal in sight. 'Keeping it simple' seemed to be the motto. Seven weeks, three quarters of a million punters in 24 cities: it covered all the bases in terms of scale, from 2,000 people coming to see 'the Cockroaches' at Washington's Warner Theatre to 90,000 at Philadelphia's JFK Stadium two nights later. The tour also marked the first time in rock history that a band had grossed over a million dollars at the gate.

Support on the tour came from either the great Etta James or Peter Tosh on most of the dates, with bands ranging from the Patti Smith Group to the appalling Foreigner, who were also given a shot. Keith especially wanted Etta, as she'd successfully fought her own battles against drugs and booze and was a brilliant blues singer from the golden age of Chess Records.

There were also small 'surprise' gigs at Atlanta's Fox Theatre, New York's Palladium and the Capitol Theatre in Passaic, New Jersey – 'a cesspool of depravity, poverty, sick oily pizza,' according to *Sounds* correspondent Donna McAllister, who described the show as 'the shortest, the sweetest and most satisfying Stones set I've ever witnessed.' She listed the live set additions from the album as 'When The Whip Comes Down', 'Miss You', 'Lies', 'Beast Of Burden', 'Far Away Eyes' and 'Shattered'. The general vibe was a back-to-our-roots, punk-friendly antidote to the excess of 1975.

McAllister's review captures the sense of the band in a state of rebirth: 'This is the only time I have actually seen the Stones play well. Oh, you can always love them and chuckle because they are always "all over the place", but this night they were serious and the music was stunning. On beat, on key, on time, and in tune, an unprecedented phenomenon. They were inarguably brilliant . . . Keith, grey-faced though he may be, slinks around the stage as always, but now plays his axe to death with remarkable precision.'

One memorable night, after the show at Soldier Field, Chicago, the Stones caught Muddy Waters and Willie Dixon at Muddy's regular club, the Quiet Knight. Keith, Ronnie and Mick got up to play a few of Muddy's own classics, including 'Mannish Boy', 'Rollin' Stone' and 'Got My Mojo Working'.

The tour would culminate on Mick's 35th birthday, 26 July, at Oakland Coliseum, CA. Just after the tour ended, the news came through that Les Perrin, the Stones' venerable press officer, had died. He'd spent the previous ten years looking after their interests during a time of unending turbulence, and was greatly mourned by the whole industry.

Still buzzing from the tour, Keith wanted to charge straight into the studio and start rehearsing for the next album. The band hooked up at the old RCA Studios in LA, where many of their sixties classics were laid down. They spent two weeks working up new songs, and worked on some of the ideas they'd come up with at the Some Girls sessions.

When word came through that Keith Moon had died on 7 September, Bill and Charlie made the funeral. But otherwise, the Stones were into one of their periodic bursts of activity. In October, they appeared on the irreverent TV comedy show *Saturday Night Live*, their first live TV spot for ten years. They were, by all accounts, royally pissed. It was the opening show of the fourth season, a coup d'etat for the programme which spawned *The Blues Brothers* from the skits of Dan Aykroyd and John Belushi. (Incidentally, the Blues Brothers, apart from looking like rock critic and Stones fan Charles Shaar Murray, featured a guy called Steve Jordan on drums, who'd later work with both Keith and the Stones.)

They did three songs from *Some Girls* and a test drive for 'Summer Romance', with Belushi joining in on vocals. Apparently, the dress rehearsal pissed all over the actual broadcast, so it was used on the reruns. Stephen Davis reported how Keith, who couldn't stand up straight, failed to deliver his solitary sentence in a drug skit. Cast member Laraine Newman quipped, 'It's interesting to be standing there working with someone who's dead.'

SNL always put itself forward as the most radically 'out-there' show on TV. Watch those old re-runs now, and it seems quite tame. With all the members of the greatest rock 'n' roll band in the world running amok on booze and drugs, it should have been landmark TV anarchy of the highest order. But Mick caused a stir just by licking Ronnie's lips in front of the camera. Maybe it was Belushi's fault, for providing refreshments from the sound-proof vault he had in his apartment. Asked about the show by *Trouser Press*, Ronnie acknowledged, 'we'd been up partying for three days straight.'

John Belushi would die of a drugs overdose in March 1982. In the July '84 issue of *Beggars Banquet*, Bill German asked Keith if he saw Belushi's death coming:

'You never expect it to happen. It's a kind of retrospective point of view. But there was a certain amount of Brian Jones type of vibrations in John Belushi . . . I never expected Brian to die either, it was a terrible shock. And Belushi was a real pussycat, basically . . . there was that extra "more, more, more" about him that you only recognise when it's too late, when it's all over and done with . . . something of Brian was in Belushi. The more they got, the more insatiable they were.'

New Barbs On The Block

Keith's future had been in the balance since that day he got busted in Newport Pagnell in May '76. 23 October was the day of reckoning. Present in court were Lily Wenglass Green, *SNL* comic Dan Aykroyd and his fellow Canadian, producer Lorne Michaels. Before the Canadian High Court, Keith pleaded guilty to heroin possession. Another piece of twisted luck came his way when it was confirmed the arresting detective had met with a fatal car accident earlier in the year. Keith's past form was ruled out of bounds, and they dropped the trafficking charges. Stephen Davis wrote that the deal and legal fees had cost Keith a couple of million pounds. However, it was still touch and go.

Keith's defence lawyer, Austin Cooper, pleaded with Judge Lloyd Grayburn for his client to be put on probation, while comparing him to tortured artists like Van Gogh, Aldous Huxley, Dylan Thomas, F. Scott Fitzgerald and Billie Holliday. He described Keith's nine-year battle against addiction: 'In 1969 he started with heroin and it got to the state where he was taking such quantities of the drug and getting no euphoria from it. He was taking such powerful amounts – as much as two and a half grams a day – just to feel normal . . .

'He should not be dealt with as a special person, but I ask Your Honour to understand him as a creative tortured person – as a major contributor to art form. He turned to heroin to prop up a sagging existence. I ask you to understand the whole man. He has fought a tremendous personal battle to rid himself of this terrible problem.'

Keith himself told the court: 'If you want to get off it you will, and this time I really wanted it to work. I've got to stay on the treatment if I want to stay off it for good.'

The judge opined that the Stones had glorified drugs in some of their songs, to which Keith replied, 'That is a misconception. I mean, about one per cent of our songs glorify the use of drugs, and Mick Jagger wrote them anyway, not me.'

Keith got off with a one-year suspended sentence, on the condition that he played a special gig at the Canadian National Institute for the Blind within the next six months. He was also ordered to continue treatment and report to a probation officer within the next 24 hours, then on further dates in May and September to confirm how his rehab was going.

So, why a benefit concert for the blind? It was down to the young girl Keith called 'my blind angel', when he told me about her in 1980. He smiled, touched his heart, and talked about Rita, a major Stones fan. 'Followed us all over the place in '75. I had to make sure she was alright, because she'd stand near the front, in all the crush. I'd just get the roadies to make sure she was alright, got a lift home and all that.

Knowing of Keith's plight, she went to speak to the judge. She obviously moved him. A classic case of what goes around comes around. 'My blind angel came through, bless her heart.'

Affirming, 'I feel good about the sentence,' Keith then left for New York. The night of 25 October, he went to see Rockpile, the band featuring Nick Lowe (Johnny Cash's future son-in-law) and Dave Edmunds (my second cousin) at the Bottom Line. He got royally pissed during his celebrations, and climbed up to jam on a couple of songs. A few days later he went home to Jamaica.

The authorities were pissed off that they'd missed their big chance to shut away Keith Richards. After the trial, Keith had been confronted with an earlier quote where he said, 'They're out to make rock 'n' roll illegal.' His reply was, 'Well, they've missed another chance at it. Don't lock up the rock.'

It made the outcry even worse, with Toronto leader writers clamouring for an appeal against the leniency of Keith's sentence – as did Prime Minister Pierre Trudeau, humiliated by ex-wife Margaret's following of the Stones camp. However, the *Toronto Globe* described the verdict as 'a model of enlightened sentencing, one which should pave the way for a more equitable and civilised treatment of convicted drug addicts in Canadian courts.' But the pressure built until the Attorney General wrote to the Justice Minister, saying that the judge had 'erred in principle' by not sending Keith down. Next day, the Federal Crown Prosecutor, John Scollin, won an extension until 3 May 1979, to appeal against Keith's sentence.

One other result of both the Toronto case and his earlier trial at Aylesbury Crown Court was that the press now habitually referred to him as Keith *Richards*. It was a cue for Keith to reclaim the missing part of his surname. For the first time since Andrew Oldham made him drop it, he'd wear his missing letter 's' with pride.

On 3 December, Keith released his first ever solo single – a swinging version of Chuck Berry's 'Run Rudolph Run'. It came out in America first, before getting a UK release in February '79, which seems a weird time to release a Christmas single. I was just finishing off the first *Zigzag* of 1979 when I tracked down an import copy, and wrote, 'Keef in his element: churning out stinging Chuck Berry licks over a skipping rhythm, scraping his partied-out larynx . . . and the B side's a shambling ghost of Jimmy Cliff's "The Harder They Come" – now the side I like best! Great stuff!'

The sleeve depicted a mean-eyed Keith, hoisting a bottle of Rebel Yell. My Keef-spotter instincts told me it dated from the UK '73 tour, and I got him to sign it after our first interview. It was the Christmas number one in my local boozer (I donated my import copy) and Keith was happy to hear he'd beaten Bing Crosby: 'I just wanted to put out a Christmas record. Why not? I had it around for a while – stick it out. And the other side – "The Harder They Come" – is an even bigger jumble. It was like a quick snatch of tape we'd done between two other songs. Did it during a break. But there's nothing on the actual record that was on the tape. Eventually we overdubbed it and wiped everything that was on there off . . . . Ronnie ended up doing most of the drums on it. There's a couple of mistakes on it. I don't care. Some of the records I like best have got mistakes all over 'em.'

In January '79, the Stones hooked up at Compass Point Studios in the Bahamas to cut some new tracks. The same month saw *Some Girls* voted Best Dressed Album of 1978 for its sleeve design in the annual *NME* poll, while *Rolling Stone* named it as Album of the Year, 'Miss You' as Single of the Year and – best of all – the Stones as Band of the Year.

At Compass Point, the Stones laid down some more rough ideas for the new album, including 'Start Me Up', which was still in the works, waiting to get started, and a Latin-disco outing called 'Dance', which would become the subject of wrangling between Keith and Mick – or all-out war, perhaps.

In February, Keith was hit with a dilemma relating to the Canadian court case. The Ministry of Justice's appeal meant that, if he returned to the country to give the charity concerts, he could be served with a subpoena and have his passport confiscated. If he didn't go back, he would be violating the terms of his suspended sentence. Two concerts for the Canadian National Institute for the Blind were announced on 20 March – the venue would be the 5,000-seater Oshawa Civic Stadium in Toronto, on 22/23 April. With Keith on Canadian turf, the Justice Minister would be able to serve the notice of appeal.

The upcoming gig jump-started the New Barbarians, who would go on to tour the States on their own steam. It would be a joint Keith 'n' Ronnie knees-up, mingling Woody's solo material, some Keef songs and Stones nuggets in a similar vein to their '74 Kilburn gigs. It would also be the nearest anyone got to seeing the Stones play during 1979. Ronnie Wood had a new album to promote called *Gimme Some Neck*, and Keith couldn't resist another excuse to go on the road. So it was rehearsals-a-go-go for the month of February at Ron's place in LA. John Belushi was there too.

The album was Ronnie's first as part of a new deal with Columbia – 'I needed the money,' he disarmingly claimed. It was more straightforward rock 'n' roll than the first two, and Keith only appeared on two tracks, singing harmonies on the Bob Dylan song 'Seven Days' and playing a sturdy guitar on 'Buried Alive', one of the better numbers. Ronnie had roped together a formidable lineup: Joseph 'Zigaboo' Modeliste from the Meters on drums – suggested by Charlie Watts, who also played, because he needed some time off – and jazz-fusion maestro Stanley Clarke on bass, making for a taut and tight rhythm section. Bobby Keys – finally allowed back on board after some years playing bars as 'Mr Brown Sugar' – and Ian McLagan were in there too, on sax and keyboards.

The Barbarians had been named by Neil Young, but had to tack on the 'New' after they discovered there was another band of the same name. (Possibly the same Barbarians who scored a minor sixties hit with 'Moulty', about their one-armed drummer.) They played first on the night of the Institute for the Blind gig, to be followed

'It's incredibly rare to find a playmate like Keith Richards' – Ronnie Wood.
The Degenerate Everly Brothers guffaw their way to San Diego.

by an almost-Stones set that saw the line-up joined by Mick Jagger and Bill Wyman.

Neil Young was nearly a Barbarian too. 'He was really involved,' said Ronnie in *Trouser Press*. 'He came down from San Francisco to meet Keith, 'cause they'd never met and, as things had it, the timing was wrong. Keith was unreachable while Neil was in LA, and then Neil had to return to San Francisco . . . He gave us the name the New Barbarians . . . It was like a parting gesture.' Jeff Beck and Jimmy Page were also up for it, but managerial red tape interfered.

There's an excellent double-bootleg of the first New Barbarians gig, called *Blind Date*. It's more or less the whole proceedings, right from the announcement by John Belushi: 'I'm just a sleazy actor on a late-night TV show, but here's some real musicians! Come on up here! Keith Richards! Ron Wood! The New Barbarians! Go nuts!' The gang toppled headfirst into the opening greeting of 'Sweet Little Rock 'N' Roller'. It was unbridled Keef, off the leash. Playing his own gig, for his own freedom. One little girl in the crowd couldn't see his elation, but she knew it was all down to her. I hope she got a lift home that night.

'Before They Make Me Run' has never sounded so suitable for an occasion. Keith sang like his life depended on it, and the raunchy interplay between the guitars was astounding. The country twang in Keith's voice, when he sang, 'there's not a dry eye in the house,' was particularly moving.

Full marks to the Judge – even though Keith had been served with notice of appeal against his sentence, which would be submitted at the end of June.

With a working band in operation, it was a logical move to take the New Barbarians on the road. There were no plans for the Stones to be gigging, so Keith and Ronnie's addiction to life on the road could be satiated. They kicked off their US tour on 24 April in Ann Arbor, Michigan, and went on to traverse the country for the following month, selling out large venues everywhere. 7 May even saw them storm Madison Square Gardens.

It was a first for Keith. His first foray onto a stage without the Rolling Stones. The first time he'd played a whole set with another drummer since Charlie first took the seat. He was starting to see that there was life outside the Stones.

NME's Charles Shaar Murray attended the Houston, Texas show on 12 May and loved it. 'It's not as spectacular and legend-soaked as a Stones show, but it has a warmth and humanity and friendliness that will never waft a stage that has Mick Jagger on it and THE ROLLING STONES on the poster outside. Whether you still believe in the great Stones myth of The Greatest Rock 'N' Roll Band In The World or whether you see them in the post-punk light as a bunch of poncey smacked-back old jackoffs, they can never be just a rock band playing for your pleasure and theirs. The New Barbarians can.'

The July issue of *Trouser Press* had a cartoon of Keith and Ronnie on the cover. Their writer, Robert Duncan, had caught up with the 'Barbs' in New York, and commented on Keith's demeanour. 'There is a new, wilful, jaunty bounce to his gait and ease to his manner in general. He is lithe, as he bops among friends and associates assembled on the sidewalk, and the smile with which he greets those friends seems genuinely friendly and far removed from the ironic, rotting grin of days past. More than that there appears to be real human colour in the face, which, remarkably because it's still daylight, is sans shades and nearly sans makeup (a hint of eyeliner maybe) . . . Keith bounces out from the shade of the hotel canopy, steps over and greets Stanley [Clarke] and greets [his wife] Carolyn and then reaches up to Carolyn to take the seven month old Clarke baby from her arms. And, in a moment, Keith slips one hand under the baby's bottom and with his free hand taps gently at the child's nose and with his mouth wrinkled up into a pucker, Keith Richards, Prince of Darkness, lately manque, begins to make baby sounds. Coochie-coo.'

If the truth be known, that incident wasn't so extraordinary. When it comes to kids, Keith's an unashamed sucker. In 2003, when my girlfriend gave him a fairy story written by her nine-year-old daughter he visibly melted, laughed and scribbled in her autograph book. He loves 'em, and Marlon ain't done so bad – neither have his daughters.

As Robert Duncan commented on Keith, 'though his Edge City Style was appealing as metaphor and appealing as any dangerous game is to the spectator, you never really wanted him to go over and the odds on that were getting shorter all the time.'

After a gig in Washington DC, Stanley Clarke – perhaps the most intriguing inclusion in the band, given his jazz background – talked about his surprising long-time admiration for Keith: ' . . . One thing I respect about him is that what he does he does to the hilt. He does it full, like, "This is me and this is what's happening and if you like it, great, and if you don't . . ." Boom. And I'm like that. I get on the plane in the morning and drink protein drinks and I'm sitting right next to Keith and he's drinking fucking bourbon, and we're still friends because I respect him and he respects me.'

But there was still the matter of the appeal against Keith's sentence. It began on 27 June, before five Court of Appeal judges in Toronto. Keith's lawyer said that his client was now off of drugs, but that a jail term would probably cause a relapse. Keith filed an affadavit with the court, saying, 'I have grimly determined to change my life and abstain from any drug use. I can truthfully say that the prospect of ever using drugs again in the future is totally alien to my thinking. My experience has also had an important effect not only on my happiness, but on my happiness at home in which my young son is brought up.' In truth, we couldn't expect our Keith to follow this to the letter – but he was sincere about giving up smack for Marlon.

The Crown Prosecutor argued that Keith should be jailed, if only to safeguard Canada's reputation for dealing with drugs. But on 17 September, the Court of Appeal rejected the clamour to send Keith to prison. Finally, it was all over.

But further problems loomed. On 20 July, seventeen-year-old Scott Cantrell shot himself in the head with a .38 Smith & Wesson revolver, at Keith's house in Westchester, upstate New York. The boy, who had been hanging out with Anita, was rushed to Northern Westchester Hospital and died soon afterwards. Anita was remanded in custody, then released the next day on bail, charged with possession of stolen property. (The gun was the one that Keith bought on the opening night of the US tour from a security guard.) She told the police that Scott had been playing with the weapon all evening, and talking about Russian roulette.

Anita was cleared of any involvement with Cantrell's death – but it could have been disastrous for Keith, given that the stolen firearm was his. The press accused her of everything from black magic orgies to animal sacrifices, while local nuns told police they sometimes heard 'strange chants, gun shots and loud music.' The incident was probably the last straw that broke the tottering camel's back of Keith and Anita's relationship.

The New Barbarians only played once in the UK – at the Knebworth Fayre on 11 August 1979, when they supported headliners Led Zeppelin on a bill which also included Todd Rundgren's Utopia, Commander Cody and his Lost Planet Airmen and cockernee pub geezers Chas and Dave. It was another long day in the stately grounds.

The band had been up all night, with Philip Chen having to stand in at the last moment for Stanley Clarke. They were customarily late coming on, didn't have a very good sound, and visibility was poor in the huge crowd. It was obviously difficult for the Barbs to get a vibe going. But, in their gloriously ramshackle fashion, they pulled it off.

And the change in Keith was noticeable. He was on the ball – obviously not straight, but no longer at death's door, and loving every moment. As *Sounds'* Pete Silverton observed, 'Keith Richards didn't fall over, he drank Jack Daniel's straight from the bottle and his shoelaces were pink.'

On a less positive note, some journalists made much of the fact that Keith was enjoying a drink.

But he'd just quit smack. That's what happens.

They even drew attention to the fact that his hair was turning grey.

That happens, too. But, for a man in his mid-thirties, Keith's barnet was faring pretty well – considering how the previous three years had been the most turbulent of his life.

Now, he was ready to leap into a new decade, with guns blazing. And there were times when he probably felt like he needed a gun, as he began to reassert his position in 'Mick's band'.

CHAPTER ELEVEN

WAITING ON A FRIEND

The Turning Point

The Stones had reconvened in Paris, in late June 1979, to work on their new album. They would continue on and off through to October. *Some Girls* would be a tough act to follow. It had been a new lease of life for the band and for Keith, and needed to be matched by another hot-stone belter.

But *Emotional Rescue* just didn't set the house on fire. A lot of it was fine, but it was not the requisite tour de force. Braver and more experimental in some departments, it still occasionally came over like the sloppy seconds after the Stones had shot their load on *Some Girls*. Unsurprisingly, perhaps, much of it was worked-up from out-takes of that album – but then, so was their far superior next album, *Tattoo You*, which was made up almost entirely of leftovers from '72 onwards.

Part of the disappointment of *Emotional Rescue* might have been down to the growing conflict between Keith and Mick. Now that Mr. Redlands' cylinders were starting to fire on full-blast, Keith would sometimes claim he was surprised when Mick saw his cleaning up as a 'power grab'. As the squabbles began, he was telling friends that he'd even heard that Mick wished he was still on junk.

'That was where it got fucked up, because Mick had got to used to holding the strings and he didn't want to relinquish one little bit,' Keith told *Mojo*'s Sylvie Simmons in 2002. 'So then I had to start to get into that, which culminated in [mid-eighties album] *Dirty Work* and the Third World War!'

The creation of *Emotional Rescue* seems to have been uphill all the way. When recording began in Paris in June, with Chris Kimsey engineering again, Mick was in the lengthy throes of his divorce from Bianca, and had to keep breaking off to go back to London. Bill Wyman is disparaging about the July-August sessions in his book, citing 'arguments, sickness, lateness and other frustrations.' That period had also seen the incident with Anita and the dead boy at Keith's house, plus Keith and Ron's break to play with the New Barbarians at Knebworth – which extended way beyond that one afternoon.

The hothouse creativity that spawned *Some Girls* seems to have been absent, as the Stones just continued revamping leftovers. (The working title for the new album had been *Certain Women* at one point, wilfully echoing its predecessor.)

Keith and Mick started mixing in November, but soon fell out. They argued about everything: the sound, the track selection, the musical direction. The storm that raged over the album's eventual opening track, 'Dance (Part One)', would turn into one of those 'good old British compromises' as the warring pair tried to placate each other. Like many Stones songs, it had started life as a jam between Keith and Ronnie, a loose, funky guitar work-out that Keith regarded as something like Junior Walker's 'Shotgun'. Then enter Mick – 'with a fucking opera,' according to Keith.

When we met the following October – ostensibly to talk about the new album – the opening track was one of the things that got Keith's goat.

'Originally "Dance" had a whole vocal thing,' he explained. 'It was swamped with vocals. Mick had decided he'd got to write this song to this track. He did a lot of work on it and he did a good job, but it totally nullified the track. I said, "Let's make it an instrumental." But Mick said, "We can't waste time on an album with only ten tracks and instrumentals." Instrumentals have got a dirty name. Everyone thinks it's just a filler, but some of the best rock 'n' roll records I can remember are instrumentals – Johnny and the Hurricanes, Bill Black's Combo … instrumentals used to be a regular part of your diet.

'We used to put out instrumentals from the very first album – "Now I've Got A Witness". Just let a band have a blow once in a while. Sometimes you can screw a track up by putting a vocal on it. You lose some of its impact because it's neither a song and it's no longer an instrumental. I'd much rather have kept "Dance" as it was. In the end it became a compromise – do the vocals again but rewrite it. You win some, you give a little, you take a little, and I wanted "All About You" on there. But if I wanna listen to "Dance", I listen to my cassette of the instrumental!'

In the end, the song appeared on the album with a chanted hook, and Mick's drawling lyric, now situating itself on the corner of West Eighth Street and Sixth Avenue.

Keith's warts 'n' all attitude to recording had clashed with Mick's more painstakingly polished approach ever since *Beggars Banquet*. The creative tension certainly worked on *Exile*, the album that Keith had more to do with than any other. But I'd been hearing about the escalating conflict in the studio since Keith started shaping up.

'Well …', he replied, choosing his words carefully. 'I always get a bit obstinate, 'specially towards him [Jagger] when I think, "Christ, we've been working on this thing nearly two years, and if I don't watch it it's not gonna come out unless I start kicking the fuckin' walls down and stuff." But that happens with every album!' Cue massive laughter. 'You ain't gonna get through two years in the studio without someone getting shirty.'

Keith had always been there as an audible presence, but aspects like musical styles and track listings had been taken over by Mick. *Emotional Rescue* was full of uneasy truces but, by *Dirty Work* in '85, the conflicts had all but split the group. Mick finally had to pursue a solo career so that he could be In Charge, to be followed eventually by a disgruntled Keith.

During the *Emotional Rescue* sessions, they would make up their differences and hitch up again at New York's Electric Lady Studios – but not before a prolific burst of activity from Keith. In November '79, he appeared on albums by Steve Cropper (of Booker T. and the MGs) and Screamin' Jay Hawkins, as well as joining Ronnie on Ian McLagan's solo album, *Troublemaker*. Keith played on a reggae outing called 'Truly', and a remake of 'Mystifies Me' from Ronnie's first album. He also noticed, with some disdain, that Ronnie was cultivating a major freebasing habit. Bobby Keys had brought the pipe along one night and Ron was off – proving the old adage, 'One hit and you're hooked.'

As the end of '79 approached, Keith was a bit down. He never hung out at

Living for the city. Keith and Stevie Wonder at New York's Xenon club, December 1979. Keith's old friend had just played Madison Square Garden.

Studio 54 with the jet-setting Mick, and his best mate Ron was immersed in a drug problem that Keith really didn't need. Sure, he enjoyed a line, but if he grabbed hold of the pipe with the same gusto that he approached everything else, he'd be a goner for sure.

It would be compounded when Ronnie and his girlfriend, Jo, got busted on the Caribbean island of St Maarten the following February, with over two hundred grams of bugle. Ron says he was set up, but, given Keith's recent trials, it was the last thing the Stones needed. Ronnie and Jo were locked up for five days, before being deported to America. In the meantime, Keith took to hanging out a lot with Freddie Sessler in Florida, or partying for days in New York on Rebel Yell bourbon. He was seeing less and less of Lil, who'd found it too hard to steer him away from the temptations of his everyday life, and Anita was still fucked-up. But Keith's 36th birthday, on 18 December 1979, would prove to be a turning point.

Keith celebrated his first clean birthday for years at New York's Roxy roller rink. It was an unlikely venue, being a roller-disco where many of the revellers careered around on skates. Bobby Keys turned up, as did London jeweller David Courts, who presented Keith with what became one of his trademark possessions: a large, silver skull ring. He's never taken it off since. Keith says he wears it to remind him that we're all the same underneath, and that death could be just around the corner. At our first interview, he let me try it on – it's a heavy old bastard – and he showed me David Courts' catalogue. (Way out of a poor writer's price range!)

It was at the party that Keith met a 22-year-old model called Patti Hansen. Friends had been telling him about her for a while, and Jerry Hall took the opportunity to introduce them to each other. The rest of the night was chaos. Anita turned up, shouting that she wanted to see Keith – maybe in the hope of a reconciliation, now that Lilly Wenglass Green was off the scene. But Keith had his other presents to open – notably, a gift-wrapped, naked call-girl. It clearly wasn't the right time to meet a new girlfriend, but Keith did call Patti, and they started to spend more and more time together.

The girl from Staten Island was already a top model, and had made a couple of films. On the fleeting occasions that I met her, she seemed totally unaffected and laughed a lot. That must suit Keith, I thought to myself. By all accounts, they're pretty similar people from similar backgrounds. Her parents were working class, too – Dad was a bus driver. And her modelling career started when she was spotted by a scout at a Stones gig in '75.

Patti was soon accompanying Keith on the rounds of New York clubs, bars and record shops for days on end. She came back from her family's place on New Year's Eve to find him sitting on the stairs outside her apartment, waiting for her. Keith liked being out of the orbit of drug dealers and hangers-on. Patti would influence him to rid himself of the final vestiges of his habit, which had trailed off into the odd dabble. Keith started filling the hole in his heart, instead of a hole in his arm. Love is better than rehab, any day. But there was never any tabloid bollocks about 'taming wild man Keith'.

Apart from that of Charlie Watts, personal relationships had never seemed to work out in the Stones. But, 24 years and two daughters later, Keith and Patti are still going strong. By 1980, Keith was ready for someone like Patti.

Mixing of *Emotional Rescue* took place at Electric Ladyland right the way through until April – longer than it took to record it! Mick and Keith, who'd both been doing the mixes, argued all the way about which tracks to use.

As usual, Keith had recorded and mixed his token solo track last, but this also became a sore point. He actually had a whole bunch of songs, as bootleg albums testify. There were the Canadian sessions, which had led to plans to release an entire solo album called *Bad Luck* in '79. Sadly, it would never see the light of day, stifled by record company nerves over the flop of Ronnie's most recent solo album.

The songs included 'We Had It All', the Dobie Gray track Keith had been smitten with in '74. In the early days, unless a song was intensely personal to Keith, Mick would end up singing it. 'Ruby Tuesday' may have been a Keith song, but it suited Mick's voice. But, as the years progressed, a Stones fan could always rely on Keith's solo spots as a source of genuine raw feeling.

Keith's heartbreakingly fragile version of 'We Had It All' would have been one of the Stones' finest moments, if allowed to escape the studio. It would be part of the impetus for his X-Pensive Winos project in the late eighties. A cracked, wounded ballad aching with the pain of lost love, oozing emotion with every broken syllable and lick of the guitar. I procured a copy in '83, shortly before hooking up with Keith again, and ejaculated my praise when I saw him. It made him chuckle with satisfaction:

'Ohh, the Dobie Gray song. That's come out too, has it? Yeah . . . I just cut that one in the afternoon when I was waiting for everyone else to turn up. Dobie Gray cut it at the same time as when he did "Drift Away". That just sort of slipped

'She's my little rock 'n' roll.' Patti and Keith.

by everyone, y'know? . . . . It was me waiting for Mick and Ronnie to turn up, or the engineer. I think it was done with the tape op, Charlie and me, basically. Chris Kimsey was on piano, I think. It was just like one of those, while we're waiting for the session to start – "I've just remembered this song!", and bashed it out.'

But, in the end, it was 'All About You' that became one of the most famous Keef tracks to make it onto an official release. Although lambasted in some typically snide reviews, 'All About You' stands out as one of the few moments of real emotion on the album. Tender but bitter, the guitar never falters, the brass wheezes, and Keith's piano playing is steady while his voice is a crackling croak. (Unsurprising, really, as he thought he was doing a guide vocal!)

It comes from deep inside, not from the singer's ego. Lines like, 'I'm so sick and tired / Of hanging around with dogs like you,' and, 'Always the first to get laid / Always the last bitch to get paid,' are undoubtedly vicious putdowns, but the last line's 'How come I'm still in love with you?' deflected any accusations of sexism. And made you wonder who it was about.

When Keith and I were talking about the album a couple of months after its release, I said it was my favourite tune. He seemed somewhat taken aback, as if it was the first time anyone had mentioned it. The ice was broken, and it melted into our Jack Daniel's.

Keith gave a short laugh and looked down. 'I enjoyed doing it. That was another of them songs which must've been around for about three years, maybe even a bit more. I wrote it in some soundcheck, Charlie was keeping time. I was convinced myself, because it came so easy, that the actual basic song, "This is someone else's and I can't remember what it is."

'For ages I was hawking this tape and saying, "Whose is this?", and they'd go, "Uh . . . hold on . . .um . . ." Nobody could put their fingers on it, so after three years I thought, "Well . . . I must've written it!" So I went ahead and finished the lyrics and that.'

'All About You' was the last track to be finished for the album, and it sounds like it. It conjures up images of Keith sitting alone at the piano, in the early hours when everybody else had gone home. He finally nailed it down at Electric Lady, having been up for the best part of a week.

'When we eventually cut the track and put the horns on it last year [1979], I still wasn't entirely convinced exactly how it should go. So I had the track and everybody was saying, "You've got a song to put on it then we should put it on the album." But I still hadn't written it. Then everybody went home and I sat down by the microphone and started it on the spot. I hadn't written anything for it. I just started doing it and after two or three hours it started to take shape. I put harmonies on it . . . although when I was doing it I still wasn't thinking necessarily of me singing it. I was just sort of writing it and doing it to keep it for myself to remember how it went, and to play it to Mick if he wanted to do it. But when it was finished, everyone said it should stay like that, so I said, "Fine, okay."'

The Jack must have been making its presence felt, because at this point on my interview tape I blurt out, 'You sound pissed!' Which he did, laughing in agreement.

'Yeah . . . I didn't try to clean it up. If I'd tried to change it I probably would've screwed it up. I like it as it is. So I staggered off into the night and left a trail of blood all up Sixth Avenue.'

When we met again in 1983 at the Savoy Hotel, Keith said the song was his way of reacting to all the shit that had gone down in the previous year. It certainly had people looking through their microscopes, with many assuming it was about Anita. Or Mick. Or Keith's farting dog, as he told a couple of writers.

'Nobody would talk to me for six months because they thought it was all about them!' laughed Keith. 'Everybody thought it was about them. Even my kids came up and asked, "Daddy, is it all about me?"! Everybody took it personally. In a way, it was just a way of finishing off the whole thing. The last thing I did on the album. Mixed it, cut my thumb open on the Jack Daniel's bottle that had smashed while I was doing the vocal, and left a trail of blood down Eighth Street from Electric Ladyland. And that was it. I said, "That's gotta be it – I'm not doing anything else for this album!" But for about six months everyone . . . Ronnie – "Is it all about me?" But it's probably more about me than anybody. It is more me than anybody. [Atlantic Records executive] Earl McGrath chucked in his job because of that song. He thought it was all about him! That had an amazing effect, that one!' In '95 Keith said that this 'litany of insults' was about Mick, as well as his farewell to Anita. Oh well . . .

Emotional Rescue finally emerged in June '80, housed in a startling thermographic sleeve – the images of the band purportedly photographed with a camera that reacted to body temperature. It became the first Stones album since *Goats Head Soup* to top the charts on both sides of the Atlantic. However, it didn't have the impact of its predecessor. The reviews took the standard line about the Stones trading on past glories – but this time, they were right.

When I tracked down a bootleg of *Emotional Rescue* out-takes and alternate versions called *Accidents Will Happen*, a couple of years later, it confirmed that most of the best tracks had been left off the album. Keith's 'Claudine' harks back to the blackened groove-power of *Exile* – but, as it was about Andy Williams' ex-wife, Claudine Longet, who stood trial for shooting her lover in the US on the same day Keith was in Aylesbury Crown Court, it was deemed too legally hot to handle. And then there was 'We Had It All'. Just this couple of tracks would have transformed the album.

Where's Me Car?

The new album had to be promoted, so maybe I'd get that interview with Keith at last. But the launch party – for which the invitations came in a plastic prescription-pill container – was a last-minute letdown. The venue was to have been the Chelsea Pensioners' gaff in Kings Road, but, despite (or maybe because of) the heavy-handed irony, it was pulled on the very day.

I'd dreamt of sitting down in a room with Keith Richard(s) for the best part of seventeen years. During all that time, I'd only had press reports, assorted books, TV interviews and hand-me-down stories to go on. It had drawn me a picture of the man: from the fanatical young punk, hell-bent on spreading his R&B gospel, to the drug-soaked Satanic Majesty swashbuckling his way through the courts of the land. Through it all, Keith had remained the Stones' rhythmic engine room. But then there was the smacked-up outlaw who fell asleep onstage. And now, after the Toronto ordeal, Keith had shaped up and got back in the saddle. He might have toppled out of it a couple of times, but by 1980 he was pretty clean – although he still indulged in other refreshments.

But all that shit is just the tip. I was more concerned with the iceberg. There's Keith the Legend, then there's Keith the Man. Many of the stories had their grounding in truth – albeit blown out of proportion – but public glimpses of the Man had been few and far between. But, as I was to find, once he warms to someone there's no longer any guard to be let down. He's not Keith the . . . Anything. He's just Keith.

I'd spent three years trying to secure an interview for *Zigzag*, the fanzine I was now editing. I made call after call to the long-suffering publicist Claudine, at former *NME* journalist and Stones confidant Keith Altham's PR firm. The schedule for Keith's imminent visit to London changed all the time. Then, I was getting pissed-up one day with a gang of mates on a boating holiday in the Norfolk Broads. When we stopped at a phone box, word came in that the man was in town, and yes, he would talk to *Zigzag* – scene of the legendary encounter with Nick Kent six years before. *Turn the boat around!* He was only giving one interview, and that was with me.

Tales were already circulating about his visits to the Altham office. Jack Daniel's bottle in hand, he'd swagger in and hold court, before zooming off down Old Compton Street in the Blue Lena at a restrained 70 mph.

Our rendezvous was to be on Friday 26 September, at Blake's Hotel, a plush little establishment owned by former actress Anouska Hempel. I arrived at the pre-arranged time and was told to ring his room on the house phone. 'Hello,' drawled a familiar-sounding voice. Somewhat flutteringly, I announced myself. 'I'll be right down.' Two minutes later, in strode Keith Richards accompanied by Patti Hansen. Grey army sweater, black thatch, big grin and outstretched hand, all aboard that unique, loose-limbed amble.

'How ya doin', man?'

All my nerves evaporated instantly with that first grin. I no longer felt like an annoying gnat that needed to be dispatched – as I had with many a lesser so-called rock star.

'We'll do the interview at the Stones office,' he announced, before a typical Keith afterthought. 'Now I've just gotta find the car!'

We embarked on some exploration around Kensington. I immediately felt at ease in his company, and he was obviously deeply in love with Patti. He must have been used to awestruck fans, but there was no play-acting or pulling rank.

We traversed those salubrious streets with an 'I-know-it's-'round-here-some-where' narrative from Keith., who also told how they'd got back in the early hours of that morning from Tramp. Finally, we rounded into a leafy square where we spotted the faithful Bentley, halfway up the curb.

No chauffeurs here. Away we went! Through Kensington, down to the Embankment, with Keith chatting away happily. By now it was approaching rush hour, so the traffic was fairly busy.

Suddenly Keith broke off the conversation. 'Oops, I'm going the wrong way!' Without a second thought, and at rather high speed, he launched into a tyre-shredding U-turn across three lanes of rush-hour traffic, blowing kisses and waving regally at the gaping motorists. There was much commotion and horn-parping, but we were soon heading the right way to Cheyne Walk, home to the Stones' office.

We backed up to the front door and strode in. 'Hi, darlin',' Keith greeted the receptionist, who was already reaching under her desk. 'Jack Daniel's?' Out came the bottle and we headed up the stairs, to a comfy room where we both slumped on a luxurious brown-leather couch. Keith commenced the emptying of both the JD bottle and my packet of Marlboros.

His interview mode was very like his driving – he went wherever his impulse took him. His langorous, cackle-peppered drawl offered up succinct comments and one-liners. Keith's a past master of the swerve, but he released tantalising glimpses of what was going on in his world. Of his family life, he was protective, about his drug use, he was astonishingly frank – though, in retrospect, now he'd knocked smack on the head, he had little fear of being busted again. And then, of course, there was music.

My front-page feature in the November 1980 *Zigzag* covered nine pages and led off with the following description, which still holds true today: 'The 1980 model Keith Richards is devoid of Rock Star flash, maturing like a caring, kind-ly old blues musician. But he still possesses an indefinable swagger that makes any of the preening idiots that still profess to be R 'n' R stars look the pathetic buffoons they really are.'

I hate the phrase 'down to earth', but Keith revels in being as normal as his wealth and fame will allow, while still existing in what experts call, 'Keith Time.' No rules, no 'petty morals', but, at his very essence, a consuming passion for the music that got him started in the first place.

We eased in by talking about the eponymous record label the Stones were trying to get off the ground, with artists like the late Peter Tosh and Jim Carroll. It was a rare first: Keith talking about the music biz!

'I think they're squealing like fat pigs,' he opined, 'there weren't as much in the trough this year as they'd expected. No way is the record business declining, it just ain't growing as fast as they'd all got used to expecting. You know – 30 per cent more in America

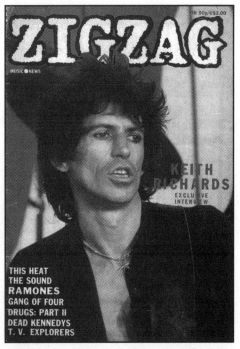

Keith on the cover of the November 1980 issue of Zigzag, *featuring my interview with him.*

almost every year for the last few years. Suddenly they only got twenty per cent more, so they start squealing and axing everybody, and giving the artists a hard time. "Aw, I was going to buy a Rolls Royce this year, and now I can't afford it because we're only twenty per cent up, and not 30 per cent up on business." And they start screaming, "Recession!" Use that as an excuse, come down heavy on the musicians.'

The Stones were powerful enough to operate their own label, within the auspices of a major. By the time of *Emotional Rescue*, they were going through EMI. After a late-eighties period with Sony, they signed with Virgin – which Richard Branson promptly sold on to EMI. By that time they'd come a further full circle, in that the Rolling Stones was the only act on Rolling Stones Records – just like when they started the label. But, in 1980, Keith really had hopes for it. The Stones were selling bucket-loads, untouched by the so-called 'recession' – whose sales figures, by the year 2000, would retrospectively seem like a boom.

'Since we have our own label, they turn round, and think, "Oh, you've got a label, you're one of us,"' said Keith of the industry types. 'Bullshit, man! We're not. We're just gonna do what we do, anyway. It don't affect us that much, at least not noticeably. We're still gonna try and get this label off the ground slowly. Apart from just ourselves, Peter Tosh has done really well, much better than anyone expected . . . He's just broken in South America real big. He did these big festivals over there, and suddenly we're getting this demand for Peter Tosh records, and we ain't got 'em! Factory didn't press enough.'

Up until the previous year, this was the sort of comment you'd have expected Mick Jagger to make. No wonder he was alarmed. Keith was paying attention to marketing strategy and A&R duties, focusing on the finer details of everything emblazoned with the Rolling Stones tongue-logo. I could never have imagined this from the ghost-like outlaw clinging to the dock at Aylesbury Crown Court, less than four years before – or from 'Keef' at any time since the Stones kicked off their record label ten years before, with 'Brown Sugar'.

Maybe hearing Keith talk record business wasn't as front-page friendly as junkie business. But the two areas met in RSR's star of the moment, rock 'n' roll poet Jim Carroll, from the East Village – the New York hotbed that had also spawned Patti Smith, writer-musician Richard Hell, and a host of artists thriving under the original shadow cast by sleaze-art figureheads like the Velvet Underground and William Burroughs.

Like Burroughs and the Velvets, heroin had played a big role in Carroll's life, and his novel, *The Basketball Diaries*, was a brilliantly graphic account of its subterranean world. His debut album, *Catholic Boy*, was lined up for released on Rolling Stones Records, trailered by the single 'People Who Died' – essentially a role call of late street acquaintances of Carroll's, some of whom had gone a hit too far.

On 26 June, the Stones had held a party to launch *Emotional Rescue* at the turbulent-but-brilliant mid-town club Danceteria. It was where the classic photos of Keith in white shirt and black vest, clutching a bottle of Jack Daniel's, hail from.

Keith with his best mate Jack, enjoying the Emotional Rescue *launch party at New York's Danceteria club.*

After the party, he was going to Jim Caroll's gig at a club called Trax to play on 'People Who Died'. That bottle of JD could have been partly responsible, but he'd been up all night on a session, carried on at the Stones' office at Rockefeller Plaza (with Carroll), then done the album launch.

By the time he clambered on stage at Trax, Keith was slaughtered. In the bar, he'd been falling into tables. On the stage, he ploughed into the track like a nuclear pig in Berry-pickled shit. People remarked how great it was to see his sizzling raunch running amok. But then, only a week later, Jagger would announce that the Stones wouldn't be touring in 1980 either. Keith, despite seeing him only a few days earlier, found out by telex as Mick left for a holiday with Jerry.

When I brought up Jim Carroll, Keith started laughing: 'Yeah . . . I did a couple of numbers with him in New York, but I was drunk so, "Yeah, alright!" Actually Mick was supposed to join me but he chickened out at the last minute. Cunt.'

The ice broken by his insult to Jagger, Keith continued talking about Rolling Stones Records: 'That album [*Catholic Boy*] should be out soon. We haven't got enough staff to work on more than one album at a time, so they're waiting until they don't have to do as much work on *Emotional Rescue*, or whatever. When that's over they'll put out Jim Carroll's album.

'He's good, and he gets better because he cut the album once a couple of years ago, and I said, "You should do some gigs for a year, and think about it again." So they recut it after a year of working, and it's a good record. It's a fairly basic sound. He uses his voice kinda like Lou Reed, almost half-talking. He'd written a couple of books before he started writing songs, so there's some good lyrics.'

Carroll may have regarded himself as a male Patti Smith, his onetime girlfriend, but his musical career would never take off. But he'd be immortalised by Leonardo DiCaprio in the film of *The Basketball Diaries*.

We spoke about *Emotional Rescue*. In September 1980, I had no idea of the extent of the conflict between the Glimmer Twins, which had built up since Keith cleaned up during the making of the album. Our interview was basically to promote the record, so Keith should have been howling its praises. Instead he came out with, 'That album's not by any means the best of the stuff that we did . . . It's just, up to a point, what was ready and what we could finish in time, because it has to be out by March or April or whatever it was.'

He went on to explain how the Stones made albums at that time – the basic blueprint that has become more disciplined over the years. They had whacked down a load of ideas and gradually honed them into album form. Hence, the next album, *Tattoo You*, was halfway in the bag already.

By now the Jack was being passed at regular intervals and a lot of laughs were being had.

So he already had the next album sussed?

'Yeah, they sent me six C90 cassettes full of stuff, not all finished, but ideas for songs, a few demos here and there and a surprising amount of finished stuff, a lot of instrumentals. Some of the stuff went back into the mid-seventies, stuff with Billy Preston just jamming, riffs . . . but there's an album there – although we'll probably put a basic album together and see what we need to finish it off. Then we might go in and record for a couple of weeks to cut a couple of new ones to add.'

So people will assume the Stones have taken two years to record just this one particular album?

'They're quite right – in a way. Having so much stuff, we've just had songs coming out of our ears lately. Also you do write quite a lot of songs in two years, try 'em out. Some songs actually take two years to get out of the mind and onto tape. You try it three or four different ways over a few months and it doesn't quite work, and then one day later someone says, "Remember that one?", and you remember it slightly differently and you get it in one, things like that.

'I mean, it's almost as bad as not having enough – not quite, that's the worst feeling [laughs] – but having a lot, it takes so long because you've got to listen to everything you've got. That takes up a load of time because you've got so much stuff.

Then you cut that down to a short list, eventually get it down to album length as far as songs go, and then start editing them down, 'cos some of them are too long.

'It's always a compromise, because it's for a specific reason. You're saying this is it, but we all know that there's lots of stuff left on the floor which a lot of people like as well. The trouble is, you just can't please everybody with one album. It's just not possible. Everybody wants to hear their idea of what the Stones is. There's the old timers who remember from the year dot, then there's the ones who believe we popped out of the ground with "Satisfaction", then there's the lot who joined us with *Beggars Banquet*, the "Brown Sugar" lot. There's people who didn't get into us until the seventies. Everyone's got their idea of what the Stones are about, which I suppose gets more and more confusing the longer you exist.

'It gets impossible if you try and live up to it. We just do what we do and hope they like it. I mean, usually more and more you find that people come up with interesting ideas on an album a year later. Me too. It'll take that long to get a perspective on the last album. I'm too close to it right now. I've only just healed up from the last sessions! [laughs] Beat me own record – nine days on a stretch! Once you get in the studio it doesn't really matter. It's timeless, like hibernation [snigger]. One tape op drops, you wake another one up!'

'So how d'ya keep awake then?' I asked, with faux-naivety.

'I dunno,' smiled Keith. 'I can only do it when I'm working really. I've got a cycle of it by now. Normally I get up and I'll be up for two or three days, but when you're working . . .'

With Keith, everything is to do with stopping the boredom threshhold crashing down. That's why he used to get back into serious heroin abuse as tours finished. Nothing else to do and energy to burn.

He went on to bemoan the lack of decent venues in London, but said he loved playing the 3,000-seater theatres in the States – 'Kept us on our toes. It's a totally different way of playing.' – that have become a tradition over the years. I asked Keith how he still related to the fans in his own country.

'I try to come back here as much as I can, just to see what's going on. Just soak it up and hang around, go and see bands. I get all different kinds of people coming up. That's the whole thing, innit? Half the time you find you're surrounded by middle-aged guys – "I saw you in the California Ballroom, Dunstable." You get surprising people coming up. Kids too. If I had longer time to spend I'd get into it a lot more.'

One thing he didn't miss was having the police on his back. But at least he could put it in perspective.

'In a way, I don't really mind all of the shit that I've had to go through. At least it kept me in touch with reality when I could well have gone off into the realms of . . . anywhere for a while! Eventually it got to a point where, if I was Joe Blow, I probably could have stayed on dope forever, as long as I could just sit in my little corner and have nothing to do.'

Before the interview, I'd made a mental note not to launch into tabloid-style 'Shocking Truth About Drug Fiend Keith' probing. The Canadian trial was still a recent memory, and it seemed futile to try to squeeze more juice out of his battered reputation. But he brought the subject up himself as our conversation gained steam. So I mentioned how he'd always be lumbered with the rock-'n'-roll-junkie-chic number. Another swig from the Jack, another of my fags, that shaking-head grin, and he was off for about the next twenty minutes. In all my years of keeping up with the Stoneses, it was the first time that I was aware of him being so candid.

'Yeah . . . I ain't gonna get rid of that one easy, am I? [laughs] Maybe if I keep my nose clean as long as I kept it dirty they'll forget about it.'

I wondered if he still got legal hassles.

'No . . . no. S'funny. [leans forward and whacks table] Touch wood! It's like they've said, "Oh, we've had a go at him, he's done his bit, we'll leave him alone, he's kept his end up." . . . which I certainly didn't do for them. I did it for the Stones and for myself, the kids, whatever . . .'

Keith was plain angry about what he considered a concerted plan to bring down the Stones via repeated drug busts. It had worked with Brian. They pried into his private life, put all the dirt in the spotlight, then accused him of being a bad influence on the kids.

'Right,' he agreed, looking seriously pissed off. 'Not only would you get done for what you got done for, you'd get done for setting a bad example. If they hadn't have come smashing through my front door no-one would've known what example I was setting! They made it public. Not me. I could understand it if I'd gone round saying, "Oh yeah, have a needle and a spoon, go off and have a good time, that's what it's all about." But I wasn't about to go 'round advertising it. They advertised it, then I had to pay for it. But fuck it, it happens to lots of people.

'I don't know how much the powers that be all work together or communicate with each other but it was like, how many more times would they have done me without it looking really like a bit of, "Let's pick on him," y'know? I was an easy target. They knew I was on the stuff. They could've come round every day! That's why I eventually had to say, "No more." I don't wanna see 'em any more. I was seeing more of cops and lawyers than I was of anybody else. To my mind, in the business of crime there's two people involved, and that's the criminal and the cops. It's in both their interests to keep crime a business, otherwise they're both out of a job. So they're gonna look for it. They ain't gonna wait for it to happen.'

By now, Keith was warming to his subject. He seemed to be letting out all his feelings about the years of being dominated by smack, with the fire and determination of a man who'd beaten it.

As we'd been talking, Keith had been leafing through an old *Zigzag* I'd brought along. It included an overview of the American heroin scene, which I'd been forced to include by my publisher of the time. I'd called it 'cheap, superficial and irresponsible' – and that opinion still stands. The first line went, 'Heroin is not chic,' followed by a quote about Stones drug references. I'd forgotten it was in there, and I knotted up inside as Keith scanned the text, grim and tight-lipped. He looked up slowly, into my eyes. Surely, an ashtray was headed in my direction – or at least a premature end to the interview.

But no. Instead, it spurred a remarkable stream-of-consciousness rap, equal parts comment, observation, confession. He'd only been off the stuff completely for six months, so it may have been the first interview he'd done clean for ten years.

'There's no way of writing about anything like that. It doesn't matter which way you angle it or state your case. Somebody's going to get turned on by it. Saying it's "not chic", that means it's chic. If you said it *was* chic . . .

'There's no way of writing about it because it's such an emotional and sensitive subject. The main thing is, why, especially in this business, do people go onto it in the first place? What are the pressures? Is it the one guy above you, that you dig the way he plays? Charlie Parker has done more to turn lots of horn players into junkies just because it happened to be known. If people had left him alone, and nobody had known he was a junkie, maybe it would've been better. Why go searching out sensational stories when you know that, just because the cops bust somebody if they're popular musicians or a superstar, there's gonna be somebody, no matter what that guy's going through himself, who's going to try and emulate it in some way?

'There's no right way of writing about heroin. There's plenty of wrong ways, and it's difficult to know. Ever since I kicked it, and cleaned up, I've been bombarded with requests and offers to make a statement about this, or address judges. I've been asked to do lectures for judges! The chance I've been waiting for – FUCK YOU! What else am I gonna say to them about dope? I'd just be embroiling myself and keeping myself in the same bag, attaching myself to the same thing that I'm trying to get rid of.

'Probably the only thing that might have any effect is, once everybody knows you're a junkie then yeah, you are an example. They've made you one, whether you wanna be or not. So the only example I can be now is to say, "Yeah, I've done it for longer than most people, and luckily came out the other end, and I'm still here, and I'm alright. Even if you're into it already and you need to kick it, at least you know, because I'm still here. If you want to, you can kick it, and the sooner the better, darlin'."

'If there's one thing I can talk about more than music and guitars, I can talk about dope! It's like guns. There's nothing wrong with the gun. It's the people who are on the trigger. Guns are an inanimate object. A heroin needle's an inanimate object. It's what's done with it, that's important. I think of all these people doing it, and not even knowing what they're doing. That, to me, is the dumbest thing. At least, by the time I got on it, I knew as much as you can know. The one thing that I've realised more than anything since I kicked it, is that the criteria you use when you're on it is so distorted from what you'd use normally. I know the angle – waiting for the man, sitting in some goddamn basement waiting for some creep to come, with four other guys snivelling, puking and retching around. And you're waiting for something to happen, and it's already been 24 hours, and you're going into the worst. How does it feel, baby? You don't feel great. If I was Joe Blow, maybe I'd still be on it, I dunno. I wouldn't take any notice of what I was saying if I was listening to it, or anybody else, 'cos when you're on it you don't.

'The only thing I can say is, if you want to, it's no big deal to kick it. Everybody wants to make like, "Oh, I've been to hell and back." You've only been halfway, baby. Nobody's been there and back. Anyway, here I am. Ten years I did it, and then I stopped, and I'm still 'ere. I've still got two legs, two arms luckily, and a bit of a head left, and that's about it. If examples count at all, that's the only statement I can make. I'm still here.

'In America it's even worse, because you have doctors coming on TV, discussions about the drug problem. These doctors . . . the more patients they get on methadone, the bigger [the] federal grant they get, so it's in their interest. They tell people who've been on it a few months, a year, "Your body can't do without heroin, you'll need methadone forever." Bullshit. You can kick it in three fucking days. That's as long as it stays in you. After that, it's up to you. I might oversimplify it in saying that, but that's the way it's always hit me. It's a physical thing for me in almost every way. If I can kick those three days . . .

'The other big problem is not cleaning them up, just sending 'em back. The same with me. The times I cleaned up and went straight back to exactly the same scene I was in before. What else you gonna do? You've been doing it for years. Everybody you know's doing it. You're kind of locked in. Unless you can break out of that circle afterwards . . . that's the next step. You're back in that same room as five years before, when you were on it, and they're still calling you up. Same people are coming around. It's a total drug, like total war. It takes over your whole life, every aspect of it eventually.

'When you're on it you'll go through any hassle to get it. "First get me the dope, then I'll do what I have to do."'

Since he's stayed off of it, Keith has talked a lot more about heroin. As this was his first interview off the gear, it was all coming off the top of his head, from his newly awakened soul. My own stupid tragedy was that I listened, enthralled, as Keith opened his heart, taking it all in – then later dove in headfirst myself. And it wasn't because of Keith Richards, either.

I became besotted with a female, who was besotted with heroin. Keith's words would often ring around my head as I dug around for a vein – or, even moreso, when I was curled up in agony – during my own ten-year battle. I may even have frequented Keith's old scoring venues, when I was living in New York for five years. He was right – it was a total war. One which my late wife – who was also from New York and, purely coincidentally, called Patti – wasn't strong enough to win.

One of Keith's scoring spots used to be the city's Lower East Side. I used to make my own regular trips down to the dark emporiums between Avenues B and D – or even lower, past Houston, to some really shady spots. The ritual was always the same, whichever bleak tenement you visited: turn up, join the gathered assembly of wretched-looking hopefuls . . . and wait.

Wait for some man you normally wouldn't piss on to give you the nod. Sometimes, you'd have to trudge up blackened stairways, past machete-wielding guards, just to do your business and leave. More often than not, you'd get back down to the bottom of the stairs and be held up, your stuff taken back off of you. If you did make it out, and the lookouts were gone, that meant the increasingly vigilant police force were in the area. Getting out of all this without a scratch, and with a bag of 'Red Devil' in my pocket, was pure adrenalin-fuelled exhilaration, followed by instant relief. But getting involved in a mass bust, and my subsequent withdrawal, was the closest thing to hell I've ever experienced.

I was a regular at this particular location between '86–'89, but Keith was there at the end of the seventies, when it was much worse. In those days, venturing east past Avenue A was totally off-limits to anyone who was white, or not on dope. Avenue D stood for Death. Most of the buildings were burnt-out, the streets were ruined and filthy, and practically unattended by cops. Simmering violence, imminent robbery and heroin etiquette ruled. The latter meant that you wouldn't think twice about ripping off someone you'd known for years. There were shooting galleries to get an instant hit. 'I carried a piece then,' testified Keith. And it was no wonder.

By now the interview had loosened up. So maybe we could talk about another delicate subject? Around this time, I'd just read *Up and Down with the Rolling Stones* by Tony Sanchez – probably the most blatant, muck-raking cash-in on the Stones' dark side published to date. 'Spanish Tony' was Keith's minder during the height of his addiction, and made sure he dished as much dirt as he could muster. (It was recently reprinted under the title *I Was Keith Richards' Drug Dealer*.) Keith emerges as a selfish junkie who changed his blood more often than his socks. The tabloids loved it, of course. But Keith dismissed the book with a grin and a shrug:

'Ohh . . . *Grimm's Fairy Stories*, yeah! Unbelievable, that. When it got to the blood change bit I thought, "Oh, here we go!" Marvellous. "Then he sprouted wings . . ." Actually, it wasn't him who wrote it, just some hack from Fleet Street. I'm the nasty, dirty, yellow snide. Oh nice, Tony. Thanks. You're my friend! Actually, it's quite clever. The actual incidents all happened, but then halfway through each chapter the description takes off into fantasy. This guy says Mick and I buried Brian, we made sure that nobody would ever see him again . . . but the guy's gotta make an angle or how ya gonna sell the book? The Fleet street hack thinks in terms of headlines. Spanish Tony had been with us for a long time, and a lot of the incidents in broad outline happened, but some of the details . . . I just gave up on the blood change! It's surprising the number of people who believe all that. No doubt some people do it.

'That one came about like this: I'd been in a clinic in Switzerland. Spanish Tony came to help us move into a house Tony asked, "What did they do to you up there?" I could hardly remember anyway and I'd only been in there about a week. I'd just crashed out virtually, went around puking in the ashtrays, ripping down the furniture and fittings for a couple of days and then I'd sort of got better, as usual. I couldn't explain all this to Tony so I said, "Ohh, they took all my blood out and gave me some fresh blood. All cleaned up!" Slowly over the years that one sentence has become one huge, "Oh, the blood change, man," y'know? It's funny – one remark because you can't be bothered to explain and before you know it that's what you are. They probably wouldn't have sold any books without that.'

Unsurprisingly, talk turned to the Press. Not just the tabloids. It's well-known that Keith loathed the people who made money out of airing his private problems. (In the case of the *News of the World*, they actually caused them.) But, in their way, the music papers sometimes weren't much kinder. The Stones were simply so huge and influential that their public fanbase didn't give a shit about what some smug sixth-form magazine-reject thought about them. After all, even *Emotional Rescue*, while it was fairly panned, has its redeeming moments.

I mentioned that some reviews had said the Stones didn't stand up to the bands of the time. (*This*, in the age of Queen and the New Romantics?) Keith has this way of getting coldly irritated. His dark eyes, which normally look capable of psychotic reaction when they're not sparking with internal mirth, momentarily freeze over into a scary kind of glower.

'Well, that's the bands they like,' he began, frostily. 'A lot of the bands they like don't mean fuck-all anywhere to anybody. Whether they might in the future, I don't know. I ain't slagging the bands. It all depends where you live. No doubt if we'd all stayed in England, we'd be playing and doing things differently than the fact that we had to move out. You start picking up wherever you live, or where you start to move around. A lot of it didn't turn out to be that different, whether I was in England or not.'

By now, it seemed apparent that Keith was cheesed off that the Stones wouldn't be touring behind *Emotional Rescue*. It was two years running that Mick had prevented him going on the road. I asked him if he was bothered by it.

'Yeah, I am a bit. I thought when we finished this last album that we'd get on the road now, but now I've sort of gotten over that and got used to the idea. I'm into finishing this other one, making it as good as we can, at the same time trying to set up some gigs. Not waiting till we finish the next album again, before we think of what we're going to do, but try and work it so we've got something to do when we finish the album. I wanna get them on the road because Mick and me have been playing one way or another – working on this album – but you forget we haven't played together with the other guys since we stopped cutting this time last year. It's a year since we even played together! So, get this one out as quickly and efficiently as possible!

'I know I wanna tour Europe. I can't see that until March or April 'cos the weather screws up tours. In the winter you can't ever be sure of making a gig, not every one. There's a lot of places we ain't played for a long time. We want to play here, but they just make it very difficult for us, y'know? Taxes. There's a lot of red tape for us to play here. On the other hand, you don't get promoters and tour managers saying, "You gotta tour England," 'cos you don't make any bread out of it. We don't expect to make any, but if they're not gonna make any bread, they're not gonna push us to play England. We have to say, "Look, we wanna play England – set it up." Otherwise, it just doesn't appear on the list of things to do, which is dumb, because there's no reason why we shouldn't play here more often.'

It was close to winding-up time, so I flung in some remark about how Keith must be 'quite pleased' how it had all turned out – considering his humble origins, and how many kids like him start playing guitar just for fun.

'Yeah, right. That's what I thought when we had two gigs a week – "Oh great! No more schlepping 'round with this artwork trying to get a job in an advertising agency," and I chucked it. "I'm making a tenner a week, ain't I? I'm alright. As long as I don't break strings, or a valve goes in the amplifier, I'll come out with a fiver at the end of the week – be alright!" So it was always like that. They just added more zeroes on the end as it went on, but as far as I'm concerned, it's the same attitude since we got our first gig: "Fine, great, wow! I'm doing what I really wanna do, and they're paying me to do it!"'

And on that note, a very pleasant afternoon drew to a close – along with the bottle of Jack Daniel's. I left the Stones office on a bit of a cloud. It's not every day you fulfil a lifelong ambition.

I could also stagger off the train back home in Aylesbury with a JD grin on my face, fall into the local pub, raise a joyful fist, and bellow, 'Fuck me! I've just got pissed with Keith Richards!' And not have to buy another drink all night.

Tattoo You

It wouldn't be such a long wait for the follow-up to *Emotional Rescue.* There had been the Guitar Auditions Album (*Black And Blue*) and the Back from the Dead Album (*Some Girls*). Now there was the Out-Takes Album. But *Tattoo You* is so much better than *Emotional Rescue.* The first track is 'Start Me Up' – the rest is an almost non-stop pleasure glide through multiple peaks, culminating in the impossibly lovely 'Waiting On A Friend'.

Keith had been presented with nine hours' worth of song ideas, demos, nearly-finished tracks and instrumentals. Chris Kimsey – who had a habit of leaving the tape machine running in the studio at all times when the Stones were in – had gone fishing and reeled in some potential forgotten gems. (Some of which Keith truly had forgotten.) There were 150 reels of tape left over from *Some Girls*, for instance, that needed a bit of spit and polish.

As Keith said, 'That's an advantage you don't think about, really, with a band that goes on for a long time,' telling *Rolling Stone*, 'Sometimes we write songs in instalments – just get the melody and the music, and we'll cut the tracks and write the words later. That way the actual tracks have matured just like wine – you just leave it in the cellar for a bit, and it comes out a little better a few years later.'

In early October 1980, the band had gone back to their favourite studios, Pathe-Marconi in Paris, to edit existing tracks and cut some new stuff. Even though there were still the inevitable wrangles between Mick and Keith, there seems to have been a better atmosphere once it was established that the groundwork had already been laid.

Reinvigorated, and infused with the spirit of rock 'n' roll, Keith was checking out his heroes in New York clubs. He saw Jerry Lee Lewis at the Ritz and joined Etta James on stage in February 1981, with a hug, a smile and a guitar for a storming version of 'Miss You'.

That same month, Keith flitted over to Hollywood to cut some tunes with Bobby Keys. In March, he went to Jamaica's Channel One studio and cut an album called *Holding Out My Love To You* with reggae veteran Max Romeo, who at one point looked like signing with the Stones. Romeo's claim to fame was in the early seventies, with a risque ska outing called 'Wet Dream'. Keith was happy to work with the shit-hot rhythm section, Sly and Robbie, but was pissed off when it appeared on a different label with his name plastered all over it. (There was even a free poster of Keith!)

Keith and Mick rounded off the new album the following month. Mixing duties were handed to Bob Clearmountain, who ensured the guitars were crystal clear in their definition. There was an economical punch to the rockers, while the slowies were lush and emotional. The record was also notable for pursuing different moods on each side – a mark of the days when vinyl ruled.

Keith's 'Little T & A', originally called 'Bulldog', had been written during the

Emotional Rescue sessions at Compass Point, and was about, 'every good time I've had with somebody I'd met for a night or two, and never seen again.' After he met Patti, it became a Keef-style love dedication – 'She's my little rock 'n' roll / My tits 'n' ass, with soul, baby.' – over a strident reaffirmation of a riff, driven below decks by a rockabilly-style rhythm twang. 'Ah, that was an old one off the tip of the tongue,' said Keith when I asked him about it a couple of years later. '"All About You" was the last one for *Emotional Rescue*. "T & A" was the last one to be written for *Tattoo You*.

'Again, it was like, "You've got this thing, you wanna do it?" "Yeah, right!" But I find if I sit down, and try and write songs in a hotel room, or wherever I am, I can't do it. I'd rather just stand in front of the microphone, and start blah-blahing away, and sort of hone it down over a few hours . . . or days. That's the only time I realise that I've got to do it, and that's when it all comes to me.'

'Neighbours' is all about Keith, and the problems he had with the other residents in his Manhattan apartment block. They didn't approve of Keith's 24-hour-music lifestyle, which resulted in his being evicted. 'I get that sort of thing all the time,' he shrugged. Keith reckoned it was the first song that Mick had written just for him – one of the only new ones on the album. The lyrics describe blaring TV, couples arguing or shagging, squawking kids, while the stomping soundtrack is suitably loud, and Sonny Rollins makes an incendiary howl. It makes its point to the extent that Keith said he wished he'd written it.

'Waiting On A Friend' was a *Goats Head Soup* artefact reworked as a celebration of the troubled-but-invincible friendship of Mick and Keith. Michael Lindsay-Hogg's video illustrated its sentiments perfectly, as Mick perched on a step in New York's East Village, eyeing up the passing girls while waiting for his mate. Soon he appears, ambling around the corner into Eighth Street, and joins him in a shoulder-slapping joke. Keith and Mick then repair to St Mark's Bar and Grill up the block, and join the rest of the band for a drink and a song.

(On my first day in New York in '83, my friends Marc and Steve took me to that very bar. We even perched on the same step as Keith and Mick!)

Tattoo You was up there with *Some Girls* – although 'We Had It All' would have made the slow side even better. It was the first Stones album for years to hit number one simultaneously on both sides of the Atlantic, selling a million copies in the US alone on the first week of its release.

Going To A Go-Go

In March 1981, relations had been cordial enough for Keith and Patti to join Mick and Jerry in Barbados for a holiday. While they were there, Keith and Mick first mooted the plan for a world tour. The Rolling Stones hadn't toured the UK since '76. After the Earls Court debacle, they were keen to get it right this time. Keith was still expressing remorse about it when we spoke in '83. 'In '76 with Earls Court, we just couldn't deal with the hall,' he lamented. 'It was a terrible place and we knew [it]. That brings you down. When it's your own town, and you don't give your best, or you're prevented from giving your best, it can piss you right off.'

By now the Stones were probably even more popular than they were in '76, so the London gigs moved outdoors to Wembley Stadium. As usual, the machine would

*Ronnie and Keith, cracking up in the 'Waiting On A Friend' video, at
St Mark's Bar & Grill, New York City.*

crank into action in America – at Philadelphia's JFK Stadium, in front of 90,000 people – and would go on until 19 December, the day after Keith's birthday.

It marked the first time that the Stones broke records and created new bench-
marks for touring. Their 50 gigs would play to over two million people and gross
about $36 million. It was the first tour to have a commercial sponsor, with
Chicago-based perfume company Jovan's logo displayed alongside the Stones' own
corporate lips and tongue.

As usual, there was conflict between Keith and Mick over presentation. Keith
wanted a no-frills approach in more intimate surroundings, but was overruled by
Mick. It was as if his penchant for the biggest shows in the biggest stadiums was
not only a means of getting the biggest pay packet, but a kind of we'll-show-'em-
who's-boss move designed to put the faves of the day in the shade.

Keith hated the fact that Mick had a cherry-picker built to hoist him over the
crowd, and the huge cartoon drapes hanging over the behemoth structure. But he
didn't attend any of the design meetings, seemingly resigned to the size of the
spectacle. And he couldn't deny that the cash would come in handy, given his legal
bills of the previous few years. All the same, he felt that some compromise could
be reached where Mick got to play his mega-gigs while he found a few smaller
places to play rock 'n' roll without any distractions.

After some rehearsals in New York in July, Keith insisted on a residential situation for five weeks to get the set sorted out. Given the phoning-in style in
which *Tattoo You* had been recorded, the Stones had hardly been together in the
same room for three years. There was also the problem of Ronnie's freebasing

habit to deal with. He was in bad shape, and was asked nicely if he'd accept half a million bucks in salary to clean up for the tour. He agreed – but the naughty boy didn't keep up his end of the bargain.

Keith went to inspect a rehearsal complex at Longview Farm in Brookfield, Massachussetts, and got along famously with the boss, Gil Markle. Victor Bockris describes the meeting in his Keith biography, having filled in from Markle's unpublished journal. Once Keith was shown the state-of-the-art studio, and the drinks supply, he didn't want to leave. He sat down at the piano and played a Hoagy Carmichael ballad called 'The Nearness Of You', then proceeded through a few country tear-jerkers.

Markle had the tapes rolling, and the results can be heard on the bootleg called *Booze And Pills And Powders*. Markle's journal relays a 'revealing statement' from Keith between takes:

'. . . I never get a chance to sing by myself like this, play the piano, without some bastard weirding out and asking me why I wasn't playing the guitar and looking mean . . . . I bet you didn't think I could play the piano, did you? Or sing classics from the thirties? Well, I can. People think I get my way a lot more than I do. You don't know what it's like dealing with the people I've got to deal with.'

That's the real Keith coming through – away from the expectations of sensation-hungry journalists. Of course, it must be great fun being Keith Richards: you could get away with falling backwards through someone's glass door at a party! But it's also meant having to live up to a perpetual image. And it's true that the average Stones fan would find it hard to picture Keith perched at the piano, caressing the soul of 'Somewhere Over The Rainbow'.

1981 also saw another turn-up when Keith re-established contact with his dad, Bert, who he hadn't seen for twenty years. The day in '62 when Keith left home to become a *Rolling Stone* was the last time they'd spoke – although Keith had written to him after the Redlands bust. The reasons were a combination of Keith's parents' estrangement, his schedule, his lifestyle, his being too out of it, and maybe a little bit of stubbornness. But Patti, who was close to her father, impressed upon him the value of maintaining contact with your parents as they get older. And Keith's dad was now in his late seventies.

Bert suggested they meet in the pub. Keith was so nervous he took Ronnie along for moral support. He needn't have worried. They got on like a house on fire, and Bert was immediately welcomed into Keith's world. They shared a mutual love of booze, jokes, dominoes and shepherd's pie. Bert could easily have come out of the woodwork at any point during those twenty years – to try to get money out of Keith, or sell stories to the papers. The fact that he hadn't exemplified how they were out of the same mould – or, as Keith puts it, 'I come from good stock.' Bert even drank more than Keith, now that his son was buying

He ultimately accompanied Keith on the Stones' European tour, which gave his son a new catchphrase: 'Dad's coming!' Keith would have his whole crew in for a party, howling along to 'Danny Boy' – a mournful lament that touches the hearts of the British, not just their Irish in-laws. Eventually, Keith moved Bert out to the house in Long Island, where he'd been paying for Anita to live with Marlon ever since their break-up.

Having established the rehearsal venue, Keith took Patti to Freddie Sessler's place in Florida while the Stones gathered at Longview Farm to begin rehearsals in mid-August. While Jagger scuttled about, sorting out the business end, Keith called up the band when it was time to crank up the set they'd be playing for the best part of the following year.

He was also in charge of making sure that Ronnie stayed off the 'base. It was difficult, because addicts can be ingenious in their strategies to procure supplies. One time, Keith got so mad he whacked Woody when he heard that he was basing in his room. Up until that point, Ronnie had been almost ostricised by the group. Even Keith had been forced to kick his arse when Ronnie passed out on stage.

But Keith is very loyal to his mates. He just wanted to see Ronnie well and back on form, like the bloke he'd originally fallen in with. Photos of the time show Woody approaching the skeletal, psycho-eyeballed demeanour of Keith on the drug tours. Different poisons, sure, but, if anything, freebase is worse than smack in its ravaging effects.

The band for this tour included Ians McLagan and Stewart on keyboards. There was no brass section, just sax-player Ernie Watts, as Mick refused to have the strung-out Bobby Keys on the tour, which pissed Keith off. Rehearsals were slightly chaotic, according to Bill Wyman. Charlie appears have been doing speed and drinking. Woody and Keith had a fight after Mr. Richards got mad at Ronnie for going back to base.

After rehearsals, the band would make up and spent a lot of time partying. But they also worked up a set that they tried out at a secret warm-up gig on 14 September at the 300-capacity Sir Morgan's Cave in Worcester, Massachusetts. Billed as Blue Monday and the Cockroaches, 4,000 fans descended on the place when a local radio station gave the game away. Riot police and helicopters were called in, but the club opened its doors so that the crowd could hear the Stones playing. Afterwards, Keith said, 'It was great . . . It was if we were playing the Station Hotel in Richmond in 1963. You don't forget those things.'

The tour proper opened on 25 September with two nights in Philly, 90,000 people attending each gig. The new stage set was unveiled, the first of three. The biggest was over 200 feet wide, 50 feet high, with ramps, lifts and platforms. It was draped with huge canvases in garish pink by a Japanese designer, showing abstract 1950s Americana depictions of a guitar, the US flag and a car.

The band had their own Boeing 707 for this tour, and played in front of an average-sized crowd of 60,000 people. The smallest gig of the tour – at Atlanta's Fox Theatre, capacity 4,000 – was also reputedly the best, with the Stones rocking their bollocks off harder than ever. Once again, they hit the huge Madison Square Gardens in New York, and various support acts across the US included Tina Turner, Screamin' Jay Hawkins, the Stray Cats, the Neville Brothers, Etta James, George Thorogood, Van Halen, Iggy Pop, Joe Ely, Bobby Womack, and a near-unknown Prince – sporting black ladies' knickers in LA.

The set for this tour kicked off with 'Under My Thumb' – the song they were playing when Meredith Hunter was stabbed at Altamont. It ran to well over two hours, with never less than 25 songs and about half of them new. At the Kansas

City show, Mick Taylor got up to play for practically the whole set.

On 22 November, when the Stones arrived in Chicago for three shows at the Rosemont Horizon, they went to see Muddy Waters, Buddy Guy and Junior Wells at the Checkerboard Lounge. Keith, Ronnie and Mick went onstage and jamming on five songs: 'Mannish Boy' (as previously performed by the Stones at the El Mocambo in '77), 'Hoochie Coochie Man', 'Long Distance Call', 'That Ugly Woman Of Mine' and 'I Wanna Get High'. Keith and Ronnie dressed up in white shirts and black vests for the gig. As Keith acknowledged, they were 'dressed up to go to work.' It was filmed for posterity, some of it popping up in the Stones' *Rewind* compilation. A few weeks later, Muddy Waters would be diagnosed with terminal lung cancer.

The December gig at the Sun Devil Stadium in Phoenix, Arizona was filmed for a Stones documentary by Hollywood maverick Hal Ashby (*Harold And Maude*, *The Last Detail*). During the grand finale of 'Satisfaction', as hundreds of balloons rained down on the band and the audience, a fan got past security and ran towards Mick. Keith simply unstrapped his guitar, hit the guy in the stomach with its neck, then carried on playing. The footage would eventually feature in Ashby's *Let's Spend the Night Together*, which ends with a shot of Keith sitting on the drum riser, Jack Daniel's bottle in hand, glowering at the circus going on around him.

There is a measure of confusion about this one. Victor Bockris has it occurring a few days later at Hampton Roads, Virginia, at a live broadcast by cable channel HBO that had a mass 'Happy Birthday' singalong for Keith. As Keith said later, 'What if he had a fuckin' gun in his hand, or a knife? I mean, he might be a fan, he might be a nutter, and he's on my turf. I'm gonna chop the mother down!'

1982 began with another falling-out between Keith and Mick. But Keith dug his heels in, and it turned out to be one of the best moves he ever made. Jane Rose had worked for the Stones' office since '74. When Mick fired her at the end of '81, Keith swiftly took her on as his personal manager. Since then she's become everything to him – looking after his affairs, and acting as a quality-control buffer with the outside world. When I lived in New York in the mid-to-late eighties, I'd sometimes visit her at the Stones' suite in Rockefeller Plaza to see what was happening with the band. It was all part of my silly pilgrimage, which would also see me walking past Keith's apartment block on East Fourth Street every day on the way to work. (I went to knock on his door once, to tell him I was bowled over by his first solo album, but couldn't get past security in reception.)

January '82 also saw Keith and Mick produce four demos for the reformed Mamas and the Papas. (But was John Phillips reformed?) In March, the Stones swept the board in the *Rolling Stone* Readers Awards for the first time since *Some Girls*: Band of the Year, Album of the Year with *Tattoo You*, Single of the Year with 'Start Me Up', Mick and Keith as Songwriters of the Year, Jagger as Singer of the Year and Keith as Instrumentalist of the Year – while the records scored best album and single in their Critics' Awards.

Mick announced the European tour in London on 28 April, at a press conference at London's trendy Le Beat Route club. Ian McLagan would be replaced by Chuck Leavell, formerly of the Allman Brothers Band, and trumpeter Gene

Barge added to the line-up, while, in a definite compromise by Jagger, Ernie Watts would be replaced by Bobby Keyes. Support bands would be the J. Geils Band and George Thorogood and the Destroyers.

What Mick didn't say was that Thorogood, the American guitar hero, had been groomed to stand in if Ronnie's freebasing got the better of him. It was continuing to disturb the band, especially Keith – who famously punched Woody in the face when he momentarily lost the plot during 'She's So Cold', at Wembley.

The tour kicked off with warm-ups gigs in Britain, starting at the Capitol Theatre, Aberdeen on 26 May, before moving on to Glasgow Apollo and Edinburgh Playhouse – big old theatres that the Stones used to play in the sixties. The Daily Mirror described the opening night as 'a rocking, roaring success, an unforgettable night of nostalgia.' On 31 May , they played a surprise gig at Londons 100 Club, before an audience of 400.

On 1 June, the Stones released a single of their version of the Miracles' 'Going To A Go Go', recorded at the Capitol Theatre, Landover, Maryland on the US tour. On the same day, the *Still Life* document of the tour came out. Even though it made the top ten, it was considered substandard against the previous two live albums, *Love You Live* and *Get Yer Ya Yas Out*.

On 24 June, the night before the Stones' first show at Wembley Arena, Keith appeared on BBC2's *Newsnight* in an interview by Robin Denselow in Paris. At the time, it was quite a rare occurrence. He was dressed in his favourite white shirt-black vest outfit of the time, leaning over a bar, quaffing bourbon. They started by talking about the early days, when his ambition didn't extend beyond 'three or four good pub gigs. We certainly weren't in it for the money. We just wanted to preach the gospel of rhythm 'n' blues. Idealistic kids.' Now, he saw his group as 'a very well-paid hobby.'

When Denselow inevitably steered the conversation to heroin, Keith said that, before Toronto, 'It didn't worry me too much, because of the nature of heroin . . . It's incredibly easy to get into, but incredibly difficult to get off,' acknowledging that, while he always maintains you can physically kick in three days, the temptation always remains there.

His parting comment was that he'd keep on playing unless there was a really good reason not to, 'like getting my arms cut off.' The interview was symbolic of the power shift going on within the Stones. Before, it would have been Mick in the spotlight, but even a shitfaced Ronnie came in to say that, these days, it was Keith telling him to shape up. (Not without good reason, either.)

The next day, I made my way to the open-air gig at Wembley. It was pissing down with rain, so I spent most of the day in the bar of the hotel next door, which had been taken over by the Stones' organisation. I did manage to tear myself away to catch the excellent Black Uhuru, but they were a little lost in the sheer size of the venue.

At Stones-time I ventured out into the damp, just as they were playing their intro music – Duke Ellington's 'Take The A Train'. The stage set looked very big indeed, even if the canvases lost their lustre in the rain and the wind. You couldn't really get caught up in it from where I was sitting, but I couldn't help noticing the difference in Keith. He was scooting about all over the place, striking the classic stances now firmly ensconced in his repertoire. Down the ramp for a solo, flicking plectrums, grinning his bollocks off, newly elevated in the eyes of the crowd. I'd never seen him like this before. Or Mick, for that matter, who was wearing American sports gear, a codpiece and a variety of embarrassing headgear, including a baseball cap – like a pretend jock in an American teenage sitcom.

It was more or less the same set as in the States, slightly pruned, and now featuring 'Go Go' and 'Twenty Flight Rock'. Out came the cherry-picker, and I was wishing that Keith would hijack it for a twenty-minute solo spot, like he did in Norway – much to Mick's annoyance.

The following year, I asked Keith how he felt about the UK gigs, in retrospect: 'Yeah, they were good, especially the small gigs. Since the Stones have been priced out of England in '71, whenever it was, it was the first time that we've come back here and played, and felt that we'd justified ourselves, to a certain extent.

'I can't say that it wasn't for us a real buzz. I mean, we did feel like we were coming home for a bit. It was a great feeling for us. Wembley particularly, but Newcastle was happening. It was the middle of summer, but it was freezing cold, pissing with rain, but the crowd were great. It was heartwarming for the band. They put their backs into it as much as they could. I don't think it's the best possible place to hear the Stones play. We could do a lot better back at the Station Hotel. But then we couldn't. That's something that everybody has to deal with, and quite likely Jagger can deal with handling a place that size better than anyone else. That stage developed, but just the idea that we could get out a third of the way out to the audience. It was a real simple idea. We should have all thought about it ten years ago. It took us that long to realise that what you needed was a couple of long ramps. You could reach a whole lot more people.'

I mentioned that I'd never seen Keith move about on stage so much. He could never have sprinted into the crowd on a ramp on the '76 tour, even if they'd had one.

'Yeah, you can see that the whole band were just waiting for you to get stuck out a quarter of a mile away. "Have I been out there too long?" Then start haring back! [laughs] Yeah, it's kind of funny. It gave us a few laughs, and it probably gave everyone a few laughs at our expense. That's what it's all about really. I mean, you don't want to take this thing too seriously. There's people going, "Oh, the Stones walked away with so many millions," but ... umm, think of the overheads! If they wanna come and see you, what can you do? You got to go out there and play, y'know?'

The '82 tour did leave a lot of pissed-off promoters looking at empty seats because everyone wanted to see the Stones. 'Yeah, I know,' chuckled Keith. 'We've been blamed for ruining everyone else's tours. Queen cancelled ... but then, as far as I'm concerned, Queen are a new wave group in comparison to the Stones. But also they could be Flanagan and Allen. Freddie alone is Flanagan and Allen. Yeah, we ruined everybody else's business. Sorry we did so well. They're gonna choose if they want to see you. I'm just glad we managed to pull it off reasonably well this time.'

CHAPTER TWELVE

BRAHN BOOTS (STOMPIN' AT THE SAVOY)

After the final date of the European tour, Keith and Patti bowled over to Cabo San Lucas in Mexico, where they'd be residing for much of the following year. On 12 November 1982, Keith's most hated journalist, John Blake of *The Sun* (who ghost-wrote Tony Sanchez's book), leaked the news that Keith would be marrying Patti in New York 'within a month'. Keith was trying to keep the wedding plans secret and wouldn't get married for over a year. No wonder Blake was on his shit list.

That month saw the Stones start work on the follow-up to *Tattoo You*. It began with Keith and Mick throwing ideas around in Paris, as the previous album had practically exhausted their stockpile of old tunes. Keith already had his solo track, a love song, in mind, and Mick helped him work it out, accompanying on drums. Then the whole group went into Pathe-Marconi studios to work up some new songs. They were playing in the same room, rolling off the buzz of touring for nearly two years.

'They recorded the same way as a bunch of kids starting out,' said Jim Barber, Keith's guitar technician for the album, in Steve Appleford's *It's Only Rock 'n' Roll*. 'It's Keith's band, not Mick's. Without Keith in the studio the whole thing is a mess.'

Bootlegs from this period boast Keith's vocal on honky-tonk standard 'Crazy Arms'. The band continued these fractious sessions, their last ones in Paris, through January, with Mick, Keith and Ronnie winding-up the mixing in May and June.

In January' 83, a spokesman confirmed rumours that Keith would be marrying Patti in the near future. But, in the middle of the month, her father, Alfred Hansen, died. She had been very close to him – which is why she insisted that Keith get in touch with the ageing Bert. For now, the wedding would be postponed. Keith served as a pallbearer at the funeral and attended the wake, on 19 January.

February saw the New York premiere of Hal Ashby's *Let's Spend the Night Together*, the film documenting the '81 US tour. It was the latest in a long line of Stones live movies, neither better nor worse than *Stones in the Park* or the later *Bridges To Babylon* video document. It was enthralling stuff for the Stones fan who'd been stuck at the back with a shitty view, but there wasn't the sense of 'being there'. Its most notable scene is the historic moment when Keith – awash in a sea of balloons – lunges at the stage invader with his guitar, then sits down with a bottle of Jack Daniel's.

That year, I'd get to speak about the movie directly with Keith. I'd taken over the editor's chair of a magazine called *Flexipop!* the year before. Up until then, it'd been a forum for the chart acts of the time, like Soft Cell, Culture Club and Duran Duran, but they often tried to go for some twisted humour. The synthesised pop-pap of the day needed raunching up. At the time, I was quite immersed in the glam-goth scene emerging in London. With *Zigzag* going down the pan, quality-wise, I thought it would be a top move to put Keith in my new organ. He was the epitome of rock 'n' roll, the look and the lifestyle that a lot of the new bands

I was hanging out with were trying to copy (and often failing miserably).

So let's have the originator! I duly put in a call to Stones PR Alan Edwards and requested an interview. (It meant I had to do a few of his less credible acts too, but what the fuck.) If I asked him now, I might get an interview in a year or so, I thought.

Within weeks I got a call saying that Keith would be in town imminently, but was only doing one interview – supposedly to promote the movie. He didn't even have to do that, as Jagger was spreading himself pretty thinly on its behalf. 'That's me out then,' was my immediate reaction.

Not at all. Keith was only doing one interview, and I was it. It turned out he'd seen the *Zigzag* piece and loved it. He wanted to hang out and talk some more. Well I'll be the Devil's scrotum!

This time the venue would be his favourite London hotel, the Savoy. Keith always booked the same suite as used by Frank Sinatra. He seemed to like the fact that the living-room view was a brick wall – no spies! – and you could get round-the-clock shepherd's pie and Jack Daniel's.

When I arrived, he was out shopping with Jane Rose. I sat chatting with Alan Edwards, who a few years later would be looking after Elton John instead (the self-important little crooner who Keith has always found a pain in the arse). Pretty soon, Keith and Jane arrived back. He was wearing his hooded designer jacket – the type that Liam Gallagher would later make fashionable – with white shirt and jeans. Even compared to a couple of years before, he looked obscenely healthy and happy, a very far cry from the tragic figure in that court room in Aylesbury. Keith greeted me like an old mate, with a massive hug and the offer of a long line of in-flight refreshments. He happily posed for polaroids, even insisting on taking some himself.

And ahh yes, the brown boots. He was currenly breaking a new pair in. Whenever Keith likes an item of clothing, he's not afraid to be seen wearing it for months on end. He'd worn those boots of Spanish leather at every gig on the '81 tour, immortalising them in the same way as he would his love of shepherd's pie twenty years later. When they became worn out from all the gigging, he'd had roadies using anything from gaffa tape to glue and nails to keep them together. US tour manager Bill Graham had often gone through hell and high water to keep the heel from falling off. When the boots gave up the ghost, Keith presented them, gift-wrapped, to Graham at the end of the previous American tour.

'It was a fuckin' disaster when they went, man,' he said, inspecting his latest replacements. 'Those babies were the only things that gave me enough grip on the stage to stop me falling over on those ramps. But in the end, I had to get some new ones.'

This particular interview out-marathoned the previous session, winding through the afternoon and covering many bases. People came and went, but we stayed chatting and guffawing in the corner, with Mr. Jack Daniel's joining in frequently. Someone's blinding Jamaican weed certainly helped the good-humoured flow. As before, the best way to kick off the conversation was to ask what was happening on the musical front. At that time, the Stones were working in Paris on the album that eventually became *Undercover*. I wondered if they were following the same method of raking in all the jams, demos, bits and pieces, then honing them down into an album.

'No, so far it's all brand new,' he said, with some pride. 'There's not even a cover version so far, which is unusual. Usually we stick a couple in there. See, this time I have no defence because I've been going in the studio for years pretending I've got loads of songs and I bang 'em out. If Charlie picks up on it, great. They think I know what I'm doing. This time I was getting some pressure – especially from Mick – saying, "Let's do some songs before we go in." So I had no defence. I didn't mind doing that anyway because I just go in the studio and do it the way I do it because I'm lazy, I guess, in a way. It's easier. It doesn't really make any difference, but this time we did work a bit. Mick and I worked a little bit for two or three weeks before the sessions started and got three or four songs together.'

What's it like this time?

'It's always hard to say with the Stones because to me a lot of it is just the Stones playing, y'know? There's some good songs. There's a real hark back to Memphis soul in a lot of the tracks. Whether or not it'll be apparent when the album comes out, that depends on the choice of tracks and what's available – or immediately available – at the time, and which tracks we actually end up working on to make the next album.

'I mean we've ended up with about 40-odd tracks. It's a pleasant position to be in in one way, but in the end it's still decisions, decisions. Do you go with this one and which ones do you actually end up using? As with *Emotional Rescue* we'll end up, no doubt, using the ones that are most advanced technically and structurally. Although there may be much better songs on tape that are not developed yet to the point where we can work on them. We'd have to recut them. To a point we're limited. Even though we might have a certain number of tracks, you've got to cut yourself down to a workable number, because if you work on them all you'll be in there forever. It'd be like painting the Sistine fuckin' Chapel! Be on your back for years. You do have to tend to go with the ones that are more immediately ready and more developed than some of the others. It doesn't mean that that's necessarily the best collection of songs you can put together. It's art and business and where they catch. If you can call it art.'

So there's no deadline on this new one?

'No, luckily, after twenty years we're beyond that. They'll get it when we're ready. It's our last album for EMI. We're up for grabs!'

The previous time we'd spoken, Keith was a bit disgruntled about the making of *Emotional Rescue*. Keith had wanted it raw and rocking, while Mick was latching onto trends like disco with an eye toward the hit single. There had definitely been friction in the air, and I wondered if that was still going on.

'In a way. Yeah, yeah, it is. It's not at the point that it was then where I was totally out in the cold on it. I've known Mick and Mick has known me since I was five years old, so I can recognise certain things that Mick's doing way ahead of everybody else because I've known him so much longer. I'm an only child but if I've got a brother it's him, because he's been there around as long as I can remember. So I probably know him better than his own brother does. But to answer your question – yeah.

'The situation is still there in a certain way. But in the Rolling Stones we're the writers and we've been together for twenty years. We can stick together through thick and thin, but there is still that certain division between Mick and me that we're both doing our best to work on. It ain't that big a thing that we can't deal with it because we've always worked to a certain point. One of the reasons that it's worked for so long is because Mick and me are able to work within a certain kind of friction. One of the main points is that abrasiveness between the two of us is what makes the pearl and the oyster. There's a bit of grit in there, y'know. It'll always be there. But it's nothing near as drastic as it was then.'

Despite what Keith was saying, I could still sense a timebomb waiting to go off. Keith's most hated journalist, John Blake, boasted in *The Sun* that Mick had given him an interview where he'd intimated the Stones didn't have long left. 'It will disintegrate very slowly,' Mick was alleged to have claimed – though he soon denied having said it. 'The band has done what it set out to do.' But not in Keith's eyes.

That day at the Savoy he was more concerned with Mick's plugging of the *Let's Spend the Night Together* movie. Within minutes, Keith was almost apologising for it. It was obviously one of Mick's babies he had no wish to be a godparent to. His mood took a darker swing.

'Ah, as far as I'm concerned, Mick's totally overexposing himself. How much can you say? You can talk about what you're doing to so many people but by then you just end up repeating yourself. It gets boring. You can't keep repeating the same thing in a short period of time. I think that's kind of dumb. But at the same time Mick wants to push the movie, which I don't particularly want to do. For what it is it's alright. I don't think it's *Gone with the Wind*, y'know what I mean? I don't think there's any point at this stage in putting something out as a full-length feature movie. I don't think there's enough interest there, except for diehard fans and that doesn't justify putting it out and pretending it's a real movie. It isn't. It's another periodical visual piece of film that the Rolling Stones have done since *Stones in the Park* and before then. *Gimme Shelter, Ladies and Gentlemen . . . .* The only difference with this one is that it was done through the Hollywood machinery, which is the reason it's been treated in a different way.

'I mean, the best one was *Cocksucker Blues*, which nobody ever saw! Hur . . . Charlie saw this and said, "I'd rather see something by Robert Frank." If you want a movie about the Stones on the road – it's *Cocksucker Blues*. Warts 'n' all. It is funny – just point the camera. Still, the new one's a good night, the sound's good and you're gonna see things that you're not gonna see from the audience. But it's a cult thing. If you're a Stones freak you're gonna go and see it. It's not something that's gonna draw people to the cinema unless they are that much into it. It's not *Psycho*. It's not Eisenstein.'

That '82 tour might have boasted the biggest stage that the Stones – or indeed any band in the world – had utilised at that time, but if you were standing at the back of Wembley Arena in the rain, surrounded by zonked punters, straining to hear a sound that was blowing in the wind, surely the movie had its place?

'Yeah, see what you missed when you were actually there. But when you're in the cinema you're gonna miss the thing that you had when you were actually there as well. Those things are events. You can't seriously expect to hear a band playing in a place like Wembley or any other of those places. You go there as an event and that's what it is. We do our best but we don't know what the fuck's going on. It doesn't depend on us. It depends on the guys that are mixing the sound. If they had a party the night before and they've all got a fucking hangover, tough luck. Y'know, a hundred thousand people – "Tough luck, the crew got stoned last night and it's not as good as it should be." But we don't know. What we hear on stage has got no relation to what you may be hearing out there. Flip the coin.'

Twenty years ago, it was still impossible to envisage how much the Stones would make the stadium gig their own. Six years down the road, the *Steel Wheels* tour would crank its spectacular bulk across the world, followed by the *Voodoo Lounge, Bridges To Babylon* and *Licks* outings. By then they would become a mighty, perfectly-honed machine, both audible and visible – thanks to advanced technology and a crew who wouldn't dare to get slaughtered the night before a gig.

Me and Keith during the Flexipop! *interview at the Savoy Hotel, London, Spring 1983.*

I asked Keith if he'd caught any of the current chart groups of the time, which led him to expound on his own working process and lifestyle.

'For the last six months I've been involved in recording and that's always my blind spot. People say, "Have you seen this film?", or, "Have you heard this record?", or, "Have you read this book?", and I realise that when I'm recording I don't take any notice, or I don't get the chance. I don't hear anything, read anything or see anything. Hear no evil, see no evil. I just totally – without really realising it – get totally absorbed into making the next album. Either I'm in the studio or once a week I crash out. I'm in the studio and then they tell me something that I haven't heard. I wouldn't be surprised if somebody had told me a couple of weeks later that England had sunk two weeks ago. I wouldn't know about it. I get that far into it. You're in the studio and you stay there until everybody's dropped around you. "Before They Make Me Run" was nine days. The same thing with "All About You".

'If I've got a song I wanna do I always tend to leave it till the very end of the sessions. We'll cut the track early then Mick'll say, "Is this the one you're gonna do? I can't do it, you do it." So I go, "Yeah, I'm gonna do it, alright then. Don't worry Mick." Hurhur. And then suddenly everybody's split and gone and I've still got this track to do. "Before They Make Me Run" . . . same with "All About You" – "We all want it to be on the album but how does it go? We've had the backing track for months but what's the tune like? What's it all about?" This album I'm ahead. I've got a track and I've got most of the vocal done already.'

He then played me an extremely rough rehearsal take, laughing as he pointed

237

out that Mick was playing drums – 'Hear that? Whoops!' – and had fluffed a fill.

What's that one called?

Keith laughed and took another swig of Jack. 'Erm, that's the one bit I've still got to figure out! I've got all the other bits, I've just still gotta decide what the hook's gonna be. This one's kind of a Beatles song. It's about time somebody wrote it. McCartney don't write 'em any more.'

The song ended up being called 'Wanna Hold You', and did indeed conjure up a more innocent era of pop music. Obviously inspired by Patti, it turned out to be the lightest, most simple celebration of love on what would turn out to be one of the darker, more experimental albums in the Stones catalogue.

'I ain't a songwriter. I never feel like I write them. I'm just a . . . an antenna, an aerial. I just sort of stand there and, if you're desperate enough, something comes out. You're just sort of a conductor . . . a medium. If there's something there zooming around the room I hope I can pick it up, but you can't force it or write it down on paper. You can't go, "This song goes like this." At least not with this band you can't. You can some of the time but most of the time it's right off the top of my head. I receive and I transmit. Sometimes it takes a while . . .'

While Keith is acknowledged as the heart and backbone of the Stones, he's only ever given one song per album or possibly two during his live spot. Which makes Mick Jagger's constant striving for a solo career all the more baffling. He already sings most of the songs, and is very obviously the front man – though Keith is the sound of the Stones.

In '83 you wouldn't dare ask a Rolling Stone if they would ever think of a solo career. Keith would probably have got out his dagger. (Even though, as I later found out, Mick was then in the early stages of formulating a solo contract for himself with the Stones' next record deal.) But I did venture to ask why they never released the tunes he sang as Rolling Stones singles – although 'Happy' did score when it came out in the US only in '72.

Keith paused, obviously weighing up what to say. 'Erm . . . Mick is very *conservative* . . .' He wrung every bit of gentle disdain out of that word. 'Not in that way . . . If you want to talk about flamboyant characters, there's Mick. But when it comes to making records Mick is very conservative. I mean, you can either take something that's very free and redo it or restructure it. I understand that and I'll go along with it too, because we were brought up in a time when you needed a hit single every twelve weeks. "Satisfaction" came out and took off and we went, "Phwoosh, fantastic!" Then you're just breathing a sigh of relief and there's a knock on the door: "Umm, have you got the new single?" "Yee-ah." So we were brought up songwriting and making records under that kind of pressure. Say it all in two minutes 35 seconds and have it ready. Before the next one's released you've got to have the one after that half-constructed and ready to go. I'm the first one to say "Get Off Of My Cloud" – forget it! As the follow-up to "Satisfaction" . . . it was like the knock on the door and, "This is what we've got." We'd sort of ride on the back of "Satisfaction".

'You can't do it all the time, but at the same time it did teach you how to learn certain things about making records and writing songs that doesn't exist now. Just because singles were king. If you didn't have the hit single an album didn't mean a thing. Now it's because of the economics of it. How much is it to make a single and get some profit off of that? Then with the profit you make off of that you can start an album. Which isn't a bad thing. The late sixties and the seventies were a real . . . they were signing everybody and giving them huge advances, when maybe they would've been better off struggling for three years and getting their act together. All these kids were getting signed up and churned out like mincemeat the other end. Just because they had two good songs . . . then ruined, finished.'

As these words come straight from the horse's mouth, we can see how a conversation with Mr. Richards takes its own meandering turns. You spark a point and end up somewhere related, but quite different. We moved back onto the gripe with the tax man he was still holding onto from our previous meeting:

'Let's be honest, you're not gonna come back and pay . . . once they've forced you out you're not gonna come back. I love England but I don't miss it that much to cough up two million quid to live here. The price of living here, sorry, it's too expensive. Like it is for anybody else. Like it is for some schmuck on the dole. And there's millions of 'em. [An estimated three million at the time.] It's horrible, but who am I to talk about that? I was dead lucky. I waltzed in here doing my hobby and made money out of it. Gonna put me down for that? I'm sorry. Anybody out there on the fucking dole queue – it could happen to them, the same as me. I'd prefer to be able to live at home but can't afford to live here.'

You still living in New York?

'I live in New York – as long as the Americans allow me in, which is a certain amount of time a year. I'm allowed to be in England 90 days a year. I'm an enforced sort of diddicoy. No man's nomad. I've been on the road for twenty years. I'm sick of hotels. I've got three warehouses full of stuff in Brooklyn. That's an enforced situation and after a while you get used to it and it doesn't bother you. I just think it's about time I found somewhere permanent to live. I love this green and pleasant land but I can't afford it. That's the weird thing with this lark – the more money you make, the less you can afford. Doesn't matter about rock 'n' roll musicians – they're expendable. But the same thing applies to physicists,' Keith lisps, having trouble pronouncing the word, 'physicists'.

'It doesn't just apply to us, it applies to anybody who's got an extraordinary talent. Why d'ya think there's a British pub in Long Beach? Because there's 50,000 of us over there because they can make more money there. You can live here and be a pauper and be a saint for England and live in a hovel . . . and work your arse off. Or you can go somewhere else and do what you wanna do and live comfortably. But they've still got their Walls pork sausages and HP Sauce!

'I wish I could live here all the fucking time, and I don't see why I can't live in my own country. If I lived here all the time I'd probably end up in debtor's prison. I'd be working out of there! Ha! I don't mind coughing up, man, but I'm not gonna slit my fucking throat. Once they force you out and you get used to not paying taxes, you structure your life that way.'

There was a knock at the door.

'Yeah, come in . . . if you can.'

It was Alan Edwards, who sat down and joined in with the interview for some reason. Taking a short break to order up more bourbon, Keith was still on one about being 'penalised for being successful'. At this point I had to turn the tape over. The next side would be sheer pinball ricochet about every topic under the sun. It's a good illustration of what it's like to go with Keith's inimitable flow. Point him in one direction and watch where he ends up . . .

I'd read in a newspaper story – credited to John Blake – that Keith was going to be making a gangster movie, based on the dying words of Dutch Schultz. The man was one of the most powerful and feared gangsters of all: ruthless, merciless, but glamorous at the same time. It turned out to be a perfect example of the way the 'Keef' legend has sometimes been made up by the press as they go along.

'Ah, that goes back a real long way. That is *The Last Words of Dutch Schultz*. There was an amazing transcript which William Burroughs presented via some friends to me. It's based on a stenographer's report. Dutch took a long time to actually expire. He got blown away in a subway somewhere in New York and his last words went on for about an hour or two. The cops were trying to pump him for information – "Who did this job?" and all that. And he was like [affects death rattle croak], "The angels have black horses." No answer at all. He was off on some vision. It's one of the few well-documented visions of premature death. The big black hole. I had this four or five-page manuscript and always said, "Yeah, that is a movie to be made." That was as much as I ever said about it. The rest of it is people wanting to make the movie and it getting to I'm supposed to be making it with them. The usual . . .'

John Blake!

'Exactly. Centre page of *The Sun*. They twisted it around like that. I've never known anyone ever come to me and say, "Yeah, we really wanna make this." I've got no claim on the thing. It doesn't belong to me. It's just something that I happened to talk about with some people. This could be an amazing movie. That's as far as that one goes.'

This kind of falsification and exaggeration has always been like water off a duck's back. How could it not be, after all those drug stories? (Though a lot of them were true.) But I wanted to know how Keith himself felt about it. He laughed.

'Yeah, I mean sometimes I get up in the morning and my old lady tells me what I did last night, and I find that pretty amazing sometimes! And so that's an extension of that. Back to John Blake again, Spanish Tony [Spanish accent] Domingez. Motherfucker.'

Whoops. Keith got back on the subject of his former minder's vile book, *Up and Down with the Rolling Stones* – ghost-written by John Blake. The subject still rankled as much as at our 1980 interview. And he really had it in for Blake now . . .

'He can't believe that I don't know it's him. *Grimm's Fairy Stories*! Each chapter would start off alright but then it'd go, "whoosh" – up into fairyland. That's why I'm very, umm . . . hey, why should I do John Blake a favour?' he reined himself in, realising he was granting the Fleet Street hack too much importance. 'I don't owe him nothing.'

It was inevitable that the two of them should run into each other one day. Keith's not one to waste his energy bearing grudges, but watch out if you cross him. His path finally crossed with Blake's in January '85, at Woody and Jo's wedding in Gerrards Cross, Buckinghamshire.

'Ah, Mr Blake, I've got a small bone to pick with you after this photo,' Keith promised as he lined up with the rest of the dearly beloved. According to eyewitnesses, Blake came over all funny and fled the ceremony. (I was happy when I heard it, because Blake would nick bits of my Keith interviews for his column without crediting them.)

'We don't need to talk about him. As far as movies go, I can't see myself doing it. I mean, I wouldn't mind because we'd all like to make a movie. I wouldn't mind! [much laughter] But after twenty years of being me I can't see myself doing the rounds of the studios, doing screen tests and auditions and doing Fu Man-bloody-Chu in pantomime [referring to Mick's recent donning of a large moustache and silken robes, for a cable TV production of Hans Christian Andersen's *The Chinese Emperor*].

'If somebody came to me and said, "I want you to do this," I'd say yeah, if it was the right movie. I might do it. But I can't see myself making a conscious decision to go to Hollywood and tussle with a role . . . competing with Dustin Hoffman or Al Pacino? I'm not gonna go up against those guys. That's their fucking job. They can't play guitar. I'm not saying they couldn't make a good record, no more maybe than I might not be able to make a good movie. I can't see myself going into it that way. You can't teach an old dog new tricks, hur hur.'

The conversation switched to David Bowie – maybe because of his faltering film career, or maybe because he came up from the same London club scene as the Stones. It proved a good launch-pad for Keith to talk about longevity in the music business. Even twenty years ago, he regarded the Stones as veteran survivors.

'Bowie's one of the few, apart from us, who has managed to ride out from the sixties through the seventies until now and still keep the interest of the public, which is what it's all about. Don't matter how good you are or how bad you are. We all know that 90 per cent of the stuff that's around today is a load of crap. The art in it is lasting. Can you imagine how sick the Beatles must've felt there when they broke up? They thought that they'd done it all and reached the pinnacle and they just broke up at the point where everything would've come their way. John got blown away, I know. It might sound callous here but it wouldn't matter what album he made, or would've made. It don't matter. The Beatles were the biggest band in the fucking world bar none. Forget us. They had a hold on the public all 'round the world. The only reason we exist is because the Beatles had that thing going and we were the opposite to that. That was our shtick really.

'The actual musical talent which is required to be a great and important recording act is ten per cent of it. The other 90 per cent is, can you live with each other? Can you live with the crap and the bullshit? Can you take the knocks? Can you all deal with it as time goes along? There's indefinable things which have got nothing to do with what you actually play. It's very rare to find guys who actually stick together, actually like each other and, even if they don't, be able to accept each other. I mean, it's one thing to make the records and be the band and be on stage. But to also be able to relate to what it means to the front row and the twentieth row, to record buyers, to the public as a whole, and to be able to assess, fairly accurately, what you are doing and what it means to the audience. To be able to understand that and be able to deal with that – because nine times out of ten you're screwing up. Most bands, give 'em eighteen months. The more successful they get, the quicker they break up.'

Alan Edwards, who'd been butting in during this part of the interview to Keith's general irritation, added that only one band came out of the whole punk generation who were still a fresh memory in '83. Yeah, The Clash, I said automatically. 'Two then – the Stranglers and The Clash,' said Alan, who happened to be looking after the Stranglers at the time.

'The Clash and the Stranglers,' agreed Keith, democratically. 'And they're the least punkish out of the whole lot! Compared to the Sex Pistols – because that's your definition of punk, right? Snotty little . . . pukey little . . . that's a punk, right? I've never understood why anybody would want to put that particular label on themselves and be proud of it. [adopts sneering tone] A punk's a punk, hur hur! The phrase that still hangs on is "new wave", which came out at the same time. People still use it now. In a way it's more valid, because each wave that comes in . . . it doesn't really mean anything. New wave? My next album – that's new fuckin' wave baby! It's the last thing I've done that's gonna hit the shore. Take it or leave it.'

The phone went. Keith broke off and shouted over to Jane Rose. 'Grab that, it could be anybody. If it's anything to do with merchandise just tell 'em to stuff it.'

It was the cue for a further diversion. 'I was in Paris and the one English paper I saw just happened to be the one with the music awards. There was some chick called Alf [Alison Moyet, then the vocalist of Yazoo] and the little poof in the skirt from Culture Club. Ronnie fancied him – until he found out it was a guy! Ronnie's in New York watching MTV and drags me up and goes, "You gotta see this chick, man!" I was already hip to it. "Her name's George, Ron." "Oh no!" He fancied the video. Jo was pissed off.' John Blake wasn't – he took that one from me for his column. But reggae must conquer all – and Stones fanzine *Beggar Banquet* reported that Boy George (who'd first hit big with the reggae-tinged 'Do You Really Want To Hurt Me?') visited Keith at his Jamaican home in mid-July '84.

From Culture Club's reggae-lite to the real thing. Keith, and to a lesser extent the Stones, had done their bit to further the music in the UK in the seventies and early eighties. I wondered if he was still as far into it as before – after the overselling of his name on the Max Romeo album, the ignominious departure of Peter Tosh from Rolling Stones Records, and the petering out of the music's golden age as the eighties wore on.

'I think that reggae here is suffering from post-Marley depression, not that Bob Marley . . . he's the least favourite of my reggae artists. But reggae music's gotten big business. I liked it when it wasn't and they didn't expect to make a buck and just laid it out. It happened to coincide with a time when black music in America just meant disco. Otis Redding was dead and you had the [Detroit] Spinners and the Chi-Lites, then it went into disco.'

The Stones also got a lot of people into funk – the pure, greasy American stuff by the likes of the Meters, who supported them on the '76 tour and part of the '81 jaunt. Around the same time, Ronnie Wood was introducing the great Bobby Womack to a white audience via his guest appearances on *I've Got My Own Album To Do* and *Now Look*. It was that same basic missionary zeal that the Stones have practised from the start, when they enthused about Chuck Berry, Bo Diddley and Phil Spector. Now it was the Meters – or rather, the Neville Brothers family ensemble that sprang out of them. And this time the Stones had gone one step further.

'I've got the Neville Brothers,' said Keith with pride. 'I've signed them up! The heart of the Meters were the Neville Brothers anyway. They're joined together now with the rest of their family. There's Aaron Neville, who did "Tell It Like It Is", which was a big hit in the late sixties. I happened to know about him a lot earlier than that because we got "Time Is On My Side" from an album that Aaron Neville's first record was also on. I knew about him for years. You've got his son Ivan, who's writing songs that Rufus are doing. With no stretch of the imagination – and I don't think he wants to be – he could be the next Lionel Richie. He's writing songs that good. This is the great thing because you've got this band there, which is all family. New Orleans. You've got the experience of that era and the guys that were in the Meters. You've got the father and the son, who are writing songs together. You've got the experience and you've got the youth within the same thing. It's as if you've got the Temptations with Michael Jackson thrown in at the same time. They've got some incredible songs together. All I did was do everything I could to make sure they ended up on our label, and it's worked out.

'Nine times out of ten it doesn't work out right. When I was working with Max Romeo, it came out on another label. You take that as it comes and nine times out of ten it doesn't pan out. But the Neville Brothers, it seems to have panned out. Atlantic are on the record they've put together. It makes it easier for us. We're just a label. We can't actually stamp the records and distribute them. All it means if somebody's on our label is they'll get that extra bit of airplay on the radio. Certain DJs will play it because it's the Rolling Stones and it's got the tongue on it. They'll give it a spin, whereas they might not if it was on any other label.'

The Neville Brothers would never hit the bigtime, but Ivan Neville would continue working with Keith throughout his career. Talk of Rolling Stones Records led to Peter Tosh, who had done well on the label but had messed with Keith. But he'd also busted open markets like South America – 'places you'd never think about' – which, in turn, gave Keith the urge to play in previously unexplored territories. This got him onto one of his favourite subjects – the road.

'There's been no doubt about the fact that we spent two years on the road being, for us, a complete reversal of the whole situation for the last ten years. It's done us more good. We've been talking between ourselves as a band. It's always been my point of view. We talked about this is the last time – if you don't play in front of an audience, forget it. Eventually you're gonna dry up. It's no accident that we've cut 40 tracks in six weeks. It's a direct result of being on the road for two years. You might not be consciously writing songs on the road but the arrow just points to certain things. Just the fact you're playing together more regularly. It makes the juices flow and it makes making records easier. And making records easier makes it easier to play on the road. You can't do one without the other. If you get to the point where you sell enough records you can afford not to go on the road – you can never afford not to go on the road. The minute you stop that, the minute you stop making good records.'

There was a rumour circulating at the time that Keith was going to release an album of country-blues prison songs. I put it to him.

'Right, coming out of the environment,' he quipped, harking back to the background that produced that classic '77 session, 'but I've always done that as far as I can remember. It's just that people have heard about them now 'cos the news crept out.

'There is a lot of stuff . . . I do Hoagy Carmichael songs. I do "Somewhere

Over The Rainbow". You wouldn't recognise it the way I do it, but so does Jerry Lee Lewis, an out-and-out rock 'n' roller. I mean, I can play anything. I like a lot of different things. I can do a lot of different things I don't do with the Stones . . . because it's something I know you don't do with the Stones. Being in the Stones, you're hamstrung a certain way. But I can still do all these extra things and put 'em down on tape. I'm not interested in whether they come out now. Never. I just enjoy doing 'em. You want someone to play a piano at a party and I'm there, I'll do it. "Sing us a song" – I'll play, "We'll Gather Lilacs".'

I've got this material on a bootleg called *Booze And Pills And Powders*, which emerged that year on The Swingin' Pig Records (though the label credits the record as Soulful Heart by the Winnie Perke Band!). Apart from 'Little T&A' in its original form as 'Bulldog', and a dub version of 'Beast Of Burden', there's some terrific stuff with just Keith on the piano, occasionally accompanied by Bobby Keys. 'Worried Life Blues' dates from the legendary Toronto sessions, while the aforementioned 'Somewhere Over The Rainbow' is funereal, wasted, but quite beautiful. And there's the Hoagy Carmichael song, 'The Nearness Of You', rendered in a truly damaged croak and quite touching. Keith would sing it to Patti, on his knees, when they got married. Along the same lines is the whispering plea of 'Honey, Don't Say Don't', which also features the bittersweet tones of Bobby Keys. Rock 'n' roll classics 'Whole Lotta Shakin' Goin' On' and 'Key To The Highway' are strident belters, while the title track sounds like one of Keith's loose backing tracks with a killer riff to hang it all on. But it was the ballads that were the big surprise. Even more of a surprise was that Hoagy Carmichael tracked down Keith in Barbados and phoned him up after he'd heard about his cover version, shortly before he died in December '81. He might have been hawking some more of his back catalogue, but he also recommended a lethal local rum concoction. Keith was touched but still didn't have a vehicle on which to release such intimate solo material. It remains unreleased simply because, he claims, it's so totally different to what's expected of Keith Richards.

Some of the ballads – including 'The Nearness Of You' – came from the three-day session in '81 when Keith christened Longview Farm, Massachusetts as a Stones rehearsal space. It's a real shame that he only ever gets to do stuff like this on his own. In terms of naked emotion, it's deeper and more personal than anything the Stones can muster. 'But that isn't the point of the Stones anyway,' said Keith, resignedly.

'Thing is you're one of the Rolling Stones. You're Keith Richards of the Rolling Stones and you play that game to a certain extent, because it's what you have to do. As long as *I* ain't bullshitted by being Keith Richards of the Rolling Stones, I don't give a damn. I don't mind bullshitting other people! You want this Keith Richards? You want that Keith Richards? Then there's your Keith Richards! You know me better, even though we've only met a couple of times, 'cos I can talk to you, in a way that I'd never talk to John Blake. I give him his version of Keith Richards. If I thought it served a purpose I'd stick him up against a wall and put a knife to his throat. And he'd write about it and get a scoop. I'd just need the opportune moment to do it. I don't see why I shouldn't. I'd dearly love to. And not just him either.'

And on that note the tape ran out. But it didn't stop there. Now it was time for some fun. 'Fresh supplies' were obtained and Keith greeted an ever-growing stream of visitors who'd heard he was in town. Soon it was like a mini-party in there.

At the time I was working at a Soho club called the Batcave, which was at the forefront of the burgeoning glam-goth movement. It eschewed the prevalent seriousness of the Gothic movement for silly fun and frolics with glam rock, disco, outrageous stage acts and the odd band. I tried to inject a rock 'n' roll element, which meant playing the Stones when I deejayed. I had to deejay that night and, much to my surprise, Keith decided he was coming too. He went on about it for hours, deflecting incoming phone invitations from the likes of Pete Townshend with a sharp, 'Nah, I'm going to the Batcave with Kris!'

Unfortunately, just as it was time to leave, Keith's lawyer turned up for a meeting. 'Gimme a call from the club, I still might be able to make it,' he said and scribbled down his room number and the name 'Mr. Hannay' – the alias he'd chosen for this particular stay, after a character in the early Hitchcock movie *The 39 Steps*.

The whole club was buzzing about a possible visit from Keith. I called Mr. Hannay about three hours later, from a payphone situated right next to the dancefloor. He'd just finished his meeting and by now the party was in full swing. 'Come back for a night-cap,' he said. Still not quite believing all this, I dutifully returned to the Savoy for another ten hours of rampant imbibing, dub reggae and top Keef anecdotes. Unfortunately – and unsurprisingly – I can hardly remember any of them!

He did let me try on that legendary skull ring again though: 'It's there to stop me getting big-headed and remind me that beauty is only skin deep. We all look like this under the surface.'

One thing I do remember is getting a crash course on the music hall comics Stanley Holloway and Max Miller. 'You've gotta hear this guy!', said Keith of Holloway, with a huge grin at about seven in the morning. He'd been talking about his love of the great comedians. Keith didn't have much time for your unfunny Ben Elton-type wankers, but went on for ages about vintage music hall-era greats like Flanagan and Allen and great comedians like 1930s lunatic Will Hay, and, of course, Tony Hancock and Tommy Cooper.

He whacked on a Stanley Holloway tape and knew every line: joining in, pointing out his favourite bits, and cracking up at the gentle East End humour (with piano accompaniment) of tracks like 'My Word You Do Look Queer', 'The Lion And Albert' and the aptly titled 'Brahn Boots'. This concerns the outrage at a funeral when a bloke called Jim turns up in 'brahn boots'. It turns out that he gave his black ones to a shoeless beggar, so the punchline is, 'Some day up at Heaven's gate / Poor Jim will stand and wait / Till an angel whispers, "Come in mate / With your brahn boots."'

Which is almost where we came in.

It had been quite some 24 hours. My first proper sesh with Keith, and he was more than the perfect host. I was expecting an aching hooter and came out with splitting sides. Next day I went looking for a Stanley Holloway album and found a compilation called –wait for it – *Brahn Boots*!

I dug it out while I was writing this, and presented it to Keith when I visited him twenty years later, before one of the *Licks* gigs. 'Ah, great, Stanley!', he said with a cackle.

CHAPTER THIRTEEN

DIRT

Too Much Blood

On April 30 1983, the Stones were grief-stricken to hear about the death of Muddy Waters. He'd been fighting lung cancer for two years and his heart had finally given out. The Stones sent one of the largest floral wreaths, bearing the message, 'In memory of a wonderful man dear to us all. We shall never forget you, Muddy.'

In May, Keith and Mick were reunited in New York for the mixing of *Undercover*. Rumours that Keith was falling out with Mick seemed to be confirmed when he took off for San Francisco – where Patti Hansen had started filming a movie called *Hard to Hold*, with former teen idol Rick Springfield. He popped over to Jamaica in June, went back to LA in July, and in the middle of it all found time to buy four floors of an apartment building on New York's East Fourth Street, a permanent home for 'no man's nomad'. It's a great spot – just off Broadway, in the same huge building as Tower Records, walking distance from the arty hubbub of St Marks Place where they shot the 'Waiting On A Friend' video.

On 16 July, Keith jammed with Jerry Lee Lewis for a TV programme called *Salute*, to be aired in September. It was a tribute to the man who was one of Keith's first great influences as he eased into his teens. Also on the bill were Little Richard and Mick Fleetwood. Both Keith and Jerry Lee – who'd never played together before – turned up in the same outfit of turquoise t-shirts, black jeans and white shoes!

'It was fantastic,' said Keith a few months later in London. 'Sometimes I've got people I wanna work with, and think I wanna work with, for years and years. It's not for me to instigate it because then it could seem phoney, like me wangling something because of who I am. I'd rather it came from the other way round. For years and years, I've been dying to play with Jerry Lee Lewis. Eventually, a few months ago I got the invitation to do it, so I did it. I wanted to do it because the guy's always fascinated me. It was much better that I wait until he asked me. I'd rather those people want to play with me rather than me force myself on them.

'This was fascinating. At rehearsals I found that I had to stop playing. I was just looking. To be behind him and watch him play. He's so unique. When he plays with his elbows and you think it's all just showmanship, but the guy plays like that, y'know? It's all part of the way he plays. It's amazing, so powerful. One of the reasons that I also did the show was that I saw a TV show that he did about a year or so ago, and he'd been very sick. They half disembowelled him, I think, but he's a tough son of a bitch.

'Then there was Little Richard, who was on the first tour that the Stones ever did in England. He was like, "Hey Keith, what are you doing here?" I was like, "Richard, I saw Jerry Lee on this TV show last year and I thought he was gonna kick the bucket. Maybe this was gonna be the last show and it's just something that I gotta do." He said, "Yeah, that's what I thought." Then we saw Jerry and he was like way bang strong, powerful. There's no way. And he said, "He's got us here under false pretences!" He was so strong. We got along real well. He's a real gent, a real Southern gent. Mellowed down a bit. He had to.'

Since the end of 1983, Mick had been negotiating a new recording contract for the Stones. They were in a good position, with the success of the recent album and tour. Columbia's Walter Yetnikoff, then quite a hotshot in early eighties New York, wanted them. Hitherto, Michael Jackson had been the biggest notch on his belt. This was the age of *Thriller* – nothing would ever be bigger, in terms of sales anyway. Having boosted Michael as a solo artist performing outside of the Jacksons, Yetnikoff could see possibilities in doing the same with a Mick Jagger solo album. He duly set about feeding Mick's ego.

In August 1984, the Stones signed a massive $28 million deal, to produce four albums for Columbia. The arrangement also included two Jagger solo albums, plus a chunk of the Stones' back catalogue. Big money – but CDs were just being introduced, so Columbia recouped within the year by regurgitating the back catalogue on horrible little silver discs.

Keith had been all in favour of a new record deal, but it was the first he knew of Mick's solo plans. Now it was set in stone, and he wasn't happy.

The extent to which Keith had been kept in the dark was revealed in an interview conducted at the end of July, with US magazine *Record*. When asked if he would ever release a solo album, he replied, 'I always say I'm not interested in that. I can't put myself in that position, and neither will Mick, ever. What do you say when you write a song? "Do I give this to the Stones, or do I keep it for myself?" To put yourself in that position versus the group is dumb, as far as I can see it.'

The interview eventually appeared in the October issue, after Mick had made known his plans. While the Stones were talking about their next album, Yetnikoff was setting Mick up to do his first. Dirty work, indeed – and the start of what Keith likes to refer to as 'World War Three'. All it would ultimately achieve – apart from rending the Stones apart until their reunion in 1989 – was gaining massive respect for Keith's own, retaliatory solo debut.

The new album would be the last for the Stones' old record deal with Atlantic in the US and EMI everywhere else. The first single was 'Undercover Of The Night', which was released at the end of October and made number eight in the UK, nine in the US. It was one of the darkest, most adventurous Stones outings for quite a while. The music was a wired cauldron of bubbling dance beats, clattering effects and a sonic dagger of a Keith riff, all combining to create an escalating feeling of urban panic. Over this, Mick howled and spat tough lyrics about repression, violence, and people disappearing in South America.

It was ambitious, politically focused, capturing the oppressive mood perfectly. It might not have been a party anthem like 'Brown Sugar', but 'Undercover Of The Night' boasts one of the great underrated Keef-riffs. Primal Scream's guitarist, 'Throb' Young, a big Stones fan, liked it so much that he heisted it ten years later for the live version of his group's 'Know Your Rights'.

The video more than matched the song. It featured footage of the band playing at Paris' Bains Douche club, with a dramatic section starring Mick and Keith filmed in Mexico City. Behind the camera was Julien Temple, who'd made the Sex Pistols' *Great Rock 'n' Swindle* movie. Temple had come up through the punk rock explosion, having also worked with The Clash, but he can't have been prepared for Keith's initiation test at their first meeting. Speaking on Channel 4's *The Tube* in October '84, the quiet, well-spoken young Englishman described how Keith had held his sword-stick to his throat, then taken him for a seat-gripping high-speed drive through the streets of Paris. Temple must have passed the test, as he started hanging out with Keith afterward.

The video shows straight-man Mick sitting by the pool of the Holiday Inn, before being kidnapped by a gun-toting Keith in a skull mask, heading a death squad who execute Mick. Temple had been one of the people present at the Savoy when I was doing my previous interview with Keith. Maybe he'd been reading Keith's mind.

At the same time, the single was also adapted to another growing trend, the twelve-inch extended dance mix. Keith wasn't into the idea of remixes at the start, maybe because he equated them with the clubs which Mick frequented. I can see his point. The motive behind remixes can often be mutton-dressed-up-as-lamb. With the Stones, it's always been the currently hippest and highest-paid members of the dance music elite they've called in: Armand Van Helden, Deep Dish, Paul Oakenfold, Fluke, the Neptunes, the Dust Brothers. But none of them, even if they were good tracks in their own right, eclipsed the original version. (The Deep Dish remix was a great club track, but it wasn't the Stones.) It wasn't until 2003 that Fatboy Slim achieved the impossible, tampering with 'Sympathy For The Devil' while preserving the song. But most of them – particularly the Oakenfold remix – got a disdainful snort from Mr. Richards:

'That's not my way of getting round things. There's only one good version. You can embellish and throw up a couple of extras, if you don't know or you're not sure. But there's really only one good version really.'

Undercover contained the Stones' most political music for years. It was the first time they had tackled the big issues since the heyday of 'Street Fighting Man', 'Sympathy For The Devil' and 'Gimme Shelter'.

Keith had talked about it when we were discussing the upcoming album. Just as he despised the synthesised pop of the early 1980s, when he came out of his acid daze in '68 he'd started hating the hippy-drippy sounds of the day. It was what had germinated *Beggars Banquet*.

'Yeah, maybe violence is playing a greater role in the world and we're that great old cliché, a mirror of society,' he reflected aloud. 'I love clichés. They're so true and so boring. In a way to me this album is a little bit of a brother to *Beggars Banquet*. It's not often we feel it's necessary, or even realise that we're doing it at the time. Standing up on our hind legs and saying something. But when there's too much crap going down, we find ourselves writing about it and singing about it. In that way this album has a little bit of relationship to that one.

'We never have stepped out of our way to be political or sociologically inter-esting. I still don't find it necessary to be the voice of any particular point of view. But it seems certain things build up in the world to a certain point, and suddenly we find ourselves writing about it and putting it out. "Undercover Of The Night" is basically about Central America and the possibilities and the confusion and stupidity there of not leaving people alone. The system.'

Undercover was released on 7 November 1983, going Top Five on both sides of the Atlantic and reaching number one in the UK. The sleeve featured a stripper covered in strategically-placed motifs, which could be peeled off from the American version. (The working title of the album had been *Undress Her*.)

At the time I thought that *Undercover* was the best Stones album since the early seventies, and still think it's undervalued. I partly agree with Keith's evaluation of it as a brother to *Beggars Banquet*, although the claustrophobic funk 'n' roll sometimes stokes the same simmering volcano as *Exile*. The rampant mood conjured by the opening title is just the right mix of modern dancefloor production technique, peak Stones savagery and thought-provoking lyrics. It set the scene for an album that cut like a knife through the booming clichés and vapid synthetics of the 1980s.

Keith's track, 'Wanna Hold You', is the breeziest, most celebratory thing on the album, whipping up a rockabilly-tinged pulse. Keith overdubs himself to mass choir level, while Ronnie's guitar sings. 'Yeah, I'm in love,' said Keith at the time, and it sounds like it.

'It Must Be Hell' is a dark observation from Mick, who comments on subjects clearly close to his heart – like unemployment, life on the street, and the decay of society. But forget the words for a minute. What is that riff roaring forth in Keith's most recognisable open-tuned tone? It's 'Soul Survivor', the closing track from *Exile*, one of the greatest guitar signatures he ever donated to mankind. Not only that, but the verse rides a mutation of the 'Honky Tonk Women' riff. As Keith explained it to me:

'Mick came out with the basic idea of that and I leant it. The Riff. I just hammered in there, in the old way. I find it difficult talking about this album or any other album – when you've just finished it and before it comes out and you've been into it for so long in such an intensive way every night. "No, Mick – less drums, more voice," and we argue. When it comes to this we know that the record's finished. You can go on forever. When we start fighting about it we know we've made it. I have this little ritual that I have to go through. I have to wait until the record's released and go along to the record store, shell out my few bucks and take it back home. And then I know that it's a record. Up until then I'm still listening to, as far as I'm concerned, a collection of tracks that might be a record or might not. I have to go, like everybody else, to the store and buy it. Break the cellophane off and put it on the turntable before I can start to hear it on the same terms as everybody else and make any rational judgements on it. I've got fifteen mixes of "Undercover Of The Night" and they're all totally different. The original version went on for about twenty minutes, maybe half an hour.'

Later that year, Keith gave another interview, which I came across on a bootleg. It contained some good stuff . . .

On fame: 'We're always very careful to avoid the estrangement of what comes with fame. I did all kinds of things to avoid it. With the Stones, despite it all, fame has never really sat that happily on our shoulders. "You're famous" – you kind of cringe a little bit. It's a bit embarrassing. There are people in this band, like Charlie Watts, who simply do not accept it at all. Charlie's attitude is part of the chemistry of the Stones really. We've been through as much as we've got in the way of success from fame and we've had a lot of other things to keep our feet on the ground.

'"The Greatest Rock 'N' Roll Band In The World." It's not our phrase. Hustling for dope in New York City with a shooter down my back. That keeps your feet on the ground. That's an example. Everybody in the band has always been very wary of being The Star, or coming on like that. In the Stones you're not allowed to be bigheaded. If one of you does get bigheaded the rest of the Stones will come and chop your feet off! It's something that can affect you as a person but it's not anything that's going to be useful in your life. It's a sure way to go down the tube.

'One of the magical things about the Stones is how, for some reason and I don't want to find out why, these five guys work the way they do and how they manage to keep it together through thick and thin. We don't ever analyse it.'

At this point, our intrepid mystery interviewer quotes Iggy Pop describing fame as 'the politics of envy'. He asks Keith if he's ever envious of others.

'Envy? I'd modify to wishful thinking,' says Keith, amidst the clink of many glasses. 'Everybody sees what they think is the ideal life – millions of birds, loads of money, flying around – just try it sweetheart! We're here to prove that that's not really the important thing about it. The important thing about it is to still carry on doing what you wanna do and do it good. The rest of it doesn't really make any difference. It's no fun zooming around in a jet every day. It's no more fun after a bit than being on a bus. It doesn't make any difference whether you're flying through the air or you're just trundling down the street. You're still in a little tin can and you're going from A to B. That's it. You got a seat and that's alright. It's nothing marvellous which is going to transform your life. That's one of the things you learn from having it thrown at you. It don't make you any happier – X thousands of this. People's idea of glamour . . . but they need it. We all need it in a way but, believe me, glamour isn't on a jet plane doing the Rolling Stones tour! Ha!'

So what excites him about travelling?

'People excite me. To a certain extent, some people excite me. Doesn't matter where it is. The more you travel around the more you realise, there's another little piece of education. People are people wherever they are. It's not any more exotic in Wigan than it is in Tahiti, quite honestly. Once you've got the frogs croaking outside and the mosquitoes biting you, you quickly lose the idea of tropical exotic glamour. It's just another place on the surface of the planet. What I try and do is make sure it's warm!'

How do you rate yourself as a guitar player?

'I'm not into ratings. Everybody hopefully is their own worst critic, most severe critic. The day I'm satisfied with what I do is the day I give up because then I've done it. It's the quest that's important. There's nothing at the end of the quest. It doesn't matter. The Holy Grail: who wants to find a gold cup full of blood? It's just the search that's important and passing it on. The greatest thing a musician can do is turn somebody on to the music. Doesn't matter if you're successful, as long as somebody picks something up from you. The greatest epitaph a musician can have – "Rest in peace. He passed it on." Music's far more important in people's lives than any of us realise. No doubt one day they'll do a scientific study and find out why. The fact is it's incredibly important. It's not a luxury. It's a necessity. One thing about music is it bypasses all of the barriers. As long as you've got ears. To me hell is being deaf. I've always had a theory that deaf people hear their own music in their own head. It doesn't necessarily have to come in ears, it's inside.

'We've got our own little vision of the Rolling Stones and we haven't found it yet. The day we think we have we'll give up. I still feel a long way away from it but I feel I'm getting closer.'

Even when it comes down to interviews, the Stones are a bootlegger's paradise.

Keith's 40th birthday was on 18 December 1983. He celebrated by finally marrying Patti Hansen, in secret in Cabo San Lucas at the Finisterra Hotel. Mick was the only Stone present – although the wedding did reunite Keith's parents, Bert and Doris, in the same room for the first time in twenty years. Patti's mother and brother were also in attendance.

The bridegroom wore a tuxedo and blue suede shoes for the Lutheran ceremony. At the reception afterwards, he sang Patti one of his favourite songs – Hoagy Carmichael's 'The Nearness Of You' – and his own sublime 'Wild Horses'.

Keith had never been happier. He was back with his dad, and had the girl of his dreams. It had taken her a while to realise that she wasn't going to get sucked into the vortex of Keith's lifestyle, and end up like Anita. But these were different times, and Keith had grown into a new sense of love and security. Anita didn't make it, because she'd broken her leg and got busted again. But the marriage did have her blessing, and she later gave Keith a 1934 Gibson guitar as a wedding present.

April-May 1984 issue of Beggars Banquet.

In the April-May '84 issue of *Beggars Banquet*, Bill German got Keith to open up on the subject of marriage. He claimed that Anita was doing so well in cleaning up that he was 'very proud of her', and that she spoke to Patti. 'I'm either very lucky or I've done something right ... Anita still knits me sweaters.' The interviewer asks Keith why he decided to make it legal with Patti.

'Because it's me now, and it's Patti, and it's a different point of view. Anita and I, in the sixties, were never interested in marriage. It seemed an archaic and dumb thing to do just to have a child . . . . And Patti and I have a different relationship. And besides, shit, I'm gonna try anything.

And if I'm gonna try anything like marriage, I'm only gonna try it once. And if I'm gonna try it once, it's gonna be with this chick . . . . For me, it's worked out real fine, 'cuz I can still talk to my ex-whatever. And there are other exes before Anita and I can still talk to them.'

1984 didn't start so well. Alexis Korner, the Stones' original mentor, passed away at London's Westminster Hospital on New Year's Day, aged 55.

In January, as Keith was trying to get recording sessions for the new Stones album underway, Mick began work on his first solo album. He was mighty pissed off when Mick informed him he'd be abandoning the Jagger-Richards compositional partnership for his solo album. Keith's attitude, when we met again a few months later, is summed up in a dismissive, 'Oh, he's just a cunt, anyway.' He'd already been through the ballistic stage at what he'd first felt to be a betrayal of lifelong trust. Now he was resigned to the fact that Mick was recording a solo album, though he suspected it might be a pile of shit. When he heard the album, he was glad not to be associated with it.

Keith and Patti spent much of February and March having a whale of a time in New York City. It was basically an extended honeymoon. They went to see *A Chorus Line* on Broadway, then checked out Buster Poindexter (former New York Doll David Johansen) at Tramps nightclub. He was playing an extended residency, hacking out booze-soaked blues and crooner standards with a supper-club band decked out in tuxedos – a far cry from when he was the glam Mick Jagger to Johnny Thunders' chaotic Keef. Keith himself couldn't resist getting up in the second set for a couple of numbers – Jimmy Reed's 'Take Out Insurance On Me Baby' and Pete Johnson's twenties classic 'Rocket 88'.

At the beginning of April, while Mick adjourned to Compass Point Studios in the Bahamas to record his album, Keith and Patti repaired to Point of View, Jamaica, for two and a half months. Some different kind of creativity must have gone on there, because, in July, Patti announced that she was pregnant.

In September, the Stones met at their London office to try and sort out their future. They were due to start recording their first album for Columbia in September, but it had to be postponed because Mick was still doing his album in New York. It was driving Keith completely mad. He spent much of his time jamming in Ronnie's studio basement in New York, putting some ideas down on tape. But Keith was still at a loose end with nothing to focus on. A fact which inadvertently led to our next meeting . . .

Shepherd's Pie & Dirty Strangers

Sometime during the autumn of '84 – and I'm ashamed to say I can't name the date! – I was sitting at home one night in Wandsworth, south London. By then, I'd also hitched up with a girl from New York called Patti – though, as I've said, our relationship would have a far less happy outcome. We'd had a slight tiff that evening, so I was feeling a bit low.

Then the phone rang.

'Kris?', asked a familiar voice.

'Yeah.'

'It's Keith here. I'm in town for a few days. Wanna come over for a drink? Savoy Hotel. Just you, right?'

Well, I'll be the Devil's scrotum for a second time!

Within minutes I was out of the door and on a 77 bus to The Strand. I've never subscribed to the male groupie mentality, but it isn't every night that you get an invitation from your all-time musical hero. Interviews are fine if you get on, but they're an arranged scenario. Here I was going for a session, at the man's invitation.

I reported to the front desk of the auspicious foyer and gave the password name, Mr. Hannay. It was the same suite as before. A grinning Keith answered the door himself. Expecting a party to be in full swing, I was surprised to find him on his own apart from one other guy. 'Meet my mate Alan.' He turned out to be Alan Clayton, the singer from a band called the Dirty Strangers who Keith had enthused about at our previous meeting. He was the one who made a gift of the ornamental swordstick Keith threatened Julien Temple with!

The Dirty Strangers were a London-based band who'd been playing blues and rock 'n' roll around the pub and club scene for years. A chaotic but hugely enjoyable knees-up, and decidedly untrendy, they seemed to remind Keith of his early days.

'There was like a weird parallel,' Keith had told me. 'The first stuff they actually managed to get on tape they did at IBC Studios, which is where we cut our first stuff . . . . Up until Christmas I was in contact with them all the time. I've only spoke to them a couple of times since then because I've been so involved with doing the Stones. I heard three or four songs that were really interesting. I managed to lay this tape on a DJ in Paris, and it took off like that. But they didn't have a record to back it up so it didn't do it. On the strength of that they got over to Paris to do a couple of shows, which is better than not working . . . . They're probably right now the only English band I know of, at all really.'

Alan Clayton is one of nature's likely lads: the proverbial diamond cockney geezer with a heart of gold and hilarious repartee, but also a fierce passion for music. There's no bullshit allowed when Alan's around. Humour, music, no bullshit – they must be the reasons why he'd accompany Keith on much of the European leg of 2003's *Licks* tour, nearly twenty years later. Alan had met Keith in '81 through a mutual friend called Joe Seabrook, who was his minder. Alan and Joe had both been nightclub bouncers together.

It appeared that Keith had been visiting London during the period when Mick was otherwise engaged, and wanted to hang out with some mates. Alan had been up to the Savoy several times already, even though he was working on a building site at the time, and sometimes had to go to work straight from an all-nighter with Mr. Richards!

Keith also had a problem. He was due to fly to Jamaica the next day and, being Keith Richards, definitely could not board the plane with the bag of killer weed and added extras someone had left in the room. 'Our mission tonight is . . .' There were also several bottles of Jack Daniel's lined up.

It was one of the most remarkable nights of my life – though I wouldn't say memorable! Within an hour, we were all sitting around chatting, joking and, it must be said, giggling a lot. The three of us approached our obliterating task with gusto. As ever, Keith's mighty boom-box was blasting out the dub and it struck me how relaxed he was, away from the press officers, assistants and hangers-on, with no microphone in front of him. Jokes were exchanged of a lavatorial nature, and out came the music hall tapes.

Keith has been portrayed as many things. I personally had always found him friendly and accommodating during the interviews. But here he was just hanging out with the boys, having a laugh. It's an old cliché, but he could have been a top bloke you'd met down the pub. In a life that nobody could call 'normal', Keith could unwind in his hometown without any pressure on him or any duty to perform.

But it was inevitable that the guitars would come out. I was sitting about three feet away as Keith picked up a large Gibson acoustic and started picking some mean and lowdown blues. He used it to punctuate his words as he talked. Close up, Keith's guitar style is awesome. He talks about how he stood next to Jerry Lee Lewis and had to stop playing as his jaw hit the floor. I wasn't playing anything – can't! – but it didn't stop my own chin crashing into the carpet as Keith closed his eyes and let fly. Chords ricocheted between scattershot flourishes and fills, delivered with brutal power or gentle affection. He struck, stroked and steered the instrument with a sublime motion that goes way beyond mere skill. For a few minutes there, Keith was in the dark heart and soul of the original blues.

No wonder his hero is Robert Johnson. When Keith first heard the music of the blues' greatest legend, he asked Brian Jones who the other guitarist was. If what I was hearing had been on a record, I'd have asked who the other two were – although occasionally he'd simply twist your heart with one solitary groin-snarling note.

At Keith's insistence, Alan played one of his own songs. Looking a trifle nervous – who wouldn't? – he acquitted himself just fine with 'Gambler's Blues'. And got a round of applause in return.

Next it was Keith's turn again. Fuck me if it wasn't 'Wild Horses'. Five minutes later, Keith and Alan were trying to scrape me off the ceiling.

The night went on. A bit of Max Miller, fresh supplies of Jack, more strumming, more of everything, until, at around six in the morning, Keith came out with his own piece de resistance. Mischievous gleam in his eye, he bounded over to the phone and dialled room service. 'Just you wait until you try this!' he announced.

Soon the trolley turned up, the porter wheeled it in, receiving a twenty-pound note for his trouble, and Keith unveiled . . . shepherd's pie! With peas.

Over the years, the man's obsession with shepherd's pie has become legendary. In 1984 it was a little-known fact, but it was probably the reason he stayed at the Savoy. It was certainly top of the list of things he missed most in the UK, along with PJ Tips teabags and brown sauce.

As the sun began to stream in through the window, Keith tottered into the bedroom and made a phonecall that went on for over an hour. It must have been to Patti, as he chuckled contentedly and spoke low and affectionately with a massive smile on his face. Eventually, he came off the phone, walked in, and looked around. 'Aah, fuck the plane!' he exclaimed, and started over again. It was only for a while though, as we were all drifting off. Al and I said our warm goodbyes, with Keith telling me to call him the next day to see if he was still around. Then he went back into the bedroom.

Next day I called the Savoy from a phone box in Tooting, where I was signing on. I got through to a laughing Keith immediately. We swapped 'good night, wunnit?' chat, but he couldn't meet up. Keith was finally going to make that plane.

Alan and me kept in touch for a while after that night at the Savoy. I went to see some Dirty Strangers gigs, and even organised a photo session in a public lavatory to accompany a feature in *Flexipop!*. But we lost contact after I moved to New York for a few years, and I didn't see him again until a chance meeting in early 2003.

We got to trying to recall that night at the Savoy. Alan remembered it, but added, 'There were so many! I used to leave there at four in the morning and go straight to the building site where I was working. Sometimes I'd be there for days on end. Reality used to hit me as I walked into the lift. It was detached from reality. I do remember Keith saying, "There's this bloke who's a journalist but he's really into music."'

That must have been when I got that phonecall. But why does he want to hang out with tossers like us, I wondered?

'If you knew all his friends, they're various sorts of people. He doesn't hang about with anyone if they're not his friends,' reckoned Alan.

These '84 sessions also resulted in Keith playing with the Dirty Strangers. The group, who'd formed in the late seventies in west London, had put all their dough into recording demos for a new album in '85. One day Alan played the six songs to Keith:

'He said they weren't right. "Do 'em again." We said, "But we can't because we haven't got any money now." So he came in and played on 'em. And he paid for the studio too.'

The all-night sessions took place in a tiny studio on Mount Pleasant, north London. I can't imagine what it must have been like for the guys, thrashing out their boogie in this cheap, cramped studio – with Keith Richards playing alongside them.

Nick Kent mentions the Dirtys' 'raucous mongrel R&B' in a Stones feature he wrote for *Spin* magazine in '85: 'A couple of days later, Richards was in a recording studio adding his guitar to a session by an unknown and unsigned group called the Dirty Strangers . . . He tuned the strings down to his famous G-modal tuning and cranked the same old leathery licks he's been locked into for the last twenty years. The sound is unmistakable. It has its virtues and its limitations. It is just as the Rolling Stones were.'

'It was good, because he just acted normal like he was one of the band,' recalled Alan. 'I'd take him back to the hotel in my white Fort Escort. He says he didn't pick up a guitar to make money – he just wanted to play. He was just playing there with us, like one of the boys. It was a buzz but it just felt perfectly normal. He just mucked in and got on with it.'

And brought in Ronnie Wood, for good measure. They did six tracks, which appeared on an album called *The Dirty Strangers*, released on the Thrill Records label owned by Prince Stash. He's the same Stash who was present at the '73 Cheyne Walk bust, and started the label just to put the album out.

'Yeah, we fell in with Keith and Ronnie, done the album and it was downhill from there on!' laughed Alan Clayton.

When the Dirties played the Marquee, the Stones turned up. For their American tour in '86 Ronnie leant them his guitars and amps, and Alan stayed at Keith's East Fourth Street apartment in New York. 'I should say I stayed UP up there. I hardly got any sleep!'

Alan has the only copy of Keith's multi-track recording for the album. It's basically what Keith laid down as the track played in the background – unmixed, unadorned and absolutely stunning. I've never heard him like that before. He's chugging away with the track, driving it like he does the Stones. Not just the riffs, but little sparks and bends, with shades of Chuck, Muddy and Jimmy Reed assimilated into a pulse that sounds hot-wired straight from his internal organs.

Alan remembers that Keith took the trouble to learn the songs. 'He wasn't busking it. He listened to all the tracks and knew all the changes. He just put everything into it. But then I edited it! Back then, I didn't care who it was. "Right, that bit can go." Looking back! . . .'

Springtime For Biff Hitler

At the Savoy, Keith only alluded to the trouble and strife going down with the Stones. Mick was hellbent on his solo career, and would spend the rest of '84 and early '85 on his personal mission. The Stones album that eventually appeared as *Dirty Work* was plagued by bitterness, non-attendance and sheer bad vibes. As its making overlapped with Mick's album, *Dirty Work* becoming known as 'Keith's album'.

At a Stones meeting in Amsterdam that October, Jagger made it quite clear what his priorities were. It spawned the famous anecdote where he got pissed and called up Charlie at five in the morning from Keith's hotel room, asking, 'Where's my drummer?' At which point Charlie got dressed, came round, and whacked him. 'I'm not your drummer. You're my singer,' said Mr. Watts. Keith loved telling that one, and later told Bill that he wished he'd done it.

Meanwile, Keith was frustrated enough to start considering outside projects, such as coordinating the music for a film about Robert Johnson called *Love in Vain*, and even a part in Julien Temple's first big movie, *Absolute Beginners*. (It emerged the following year with David Bowie and Liam Gallagher's future ex-wife, Patsy Kensit, but *sans* Keith.)

1985 – the most troubled year of the Stones' career – started well enough, as Ronnie married Jo Howard at Denham, Buckinghamshire on 2 January. All the Stones turned up, apart from Mick, while the wedding band was the Dirty Strangers. Keith and Charlie were joint Best Man.

Later that month, sessions finally started for the new Stones album with quintessential eighties producer Steve Lillywhite (Peter Gabriel, U2). But there was instant friction, as Mick turned up with no new songs, having emptied his udders into his own milk bucket. 'I thought it would be something that he couldn't do with the Stones, rather than an obvious commercial rock 'n' roll album,' Keith complained about Mick's solo project to *Musician* magazine. 'If it was Irish folk songs with a lady harpist, I would have respected it. If he had some burning desire to do an album like *Mick Jagger Sings Frank Sinatra*, or *Mantovani*, I would have understood

. . .' But all he'd done, according to Keith, was fuck up the Stones' recording process.

The Stones soldiered on, often without Mick, for five months. Bill Wyman totted up over two hundred tapes, and listed a tasty string of covers in *Rolling with the Stones*: songs by Chuck Berry, Howlin' Wolf, Fats Domino, Buddy Holly, Elmore James, Elvis and Muddy Waters. It gives the sense of a band just hanging out, having a laugh. Some more diverse titles include vintage classics like 'The Nearness Of You', Santo and Johnny's 'Sleepwalk', Bobby Darin's 'Splish Splash', 'Putty In Your Hands' by the Shirelles, the Everly Brothers' 'Claudette', 'Soothe Me' by Sam Cooke, and the Ventures' guitar rave-up 'Perfidia'. I'd particularly love to hear Keith doing George Jones' 'Burn Your Playhouse Down'.

The working titles for the album tracks give some inkling of Keith's mood: 'Had It With You', 'One Hit To The Body', 'Dirty Work' and 'Fight' all made it to the album, with Keith making sure Ronnie got a co-writer's credit. Keith would keep 'Talk Is Cheap' for the title of his first solo album while discarding the instrumental track of that name.

Peter Doggett's bootleg guide in *Record Collector* says that some of the Keith-dominated out-takes from *Dirty Work* are as good as the album. An exclusive *Dirty Work* studio preview in *Beggars Banquet* mentions his song 'Deep Love' as being on the finished album, but three Keith vocals on one Stones album seem to have been too much for Mick, so they swapped it for the weak 'Hold Back'.

Mick's first single from his solo album, 'Just Another Night', was released at the beginning of February. It stiffed at number 27 in the UK, but got to number ten in the US. All the promotional interviews inevitably asked about the Stones, which gave Mick the chance to vent his spleen about things like the drug busts ('boring and time-consuming') and to tell the *Daily Mirror* that the Stones were like a long marriage, while the solo fling was his mistress. And, as with his women in real-life, it seemed he had no intention of staying faithful.

She's The Boss was released a month later. The album that 'should have been a ginormous event', according to Keith, smacked of desperation. By dragging in hot eighties producer Trevor Horn, who'd caused such a sensation with the short-lived Frankie Goes To Hollywood, Mick was treading in all the boomy-plastic-drums shit that Keith avoided like the plague. And he'd later tour behind it with another band, playing Stones songs in the set. The album made the lower reaches of the Top Ten on both sides of the Atlantic, but its real achievement lay in igniting what Keith referred to as 'World War Three'.

There was a joyous interlude beginning on 18 March, when Patti gave birth to a baby girl at the New York Hospital. Keith was present at the birth, and they named her Theodora Dupree – her middle-name after Keith's beloved musician grandfather.

In April, the Stones regrouped in Paris for more sessions. The release date for the next album had already been put back from June to September, in deference to Mick's solo work. They still managed to wind up with 30 tracks for *Dirty Work* by mid-June. A string of guests popped in, including Jimmy Page. Keith and Ronnie also took time out to check blues guitarist Lonnie Mack two nights running at the Lone Star Cafe. The first night was empty. Keith said he and Ronnie would play an extended blues jam on the second night – and it was crammed.

And then came Live Aid. That ballooning monster of a charity function, instigated by Bob Geldof – once the arrogant frontman of a second-rate new wave
band, now a saint raising shit-loads of cash for some desperately needy people. Bill
Wyman says in his book that Geldof flew to Paris to persuade the Stones to perform. According to the *Beggars Banquet* fanzine, the band didn't believe the money
would find its way past the regional politics and into the kids' mouths, and agreed
that they shouldn't do it. But Mick was already billed as playing, supposedly giving in to 'emotional blackmail' when his name appeared. Other sources claim he
steamed in at the chance of exposure to over a billion people worldwide.

In May, Mick announced he'd be peforming with Hall and Oates' backing
band. Geldof had guaranteed him the prime spot before the US headliner – Bob
Dylan. In inimitable style, Keith and Ronnie inadvertently trumped him by joining Dylan for his set. All they knew in advance of the set was that the crowning
moment was to be 'Blowin' In The Wind', before the cringe-worthy syrup of 'We
Are The World' – from the sublime to the ridiculous in one easy swoop.

Ronnie told Bill German he had been responsible for press-ganging the reluctant Keith into playing at Live Aid with Dylan. Bob had called to say he was in town
to do a gig in Philadelphia, and didn't have a band. Ronnie started hatching a plan
for he and Keith to join Dylan, when he twigged what event he was talking about:

'I got Keith to my house [in New York] for the first night of Live Aid
rehearsals . . . . So Bob arrives and the first thing he says, "Hey, are you guys gonna
do the gig on Saturday or stay home and watch it on TV?" Keith then began to
strangle me, and said, "What did you get me round here for?" He literally went,
"You bastard, you wasted my time. We got an album to make." . . . . Luckily, Bob
went to the toilet and I happened to be walking upstairs when he came out and
said, "Do you think one day you guys would ever do a gig with me?" I said,
"What're you talking about? We're ready to do one right now with ya." . . . . So
he runs downstairs, grabs Keith, bam, "Would you play this gig with me?" And
Keith goes, "What the fuck do you think we're here for? Of course I would!"'

The Dylan spot came over as the realest moment of the day – even if our gallant
duo seemed to be struggling to keep up with Bob's obvious improvisation, were playing acoustically after a day of electric bombast, and couldn't hear anything onstage.

As Ronnie put it, 'as we were facing out at the show and literally blowing in
the wind, it was going out and just getting lost. By that time, the stage crew were
drunk or celebrating or giving up, so we had no monitors, nothing. That's why I
liked the set so much, because Bob sang so well and in tune, and his lyrics were so
poignant and relevant. When I listened to a tape, I realised how appropriate the lyrics
are. One was about a guy who kills his family of seven through starvation ['The
Ballad Of Hollis Brown']. And "Ship Comes In" makes reference to Ethiopia.'

It's a well-worn story as to how Dylan changed the set at the last minute. 'We
were told to do "Blowin' In The Wind",' said Ronnie, but Dylan decided to do 'It
Ain't Me Babe' before they went on, which they rehearsed in the wings. But then
he started with 'The Ballad Of Hollis Brown', and told them he wanted to follow
up with 'All I Really Want To Do'. Or something.

Bob, Keith and Ronnie were still standing there when 'We Are The World'
got underway, with Lionel Richie coming out to give them a hug. Then they kind

of melted into the throng, with Keith perched on a monitor pretending to direct the ensemble. Whatever the relative strengths of their set, in no way had it been another Live Aid career move. If anything, it was the opposite – flying in the face of the opportunism running rampant in the name of charity. (Farm Aid would also be born of Dylan's set, inspired by a remark he made about relieving the US farmers' debt crisis.)

After that it was back to New York City, to mix the new album at RPM studios. On the night of 19 July, Keith popped into a mid-town studio to lay down a track with the inimitable Tom Waits. He was only supposed to do one, but ended up playing on five, three of which later appeared on the *Rain Dogs* album: 'Union Square', 'Big Black Love', and a country ballad called 'Blind Love'. The sound is sparse and bluesy, with Keith supplying laid-back embellishment.

The following week, Keith and Ronnie dropped in on Don Covay, who was recording at another studio, and repaid him in kind for the backing vocals he'd done their album. The presence of Covay on *Dirty Work* had brought the Stones, who had covered his 'Mercy Mercy' in 1964, full circle.

Keith also popped up in early August at another New York studio, to play on a track called 'My Mistake' for Stray Cats spin-off Phantom, Rocker and Slick, while Keith and Ronnie collaborated with Bono of U2 on a track called 'Silver And Gold' for the Sun City anti-Apartheid album. Bono had recorded the vocal in his hotel room, simply turned up at the studio, handed it over to Keith, and they laid down the track on the spot.

It was also around this time that Annie Liebowitz conducted the photo session for the *Dirty Work* album cover, with the Stones looking pissed-off and disaffected. They acknowledged Bobby Womack's contribution to the album by appearing with him on an interview for MTV. The next day, Bill German stumbled into a full-on session at RPM studios, which saw Keith, Ronnie, Charlie, Womack and Covay jamming into the next morning. Apparently, Keith sat down at the piano to give a rendition of Carole King's '(You Make Me Feel Like A) Natural Woman', and Keith, Don and Bobby performed joke-falsetto versions of 'Satisfaction' and 'Time Is On My Side' 'that left Keith lying back on the piano stool cackling.' A few nights later, Keith and Ronnie's mates the Dirty Strangers were over for a few club dates in the area. Even Bert and Anita went to check them out at Danceteria.

For a supposedly dark period, a whole lot of fun was being had. But much of *Dirty Work* seems to have been made without a full complement of Stones. Jagger had taken to using a separate room in the studio when he made one of his rare appearances. The nucleus seemed to centre around Keith and Ronnie plus whoever else was about, including drummer Steve Jordan from chatshow host David Letterman's show band, Rolling Stones Records signing Ivan Neville, and session bass man Charlie Drayton. Pretty soon, all three would join Keith in his X-Pensive Winos solo project – though this floating core of surrogate Stones first awarded themselves the jocular title of the Biff Hitler Trio.

At this time, much to everyone's alarm, Charlie had developed a problem with heroin, speed and booze. As he later reflected, 'I don't know what made me do it that late in life – well to Keith it wasn't late enough! . . . . The mid-eighties were

Keith in the studio with Alan Clayton (fourth from left) and the Dirty Strangers.

the toughest time for me. That's when I was going through what Keith was going through in the seventies.'

If a Stones tour had looked doubtful before, it went out the window after 19 August when Charlie, who'd gone back home to Devon, fell over in his wine cellar and broke his leg in three places. With his jazz side-project, the Charlie Watts Orchestra, now closer to his heart than the war-torn Stones, Charlie made the most famous remark of his career: 'In 25 years with the Stones, I've spent five years working, and twenty years hanging about. I'd have been dead years ago, if I'd thought about it.'

Farewell To The Boogie Man

On 12 December 1985, Ian Stewart died of a heart attack in the waiting room of a west London clinic, aged 47. He was going for a check-up after suffering respiratory problems for a few days. It hit hard. Stu was the sixth Stone, and had been there from the very start.

The funeral took place at Randall's Park Crematorium in Leatherhead, Surrey. All the Stones attended. The music was 'Boogie Woogie Dreams', and the Reverend Alastair Dyke described Stu as 'a musician's musician'. 'I'm feeling really numb,' the tabloids quoted Keith as saying. 'He's going to be sadly missed.'

'It would need a book as big as this chapel to pay tribute to him,' said Charlie. '"Desperate Dan" is what we called him,' said Eric Clapton of Stu's likeness to the comic-book character. 'That is the way he would like to have been remembered.' Shirley Arnold, who'd worked as a secretary for the Stones for years, said, 'Over the years there have been so many people around the Stones who have died one way or another, but you never thought it would happen to Stu. He was such a private guy. That funeral, and Mick with tears in his eyes. I'm sure if Stu had seen it he would have found it all quite amusing.'

When I heard the news, I could only think of Keith that day in the Stones' office, five years earlier, laughing his head off about the early days when they were rehearsing above the Bricklayers Arms in Broadwick Street, and Stu would be leaning out of the window, ogling the strippers. 'But could he play boogie-woogie!' acclaimed Keith.

Stu deserves a major tribute. He was very close to Keith, and had planned to visit him after the doctor's appointment to try and sort out the messy situation surrounding *Dirty Work*. As ever, Stu's loyalty and down-to-earth logic had held them together through the worst. His death probably wounded Keith the most. 'His passing was the final nail in the coffin,' he lamented. 'We all felt the glue had come undone. Very few people realised how important he was to the Stones . . . The combination of that and Mick's defection left me in limbo.'

In the *Beggars Banquet* tribute, Keith reflected, 'I thought he'd be the one holding the shovel, the one to bury all of us. What a hole he's left, such an obvious gap. He would always be there to comment on everything and sometimes you would think he was crazy. But then you'd go and realise that he was right all along . . . . I'd had other friends pass on, and you go, "Gee, it's a shame," but Stu was different. I could think of a hundred other fuckers who should have gone instead of him! He wasn't even on my list!'

Ian Stewart shunned the limelight. He let the groupies, drugs, and scenes of wild debauchery run past him, while he stuck to the job of keeping the Stones' show on the road. From lugging amps in the back of a van in the early sixties to directing proceedings in the mega-stadiums years later, Stu was always there. He'd bring the group down to earth if their egos puffed out too much, with some colourfully-phrased commonsense.

He only allowed himself one moment of recognition, in 1975, when *Creem* – who probably devoted more space to the Stones than any other publication during the seventies – printed a lengthy interview with Stu by respected rock journalist Lisa Robinson.

Describing the Beatles as 'nice lads who write pretty songs, but they are horribly overrated,' he also reduces his enormous role in the band with humble comments like, 'Even though Brian and myself started this group, there probably would've been a Rolling Stones in some form with Mick and Keith, because that pair – with other musicians – were going to make it anyway. So I don't feel that, apart from losing a lot of sleep and buying hamburgers when they were broke . . . I really haven't gone and done all that much. I mean, they had to go through a hell of a lot just being the Rolling Stones.'

Most intriguingly, Stu revealed that between '64 and '67, 'nearly all those records are just Keith taped over three times,' while Brian explored other instruments before becoming 'too out of it to play at all'. The way he was pushed out of the group by Andrew Oldham still rankled – 'it wasn't very nicely done' – and he obviously resented how it stopped his development as a piano player, as 'there are really a lot of guys going around who are really mediocre piano players.'

But, when asked about Keith, he said, 'he really is like the pulse of the Stones, and he leads the band and he's never displayed any flashy guitar techniques or anything. And Keith is the best rock 'n' roll guitar player there is. Yet people don't realise that because he doesn't do a lot of solos . . . he's always left gaps. He's great at tempos and things like that.'

As might be expected, Stu laid into all the trappings of excess, 'all the bullshit that goes with it. All the sort of huge entourage and kind of caravan following the Rolling Stones about, all the little egos running about.' He hated the fact that Playboy bunnies got block tickets for a Chicago gig, whereas Howlin' Wolf couldn't, and extravagant 'distractions' like the Lotus stage.

Robinson asked how much Mick controlled the show.

'Oh, I think he controls everything. Not so much the music, Keith leads that really. See, basically Keith can't be bothered to go to any of these meetings where people have to decide these things. And although he'll tend to bitch a little bit afterwards, he's quite happy to let Mick and Charlie go over these things and draw the stage and say, well, do it. Because Keith is certainly not worried about the money thing.'

And if Stu had to describe his position with the band? 'I always put company secretary.'

On 23 February 1986, the Stones played the 100 Club in London's Oxford Street as a tribute to Ian Stewart. They played an R&B set, including many of their earliest tunes, picking numbers at random as they went along. It was high-energy, lowdown and dirty, as if it came booming straight out of the Crawdaddy. That night, any differences that had festered between Keith and Mick over the previous months seemed irrelevant as they remembered their great friend. They left the club arm in arm.

The band were still devastated a couple of months later, when Keith appeared on BBC Radio One's *My Top Ten*. Talking about the big question of going on tour behind the new album, he said, 'I don't think we'll be touring this year, although nothing is carved in stone . . . I've no doubts we will tour again. It's just that this year the timing has been a little uncoordinated . . . . I don't know, man. Stu's death was the main reason this time around. It's difficult to do anything at the moment, let alone tour. I was talking to Charlie the other day, and he's still waiting for Stu to come bouncing through the door. It hasn't sunk in all the way yet. We're all so used to seeing him, then not seeing him for a few months, that it just feels like a gap right now. I guess we'll have to get used to it eventually. For the band it was a big wallop and, as I say, we're still in semi-shock.'

They will always remain so. As Keith grows older, he seems to have taken on Stu's mantle – he cuts the Stones down to size, while bigging up Charlie Watts. The loyalty and love of music that motivated Stu through times both euphoric and horrendous lives on in him. Sadly, Stu bowed out when the group he co-founded and believed in was in a state of disarray, after the teeth-pulling creation of *Dirty Work*. But he'd be happy with the way that his boy Keith has taken up the baton. Keith still occasionally refers to the Stones as 'Stu's band'.

Dirty Work would be dedicated to Stu. After Keith's lovely closing ballad, 'Sleep Tonight', there was a burst of Stu's boogie-woogie piano. Rolling on up to heaven.

Too Rude

The first taste of the new Stones album was a cover version of Bob and Earl's huge '63 hit, 'Harlem Shuffle'. According to Keith, he had been on at Mick to do it for five years, finally getting the track together in Paris. It was a soul-strutting sixties groover, given a Stones-spray and some incendiary co-vocals by Bobby Womack, unfortunately mixed too far down. As a single, it was the Stones' first stab at someone else's song since their first three releases, all of which were cover versions. Released on 15 March 1985, 'Harlem Shuffle' hit the Top Ten both in the UK and in the US.

Dirty Work itself was released on 24 March, reaching number four in the UK and the US. (It was originally going to be called *Nineteen Stitches*, after an assistant engineer who fell through a glass coffee table.) I was expecting a clash of negative sparks with an over-polished production. But, while it's not an all-time Stones classic, Keith was at the reins throughout and there's a welcome rawness. It boasts one of his finest songs, in 'Sleep Tonight', and there are no half-assed disco excursions. And, as Keith said, there were few direct battles with Mick, because he was hardly ever there. Keith and Ronnie were on top form, the dynamic mating of their guitars undiminished by the feuds, Ronnie's recently-conquered freebase habit, or the sheer pressure. But Charlie, who had recently got into heroin, doesn't feature on all the tracks.

'Too Rude' is a delightfully ganja'd-up reggae outing by Keith which sees him dueting with the wonderful Jimmy Cliff, whose 'The Harder They Come' was the song that got Keith into reggae in the first place. 'Too Rude' was unearthed from one of Keith's many reggae tapes. Compared to the rest of the album it's cool and chilled, splashing in a bath of dub. Keith would later play this one live with his X-Pensive Winos.

But Mick had been hanging out with his new mates, Duran Duran, and their sterile synthesised white funk had an influence on his contributions to the album. Mr. Richards was unimpressed when Duran Duran visited the studio, and expressed shock at the way the Stones recorded live together in the same room.

It prompted this classic snarl in *NME*: 'You get Duran Duran come down for a day, walk into our fucking sessions and say, "What are you doing in that room together?" It's called playing music, man. That's the only way we record, you snotty little turd.'

The album's title track is a hotwired stream of pure vitriol, with lyrics about people sitting back and letting others do their work for them – 'Find some fucker, find some jerk, do it all for free . . . I hate ya, you're a user.' It doesn't let up with Keith 'n' Ron's ensuing creation, 'Had It With You'. It could be about a love-hate relationship gone pear-shaped, or it could the death knell of Keith and Mick's partnership: 'I love you dirty fucker . . . It is such a sad thing / To watch a good love die / I've had it up to here, babe / I've got to say goodbye.'

Keith later joked that the album should come with a sticker saying, 'Forgive Them, For They Know Not What They Record.'

But, if 'All About You' had heralded the dawn of the Keith Ballad, his beautiful closer, 'Sleep Tonight' set a precedent which would continue through the next three Stones albums and up until the new studio tracks on the *Forty Licks* hits

Capturing all five Stones in one room for the Dirty Work *album.*

compilation. For this Stones fan, these songs are as big a contribution to modern music as the lethally invigorating touch he dealt the sounds of Chuck and Muddy. It's pure soul – bare, vulnerable, with only the minimum technique and polish.

'Sleep Tonight' emerged from a low-lit Paris amble with Ronnie on drums. It's a soul lullaby which, once again, got people wondering about the subject: 'This darkness, baby, it's chilling me / Stars stare down in sympathy.' The last verse is indeed chilling, as Keith oozes, 'You better get some sleep tonight / Warn all your friends . . . It ain't revenge / You understand / I just wanna know / Who dealt this hand?'

Like 'All About You', Stones-watchers thought it was about Mick – or Anita – or maybe even Keith himself, because of the hook-line, 'You better get some sleep tonight.' Steve Appleford wrote in *It's Only Rock 'n' Roll* that it acted 'like a premonition of the impending departure of Ian Stewart'. With that in mind, and the thirty seconds of boogie-woogie piano that close the album, the song takes on a new poignancy.

The music is a sweeping, gospel-tinged panorama of choral vocals, tasteful sax and delicate piano. The one track on the album to have truly stood the test of time, it also feels like the first time Keith had started using the full character and cracked richness of his voice. 'That's Keith when he really exposes himself,' said engineer Dave Jerden in Appleford's book. 'He would sit in the control room and play that on acoustic guitar. That's really what Keith is. Keith has got the tough image, and rock and roll image, but he's really a sweet guy.' He added that Mick was so used to trying to make himself heard in front of screaming crowds that he still yelled to mike-busting effect, whereas, 'Keith's got a real controlled voice.'

Talking to LA's *Herald Examiner* in '86, Keith said, 'Before I was just singing one song now and then, and in circumstances like that, you don't really get to open the pipes up. On this album, with Mick not being around, I was in front of the microphone all the time, because you get a much better response out of the Stones if somebody's bellowing away on vocals . . . I remember telling Bobby Womack that I hadn't done so much singing since I was a soprano in Westminster Abbey. Come to think of it, that was probably the most prestigious gig of my career.'

Keith played down his greater hand in the making of *Dirty Work*, in *Musician* magazine: 'It's a Stones album. If I've had a little more to do with it and a little more control over this one, it's the same to me as the middle seventies when Mick would cover my ass when I was out of it . . . . We cover each others' ass. We've done it very well for each other over the years.'

It was a very diplomatic approach. But then, by the time he found out Mick didnt want to tour Keith was the last to know. It was already common knowledge among the press when Mick sent a telegram as he left for a holiday in Mustique. The words, 'I don't need you bunch of old farts, you're just a millstone around my neck,' didn't go down a storm.

Pith helmets on, chaps! Keith and Mick proceeded to engage in some fierce sparring via the press. By this time, Keith was bolstered by the knowledge that he could bring an album home alone, *Dirty Work* having elevated both his status and his confidence.

'I CAN'T FACE TOURING WITH KEITH AGAIN!' screamed the centre pages of *The Sun* on 3 March 1985. 'Right now, Keith and I disagree about almost everything,' Mick was quoted as saying. 'That especially includes music . . . . I cannot face months of us living in each other's pockets when we cannot agree on even the simplest things . . . . I could see it all ending in a fight between Keith and myself on stage in front of thousands. That would be crazy.'

But then the same feature brought in a fuming Keith: 'We've got a new single and a new album, and we should be touring to go with them. But it all depends on Mr. Jagger. I cannot put a gun to his head, but he knows how I feel.' As it becomes more like a lovers' tiff by the sentence, Mick returns with, 'I don't want to get in a slanging match with Keith, but our relationship has not been very good for three years. In fact, things between us have been pretty rocky. Don't ask me why. Why don't guys get on with their wives sometimes? . . . . I think our problems will eventually be sorted out, and the bad feelings will resolve themselves. But Keith and I have to take our time to work out our differences.'

It took another three years, to be precise, before this feud finally burned out. But in spring '85, it really did seem like the Rolling Stones could be over. Keith laid the blame firmly at the feet of Mick appearing in the *Daily Express*, under the headline, 'I'M SO BROWNED OFF WITH JAGGER.'

'I can take Mick's idiosyncrasies,' Keith told David Wigg, 'and I can ride them out and take advantage of the offers that have come my way, which I have always

I'm so browned off with Jagger

IS IT all over now for the Rolling Stones because Keith Richards can't get no satisfaction from Mick Jagger? The longest running romance in rock seems to have ended.

Keith Richards, opening his heart to me over his stormy row with partner Jagger, exclaimed: " I am browned off with him because he doesn't want to work this year, and he's browned off with me because he says I'm trying to call the shots. We used to pride ourselves on overcoming a crisis and watching the rest of the bands squabbling. It is the menopause for a rock 'n' roll band.

" I can take Mick's idiosyncrasies, and I can ride them out and take advantage of the offers that have come

By DAVID WIGG

6 We can't take his attitude to the Stones . . . I shout care, but nobody can get anything out of the lad

Stoney path ahead . . . for Keith Richards, and Mick Jagger (inset above)
Picture: DOUGLAS MORRISON

World War III: Keith fires another missile at Mick in the Daily Express, *June 1986.*

said no to before. Now I can spread my wings. For the rest of the guys his behaviour is churlish. It is not a God-given right to let everyone hang around waiting – like, "I will let you know when I need you." That is the kind of feeling the band have got from Mick . . . . I would like to know whether I am in a band.'

Wigg suggested that maybe Mick was feeling self-conscious about cavorting about the stage at the age of 43. This obviously wasn't the case, as he'd be doing it again in just a few months on his solo tour. But Keith agreed. 'Yes, it's a dangerous age for lead vocalists! Maybe it is a Peter Pan attitude – the last fling!'

The music press went into the question of the Stones' survival with a lot more depth than the tabloids, with Nick Kent contributing a cover story to the August *Spin*, headlined, 'IT'S ALMOST ALL OVER NOW.' But Keith's escalating activities meant that he wasn't getting mad anymore – he was getting productive. And Chuck Berry was about to change his life for a second time.

CHAPTER FOURTEEN

SOLO SURVIVOR

Hail! Hail! Rock 'n' Roll

Finally, Keith quit standing in the shadows. After stepping off the QE2 in New York on 5 June 1986, he ploughed headfirst into a ferocious schedule of extracurricular activities. With Mick embarking on a second solo album, Jane Rose was making sure that Keith kept busy.

First he flew on immediately to play a blues festival in Chicago with Chuck Berry in front of 70,000 people, on 6 June. The next day, he went with his on-off friend Chuck to see Dr John, who was playing a local bar. After that, the pair went to see Junior Wells at Muddy's old hang-out, the Checkerboard Lounge, and ended up jamming there.

The relationship between Keith and his old hero seemed to be improving, since he'd inducted Chuck into the newly established Rock and Roll Hall of Fame in January. Even if Keith admitted, 'I lifted every lick he ever played.' It was a good job, too, as Keith had been asked to take on the unenviable task of musical director for a documentary film about Berry. Directed by Taylor Hackford, of *An Officer and a Gentleman* fame, it was planned to coincide with Chuck's 60th birthday. The climax would be a concert in St Louis, and it was Keith's job to put together and direct a backing group for the occasion.

On 7 June, Keith nipped over to Los Angeles, caught an Etta James show and got up to join her on 'Miss You'. On 11 June, he was back in New York for a return appearance on NBC's *Friday Night Videos*, accompanied by top session men Marcus Miller and Paul Shaffer, leader of the house band on David Letterman's show. Keith pre-empted Mick's raiding of the Stones' back catalogue by playing impromptu versions of 'Around And Around', 'Wild Horses', 'Tumbling Dice', 'Jumpin' Jack Flash' and 'Honky Tonk Women'.

On 7 July, Keith, Ronnie and New York session drummer Steve Jordan went to Detroit to record a version of 'Jumpin' Jack Flash' with Aretha Franklin, for the movie of the same name starring Whoopi Goldberg. Keith had first jammed with Jordan at Ronnie's house. Since then, the drummer had played on some of *Dirty Work*. Keith liked his style, but still rejected him for the Berry movie's band on the flight back to New York.

At the end of August, 'Jumpin' Jack Flash' was released as a single and appeared on the First Lady of Soul's *Aretha* album. Although Keith had guested on other people's albums before, it was the first time he'd received such prominent billing. He also appeared on the single sleeve, smiling devilishly with Aretha, and cavorting in the video with Whoopi Goldberg. (The single got to number 21 in the US charts. At the same time, Jagger released the title track for a film called *Ruthless People*, which only made number 51.)

After the Aretha sessions, Keith turned his full attention to the Chuck Berry project. On 12 July, he flew down to visit Chuck in Wentzville, outside St Louis. His own personal Gracelands, it came complete with Berry Park, an entire fairground on the adjoining land.

They discussed who to recruit for the band, and Keith also got to meet Chuck's 91-year-old dad. Although he had the Playboy channel running constantly in his house, Chuck also showed Keith jam session footage on the other screen, from when Keith had inducted him into the Rock and Roll Hall of Fame in January '86. It solved his problem as to who to recruit as drummer: there was the man right there, Steve Jordan. Keith hadn't really thought beyond Charlie Watts, and phoned Jordan straight away to reverse his decision. He'd also found himself a new collaborator.

But Keith's main objective was to employ the services of Johnnie Johnson, Chuck's long-time piano-player. That was easy enough, as he still played the local clubs six nights a week. It was Johnnie's trio that Chuck took over in the early fifties, planting his sharp lyrics and unique guitar style on top of Johnson's traditional blues and country arrangements. Chuck then took all the credit and the money, while Johnnie continued to play clubs and drive a bus.

Keith had already figured out that Johnson arranged the music because the songs were all in piano keys, not guitar keys. He became aware of just how much Johnnie contributed to those Berry classics during long conversations over the rehearsal period. Chuck might complain about being ripped off by the white man, but Keith felt he'd done exactly the same to his old songwriting partner – a partnership which, if credit were given where it was due, would be on a par with Lennon and McCartney or Jagger-Richards. Johnson didn't complain, but Keith wanted to set the record straight.

Going by the film, it seems that Keith got the biggest buzz of all from playing with Johnnie. It was Ian Stewart who first pointed out his contribution to Keith back in '62. Now, less than a year since Stu's death, he felt honoured to be playing with one of the man's main inspirations. Keith's jaw drops as he watches the enormous fingers of Johnnie Johnson weave their boogie magic.

Keith's relationship with Chuck Berry over the years has blown hot and cold. Of course, Berry made bucketloads of cash from sales of Rolling Stones records containing his songs. His name was up there now with the greats, largely thanks to the publicity he got from the Stones and namechecks from Keith. Thanks to the Stones' 1960s cover versions, hordes of young fans knew songs like 'Come On', 'Bye Bye Johnny', 'Carol', 'Around And Around', 'You Can't Catch Me' and 'Little Queenie'. Sometimes he'd gratefully acknowledge it. Other times he'd put the Stones down.

Chuck was supposed to headline the UK tour the Stones played with the Everly Brothers in '63, but was serving time for transporting a minor across the state line for immoral purposes. He'd brought in a fourteen-year-old Indian girl to work in the cloakroom at the night-club he'd opened in St Louis. She was also turning tricks. It's been said that it was this stretch in jail that instilled such lifelong bitterness in Chuck Berry.

In May the following year, he was out. He toured the UK on the back of his newfound popularity, but snubbed the Stones when they went backstage to say hello. However, during the Stones' first US tour, Chuck walked in on their first

Chess recording session in Chicago and was very friendly - probably because they were recording one of his songs.

He supported the Stones on some dates of the '69 US tour, but there was an incident on the '72 tour when Keith jammed with Chuck at the Hollywood Palladium and was thrown off for being too loud. Chuck claimed afterwards that he didn't recognise him. That was the excuse he also used in June '81, when he gave Keith a black eye backstage at New York's Ritz. He later apologised to Ron Wood, thinking he was Keith. It was only the fact that it was his main musical inspiration dealing out the disrespect that cancelled Keith's usual take-no-shit attitude.

In July '83, Chuck did recognise Keith at LA International Airport, but dropped his lit cigarette down the front of Keith's shirt in the resultant bear-hug. 'Every time him and I get in contact, whether it's intentional or not, I wind up wounded,' Keith told Stanley Booth.

However, at the Hall of Fame induction they'd got on like a house on fire and the jam was kicking. It gave Keith the impetus to stick out what were going to be a very trying few weeks. After all, given Chuck's long-term resentment towards the white-run music industry and the way he was ripped off in the early days, what would happen over the entire production period of a movie? *Chuck Berry, the archetypal industry outsider, was gonna have a Rolling Stone telling him what to do!*

For Keith, it was something that had to happen before Chuck died. Otherwise, he'd be remembered as the sometimes shoddy walking cliché who turned up at gigs, demanded the money and refused to play a minute over the alotted time with a dodgy pick-up band. Even worse, his legacy might have ended with 'My Ding-A-Ling', the excruciating wanking song which became his biggest hit in the early seventies.

On bass guitar, the well-connected Steve Jordan recommended Joey Spaminato of NRBQ, who were still playing the New York club circuit after a string of eclectic, R&B-influenced albums from the late sixties onwards. On keyboards, Keith brought in ex-Allman Brother Chuck Leavell, who was on *Dirty Work* and has played with the Stones ever since. On saxophone, it was Mr. Bobby Keys - back in the Stones camp again.

The concert was to take place at St Louis' Fox Theatre on 18 October. It was a sweet irony for Chuck, who was refused admission as a kid because of his colour, as he would take delight in explaining in the movie.

But first there was a slight detour. On 28 July, Patti gave birth to her and Keith's second daughter, Alexandra Nicole, at Lennox Hill Hospital, NY. They soon decided they needed a new family home. Their places in Manhattan, Jamaica and Paris were fine, but none of the locales were ideal for kids to grow up in. The UK was still out of the question, and Keith wanted a base where he could unpack the three warehouses full of possessions he'd accumulated over the years. Consequently, the Richards family moved into a large house in Westin, Connecticut, about an hour north of Manhattan. Idyllic, peaceful, surrounded by dogs and kids, Keith still saw fit to christen the house Devil's Den. It was here that he could chill out and plough through all the records he'd been picking up since the sixties, while working out ideas in the little studio he'd construct in the basement. The Richardses have been there ever since, although Keith would still hop about in his semi-nomadic lifestyle. And Jamaica was never too far away.

In fact, in August Chuck visited Keith at Point of View, but, being away from his home turf, found it impossible to relax. It was there that Keith observed how Chuck and Mick were very similar, in that they both had to be in control. He knew he was in for trouble and strife when the band rehearsed at Chuck's place in Wentzville the next month.

Rehearsals entailed the predictable stand-offs, raised voices and disagreements. Nobody had ever told the stubbornly independent Chuck what to play before, and the film shows Keith struggling against all odds. When he asks Chuck to adjust his amp level, there is a face-to-face stand-off which is quite frightening. Keith's glare is bordering on psychotic and a mad Chuck Berry is something to behold. Just when it looks like fisticuffs are bound to occur, the pair cool off. Keith later said that he chewed on a .38 bullet at rehearsals to keep his legendary temper down.

He must have been gnashing down hard when Chuck turned the tables and made him repeat the intro to 'Carol' – which the Stones had played hundreds of times – over and over until he felt Keith had captured the original. Chuck must have swallowed hard when Keith confronted him about the possibility that it was Johnnie Johnson who wrote the music. To irk Keith, he started addressing him as 'Jack', while Keith called him 'Charles' - amongst other things. At the soundcheck though, Keith did kiss a reluctant Chuck while trying to persuade him to sing a few lines to check the levels.

When the film premiered at the New York Film Festival, Keith sat in a box with Patti and Chuck - clenching his buttocks. As he said later, 'I suddenly realised we were coming to the point in the movie where I suggested that maybe Chuck didn't write the music, that Johnnie Johnson actually provided the melodies, which I'm still firmly convinced of . . . I realise that I want a parachute. I wanted to get the hell out of there. But he thought it was all great. Loved the fight, saw it for what it was. Since then, he's been a sweetheart . . . Asshole that he can be, I still love him.' Ultimately, the film may have played a part in Chuck being given his own star on Hollywood Boulevard.

After all the stand-offs, the concert was an undeniable success. The band all sported early sixties-style beat group uniform - the first time Keith had worn one since the Stones' TV debut playing 'Come On'. Keith also managed to produce the best live sound Chuck has ever had, with a skin-tight rock 'n' roll band – though Chuck changed the set list as soon as they hit the stage. They were joined on several songs by guest duettists, including Etta James, Eric Clapton, Robert Cray, Linda Ronstadt and Julian Lennon.

At the end of the film, Keith is propped up in a chair, reflecting on the previous mad month. He looks like he's been up for a week, and the strain is showing. His enthusiasm is obvious, but he was also obviously sagging:

'I mean, we rehearsed for ten days, got on stage, and boom, out the window! Totally different arrangements, some in different keys. Everybody's looking at me on stage and I just looked at them, y'know - "Wing it boys!"'

That he'd succeeded, and the concert was a total success, made for one of those triumph-over-adversity moments like the end of *Rocky*.

'When you're working with Chuck you've got to be prepared for anything, anytime. But I still can't dislike him. I love him and I love his family. I've done what I wanted for him. I think it's the best Chuck Berry live you're ever gonna get. I can't see him doing it again. It's good. We both came out of it with a bit more

Chuck checks Keith's ding-a-ling during the Hail! Hail! Rock 'n' Roll *gig.*

respect for one another. Now I'm gonna sleep for a month.'

In Stanley Booth's biography, *Keith*, he talks about his 'missionary zeal' for the Berry project: 'I know I've got to swallow a lot of shit, probably on camera, to do this, but if I can do it, if I can show that bit of myself, then at least everybody knows who the fuck I am . . . if anybody wants to know then they can see a little bit more. Also, if I can go through that fire it can kind of harden me up to the point where I can commit to do my own record.'

Cheap Talk And X-Pensive Winos

After recovering from the Chuck Berry experience, Keith zigzagged between Jamaica and New York. On the first night back in NYC on 21 November, he jammed with Robert Cray at the Bottom Line. Two nights later he joined Eric Clapton onstage at the Ritz, playing on 'Cocaine' and 'Layla'. After a week back in Jamaica, he came back to NYC on 3 December and caught the Charlie Watts Orchestra at the same venue. Charlie's solo venture was a 33-piece orchestra playing jazz standards. The great man sat behind his kit, radiating contentment - even if some of the crowd were shouting for Stones songs. Then it was back to Jamaica on the sixth, where Keith celebrated his 43rd birthday with Patti and the girls. They flew to NY the following day, and spent both Christmas Eve and New Year's Eve with Patti's family.

Keith still found time to visit the Neville Brothers in the studio, where they were recording their *Uptown* album for Rolling Stones Records. He ended up playing on a track called 'Midnight Key'. Shortly after, he was wandering around his Lower Manhattan neighbourhood when he happened upon the Lone Star Cafe, surprised to see that Mick Taylor was playing with his New Electric Band. Keith stunned the crowd by getting up to play a fourteen-minute version of 'Can't You Hear Me Knocking?' with Taylor, as well as 'Key To The Highway'.

On 21 January, Keith carried out another induction into the Hall of Fame at the Waldorf Astoria. This time it was another of his collaborators – Aretha Franklin, who was the first female to be honoured. Keith kept his speech short: 'What can I say about Aretha? You're in, baby!'

The reason for all this commuting to Manhattan was that Keith was attending meetings with record companies interested in signing him as a solo artist. The final jolt into making this move was Jagger's decision not to tour with the Stones. Instead, he was planning to tour behind his second solo album, *Primitive Cool*, with other musicians. Keith was incensed. He'd never wanted to be a movie star, a politician, or anything other than a Rolling Stone. And he certainly had no previous desire to make a solo record. Jagger had forced his hand.

There had been rumours about the '77 Canadian trial sessions seeing the light of day in '79, along with out-takes from that period like 'We Had It All' and 'Let's Go Steady'. A single called 'Bad Luck' was actually on the Rolling Stones Records schedule for April that year, but nothing ever materialised - apart from Keith's version of Chuck Berry's 'Run Rudolph Run', and a string of bootlegs.

I broached the subject during our 1980 interview and he was still dismissing the idea. 'People always ask me 'cos they know I did those tracks. I mean I do 'em because the opportunity's there in the studio. For some reason nobody else has turned up. At the time I do them I just do 'em!'

'I'm still in the same state of mind as always, like Mick. I'm not interested in splitting myself up to the point where I'm going, "I'm going to keep this for me - that's a nice song, I won't give it to the Stones." Put yourself in that position. It's stupid. One thing at a time. If I'm in the Stones, I'm in the Stones and I make Stones records. If I'm not in the Stones, I'll think about doing my own record. I don't wanna split my loyalties.'

Which is exactly what happened when Jagger insisted on making two solo albums. Keith was left for months on end without the Stones, burning to get back on the road. As he says, if he's not working, he gets bored - and that's when he gets into trouble.

So, after much soul searching, Keith decided to make his own solo album. As he told Stanley Booth, 'If I hadn't played on the Chuck Berry thing, I don't think I would have had the balls myself to do the solo record . . . The singing part never bothered me. It's not the most beautiful voice in the world any more but the Queen liked it. When it was at its best, before it broke. It's not been my job, singing, but to me, if you're gonna write songs, you've got to know how to sing.'

1987 was beginning in time-honoured style. When *The Sun* asked him about the constant bitching between him and Mick, Keith replied, 'You'd better ask the bitch.'

In February, Keith and Steve Jordan checked into the small Studio 900 on Broadway and Nineteenth Street – walking distance from Keith's Fourth Street apartment. Here they wrote songs together and gradually brought in the players who'd appear on the album. Once he became used to the idea of working outside the Stones, Keith started to like it and subsequently rose to the occasion.

They kept writing and playing until April. Opposed to the accepted routine of hiring session men, Keith insisted his album would feature a proper band. 'The whole joy of making rock and roll music is the interaction between guys playing, and trying to capture that on tape,' he said. By now, they'd got Ivan Neville, the son of soul legend Aaron, on keyboards. Top LA session man Waddy Wachtel - who'd played with Gram Parsons' old partner, Emmylou Harris - came in on guitar (and would end up co-producing Keith's second solo album). Charlie Drayton took up the bass.

Keith named his new band the X-Pensive Winos, after he caught some of them passing a bottle of Dom Perignon behind the drum kit at rehearsals. On the last night at Studio 900, 8 April, a fire broke out in the building, so the band dragged their equipment out onto Nineteenth Street and carried on jamming until the fire brigade arrived.

In July, Keith signed with Virgin Records to make two solo albums. The main condition was that there would be no record company interference.

On 15 August, the band started two weeks of recording at Le Studio in Montreal. Keith had returned to his *Exile* strategy of gathering his group under one roof, away from the distractions of home. Respected New York session singer Bernard Fowler, who first got noticed in the early eighties as part of disco outfit the Peech Boys, supplied backing vocals alongside the occasional presence of Sarah Dash, formerly of Labelle.

The new blood weren't going to sit about waiting on 'Keith Time', either. He was goaded into action, and it was a far cry from the laborious procedure surrounding the previous Stones albums. There would even be songs left over, like 'Almost Hear You Sigh', 'Slipping Away' and 'Can't Be Seen', which would end up on the next Stones album. One gorgeous soul ballad, called 'Make No Mistake', echoes the origins of 'Satisfaction' in that Keith woke up in the middle of the night and whacked down the idea. As he sings, 'oh, this is just a dream.'

As Keith told Stanley Booth, '. . . I ask myself, "what am I so scared about, doing something on my own apart from the Stones?" Was I just being chicken? Was I just trying to keep the Stones together because I was scared of being left out there on my own? What was really my reason for this desperate fight? Was it that I wanted to keep in the cocoon and not break out, and the fact that I got forced out maybe has been a great thing for me?'

Mick's album, *Primitive Cool*, was released in September amidst a blaze of publicity. It fared badly compared to the previous Stones album, or even his own last effort. Two of the tracks – 'Kow Tow' and 'Shoot Off Your Mouth' – were obviously aimed at Keith. For his replacement, Mick employed the services of Jeff Beck who nearly joined the Stones as second guitarist in '76. But Beck refused to join Mick's touring band because he found the money insulting.

Keith chose the name of his album by getting Jane Rose to look in his box of song titles. 'Talk Is Cheap' leapt straight out, after an unfinished *Dirty Work* song. His game plan for the album, if it could be called that, was to keep it natural and organic. Eighties music was saturated with synthesised sound – 'toy department stuff,' as Keith called it. He was looking for the antidote, bringing in fiddles, accordions, percussion influenced by South African music and a distinct vein of Southern soul. Keith had only hinted at the latter obsession in his past ballads, but the spiritual simplicity practiced by producers like Al Green's Willie Mitchell was able to blossom within the structure of the new songs. To this end, early '88 saw Keith and Steve travelling to Memphis, then Montserrat and Bermuda, assimilating sounds and recording vocals. He even got classical guitarist Benjamin Verdery to pick him the best possible acoustic guitar to enhance the album's sound.

Meanwhile, Mick was playing to huge crowds in Japan. This annoyed the other Stones, who were still denied access to the country because of Keith's drug busts and reputation (though Ronnie was touring America and Japan during this period with another Stones hero, Bo Diddley, under the name the Gunslingers). He was also trotting out pale imitations of Stones numbers to bolster most of his set. Keith called them 'Jagger's little jerk-off band,' and Charlie later opined, 'Mick's decision virtually folded up 25 years of the band.'

With his tour finished, Mick suddenly decided he wanted to be in the Rolling Stones again. The band met in London in May to discuss starting the whole process anew the following year. But Keith was now nearly ready to unleash his own album, and had lined up a US tour for later that year. It gave him some satisfaction to say the Stones would have to wait.

When *Talk Is Cheap* was finished and Keith embarked on the promotional trail, he slipped into dream interviewee mode, telling *Rolling Stone*'s Anthony de Curtis, 'There's very few records that you make, or at least that I've made, that you wanna hear by the time you finish it. You're just so full with it. It's the last thing you wanna hear. But this one – I don't know if it's because it's a novelty, my first solo album – but I actually sit around and enjoy listening to it, put it on while I'm taking a shower.'

He expounded on the Jagger situation: 'Mick's and my battles are not exactly as perceived through the press or other people . . . Last month or so I've been in touch with the other Stones. Mick suddenly called up, and the rest of them: "Let's put the Stones back together." I'm thinking, I'm just in the middle of an album. Now what are you trying to do? Screw me up? Just now you want to talk about putting it back together? But we talked about it.'

Keith told Lisa Robinson that Mick had done his hi-tech solo thing because he 'was afraid the Rolling Stones could turn into some sort of nostalgia dead end, I see the Rolling Stones on the cutting edge of growing this music up and the only band in the position to do it. As I said to him, "Listen, darling, this thing is bigger than both of us."'

It would become Keith's catchphrase from now on.

When the first Keith Richards solo material appeared, I was working in a New York record store called Bleeker Bob's which specialised in rare Stones stuff and brazenly sold bootlegs. It was amazing to note the similarity of regular Stones buyers' reactions. I can't remember selling one single copy of Mick's solo records, but when Keith's first single, '(You Shouldn't) Take it So Hard', came in the demand was clamorous. People had been asking for it for weeks.

The single first appeared in August as a twelve-inch radio promo, with a picture sleeve and the same track on both sides. These started changing hands for around $30. It was a good omen for Keith's new solo career. Opening with classic Keef-chords, it swung and punched like a man just let out of his straitjacket.

There was a new maturity to Keith's voice too. His two most recent vocal outings with the Stones – 'All About You' and 'Sleep Tonight' – had been gasping ballads oozing cracked soul, working the night shift on their respective albums. But now Keith was singing loud and proud over one of his big fella riffs, with startling assertion. The track sounded warts 'n' all, real and timeless, compared to the session-sheen Big Rock sound of the Jagger outings. On 4 October, *Talk Is Cheap* was released.

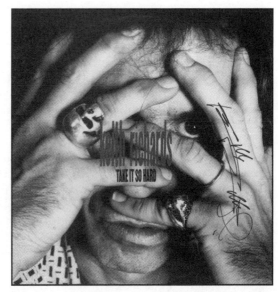

Keith signed this rare US promo for 'Take It So Hard'.

The album more than lived up to its visual promise, just a photo of Keith with his skull ring, his gnarled hand over his guitar strings. He continued to sing with the new richness in his voice throughout, the shit-hot and sympathetic unit behind backing him with the kind of space, grace and funk you didn't even get with the Stones. It wasn't *better than*, just as exhilarating in its own way. The Winos' sound incorporated all the man's favourite styles: dub reggae, Southern soul, fifties rock 'n' roll and pure, unadulterated raunch, all bouncing happily up and down on the same bed.

The opening cut, 'Big Enough', is arrestingly different from the expected Big Riff. It also features Bootsy Collins, space bass practitioner from the planet P-Funk, pumping and popping the strings that drove George Clinton's mothership and James Brown's 'Sex Machine'. The groove is bare and funky, spurred by Keith's JB-tinged riff. The track was deemed club-friendly enough in '89 to be pressed up as an extremely limited white label club promo (probably a bootleg), featuring acid-house mixes from dance producer Charley Cazanova. It still remains one of the big guns in my DJ sets.

The album moves on through 'Take It So Hard' into the urgent street-rock of 'Struggle'. The sound is sparse, funky, bombast-free, letting Keith's vocals breathe. He really does boast a new voice on this record. Bill Wyman might have commented that 'he's hardly Pavarotti', but it's irrelevant.

The swinging fifties jump-blues frolic of 'I Could Have Stood You Up But I Didn't' follows, before the first ballad, 'Make No Mistake'. Easy and gentle, with a lovely counter-vocal from Sarah Dash, the horns wheeze and Keith's voice alternates between an endearing stumble and pure emotion. It's intoxicatingly gentle. The track which attracted the most attention was 'You Don't Move Me', which emerged as another limited twelve-inch promo. It was Keith's barbed retort to

Jagger's 'Shoot Off Your Mouth'. One day in the studio, when Keith was pondering what to do next, Steve Jordan suggested he write about Mick if he was stuck for subject matter. Keith later claimed he used Mick as a jumping-off point for a song about falling out with friends. Over a skeletal dubby skank, Keith rips into lines like: 'Why d'ya think you've got no friends? Drove them around the bend. / You don't move me any more.' His strongest vocal on the album, it's tinged with a certain sadness and accentuated by a mournful backing choir.

'How I Wish' is sheer uplifting rock 'n' roll, featuring one of the album's classic Keef riffs. It showcases a major difference between Keith solo and the Stones in its use of backing vocals – Keith's are very male-dominated, even gospelly, in the manner of the Swan Silvertones. 'Whip It Up' is an elastic-funk dub-rocker, while 'Rockawhile' is a creeping snake of a tune, lazy and insidious. Another soul-soothing ballad, 'Locked Away', steps into the Memphis soul stew, with added spice from the accordion of Stanley 'Buckwheat' Dural and Michael Doucet's fiddle. As the poignant track unwinds, the chorus gains intensity – 'You ought to be locked away.' Finally, Keith slips in a wry, 'I ought to be locked away.' The album goes out on the juggernaut funk of 'It Means A Lot' which, by the end section, is just Keith hacking block chords for dear life over a relentless Winos chug. Simple but deadly.

The first Keith Richards solo album is unpretentious, not aspiring to any higher plateau or the rock history books. But it's a great record, and moved him forward in his eternal musical quest. If he hadn't done it, he probably couldn't have reached the emotional depths of his later soul-plumbing Stones outings like 'Through And Through' and 'Losing My Touch'.

The album went on to sell a respectable million copies around the world and stayed on the US charts for 24 weeks. Whereas Mick's effort received a cool press reaction, *Talk Is Cheap* received highly positive responses, the most effusive of which was Joe Bosso's review in *Guitar World*: '*Talk Is Cheap* rings with life . . . It's the sound of Keith rediscovering and challenging himself.' Then the killer punch: 'Although no other Stones played on it, *Talk Is Cheap* is the best Stones album in seventeen years.'

Whereas Mick's US tour of large venues was cancelled due to poor sales, Keith effortlessly sold out a fourteen-date American jaunt in November, which mainly concentrated on large theatres. It opened at the Fox Theatre, Atlanta, on 24 November, visiting Memphis, Washington DC, New York's Beacon Theatre – where the 4,000 tickets sold out in a few hours – Philadelphia, Boston, Cleveland, Detroit, Chicago, San Francisco, Los Angeles, and ended up at the Brendan Byrne Arena in New Jersey, on 17 December, in front of 22,000 punters. Afterwards, Keith celebrated his 45th birthday with 500 guests and was presented with a gold disc for his album. No sign of Jagger though.

Unlike Mick, Keith stuck mainly to his own songs, starting as he meant to go on with 'Take It So Hard'. From the Stones' catalogue, he also whipped out rousing versions of 'Happy', 'Before They Make Me Run', the dubwise 'Too Rude', and even 'Connection' from *Between The Buttons*. One of the set's high points was a stellar take on 'Time Is On My Side', which turned into a *tour de force* for Sarah Dash. *Rolling Stone* called the gigs 'definitive and essential rock 'n' roll'. Within weeks, the Rolling Stones shop in Tokyo was selling Red Stripe beer t-shirts just like Keith had worn on tour.

So ended one of the best eighteen-month periods of Keith's life. He'd broadened his career horizons, was in good shape, and life at home was bliss. What's more, his other band were about to return, bigger than ever.

As Keith later said in *According to the Rolling Stones*: 'When I look back on all of that now – and a little part of me probably thought this even then – I think, "Well, we'd been working together since 1962 through to the mid-1980s, we'd been jammed up each other's jacksies forever, so it's hardly surprising that one of us would feel, 'Is this all there is?'" It happened to be Mick who went for it first.'

Steel Away

So, as 1989 dawned, it was make or break time for the Rolling Stones. The band hadn't toured for seven years - their longest lay-off from the stage yet. But, as Keith said, Mick forcing him out on his own was probably the best thing that could have happened to him. He'd proved he could do it. If there had been any been doubts before about who stoked the Rolling Stones' engine room, there were certainly none now.

With the bad air of the mid-eighties gradually starting to clear, Keith and Mick arranged to meet up in Barbados on 13 January. Keith told Patti that he'd either be away for two hours or two weeks. 'Because I'll know in 48 hours whether this thing was going to work or if we were just going to start cattin' and doggin',' as he later told *Rolling Stone*.

Initially, the years of pressure and potshots erupted into the inevitable shouts and insults. But it soon dissolved into pure knockabout, with each one laughing at what they'd said about each other. Mick had been bowling through the frantic, aptly-titled 'Hold On To Your Hat' when Keith turned up in Barbados. That's when he knew it could work again.

'When we got in that room and sat down with our guitars, something different took over. I can never think of starting something up again in order to make it the last time. This is the beginning of the second half.'

The pair then engaged in a writing frenzy, which would yield their quickest album since the mid-sixties. There were no reupholstered out-takes, not even any covers, as they buried the hatchet and beavered away at pop-reggae singer Eddie Grant's studio. By February they'd laid down the bones of twelve new songs, with 40-odd bits and pieces in the wings.

Two years later, in an interview with Roy Carr in *Vox*, Keith reflected, 'Why have Mick and I stayed together all this time? Well, we do so somewhat reluctantly. It's when we stop working that Mick and I start sniping and bickering at each other. There are hundreds of things that Mick and I vehemently disagree upon . . . If we sit down in a room together with just a keyboard and guitar, all that other stuff suddenly becomes irrelevant.'

They kissed and made up just in time for the Stones' 18 January induction into the Rock and Roll Hall of Fame, at New York City's Waldorf Hotel. Keith and Mick were joined by Ronnie Wood and Mick Taylor. Accepting their award from Pete Townshend, Mick paid tribute to both Brian Jones and Ian Stewart.

'Guys, whatever you do, don't try to grow old gracefully. It wouldn't suit you,' was Townshend's punchline. The customary all-star jam session featured Keith, Mick and Ronnie leading 'Start Me Up' and 'Honky Tonk Women'.

'. . . the pearl and the oyster. There's a bit of grit in there, y' know. It'll always be there.' The Glimmer Twins return in 1989.

Keith and Mick then went back to Barbados and recommenced work on their new tunes. The complicated 'Mixed Emotions' featured one of the first Keef riffs to spring out of the sessions. With lines like 'let's bury the hatchet' and 'button your lip, baby', it would be widely interpreted as a comment on the war between Mick and Keith. Jagger would insist it was about a female acquaintance.

'I wrote this very early on in the session,' said Keith in the blurb accompanying an early nineties Stones compilation. 'People are always accusing me of attempting some sort of pun here, you know – Mick's Demotion, but it isn't true. It just goes, "You're not the only one, with mixed emotions / You're not the only ship, a-sail on this ocean."'

Keith also had a couple of ballads – 'Almost Hear You Sigh' and 'Slipping Away' – which he hadn't finished in time for *Talk Is Cheap*. They became the most soulful and genuinely moving songs on the new Stones album.

In early February, Keith joined the Winos to film a video at the North River Bar in New York, complete with a guest spot from the immortal Memphis Horns. He was back in Barbados a few days later, joined by Charlie, before Bill and Ron showed up in early March. Actual recording would take place at George Martin's AIR Studios in Montserrat at the end of March.

It took about a month, with some of Keith and Mick's differences of opinion surfacing as they went on. Keith still liked to take time to get things right. Mick brought in computer-synthesiser wizard Matt Clifford to speed things along and add the hi-tech edge he desired. Charlie took it upon himself to try to keep the peace.

During the recording, Bill was sent off to Antigua for a week to escape the media hordes having a field day with his engagement to nineteen-year-old Mandy Smith, who he'd started dating when she was thirteen. The last thing the band wanted was the paparazzi poking their cameras into the sessions, so Ronnie switched to bass for the sessions. Out-takes included a song about underage girls called 'So Young'.

Keith took his own brief hiatus, to be honoured in his own right by a music industry to whom he might have been an embarrassment ten years earlier. On 31 May he was saluted as a 'Living Legend' at the first annual International Rock Awards, held at New York's Armory. Eric Clapton presented Keith with a twelve-inch statuette of Elvis Presley, before he brought on the X-Pensive Winos and tore into 'Whip It Up'. The obligatory all-star jam followed on 'You Keep A-Knockin'', where they were joined by Clapton, Tina Turner, Dave Edmunds and Clarence Clemmons.

The album was mixed at Olympic Studios during May and June. The whole thing was done and dusted in less than five months, which was incredible for the Stones. While Keith was content to follow his usual organic recording processes, Mick and the rest of the band hurried things along so they'd be ready in time for the upcoming tour. Charlie worked Keith particularly hard, perhaps because he'd had such a good time playing with another drummer.

'This music, it's certainly not Beethoven or Mozart,' said Keith during the mixing sessions, quoted in an authorised Stones book called *Images of the World Tour 1989-1990*. 'It's got nothing to do with intricacy. It's got to do with a bunch of guys making accidents together, spontaneity and an immediate form of communication.'

Pressure to complete the album was on account of a world tour that would redefine the stadium spectacle. Not only in terms of its huge scale – reflected in the stage, the crowds, the personnel, the revenue – but also in the strategy of bringing in sponsors, and selling the blanket rights of the tour to one promoter to make sure the Stones organisation wouldn't shoulder any losses. Hence the rights to promoting the gigs, and to TV, film and merchandising, were all sold to Canadian promoter Michael Cohl, on a deal that guaranteed the Stones around £50 million. Budweiser, the 'King of Beers', came in as sponsor, while Cohl's firm would also get a cut of the profits in return for forking out an enormous amount on the stage set.

The set was a vast, sprawling industrial ruin, designed by architect Mark Fisher and costing around $4 million. With a brief to evoke the urban decay of films like *Blade Runner*, it was an awe-inspiring mass of old pipes, chutes, girders, ramps and catwalks, set-up with video screens, pyrotechnics and one of the most advanced light shows ever seen. It actually reminded me more of the decaying grandeur of Tim Burton's *Batman*, which was around the same time.

The Stones took the stage to 'Start Me Up', behind a three-hundred foot wall of fire against the metallic grey backdrop. It was the biggest stage set ever constructed, eight storeys high and wider than a football pitch. The fake radio towers went up so high, at 130 feet, that red aircraft collision lights had to be fitted. The end-of-show finale utilised nearly 50,000 fireworks, £100,000 worth of aerial shells and a ton of flash powder. As lighting designer Patrick Woodruffe said, 'It had to reflect the Rolling Stones story in 1989. It had to have dignity. It had to be tough, hard and current, rather than nostalgic and beautiful.'

The Stones also knew that – given their long absence from the world stage – they themselves would have to be all of these things. It was in another league to the '82 jaunt with its garish backdrops, and Keith was not initially impressed by the scale of the spectacle. That was Mick's thing. His department was strictly delivering the music.

On 11 July, the Stones announced the album and tour in New York City from an open flatcar on a train, which had brought them into Grand Central Station on its wheels of steel. I was one of several hundred people in the crowd. Asked if they were doing the tour for the money, Keith leaned over and replied, 'It's the glory, darling. The *glory*.' The media circus had begun, but afterwards the band retired under heavy security to a girls' boarding school at Wykeham Rise, near Washington, Connecticut - just up the road from Keith's new house. With designers finishing the new set, local residents formed a 'Roll the Stones Out of Town Action Group', complaining that the band had almost taken over the entire vicinity. Meanwhile, many of the tickets for the tour – due to start in Philadelphia at the end of August – had sold out almost immediately.

The touring band now also included Chuck Leavell, Matt Clifford on samplers and synths, three backing singers – Lisa Fischer, Bernard Fowler and Cindy Mizell – and the four-piece Uptown Horns. Keith insisted that Bobby Keys come in to lead the horns, which made in total for a fifteen-piece band. It would also be the first ever Stones tour without the presence and occasional boogie-woogie piano of Ian Stewart.

Steel Wheels, the album, featured 'Almost Hear You Sigh', a yearning song of lost love with a co-writing credit for Steve Jordan, served free of bluster by Mick. I'd love to hear Keith's original demo. His acoustic guitar solo – on his recently acquired Velasquez guitar, as shown on the sleeve – is sublimely intricate.

'Slipping Away' closes, one of Keith's most touchingly sensitive vocals. The power of true soul music is that it can make the listener cry. 'Slipping Away' is in the grand tradition of Al Green, a well of bottomless emotion as Keith wrenches every morsel of passion and pain from the depths of his battered soul.

The Stones would re-record the song for the semi-live album, *Stripped*, in '95. 'We realised, "Wow, that song kind of slipped away." It just kind of tailed off at the end of *Steel Wheels*. We realised what potential it still had, and the band and especially the horn guys said, "You've got to do that!" So, in a way, I agreed to do it at gun point. But when I got into it, I really liked singing that song. It's got some depth.'

'Just as you have touched my heart, we split up and we're apart.' He could be singing about Gram Parsons, or any lost loved one. It's a classic Keef ballad, which would set a benchmark for subsequent albums. When the Stones performed it at Twickenham in 2003, Keith became overcome with emotion and tears welled up in his eyes. It was the night's real highlight.

There was also a rocker saved over from *Talk Is Cheap* which became 'Can't Be Seen', his other vocal showcase on the album. It's an urgent, rockabilly-tinged romp concerning forbidden romance, with some uplifting harmonies. With the regular services of Lisa Fischer and Bernard Fowler, complex backing vocals were now a staple of the Stones' sound.

If not over-studded with classics, *Steel Wheels* was a strong record which would have been impossible to imagine during the previous year. Or as Keith put it in '94, 'There's a part of you that feels the Stones will be here forever, but you know that can't be. The truth is, things were a lot more fragile for us during the eighties than anyone realised, including the band. It's only now that I can look back and see how close it came to coming apart.'

And it wasn't only due to the feud with Mick. Bill Wyman had been close to throwing in the towel, embroiled in a media furore over his relationship with Mandy Smith – 34 years his junior, he would marry her in '89, but their relationship dated back to a time when she was under the age of consent. The decade had also seen Ronnie fighting his own demons with an escalating freebase problem. Even Charlie, after years of abstinence, had got deeply into booze and smack. This had greatly worried Keith, who'd already lost Ian Stewart and saw Charlie as the remaining solid link in the chain. But, as he later told *Rolling Stone*, 'I drove up to the rehearsal space and I heard him playing. I just sat in the car for five minutes and listened, and I said, "Yeah, no problem. This year's made."'

As usual, the Stones' publicity machine was cranking up. The *Sunday Mirror* quoted Mick as saying, 'It was really easy working with the guys again . . . Though Keith is more sensitive than I, we didn't have any major rows. We're not an old married couple who can't live together and can't live apart: We're two men who've been friends for 30 years. Occasionally you want to strangle even the closest of friends.'

My own first gig on the *Steel Wheels* tour was at New York's Shea Stadium, in the borough of Queens. Playing over six nights in October, 230,000 tickets were sold for the Shea Stadium gigs alone. I only knew the place from its reputation for the last ever Beatles show in '65, and the Clash video for 'Should I Stay Or Should I Go?'. I'd thought Wembley Stadium was big, but I was overawed as I took my seat about 30 rows from the front.

The atmosphere, that buzz, was absolutely unique to Stones gigs. I'd not witnessed them before on foreign soil, and was experiencing for myself the grand US tradition of beer, burgers and cries of 'ROCK 'N' ROLL!!' And nobody had ever seen a stage like that before. It was vast, sprawling, the lights deep within giving the appearance of a leviathan-like life of its own. I'd seen some big stage sets in my time, including the Stones' own lotus set, but this was the next step beyond, a true vision of the future.

When the Moroccan strains of 'Continental Drift' started easing in, it was instant lift-off. *Whooomph!* Keith's opening chord-chomp on 'Start Me Up' announced a three-hundred-foot wall of fire. The smoke cleared, you could make out Mick, then Keith, resplendent in his regular attire for the tour: brown military-style jacket, bandanna, jeans slashed with bleach and a silk shirt, which would be peeled off to reveal a favourite t-shirt. He was particularly partial to one carrying the legend, 'Ubergruppenfuhrer'. He also sported a pair of Patti's knickers stuffed in his back pocket.

It was a whole different ball game to the early eighties. This time the Stones were dipping into their back catalogue beyond the obvious favourites – as with 'Ruby Tuesday', where Jagger donned a psychedelic coat while Keith and Ron picked acoustic guitars with an elegant flourish. They were modernising the original vibe while keeping the magic intact. '2,000 Light Years From Home' had never been played live before, and sounded like it was being beamed in from a soul bar on Mars. During 'Honky Tonk Women', two giant inflatable hookers (named Ruby and Angie) reared up at the sides. Then came 'Sympathy For The Devil', with its *piece de resistance* of Mick disappearing and reappearing a hundred or so feet above the main stage, via a hidden elevator.

The Chairmen of the Board prepare to hop on the Steel Wheels.

It also marked Keith's main chance to stretch out on the guitar, as he went for a sprint around the walkways. The tour saw him buoyed with a new assurance, an energy and attack which hadn't been there before he struck out on his own. As ever, the post-gig party was in Keith's room.

Predictably, he had a tough time getting into Canada for two Toronto shows at the beginning of December. After giving his bags a good going over, the customs men found a small knife which they confiscated. They offered to give Keith a receipt, so he naturally asked if he could get the knife back when he left the country. When they said no, he replied, 'Then why the receipt, man? Have it on me. It's a gift!'

I caught the Stones again at the Pontiac Silverdome, near Detroit, on 10 December. It was your ultimate faceless American sports arena, and the sound seemed to suffer. (Plus I had a crap seat.) But all was rectified on 19 December, when I managed to blag a ticket for the show that was being televised on pay-per-view from Atlantic City Convention Centre, New Jersey. As they were 250 bucks a pop, I was chuffed.

In front of a strangely mixed crowd of Stones diehards and casino high-flyers from the 'Las Vegas of the East', the Stones wheeled out the usual set plus some special guests. Old mucker Eric Clapton got up for 'Little Red Rooster'. It became a very big night for Keith when John Lee Hooker took the stage – even if one story has it that the veteran bluesman downed most of his backstage rider first. Hooker was joined by Clapton too, for his own 'Boogie Chillun', then there was a histrionic version of the rarely performed 'Salt Of The Earth' in which the Stones were joined by Axl Rose and Izzy Stradlin from Guns 'N Roses.

The gig was also notable for another stage invader incident, which Keith quelled with his trusty guitar. He later spoke about it in August 2003, when an

NME reader asked, 'what's the best guitar for clubbing unwanted interlopers?'

'Some guy suddenly got onstage, foaming at the mouth sort of thing. He'd knocked down a couple of security guys and he'd gotten over to Charlie's drumk-it . . . I was playing a Telecaster and we were in the middle of "Satisfaction". And I have to say the Fender is far better than the Gibson for bashing purposes because it's perfect – the curve on the Telecaster fits perfectly the back of the neck. So I put him down. Out. And, amazingly enough, the Telecaster was still in tune! I did-n't miss a beat, man! . . . . I remember they put the guy in jail and I bailed him out the next day.'

The tour wound up at the same venue the following day. By that time it had played to over three million people and grossed around $100 million. Once again, it was the biggest rock 'n' roll tour to date.

Whereas the *Steel Wheels* tour ploughed through the United States as winter was setting in, the European leg would occupy summer evenings. This meant that the first half of the set would be in daylight – rendering the future-shock nightscape less effective. Some of the venues were also too small to accommodate the full set. So they renamed it the 'Urban Jungle' tour and came up with a new stage set: a sleazy tropical plantation, still with girders and walkways, but with garish yellow and orange drapes and palm trees hanging over them. Having returned to the UK less than a month before, I was delighted to catch a couple of shows at Wembley Stadium. I managed to score a ticket from the Stones' new publicist, Bernard Doherty, a favour he's since granted me about ten times in total.

The set itself didn't differ much from *Steel Wheels*, apart from Keith bringing in 'Can't Be Seen' and the addition of 'Terrifying'. In fact, the production was so com-plex that they had to have the same choreographed set for each night. 'Street Fighting Man' was now a major production piece. Enter the inflatables again – this time in the shape of four rabid dogs called Top Dog, Skippy, Kennel Dog and Shagger, with big knobs and gnashing fangs. After goading the hounds throughout the song, and pok-ing them in the knackers with a pole, Mick ended up being eaten by Shagger.

Before the Glasgow gig, Keith cut the middle finger of his left hand on a guitar string. He played the gig, but it went septic, causing two Wembley shows to be rescheduled. Alan Clayton was sitting with Keith when it was announced on the news - to which Keith stood up and raised the infected digit at the TV.

Keith reflected on the gigantic spectacle in his *Vox* interview with Roy Carr. Carr wondered if it was really what the Stones intended.

'Everything has to be exaggerated,' acknowledged Keith. 'You have to put in a lot more physical movement and perform much longer shows. Under such condi-tions, it can be difficult trying to keep both your origins and fellings intact and blow it up to that scale. Personally, I'd rather be playing 3,000-seat theatres where you can be much more subtle musically and physically.'

But the main thing was that the Rolling Stones were back in business, howev-er huge and bloated. Meanwhile, Keith was still contracted for a second solo album.

CHAPTER FIFTEEN

THE HOOCHIE COOCHIE MAN

The Bill Is Gone

Keith ended 1990 by mixing the Stones' fourth live album, finishing up in January '91. That month, the Stones also went into London's Hit Factory studio, with Chris Kimsey at the controls, and recorded two new songs. It would be Keith's last work with the Stones for over two years.

On 4 March, one of the new songs, 'Highwire', was released in the US. It had been prompted by the Gulf War, being recorded around the time allied forces started bombing Baghdad. The song was hastily added to the Sony release schedule, but was hampered by radio bans on both sides of the Atlantic.

'Highwire' was one of the last Stones songs to feature Bill Wyman, who was finally following through on a long-stated intent to leave the band. He'd actually be given nearly two years to come up with his final decision by the others, but had made his mind up during the last world tour. He would finally announce his decision on national TV in early '93.

Bill said he wanted to concentrate on his own music, running his memorabilia-stacked restaurant, *Sticky Fingers*, and turning his Stones archives into books. He'd grown to hate touring too, especially flying, and his doomed marriage to Mandy Smith may also have had something to do with it. 'I'd been with the Stones for over half my life and it was time for a change,' he'd write in *Rolling with the Stones*.

'At the end of the Urban Jungle tour Bill said he was leaving the band,' recalled Keith in *According to the Rolling Stones*. 'I got really pissed with him. I threatened to do everything in the world to him, including death at dawn — as I always say, "Nobody leaves this band except in a coffin." But he'd made up his mind.'

Unlike Mick Taylor, there wasn't an ideal replacement waiting in the wings, and Keith believed the Stones' music depended on its rhythm section. Losing half of it would be like losing a limb.

After the Stones initially bonded through their musical ambitions, Bill and Keith had grown into polar opposites. Wyman always despised hard drugs and hated what they did to the band. Keith laughed at the bass player's constant pursuit of female company, claiming, 'he only thinks with his dick.' Bill could recall what date they played Glasgow Apollo in '73, and stuck it down in his memoirs. Keith probably didn't even know where he was at the time. Bill also didn't approve of the long-running feud between Mick and Keith, and, as his book constantly stresses, felt he wasn't getting his fair shake of the Stones' financial sauce bottle.

It was no secret that Keith and Bill didn't communicate for years. Bill thought Keith hated him. But when Keith was writhing on the bathroom floor in withdrawal hell in Toronto, it had been Bill and Ronnie who scored smack off the street to ease his pain. When Keith was undergoing his detox programme, Bill sent supportive letters – and got one back, decorated in pressed flowers. Keith also sent him a set of pencil portraits of blues legends by celebrated West Coast artist Robert Crumb.

The Only Offender

As the curtain came down on the Stones' late-eighties renaissance, Keith ploughed into a period of intense extracurricular activity. In New York, he produced and played on two tracks for an album by Johnnie Johnson, *Johnnie B. Bad*: Keith sang lead on his old fave 'Key To The Highway', a strident blues treatment which recalled the version laid down during the late seventies with Stu, and co-wrote a track called 'Tanqueray'. It must have given him satisfaction to know the album came about thanks to the attention Johnson received through the Chuck Berry film.

After taking his family for a holiday in Antigua, Keith returned to New York at the beginning of March to shack up with Steve Jordan and start work on his next solo album. But even this was punctuated by outside activities

In April, he nipped over to San Francisco to play with and produce another of his lifelong influences – John Lee Hooker. The charismatic Chicago blues architect's strange way of attacking his guitar had reshaped the way that the mid-teen Keith played his. Hooker was one of the American bluesmen who gained an eager new audience in the early sixties via the Stones. He supported them several times over the years, and played with them at their Atlantic City gig in '89.

Hooker was now 73 years old, and revisiting some of his old songs with invited guests for an album called *Mr Lucky*. He told a journalist that he considered Keith as someone who 'knows what the blues is'. When he asked Keith what song he'd like to play, Keith opted for 'Crawlin' Kingsnake', one of Hooker's earliest tracks, dating from 1949 and covered by the Doors in the early seventies. John Lee Hooker passed away in 2001, but his unique stomp boogie and night-stalking rumble live on in Keith, especially when his playing gets evil.

While in San Francisco, Keith also hooked up with Tom Waits, who was cooking up a mad brew for his next album. They ended up working on three tracks which appeared on the resultant *Bone Machine*. His next high-profile appearance was in October at Spain's Guitar Legend Show in Seville. *Guitar World* reported the man having the time of his life, hanging out with Les Paul and Bo Diddley.

His appearance was introduced by co-headliner Bob Dylan. They launched into an enthusiastic version of 'Shake, Rattle And Roll' together that continued the raggedness of their Live Aid appearance. Keith continued with covers of blues standard 'Going Down' and Eddie Cochran's 'Something Else', before launching into the Stones' 'Connection', with Steve Jordan on drums.

It's been observed that Keith was drinking particularly heavily at this time. Watching a pirate video of the Seville gig, I can concur. When I met him the following year, he was slaughtered – but that was after a gig. It wasn't dampening his enthusiasm or his ability to deliver the goods. As Tom Waits described him, he's 'a great spirit . . . Like a pirate, and he's a complete gentleman.'

It's an old cliché that booze takes over when heroin is sent packing. Technically, Keith may have been an alcoholic at this time – but I'm sure he'd regard it as 'maintaining', in the way that a heroin addict keeps afloat by topping up. His sturdy metabolism seems to enable him to imbibe vast quantities of bourbon, or vodka, and not fuck up – like the old bluesmen, who played and drank till they dropped at a ripe old age.

On 19 November, the Stones signed with Virgin for around £30 million, contracting them to three albums with the back catalogue from 1970 onwards thrown in. Bill didn't sign. On 26 November, Virgin released *Keith Richards And The X-Pensive Winos Live At The Hollywood Palladium, December 15, 1988.* The reason for the three-year gap between recording and release was that it was made available to counter poor quality bootlegs. The Winos now had their own logo on the packaging - a piratical tattoo-like design featuring a skull-encrusted coat of arms.

In January '92, at what was becoming his annual appearance at the Rock and Roll Hall of Fame Awards he posthumously inducted Leo Fender, the man who invented the electric guitar. Fender had died in March, but Keith's glowing tribute had clearly been preparing itself for years: 'I think the stroke of genius, really, was not his inventing the electric guitar but inventing the amplifier to go with it. This is the Hall of Fame. Well, here's the fame, it's been a long haul . . . He gave us the weapon – caress it, don't squeeze it.'

To be closer to his work, Keith stayed at his East Fourth Street apartment, near to Steve Jordan. The pair started writing and honing the ideas which had sprung up the previous year. The strategy was that there wasn't one. It was Keith's 'Incoming!' theory at work. In interviews of the time, he placed emphasis on 'emotions', 'feelings' and 'vulnerability', and his belief that he was making an honest soul music album.

'We tried to avoid making too much sense of this record,' he later told an interviewer. 'To me, ambiguity and provocation and mystery is far more powerful and important. It's kind of like life – you're not quite sure what's going on. I still keep going. It's to do with accepting things, being able to ride it and at the same time not cutting it off. If things don't hurt at all, you're numb, and that's the worst.'

Both Keith and his music had matured, like a fine wine. Both were deeper, richer and, at the same time, funnier. Echoing the song, Keith was now *happy.* From the numbed seventies, through the wartorn eighties, he'd now reached fulfilment – musically and personally. He'd continue to mine the deep soul vein he'd found with the Winos, with humility and passion.

And he was elated to be back with the boys. After a month with Jordan, the rest of the band had arrived in February for Studio 900 rehearsals: Neville, Wachtel and Drayton, later joined by backing singers Bernard Fowler, Babi Floyd and the wonderful Sarah Dash. They approached the recording as a seasoned road unit, with Waddy Wachtel elevated to co-producer status to bring some order to the proceedings.

Recording took place at The Site in San Rafael, California, between 18 March and 1 April, with overdubs and mixing back in New York, finishing on 6 September. Keith moved into the studio and stayed up around the clock.

Main Offender would be the most 'New York' record Keith had been involved in – and there's not one mention of the place in the lyrics. It sounds just like the area of Lower Manhattan it was composed in, atmospheric, funky, shot through with all strains of life. All the band were New Yorkers, apart from Ivan who was from New Orleans, and Keith, who claimed, 'I'm an honorary New Yorker,' anyway.

After a welter of pre-release publicity, *Main Offender* was released on 20 October. That evening Keith did a signing session at New York's Tower Records – in the same block as his East Fourth Street apartment. It attracted over 3,000 people and caused widespread gridlock conditions akin to the Stones-fever days of the 1960s.

The album gets off the launch-pad with the churning grind of '999', before settling into the Winos' patent bare-boned funk-rock of 'Wicked As It Seems' and the melodically cheerful 'Eileen'. Keith celebrates Jamaican roots culture with the eerie, semi-spoken 'Words Of Wonder', before the more low-slung 'Yap Yap', 'Bodytalks', 'Runnin' Too Deep', 'Will But You Won't' and the soul-searching 'Demon'. There's only one ballad this time, 'Hate It When You Leave', but it's the best track on the album, recalling the immortal strains of early Motown and Southern soul with its sombre woodwind. It's the strongest vocal on the album too, soaked in vulnerability and emotion. As Keith's message on the inner sleeve said, 'Angels told me!'

Keith took the Winos on the road between November '92 and February '93. The first gig was on 7 November in front of 45,000 people at the Velez/Sarsfield Stadium in Buenos Aires. Keith had been pushing for the Stones to play South America since the seventies, and finally beat them to it with his other band. The European leg of the tour kicked off on 27 November in Copenhagen, before moving on to Cologne, and a 'secret' gig on 2 December at London's Marquee, which was now located on Shaftesbury Avenue.

I'd just been taken on as a tour DJ for Primal Scream, the most notorious Stones afficionados in the UK, and their management turned Keith's solo gig into a full-scale outing. We met in the pub and were well into the spirit of things by the time we hit the Marquee. When the Winos came on, the packed club went crazy. Scream singer Bobby Gillespie and myself charged through the throng down to the front, not quite believing that we were witnessing Keith in full solid gold action from a distance of about ten feet. When not clapping and dancing our bollocks off, we could witness his every smile, strum, slurp of booze, or inter-band guffaw.

When Keith hit that little stage and the first chord to 'Take It So Hard', it kicked off a euphoric rush which didn't let up for 90 minutes. By the time he hit the familiar spine-tingling intro of 'Gimme Shelter' the place was in uproar. It had taken a couple of songs to get used to Keith fronting a band centre-stage, but he was in total control and worked it with a panther-like stealth. Chords crackled out of his hands, which occasionally flew off of his guitar in visual counterpart. Sometimes his right leg would kick up, before he went off on the prowl in search of another incoming monster-motif, firing off of the energy and funky precision of his Winos. They almost seemed to be using space as another instrument, but the overall feeling of celebration could only spill out into the crowd and make them howl.

After that the Winos went on to Rotterdam, Paris, Barcelona, Madrid, then returned to London for two nights at the Town & Country Club, Kentish Town, on 17-18 December – Keith's 49th birthday. While in London, Keith tried to pin down Bill Wyman for a face-to-face talk about his decision to quit the Stones. But

Bill's mind was made up, and they didn't even meet.

The Town & Country was a perfect venue for Keith, a nice 3,000-capacity theatre. I was with the Scream crew again on the first night, and it was as good as the Marquee. On a larger stage, the full power of Keith's newfound stagecraft and the wickedly sympathetic Winos could be felt with staggering impact. (The fact that most of our group had dropped some ecstasy stuck an extra slant on it too.)

The '92 set took in the high-points of both albums, plus 'Too Rude', 'Before They Make Me Run', 'Happy' and 'Time Is On My Side'. The gigs were also notable for a seven-minute crawl through 'Gimme Shelter'. In the hands of the Winos, the song became an ominous warning burning on a slow fuse. It was one of three songs recorded at this gig which were included as bonus tracks on the American single release of 'Eileen' in April '93.

Afterwards, we all adjourned to the after-show party in the upstairs bar. The Scream team occupied the table next to Patti, Marlon and Bert. I made some kind of cheery greeting and they responded pleasantly, maybe wondering who this bunch of lunatics were. Bert sat surveying the music-biz circus with a kind of proud smile.

Then Keith staggered in, clutching a pint glass full of vodka with a splash of orange. As it had just turned midnight, I realised it was now Keith's birthday. To my total surprise, Keith spotted me, grinned and made a beeline through the music-biz mob straight to our table. He gave me a bear hug and a 'How ya doin', man? Long time, no see,' while I wished him happy birthday. Of course, he was soon ushered away, but it made my night. And you should have seen Primal Scream's faces.

After a couple of hours we went back to the studio. Guitarist 'Throb' Young peeled off the most beautiful guitar solo during one of the Memphis soul ballads they were recording. 'It must be the spirit of Keith!' someone said. So was the partying that didn't end until around eleven o'clock the next morning.

Keith spent Christmas at his Devil's Den with Patti and the girls, plus Anita and Marlon. On 28 December, the Winos filmed a concert for Chicago TV's *Centre Stage* series. On New Year's Eve, they played at the 2,000-capacity Academy in New York, supported by Pearl Jam. This time, Bert, Anita and Angela came along – Bert never missing a gig these days.

So ended a great year. *Main Offender* had only reached number 50 in the UK chart, while just making the US Top 100. But Keith had come out of it with even more credibility and respect.

It was bolstered further when the Winos toured the US, playing 22 gigs in sixteen cities. The tour wound up with six triumphant sell-out shows at New York's 4,000-capacity Beacon Theatre between 19-24 February

Job done. Now it was back to the Stones.

Voodoo Child (A Slight Return)

1994's *Voodoo Lounge* broke the longest gap yet between Stones albums. It had been five years since *Steel Wheels*, although there had been the barrage of solo projects including, latterly, Mick's third solo album, *Wandering Spirit*, and Ronnie's fine, bluesy *Slide On This*.

The next album would be the Stones' first under their new contract with Virgin, and their first without Bill Wyman. When the Stones had first burst out of the R&B club scene, their individual images were a lot less polarised. They were a group with a frighteningly modern look and sound, and Bill complimented that as Old Stone Face. He sat on Charlie Watts' big beat with an understated sense of swing that later worked brilliantly on tracks like 'Miss You'. The fact that he was now walking away from the Stones, unscathed, rattled Keith to the extent that he simply wouldn't believe it. It was only after Wyman went public in January '93 that it really hit home.

'I was incredibly mad at Bill,' Keith admitted later in *NME*. 'I even thought of making him play at gunpoint.' He told *Rolling Stone*'s David Fricke that he was 'devastated' when Wyman left. 'I was ready to kill Bill Wyman. How dare you? Nobody leaves. Especially from that end of the band. I kind of appreciated Bill in a way later. He was being true to himself.'

Keith delivered his final verdict in *According to the Rolling Stones* : 'It was a huge surprise when he actually said, "I'm going to leave the group." Nobody says that – that's a kind of *Spinal Tap* line – but I eventually had to accept it.

'After all, the only thing Bill did was to leave the band and have three babies and one fish-and-chip shop!'

Before the search commenced to find a new bass player, Keith and Mick had to rekindle their relationship, both creatively and personally. They ended up back in

The Bill has gone, but the four remaining Stones reconvene in the Voodoo Lounge.

the kitchen, just like 30 years earlier, at Mick's gaff in Richmond, Surrey.

'We did sit around in Mick's kitchen in February 1993,' recalled Keith in *Stripped*, an authorised Stones book about this period. 'All I can remember was we were kickin' ideas around and talking and I came out with one word. "Focus." We were talking musically first, but really my mind came out with "focus". We'd all be looking down the same 'scope. We've all got the other's ingredients. All we need to do is focus.' This time, Keith was determined to assimilate all the disparate Stones elements into a healthy central nervous system.

Charlie came to work on the new album the happiest he'd been for years. Like Keith, he'd fulfilled a personal dream – his own 'jazz-orchestra' big band – and proved he could thrive outside the Stones. The *Sunday Times* published an extensive feature on the Stones by Robert Sandall, where Keith explained how the drummer had become the perfect bridge between himself and Mick.

'These days Mick and I find it easier to go through Charlie rather than talk things through face to face. The trouble I find with Mick is he's got ants in his pants. He can't lie in a hammock for the afternoon . . . He dissipates his energy and really gets up my nose, contradicting everybody, creating confusion. Artwork, for instance, is not his forte, but he's always dabbling in it. Charlie's a great one for sorting those things out.'

Rehearsals commenced in April with Keith, Mick and Charlie at Eddie Grant's Ocean Wave studios in Barbados. Keith was still on a roll from the Winos, and squirted the bacteria for around 150 songs in ten days.

On 4 June in New York, Keith represented the Jagger-Richards partnership at their induction into the venerable Songwriters Hall of Fame. Apparently, it had been a deathbed wish of veteran showbiz legend Sammy Kahn. Keith reckoned it to be the greatest acknowledgement of his career. His acceptance speech included the line, 'There was really just one song ever written. That was by Adam and Eve. We just do the variations.' He later said it was the only award he ever stuck on his mantlepiece, so flattered was he to be honoured along with the likes of George Gershwin and Irving Berlin.

Now all he needed was what he would come to call the Rolling Stones Mach IV.

Bass-player auditions were held in June. These proved unfruitful despite the collective pedigree. Hopeful candidates had to run through classics like 'Brown Sugar' and 'Miss You', before jamming the blues to see how they sat with Charlie. The array of names included Living Colour's Doug Wimbish, who'd also played with Mick, Joey Spaminato from the band Keith put together for the Chuck Berry movie, Lou Reed stalwart Pino Palladino – who would later, at very short notice, replace the departed John Entwistle in the Who – and even Noel Redding from the Jimi Hendrix Experience.

The same week as the auditions, Ronnie finally got made an equal member, or 'junior partner', of the Rolling Stones. This was mainly at the insistence of Keith and Charlie. When he'd joined the Stones, Ronnie had accepted a cash payment and on-the-road wages, instead of royalties. Now he'd get a share of the profits and have a say in the band's future.

Ronnie offered the band the use of his home studio in Kildare, outside Dublin, to work up the new songs. His house contained an art studio, a recording studio, and even a pub! The band took him up on it. In July, they got down to eight weeks of serious rehearsing and recording demos. Initially Ronnie and Keith handled bass duties. Then along came Darryl Jones from Chicago, who'd contacted the Stones office and offered his services. He'd played for five years with Miles Davis and toured with big leaguers like Madonna and Clapton. Ronnie liked him immediately because he'd passed his initiation test of accepting the Guinness he was offered when he walked in.

The final choice was between Mick's man, Wimbish, Keith's mate, Spaminato, or Jones, who everyone liked. Keith passed the final decision to Charlie Watts. 'I put him in the hot seat. Only once in 30 years! . . . He plumped for Darryl straight off and he slotted straight in.'

'I saw Charlie's face when he started playing with Darryl,' he added in *According to . . .* 'It was the jazz connection, and also the fact that Darryl is very accomplished.'

The big man did indeed add a different kind of swing to the Stones' rhythm section. Once he'd learned to follow Keith's own metronomic pacesetting, he was home and dry.

'Not the new boy any more!' bellowed Ronnie Wood.

In Dublin, Keith had moved in to the 'granny flat' which Ronnie had built for his mother above the garage. Of course, the place was immediately Keefed-up in the usual fashion, with a sign hanging in the window saying, 'Voodoo Lounge'. Hereby hangs a tale, as related by Keith in *Stripped*:

'I was in Barbados with Mick and Charlie at Eddie Grant's studio . . . One night I was going from the house to the studio. It was a real tropical evening. Thunderstorms, rain . . . I saw this animal standing in the corner and it was a small cat, so I tried to put him back with his mother, but the cat was the runt of the litter so was rejected. So I picked it up and took it to the studio and said, "this cat is Voodoo."'

'Whenever I work, I have a sign up on my amps saying "Doc's Office" . . . and then I added in my head, "Doc's Office And Voodoo Lounge" . . .' Thus did a runty little cat, who Keith adopted and took home to Connecticut, come to have his name plastered on billboards all over the world.

The sessions at Ronnie's gave the album its shape and, indeed, focus. Keith compared the mood of the sessions to *Exile On Main Street* – in terms of hothouse creativity under one roof, rather than excess. American producer Don Was was brought in for the job of co-ordinating, steering and whittling down the welter of song ideas ejaculated in Barbados. I first came across Don when he was half of a duo called Was (Not Was) in New York in the late seventies. They'd come up through the club underground, eventually hitting big with a tune called 'Out Come The Freaks'. Don had moved on to production, scoring with Bonnie Raitt, the B-52's and Brian Wilson. He fitted in well with the Stones' work ethic of building up from a groove at ground level.

Don was quick to big up Mr. Richards during a piece on Keith in the October '94 issue of *Guitar World*. 'I learned more about music working with this guy for five or six months than I could in years' worth of the Berkeley School of Music. There's certainly this conception of Keith being this drug-burnout, *Spinal Tap* character. It's wrong. He's a brilliant, vibrant character . . . a very deep guy who I think may be at the most creative period in his life. He plays like a jazz musician . . .'

Keith's slant on Don (Was) was, 'I read Don my usual riot act, you know: Are you sure you wanna be the meat in the sandwich? . . . . Because most of the guys we've used are scared to step in between Mick and me. It doesn't happen so often now, but when it does it flares. I'd be like, "what are you doing singing a song called 'Attitude' with your feet on the sofa, man?", and Don would instantly step in and break it up.'

The Stones returned to Dublin in early November - this time to U2's Windmill Lane Studios, where they worked for five weeks. Again, Keith became so immersed in the proceedings that he all but moved into the studio. Unlike most album sessions since the early seventies, he actually seemed to be getting on with Mick, celebrating their long friendship with the ironically-titled 'Sweethearts Together', which they sang face-to-face. By early December they'd finished recording. The tracks were tough and bluesy with splashes of exotic rhythms. Ah, but the mixing was still to come . . .

Keith had a double celebration on 18 December, turning 50 on the same day as celebrating his tenth wedding anniversary with Patti. The celebrations took place at New York's Metropolis Restaurant. The 150 guests included Eric Clapton, Bobby Keys, Kate Moss, U2's Adam Clayton with Naomi Campbell in tow, plus Marlon and Angela.

Mixing took place in Los Angeles between January and April. Despite their mellowing attitudes, there was the traditional conflict between Keith's raw vision and Mick's desire to be contemporary, which had sparked their studio battles since the seventies. *Exile* became the masterpiece that it is because the seams still showed. Keith has said that *Voodoo Lounge* was created in the same spirit, but Don took it to LA and gave it a good nip and tuck. The chart-friendly result was ultimately out of the hands of the Stones. When their baby emerged, all the dirt had been wiped carefully from every crevice. But you can't fault Don Was for delivering the mainstream Stones album they needed to consolidate the success of *Steel Wheels*. It became one of their strongest sellers, moving over five million copies in the first year and scoring a Grammy for best rock album. And Don Was is still working with them.

For a couple of days in February, Keith undertook a quick visit to Nashville to record with another of his lifelong influences - the great country singer George Jones. He had been every bit as wild as Johnny Cash in his day. Then he matured into the ultimate broken-hearted barfly, lamenting lost love over a bottle of bourbon. Keith first encountered his music in his adolescence at the same time as he had Hank Williams. George had also been a particular favourite of Gram Parsons, and his music formed part of the lessons in country music that Gram gave Keith, along with that of Merle Haggard and Jimmie Rogers. Keith and George duetted on his tear-stained ballad 'Sorry It's Not You'.

'I did the Jones duet for Gram,' Keith told *The Observer* the following year. 'That's a song he taught me and which we used to play endlessly, even when we were being supposedly cured. We'd be in cold turkey and playing would be our therapy. After a few days we'd say, "OK, we're clean, that's it," and off we'd go, stay clean for a week or two. Those were the days . . . silly days.'

A couple of years later, Keith would also run into Johnny Cash himself – in the toilets at an LA awards ceremony. A surprised and delighted Keith reportedly announced, 'We need a camera. I'm having a piss with Johnny Cash!' Mr. Cash zipped up and left.

The first major press about the new album came in an interview with David Fricke in *Rolling Stone*. In it, Keith talked about his idiosyncratic songwriting regimen:

'There's no such thing as boredom if you've got a guitar. Sleep is important. I once stayed up for nine days. I gave up doing that because when you do fall asleep, it could be anywhere. I fell asleep on top of a speaker once in point nought of a second. Nine days is my record and I'm leaving it that way. It's a lot of fun not sleeping for two days because you don't need to take anything. You're in another world.'

Chuck Leavell talked about Keith's songwriting in *Stripped*: 'Keith has this amazing ability to write songs that sound like standards in their melodic content like "Slipping Away". They have a certain chord structure that are unusual but standard. That's what comes of him listening to people like Hoagy Carmichael. He's a big fan of those kinds of writers.'

When I was in Miami in '97 I happened on a record store across the road from the hotel. It was bootleg heaven. I paid about 150 bucks for the four-CD boxed set *Voodoo Brew*, a rough-diamond cut of the eventual product, which also contained an elaborate booklet centred around the *Rolling Stone* photo session and interview. Three of the CDs feature work-in-progress versions of *Voodoo Lounge* tracks, along with studio chat. In several cases, the finished songs before they got smoothed down in the mix were superior to the released versions.

The CD subtitled *Keith Plays His Favourites* sees him alone in the early hours with an acoustic guitar, picking and crooning through old faves like 'Salty Dog', 'Cocaine', 'I Get A Kick Out Of You', 'Love Is Strange', 'Girl Of The North Country', 'John Wesley Harding' and 'Please Please Me'. There's a riveting ballad called 'Goodbye To Love', plus original items and throwaways like 'Love's Tough Shit Baby', 'Keith's Boogie' and 'Scotty Moore Riffs'. Keith talks throughout, while trying out licks, and it took me back to that London hotel room in '83. 'You can't keep the country out of the boy,' he says after folk standard 'Salty Dog'. He's rarely heard in this manner, and it's fascinating.

'Innovations,' Keith reflected aloud in Fricke's *Rolling Stone* interview. 'A willingness to experiment. That's what feels like the Stones. It wasn't like the other periods where, like everybody else, we were trying to sound like the Stones. We had to get over that. We already are the Stones.'

Asked about this spirit of experimentation by *Guitar World*'s Gary Graff, he elaborated: 'A lot of what came out on this album came from what we did in the time between the Stones stuff. When you're working with other people you stroke a lot of other areas you were unsure of going down before. You just kind of grow, you know? It's better than doing nothing, which was our big problem.'

That year, Bernard Doherty asked me to write a piece about *Voodoo Lounge* to go in that album's promotional package. My first impressions from the advance tape read, 'Keith conjures an achingly lonesome country wail on "The Worst", and opens his heart again on "Thru And Thru" . . . .

Voodoo Lounge wasn't an instant Stones classic, but it's a sleeping beauty and marked a turning point for Keith. His two vocal tracks stand up alongside his best ballads.

'Thru And Thru' deserves special attention. Like 'Slipping Away' on the previous album, many critics hailed it as the best track, and this six-minute emotional epic is still one of Keith's finest.

He talked about the song's birth in the *Voodoo Lounge* tour programme: 'In Barbados one night I'd gone out with Pierre who works with me. Four or five in the morning we got back. I said, "Let's go to the studio. Incoming, Pierre!" I had no idea what it was, but had to switch on all the gear and get it all lined up. Something had just clicked in the car on the way home. And if I let go – if I go to sleep now – it's gone. Waiting for the machinery to be turned on it all came out. Then what do you do with it? It would've probably have been a backburner job if it hadn't been for Charlie saying "let me take the drums down the stairwell." He brought in that extra thing and then we built it up. There's a little bass on it and Pierre put a little acoustic guitar in it, but otherwise we left the track as it was, and apart from a little wizardry here and there, that was about it.'

Keith grew this one himself. Not even Ronnie plays on it. There's a famous tale relating to Guns 'N Roses guitarist Slash, who was visiting the studio, getting knocked back when he suggested he should play on the end of the track. 'I like ya kid, but don't push your luck. You ain't coming anywhere near my fucking track,' spat Keith, trying to dampen the fuses behind his darkening eyes. No-one was going to lay a finger on his new baby. In the grand tradition which Keith has followed since the late seventies, his magnum opus was the last track to be finished for the album. And he finished it himself, with Bernard Fowler and Ivan Neville supplying exquisite backing vocals.

'Thru And Thru' works via its cavernous emptiness, with the spotlight on Keith. Charlie doesn't come in until halfway through, along with backing singers including Wino Ivan Neville. It was Keith's most effective and starkly honest vocal to date. Thanks to the desolate backing, you can just picture him sitting in his room at five in the morning: 'Any minute, any hour / I'm waiting on a call from you . . .' Then the killer punch: 'What I heard really pissed me off / 'Cause now I got those FUCKING blues . . .' It hasn't been played live much, although it was one of the highlights of the New York gig on the 2003 *Four Flicks* DVD. You could have heard a pin drop in Madison Square Gardens as Keith performed the song.

He talked about it in *According to the Rolling Stones*: 'On an album like *Voodoo Lounge* there are songs that people won't get for ten years – and then suddenly they get what I've been doing. "Thru And Thru" was exactly like that. It took off when it was put on the soundtrack of *The Sopranos* along with "Make No Mistake" from the X-Pensive Winos. Suddenly everybody was saying, "What's that wonderful record?". . . . if you don't get it now, you don't get it in ten years, or you don't get it until after I croak, it doesn't matter to me – you'll get it one day.'

'The Worst' is a country lament for lost love with a big George Jones influence. It's almost a Keith confessional, as he sings, 'I said from the first / I am the worst kind of guy / for you to be around . . .' He admits that he can't be trusted, should be blamed for everything, and ought to be passed on by. It's bare and moving, complimented by crying pedal steel from Ronnie and an Irish fiddle.

'I wrote "The Worst" in Barbados in the kitchen. So I said, "that's a pretty melody but what to do with it? I really didn't know. That's where Ireland comes in, because Ireland has its own great traditional music - Frankie Gavin on the fiddle there. It's not country music as such, but it's the roots of it. It's that Irish feel.'

The sessions were also notable for Keith and Mick getting along during the recording. 'Mick and I have been singing straight into the night together, which we haven't done for a long time,' said Keith. 'In fact it was Don Was who said "go and do it together."'

Ronnie agreed: 'The great thing is, Mick and Keith are getting along so much better now. Whenever they thought a little feud was coming up, they would say "oh I guess we'd better do 'Sweethearts Together' to cool things down." They do nice harmony.'

This track is a kind of sixties-slanted Drifters teen ballad, but is also an ambivalent affirmation of the long-standing relationship between Keith and Mick. Keith: 'My life with this band, it's had its ups and downs, but at the moment, I haven't known them to be enjoying what they do so much for a long time. I feel very focused on what they're doing. It's a good feeling. When you're not quite sure what you're doing that can be a drag. But you do it and, if you hang in long enough, then you get the return.'

Q, whose review dismissed the album as 'neither dog's dinner nor sumptuous banquet', carried one of its periodic Stones cover features in August '94. Adrian Deevoy asked Keith how he saw his image these days:

'It's something you drag around behind you like a long shadow. Does it really belong to you? Some people still think I'm a junkie who lives in a coffin. And even though that was nearly twenty years ago, you cannot convince some people that I'm not a mad drug addict. So, I've still got him in my baggage. But I'll get a lawyer in an expensive suit and cologne coming up and shaking my hand one minute and some fifteen-year-old kid is asking me about Telecasters the next.'

Deevoy was even brave enough to pop the question (probably prompted by Anita Pallenberg's speculation on Mick's supposed bisexuality) of whether Keith and Mick had ever had sex together. Fortunately, Keith was laughing. 'No, we've never had sex with each other. I never fancied bum. At least not male bum. I might have accidentally slipped into a couple of females . . . Second hole down from the back of the neck, son. That's the one you want.'

Lounge Lizard

On 4 May, the Stones announced the *Voodoo Lounge* world tour from John F. Kennedy's old yacht, moored on the Hudson River, New York. They'd open in Washington on 1 August, traversing the States before moving on to Mexico, South America, South Africa, Japan, Australia, New Zealand, before ending up in Europe in summer '95.

They rehearsed for six weeks in the gym of a boys' boarding academy outside

Dramatic launch: The Rolling Stones arrive to announce in New York their world tour, on board a boat once owned by President Kennedy

This tour won't be the last time says Jagger

The Stones announce the 1995 Voodoo Lounge *tour at New York harbour.*

Toronto, with the rejuvenated Charlie Watts driving along proceedings, running through old songs which hadn't been touched for years. The Stones were determined to steer clear of what Keith called *Voodoo Lounge: Live At The Stadium.* They would play the CD version, while the band traced their parts, then play it on its own a couple of times. If it was firing, Ronnie would sprint over to a big board and scribble down the name of the track. It was also useful for teaching Darryl Jones a big chunk of their back catalogue.

NME published a feature by Rich Cohen, who was present at one of the rehearsals. Keith threw down the gauntlet: 'On any given night, we're a still damn good band. And on some nights, maybe even the best band in the world. So screw the press and their slagging about the 'Geritol Tour'. You assholes. Wait until you get to our age and see how you run. I got news for you, we're still a bunch of tough bastards. String us up and we still won't die.'

That last sentence was plucked out and used in the PR campaign.

As Cohen reported, Keith was in combative mood: 'We're the only band to take it this far. And if we trip and fall, you'll know that's how far it can be taken. If there's someone out there doing it better than us, they can have the gig. But I ain't heard it so far.'

The first single from the album, 'Love Is Strong', was released on 4 July, making number fourteen in the UK but only 91 in the US. But it boasted a great video, featuring the band as giants straddling the New York cityscape. Keith looked particularly effective, leaning against a skyscraper in the skull-emblazoned shirt that would be his favoured item of clothing on tour.

The latest Stones look for their album artwork fitted Keith's fixation with death's heads: all swirling skulls and spirits, while the tongue had sprouted lethal-looking spikes. It was a smart touch to feature an old black-and-white photograph of the Devil and his grinning skeletal mates leering at the dinner table in the centrefold. Entitled 'Satan's Play Room', the satanic sculptures were taken from a book called *Satan's Daily Life at the End of the Nineteenth Century*, by Jac Remise. The Stones used the Devil's feast 25 years after 'Sympathy For The Devil' . . . and *Beggars Banquet*!

The album was released on 11 July, making number one in the UK and two in the US.

The Stones played one of their traditional warm-ups on 19 July at the tiny RPM strip club in Toronto. The touring band was itself stripped down: just Chuck Leavell on keyboards, with Bernard Fowler and Lisa Fischer supplying those essential backing vocals, and brass construction from top session guys the New West Horns – Andy Snitzer, Michael Davis and Kent Smith, led by Bobby Keys. Lisa talked about working with Keith in *Stripped*: 'I met Keith in a recording studio and everyone was telling me he's really freaked out and out of his mind . . . and Keith walks in and says, "Heeeey bayyybeeee how yaaa doing?" I realised he meant, "How you doing baby?" At first it was, "okay, I better get used to the accent and the gravelly sexy voice." So after a while I started to call him Cookie Monster [from *Sesame Street*], so I just loved him immediately. He's such a sweet, warm person, so you have to get past the stories people tell you.'

Keith later returned Lisa's affection, telling *NME*, 'I said, "one strong chick singer." . . . and Lisa Fischer can handle being the only chick in a band like this - backstage as well. There's a lot of teasing, ha ha. Respect.'

Around a thousand of the world's press were flown in for the opening night on 1 August at Washington DC's RFK Stadium. I managed to pitch it with a dance music magazine I was writing for called *Jockey Slut* – on the basis that the Stones were the first British white kids to translate dance music as originated in the ghettos of America into their own hybrid. Our dance kids had to be told! Up until then the rave generation had probably only admired Keith because he'd taken more drugs than them.

Immigration gave me a hard time. Customs gave my bags a good shakedown too. But there was Stones fever all around, as many of their team were staying here too. The whole city was crawling with media, diehard fans and people connected with the tour. (President Clinton, however, who the Stones had asked to introduce them, had a convenient appointment in New Jersey.) On the day of the gig, I also discovered a bourbon called Knob Creek . . ..

Look at that snake! That was my first reaction when I staggered into the massive stadium and clapped eyes on the towering lighting rig in the form of a cobra. The cyber-city stage seemed even bigger than *Steel Wheels*.

Visual head honcho Patrick Woodruffe described Keith's attitude to all the visual excess in *Stripped*: 'Keith is not against all that thing, but he's more instinctively focused on just his space and his patch, driving the band, playing the music . . . Keith is, in his own way, very theatrical. He is the personification of rock 'n' roll. He is a man with an eye, for someone who dresses like that must see the theatre and drama of their performance.'

The US stadium shows used one and a half million watts of power, 1500 lights, half a million tonnes of steel and around 250 people to get it all working. It cost $4 million. All of this inspired by Keith's adopted cat!

First the snake started hissing smoke belches, the crowd roaring in their Budweiser heaven. The lights loomed and Charlie started up that pounding Bo Diddley tribal rhythm. 'Ahm gonna tell you how it's gonna be!' signalled 'Not Fade Away'. Now the snake was belching fire and light while the whole stage erupted into action. It was kind of saying, 'Darling, I'm home!' And how.

For Keith's spot, he answered my prayers and delivered a wrenched version of 'The Worst', before 'Happy'. 'Monkey Man' was played for the first time live, 'Sympathy' saw Mick in witchdoctor evening dress, and 'Honky Tonk Women' provoked some outrage as the biggest video screen in the world flashed a series of girlie images, including a sneaky blowjob.

It was a great gig, even if there were some sound gremlins and first night teething problems – and a redneck whacked me in the face, sending me down a flight of steps when I jumped on his seat. (I'd gone to the toilet and forgotten where my own seat was. It made the gossip column of *Music Week*, anyway. Blame the Knob Creek.)

One of my accomplices on the jaunt was *NME*'s Gavin Martin, who singled out 'the mercurial firepower, broken riffs and serrated swaggering interplay between Keith Richards and Ronnie Wood. I remember on the previous occasion I saw the Stones, in 1982, this pair were barely able to stand. The playing was bludgeoning, messy, they were dragging each other down, but the authority they now parade is a revelation . . . Richards' solo spot on "The Worst" is further evidence of his new assured standing.'

In the seventies Keith lurked at the back by Charlie's drumkit. The next decade saw him coming out until he was assertive enough to cajole Mick, safe in the knowledge that he now epitomised the essence of the Stones. The Glimmer Twins would never simply down tools and start scrapping up there (although Keith has been known to plant one on Ronnie). But the day that the conflicts born out of the solo projects, the different lifestyles, the different musical directions is no longer there is the day much of the fire evaporates from the belly of the Stones.

The tour book answered a question that's often niggled me when watching them: just what are Keith and Ronnie whispering and cackling about while they're hacking away behind Mick?

Keith: 'He just comes up and says thing like, "I love you," or "I hate you," or "where did you get that jacket," or "I thought that was alright," or "what happens next? I don't know!" Those kind of things. Or Mick will come up and say, "What's Ronnie doing?", or "what are you doing?" That's the great thing - no matter how much you rehearse, there's always that element of looseness where the number can always change the whole face of the song, and everyone looks at each other and says, "where did that come from?"'

Keith describes his uncanny onstage interplay with Ronnie as being down to 'sympathetic particles'. When asked about the definition of guitar parts in *Guitarist* magazine, Ronnie explained, 'it's decided on the night between us. Keith and I call it an ancient kind of weaving and we just do it. We never used to argue about solos but we do now! We have some great arguments, on stage and off, mainly to entertain Charlie, I think. He's usually sitting there cracking up behind his drums.'

I also caught the tour at New York Giants Stadium in August. Before the gig I went to the hotel where the band's entourage were staying and said hello to Bert. I must have had some money at the time as I hired a limo, and spent about a hundred quid on a Stones-logo denim jacket.

Charlie Watts got a hooting ovation lasting over two minutes during the band announcements. It's something that started up on this tour and continues to the present day, with Keith and Ronnie often dropping to their knees in Watts-worship. 'It's a weird thing but that's been happening since the very first show of this whole tour in Washington,' said Keith in *NME* on the eve of the UK gigs. 'And it's a totally spontanit . . . spintanont . . . urgh, I'm starting to slur . . . it's a spontaneous thing - there we go! C'mon Keith, wake up! Hahaha! . . . and it started there and it just spread.'

On 7 September the Stones were presented with a Lifetime Achievement Award by MTV. It was the only good news in a month of casualties: first, the band learned that Nicky Hopkins had passed away in Nashville at the age of 50, from Crohn's disease. It's hard to imagine any of the classic late sixties/early seventies albums without his presence. Then Jimmy Miller died of liver failure at the age of 52. The last record he'd worked on had been with Primal Scream, who openly admitted the debt they owed the Stones. (The crazed Miller was still carving swastikas into the control desk.)

The *Voodoo Lounge* tour wouldn't wind up its American leg until Vancouver on Keith's birthday, 18 December. He had to miss Marlon's wedding to Lucy, daughter of fashion designer Loulou De La Falaise, in Italy, with Patti going along instead. Still, the tour ended up breaking records once again by grossing $140 million.

On 14 January, the next leg of the tour started in Mexico City, realising one of Keith's ambitions by taking the Stones on a jaunt through South America, then moving on to the post-apartheid South Africa. All the shows were fantastically successful, accompanied by absolute pandemonium that recalled the Stones-fever days. The tabloids reported that Keith was lobbing fruit out of his hotel room at the fans below - which he was, but the tabloid stories painted it as the actions of a madman. When asked about it by *NME*'s Brendon Fitzgerald, Keith explained, 'They were hungry and thirsty! They were out there going "Ole ole ole ole! Reechards Ree-chards!" Amazing. It was like the sixties, except there were like more guys now!' Keith told the same writer that the Stones still weren't allowed into China because they'd cause 'cultural pollution'.

In March they played Japan, where they sold out the Tokyo Dome for six nights running. The band and Don Was also popped into the studio and started rearranging some old tracks for a projected 'Unplugged'-style acoustic album. Some would appear on the album later entitled *Stripped*, including 'I'm Free',

'Slipping Away', 'The Spider And The Fly', 'Love In Vain', 'Shine A Light', 'Wild Horses', 'Black Limousine' and a version of Willie Dixon's 'Little Baby'. It was followed by an Australian leg of the tour, including the first time they'd played New Zealand for 29 years.

Ten years earlier, when I was sitting in Keith's London hotel room, he'd launched into his frustration at the Stones not being able to play new territories: 'It makes you realise that we're all going round this same fucking running track and it's so difficult to break out. You do the US and Europe, then you do Australia. But you're leaving out huge portions of the world. All you need to do is go there. At the same time it's so much easier for the promoters and the business people to keep you going round the same old track. They've got it all organised and it's so much hassle for them to get you to play South America or Africa or Russia. By now I'm sick of playing – well, not sick of it, I'm not sick of playing to anybody – but I don't see why by now I haven't managed to get out of that single rut of just playing the US and Europe and Australia. It's because they can make enough money out of forcing us to go around the same old track time after time after time. They've got no imagination. It's not required of 'em. This means you have to get the actual musicians in the band to force these things to happen. [getting quite heated] I'm sick of it. One more rut. What I want is not one more "farewell" American tour, but bust their balls and get us into Russia.'

This conversation came back to me as I scanned the '94 tour dates, realising how most of the world had now thrown itself open to the Stones. Even Keith's ambition to play Russia would be fulfilled toward the end of the nineties.

The Stones rehearsed their low-key semi-acoustic set in Amsterdam through May, with three nights at Amsterdam's infamous Paradiso club. I've deejayed there about ten times, and it's always packed to its 800 capacity and very relaxed. (The customary weed stall in the foyer must help.) Keith reckoned the gigs, which would form the bulk of the *Stripped* album, were the best shows the Stones had ever played.

The European leg of the *Voodoo Lounge* tour started in Stockholm at the beginning of June and hit Britain in July. Keith made the cover of *NME* in another of his periodic music-press appraisals as 'the very essence of rock 'n' roll'. Pennie Smith's cover shot depicted a kohled-up man in black, with the banner, 'Monster Of Rock! The Creature From The Jack Lagoon'. The headline inside was that old warhorse, 'Sympathy For The Old Devil'.

Writer Brendon Fitzgerald had plugged me beforehand for handy hints about interviewing Keith. He was obviously nervous. 'Just be yourself – he'll suss if you're into the music and you'll be sorted,' I said. He caught Keith in a good mood, classically describing him as possessing 'the demeanour of a tipsy pirate well satisfied with his plunderings . . . a pool hall Dudley Moore in *Arthur*.'

The Stones' big one was 19 July at the 4,000 capacity Brixton Academy. It was the smallest venue I'd ever seen them play, and they performed a set of lesser heard classics. The morning before had seen 2,500 tickets snarfed up from the Virgin Megastore in Oxford Street after the hordes had camped out all night. There were also about 800 friends and liggers, including Marianne Faithfull, Mick Hucknall, George Harrison, Joe Strummer, Duran Duran and Michael

The 'Cookie Monster' on the rampage in Stockholm, on the Voodoo Lounge *tour.*

Hutchence. This was something very special indeed.

As usual, Keith kickstarted the set and sent the place into orbit – this time with a churning 'Honky Tonk Women'. A sleazy 'Live With Me' saw Mick mopping Keith's brow mid-song. A startling run of 'Dead Flowers', 'Sweet Virginia' and 'Far Away Eyes' preceded a soaring 'Love In Vain', revisiting the earliest days at the Crawdaddy. By now I was a gibbering wreck. A further surprise was 'Shine A Light', from *Exile*. Mick once said that most of *Exile* was unplayable live, but this was transformed into gospel heaven with Chuck Leavell excelling on Billy Preston's old piano parts. They just didn't let up, with Keith's double header of 'Connection' and 'Slipping Away' before the killer punch of an epic 'Midnight Rambler'.

It was a once-in-a-lifetime celebration. Afterwards, I ended up at the Stones' favourite Landmark Hotel, opposite Marylebone station, in the bar with Chrissie Hynde, Annie Nightingale and Bobby Keys. He was armed with a video camera and turned out to be one of the funniest blokes I've ever met, giving a running commentary as he filmed us talking to him. Some of us ended up in Freddie Sessler's room. It was the first and only time I ever met the buddy who'd been with Keith since the sixties. I was there until ten o'clock the next morning – and can hardly remember a word that was exchanged! Freddie, who was very witty and very wise, let me scrawl 'what a gig' to Keith on a napkin. I had to be in the studio myself the following day, but ended up crawling into a straw hut in the garden, still buzzing. What a night.

The *Voodoo Lounge* world tour eventually finished up in Rotterdam at the end of August, although there was another secret gig at London's Bagley's Warehouse for the 'Like A Rolling Stone' video in September. Keith talked about covering the classic Dylan song to Brendon Fitzgerald: '. . . the first thing Bob Dylan said to me, it was in the Ad Lib, Leicester Square. He walks over, I'm sitting there with John Lennon, we're talking – Bob's just arrived in town . . . first thing he says to me, "I coulda written 'Satisfaction' but you couldn'ta written 'Desolation Row'" . . . . and well, you're probably right! . . . and now I'm playing "Like A Rolling Stone". The title's just so inviting, innit?'

Brixton Academy paved the way for the upcoming live album, entitled *Stripped* when it was eventually released in November. (The original title was *Butt Naked*.) Keith once again took on promotional duties, interviewed this time by former *NME* editor Neil Spencer for *The Observer*.

The man played down his evergreen 'Keef' image: 'I'm a lot of different guys. In fact, the mythical Keith Richards is the one that no one wants to meet, including myself. I can pull him out if I have to, if something gets me going, but most of the time I'm the same as anyone else. I'm just one of the lads. Imagine, I've got two little daughters who love me and Keith Richards is their dad. What does that make them, members of the Addams Family?'

Spencer wondered how he regarded the numerous deaths and casualties surrounding the Stones over the years. Keith was philosophical:

'After a while you develop a certain dressing room fatalism . . . . If you look at Kurt Cobain's suicide, things aren't that different these days. There are many ways to go in this business, some self-inflicted, some just down to the amount of travelling you do . . . . And when you look at the casualties – well, some regiments would be drawn out of the front line if they endured our casualty rate.'

So have the Stones acted out their careers to a dangerous script?

'When it's projected onto you, there's the temptation to say: "OK, you want to play that game, I can probably play the Prince of Darkness pretty good . . . ." But no, I've always felt that idea was projected from the outside, especially that cabalistic business. OK, so I knew Kenneth Anger, big deal. I certainly would never go into it like – bless his heart 'cause I love him – Jimmy Page, who spent half his life worshipping Aleister Crowley. I find that a waste of time. It's a backwater.'

Determinedly back in the mainstream, the Stones would be making their next decisive move almost immediately.

CHAPTER SIXTEEN

BLESSED POISON

Prophecy Must Fulfil

After the tour, Keith was in his usual adrenalined state – the one that used to get him into trouble. Following the *Steel Wheels* jaunt, he'd had the second Winos album to dive straight into. Now, after two years immersed in the latest album and tour, Keith had family life at home in Westin, Connecticut to look forward to. But first he had to calm down, chill out and ready himself for it. For Keith, it was never as easy as just scooting back, walking in the door with a weary 'Darling, I'm home!' and flopping down in front of the TV with a beer.

'There's a certain period of adjustment required between the last show of a tour finishing and suddenly finding yourself back home, where there's no motor-cycle escort and you still forget that the red light means "Stop",' he says in *According to the Rolling Stones*.

In the seventies, Keith would leave a tour and head home to Anita and the arms of Morpheus. Victor Bockris paints a bizarrely different picture of the kind of domestic bliss Keith went home to in November '95, and the increasingly devout Christian way of life Patti had been pursuing in the leafy suburbs of Connecticut: the kids going to strict Christian schools; grace being chanted before meals; often finding himself in the doghouse for his ingrained and totally opposite way of life.

This would piss Keith off, as he was brought up in a family with no time for organised religion and had never attended church when he was growing up. At least three books have quoted Keith as saying, 'Dead guy on a cross? Shit logo.' Bockris, who names his source as two anonymous house callers, says Patti disapproved of Keith's 24-hour party person lifestyle. Understandably, perhaps, but it was obviously impossible for Keith to change into a church-going suburban American dad overnight.

That kind of lifestyle must have seemed as alien to him as the idea of joining the Marines. His idea of shaping up would be to stay up for only two days instead of a week. But he could grin and bear it on the basis that he sometimes went out to work for two years! And, of course, he loved Patti and the children, and both sides would eventually reach a happy compromise. By the end of the decade, Keith would become more domesticated, getting up with the kids and taking them to school when he was at home.

Meanwhile, Keith would hole up in his large, oak-paneled library or his basement studio den. The ironically-named Devil's Den was the first properly-rooted family home that lifelong nomad Keith had owned, and was a major step up for Patti from her working-class Staten Island roots. But, once the family were ensconced, Keith ventured forth to make the Chuck Berry film, his first solo album, a Stones album, his second solo album, then another Stones record, touring behind all of them. With the periods he also spent at Ronnie's farm, Redlands and Point of View, Keith simply wasn't home much during these years, and wouldn't be until the end of the decade. Meanwhile, Patti had plenty of time to get to know the local community and rearrange the furniture.

The November '95 issue of *Loaded* trumpeted a Keef interview. The pioneering lads' mag used to be a great laugh for the eternally stupid hedonist, and the feature seemed like a marriage made in heaven. Jon Wilde asked about sex, groupies and wanking. But, breaking away from the mag's usual stream of thigh-slapping whoopee, Keith talked about his special regard for the female species.

'I mean, chicks are endlessly fascinating to me,' he said. 'They're always an education. I can have a load more fun with chicks than with a bunch of guys. When men are left to their own devices, they're always jousting, trying to put one over on each other in a boring, macho way. But women have a different point of view on things and they're not afraid to point out that I've been behaving like an asshole. And I kinda like that.'

However, after the world tour, Keith decided to head first to his sanctuary of more than 20 years – Point of View in Jamaica. Patti was not happy.

But Keith loved Jamaica: the people, the music, the vibe and the weed. Despite the hideous ordeal experienced by Anita, and the bad experiences he'd had at the hands of artists like Peter Tosh and Max Romeo, he still felt like it was his spiritual home. He also had another family here, who'd grown up around a bunch of Rastas he'd met on the beach in '72.

'I like hanging with black people, man. It's so much easier,' he told *Mojo*'s Barney Hoskyns in '97. 'They think I'm one anyway. I'm just in disguise. I've spent half my life hanging out in back rooms with black guys. They accept me. I don't think about it. I find there's a lot less tension in the air. They're less self-conscious. Hanging around white people there's always a little tinge of stress. To me, the other side of the tracks is where I can really rest.'

So Keith went there to adjust before going back to Westin – and ended up realising a personal dream of over 20 years. Back in '72, after Keith had bought Point of View within weeks of arriving, he soon fell in with the local Rastas in Ochos Rios and started jamming with them.

'That was one of the best things I did, to hang about in Jamaica after we'd done *Goats Head Soup*,' he told me in 1980. 'I stayed there for nearly a year. I don't get down to Jamaica as much as I'd like to. Every time I go down there I have a great time with this little of band of Rastas I've played with for years. Just drums and chanting. They really keep me at it.'

The form of music Keith was talking about is Nyabinghi – spiritual lyrics chanted and sung over a hand-drum pulse based on the human heartbeat. The Rasta equivalent of gospel or the blues, it's basically Rastafarian hymns. Keith said the music 'wasn't reggae – more these ethnic chants which are basically African but have this strong injection of a kind of Southern Baptist spiritualist feel.' It is an amazingly soothing sound, hypnotic and endless. Bob Marley used it beautifully on 'This Train', but homogenised it on his 'Rasta Man', which Keith reckoned 'sounded like Millie' of 'My Boy Lollipop' fame.

I first read about Keith's interest in this music in *Zigzag*, just before I started writing for them. Following his 'passing it on' theory, I picked up albums by all the practitioners I could find, such as Ras Michael and the Sons of Negus and Count Ossie and the Mystic Revelations of Rastafari. Even they were 'still no way the real thing', according to Keith. It led me on to roots reggae itself, which the Stones had yet to tackle, 'because,' Keith explained, 'we didn't think we were capable of doing it to the required standard.'

In the years since then, the Stones have become confident enough to wade into reggae's waters on tunes like 'Luxury', 'Cherry Oh Baby', 'Send it To Me' and Keith's 'Too Rude' on *Dirty Work*. Keith proved his standing in the Jamaican reggae community in '79 by guesting on guitar with island heroes Black Uhuru on their classic single, 'Shine Eye' – although he didn't know it at the time. 'That was those sessions I did with Sly and Robbie,' he told me. 'It was just a backing track when I did it, then somebody said it'd come out with Black Uhuru singing on it.' But with the Nyabinghi drums, Keith felt that he'd happened on a musical form which had never been properly documented. Reading that Kent interview now, it's apparent that Keith started trying to get what became his Wingless Angels project off the ground back then.

'It got so good at one point that I loaded all their gear – these drums and some amps of mine – into a Range Rover and took 'em all down to Dynamic Sounds in Jamaica to record. Ultimately I realised that they were pretty much totally inhibited by all the machinery in the studio so the next time - and this is going to be my big mission – I'm going to do it right, which is to take the equipment to them . . . it'll be interesting to find out just how many of the band are alive or out of jail.'

When Nick asked Keith how he wasn't ripped off in this notoriously tough country, he described another essential link in the story. 'I was fortunate in that respect in that they dug the way I played and pretty much accepted me. Sure, there was the occasional hassle for the extra $10. I paid the Rastas for the session work they did. In fact, it got to the point where they laid this great honour on me when they left their drums at my house.'

Ah, the drums! In '75, one of the Rastas made Keith a set of *akete* drums out of goatskin and cowskin. He handed them over with the advice that it would take twenty years for them to mature and sound right. By November '95, the drums were ready. No sooner did Keith get in the front door than the brothers came around, asking when he wanted them to play those drums.

'I went to Jamaica to kick back after the *Lounge* tour, and there they were, ready to go,' Keith told Barney Hoskyns. 'It had nothing to do with me: Jah was leading the way. The guy who made those drums for me in 1975 told me they took 20 years to sound good and I guess he was right.'

Keith named the guys Wingless Angels because they wanted to go to heaven, but didn't have wings – a typically Rastafarian metaphor. Of the original bunch that Keith and Anita had met on the beach, up came veteran reggae singer Justin Hinds, of the Dominoes, Locksley Whitlock, Vincent Ellis (aka Bongo Jackie), Winston 'Blackskull' Thomas and Milton 'Neville' Beckerd, who also looked after Keith's house, plus Warrin Williamson and Sister Maureen Freemantle. The Angels hailed from Steertown, a no-go area up in the hills. After befriending Keith and

Anita, they all but moved in. Sometimes the place resembled a Rasta version of Nellcote. But Keith was always happy to see them whenever he went back. They called him 'Dreader than Dread'.

Keith finally got around to recording them all. He opened up one wall of the living room overlooking the bay for the boys to set up. They asked Keith to join in and he played like he had done from the very first sessions – 'This sort of funky, chicken-scratch riffing, throwing in some nice chords now and then to back up the chants,' as he told me with an obvious sense of wonder. The group started playing a Grounation ceremony - which involves playing from sunset to sunrise for six days straight, while chanting over the pulse and praising Jah.

The seemingly random events took another turn when the Jamaican film board donated a mobile recording studio. Ever since *Goats Head Soup* – and, of course, the rise of the Wailers – the place became a hip location to record. The next day, producer/engineer Rob Fraboni, who knew Keith and the Stones, turned up after he'd just got married on the island. Suddenly the proper recording started. Keith maintains none of it was pre-arranged, but bang went the vacation. (Imagine the phone call: 'Hi baby, I'll be late home. I'm making an album.')

Then Island Records supremo Chris Blackwell turned up when they'd started recording and said he'd release it on his label. If this wasn't Jah's guidance, then it must have been Keith's lucky week. The tracks would include 'Rivers Of Babylon', 'Morning Train', 'Enjoy Yourself Love', 'Write My Name'/'Good Morning', 'Love, Love' and 'No Dark Here'. The results were sonorous, blissful and mesmerising.

But Keith still didn't have any definite plans for the recordings. He spent the next eighteen months playing with the tapes, overdubbing elements like his custom-made six-string bass, and working out how to expand the sound with extra players. His acoustic guitar work on the music is different to anything he'd done previously, although the very bottom of the blues still reverberates within.

Another fortuitous visitor who happened to be in town was Irish multi-instrumentalist Frankie Gavin, who'd played that sublime fiddle on 'The Worst'. He brought in the extra dimension of traditional Celtic music, even sea shanties, which Keith decided he wanted. They fitted startlingly well.

'I realised these songs were old English and Scottish and Irish hymns, reworked and adapted, and I thought about that Celtic sound over the African chanting . . . when I got back to Jamaica, I was sittin' there with the brothers, and after the first track Justin Hinds stood up and said, "It's magic to be able to hear it like that." And then they all stood up and took another draw on the pipe. It was a great relief.'

On a roll, in March '96 Keith got the X-Pensive Winos to fly to the island and try their brand of funk in the same situation. Maybe it was down to the lethal weed, but this time it didn't catch a fire. Maybe it was just too far a cry from lower Manhattan. (The following year, when I was running a record label, Steve Jordan sent me a tape of two songs he had written. They were good, but sounded like a more dance-oriented Winos without Keith.)

The *Wingless Angels* album finally sneaked out in '97, on Keith's Mindless

Records label via Island. It's a haunting soul massage, utterly entrancing. But there was no fuss and little press, although Keith would mention it in interviews. In October '97, Alan di Perna of *Guitar World* asked him why African-derived musical forms spoke so deeply to white Europeans. It provided a rare glimpse of Keith's own fundamental beliefs. 'It's bones. 'Cause probably we all come from Africa. We just went north and turned white. But if you cut anybody open, bones is white and blood is red, man. It's kind of deep, you know. And I think maybe it speaks to us in that way. Ancient bone marrow responding to the source. That's the only one I can come up with . . .

Keith talks to his favourite magazine, Guitar World.

All it points out is the superficiality of racial differences.' When Keith flashes his famous skull ring, with the comment, 'Hey, beauty's skin deep,' di Perna asks what his Rasta mates think of it. 'They know what it means,' he replies, launching into patois. 'This is what we all like under the flesh, brother. Take off the hair, pull off the skin, you're looking at the I and I.'

So is he a spiritual person?

'Yeah, but not religious . . . . That's why I did the Wingless Angels album: very spiritual music. But mine is a very nebulous spirituality. I wouldn't care to put a name on it. I don't want to place any bets [assumes American gameshow host accent]: "Oh, you picked the wrong god. Sorry, it's Allah." . . . . Hey, give thanks and praises, whoever you are, wherever you are, whatever you are. I never got a postcard from anybody that left. Maybe they don't sell stamps up there.'

Ironically, Keith had gone to Jamaica to chill out before he went back to the Christian atmosphere at Westin, and ended up making the most profoundly spiritual statement of his career – maybe in subconscious retaliation. Judging from the record, it did wonders for his soul.

Prophecy must fulfil indeed.

Babylon's Burning

Patti had hooked up with a local Baptist church while Keith was away. Bockris relates an amusing story about the '96 Thanksgiving dinner at the Devil's Den. The anonymous source describes a scenario where, during a droning grace by the local preacher, a somewhat sozzled Keith jumped on the dinner table and demanded the guy get out of the house, declaring it was all a load of bollocks. If true, it gave Keith the chance to finally vent his spleen in a more upfront way than Wingless Angels. True or not, it conjures up a great picture.

In May '96, Keith became a grandfather for the first time, when Marlon's wife Lucy gave birth to Ella Rose Richards. In mid-2000, the couple would present Keith with his first grandson, Orson, too. As the decade wore on, his extended family became increasingly more important to Keith, even if he was away for large chunks of the time.

In summer '96, Keith also got to play with another of his lifelong heroes – Elvis's old guitarist, Scotty Moore. As he'd got into Presley from '56 onwards, Scotty was one of the major figures keeping him in his bedroom practicing. Keith has often said that his favourite guitar solo of all time is probably Scotty's rampant string-splatter in the middle of 'You're Right I'm Left She's Gone'. Now here he was in the Woodstock, NY bar owned by Levon Helm of the Band, playing and singing 'Deuce And A Quarter' with Scotty and Elvis's drummer, D. J. Fontana, for their *All The Kings Men* tribute album. Both men were in their seventies, and Keith was amazed to see Fontana still managing to play with a catheter and a colostomy bag in his pocket. Scotty had planned to show Keith a thing or two about drinking, but got absolutely pickled while Keith soldiered on until dawn. Who else was there left to play with *now*?

Keith wanted to call up the troops again in late '96. It became clear why Mick may have opposed Ronnie becoming a fully-fledged Rolling Stone in '93, as Keith and Ronnie announced they wanted to record another album and go on tour straight away. Charlie was away on tour with his jazz orchestra, but tended to side with Keith on group decisions.

So Mick, who was busy setting up a film company and about to record yet another solo album, didn't really have much say. But he did throw a spanner in the works by insisting that, if he committed to recording, the two songwriters be allowed to bring in their own producers to work on their own tracks. It was a crafty move, as Mick would effectively get to make at least a part of his solo album with the best backing group he could wish for.

In order to keep the Stones moving, Keith agreed. He eventually saw things the same way, which is why he ended up with three vocal tracks on the album, the most on any Stones record. It ended up like three EPs on one album – by Keith, Mick and the Stones.

Things started promisingly enough, as Keith and Mick began writing at the tiny Dangerous Music studios in New York's Greenwich Village. Initially, it went so well that an excited Keith wanted to bring in the band, with Rob Fraboni producing, and do the album there and then, in as live and random a fashion as possible. It was overruled by Mick, complaining the venue was too small, but Keith already had his vibe going. More writing followed in London and Barbados, with recording booked at Ocean Way in LA between February and June, with Don Was.

Events took a bad turn for Keith as '97 progressed. Although things were now settled at home, one of Patti's sisters was seriously ill with cancer. The Wingless Angels were in disarray before their album had even been released: Bongo Jackie was ill, some of them had since got into crack, all of them were demanding more money. Keith, who had been considering taking them on tour, was forced to cut them off, apart from the faithful Neville.

What with the demise of the Winos, Keith was not in the best frame of mind when he turned up in LA. He then discovered Mick had already started work with a bunch of trendy dance music producers. Men who used drum machines to make music seemed like a bridge too far – though the fact they were using Ocean Way, the same studio where Phil Spector and Frank Sinatra recorded some of their classics was a placatory factor.

'For the recording of *Bridges To Babylon*, Mick and I agreed that instead of us coming together, he would cut some tracks his way and I'd cut some tracks my way,' recalled Keith in *According to . . . .* 'I had no idea that Mick thought that meant he had a licence to have a different producer for every song.'

Mick brought in sampler kings the Dust Brothers, who had risen from late eighties hip-hop with bands like the Beastie Boys through to artists like Beck. Danny Saber was a more viable prospect, in that he'd come from the UK underground and worked with ex-Happy Monday Shaun Ryder's Black Grape, as well as rock bands Garbage and U2. Worst of all was R&B supremo Kenneth 'Babyface' Nelson, who worked with stars like Janet Jackson.

Keith retaliated by bringing in his own firm: surviving Wino Waddy Wachtel, indispensable guitar-tech and musical sparring partner Pierre de Beauport ('Minister of Production', according to the sleeve), Bernard Fowler, Winos engineer Don Smith, P-Funk keyboards maestro Bernie Worrell and backing singer Blondie Chaplin, who'd worked with the late-period Beach Boys. Darryl Jones only played on three tracks, but two of them were Keith's. Along with Ronnie and Charlie, these guys would help Keith realise his own visions for the album.

Keith didn't mind the young Saber, whose front and groove tactics would enrich the Stones' 'Gunface', but wasn't enamoured with the Dust Brothers – though three of Mick's tracks they worked on all survived.

But Babyface didn't fare so well, being dropped from the credits when his contributions were mixed out of 'Always Suffering'. Though he unwittingly provided Keith with a story to tell about their first meeting: 'I said, "So you're Babyface? You cut with Mick, your face is going to look like mine. You may be Babyface now, but you're gonna be Fuckface like me after you get out of the studio with that guy."'

The sessions may even have been the most tense yet between Keith and Mick. When Mick worked with the Dust Brothers he was in another studio altogether. At best, they worked in separate rooms at Ocean Way. Don Was went from the community spirit of the *Voodoo Lounge* sessions to trying to hold things together and get an album out of all the feuding. Keith initially hated the fact that Mick was trying to buy hipness, the way he'd tried to on his solo albums. Eventually, Mick walked out, something he never even did during *Dirty Work*.

This left Keith in complete control in the latter stages. By now he was functioning on adrenalin, neat vodka and a few drugs. Some reports said he was doing smack again, but, if he was, it wasn't for long. All these factors combined with the creative tension to thrust Keith upwards like some kind of rock 'n' roll Terminator. Nothing could stop him now, and he completed the final three tracks on his own terms.

The album's working title was *Blessed Poison*, before being rechristened *Bridges To Babylon*. 'Babylon, you see, is the outside world, and our music is the bridge between that world and mine,' said Keith in France's *Rock & Folk* magazine, bolstering his Rasta credentials.

The album, although very strong in places, lacks the sense of unity of its predecessor. Keith and Mick were recording in different studios with different producers, and it sounds like it, Jagger's tracks sometimes sounding like *Primitive Cool* out-takes. (In fact, a couple were intended for his next solo album.)

Homing in on Keith's tracks, 'You Don't Have To Mean It' was his liveliest reggae outing to date. Charlie now had his own firm handle on the island groove, Keith sounds thrustingly assured with his vocal and guitar delivery, and Rob Fraboni has the right dubwise approach to his mixing. The lusciously hazy brass is pure early seventies Studio One.

'Yeah, I think I really got it right on this one,' said Keith. 'Even my Jamaican brethren say so.'

'Thief In The Night' is of a darker hue. A brooding soul ballad with Keith hissing unsettlingly direct lyrics like, 'You can call the police on me baby / Set me up and then bust me . . . .' Some said it alluded to the problems at home. Keith later said it was about a guy trying to get back into his house, having been thrown out. Whether this meant Keith himself, or the local preacher, is the stuff of speculation.

'Thief' effectively segues into 'How Can I Stop'. In Keith's grand tradition, it's the final track on the album and the last one to be finished. After 'All About You', Keith had taken the form of the ballad as a framework on which to slowly build the mood and present vocals which sound like he's whispering into your ear. Its strain of deep soul pitches straight to the heart. 'How Can I Stop' invokes the spirit of close-harmony seventies outfits like the Chi-Lites or the Delfonics. Sweet, sad and swooning.

The words are particularly vulnerable, wracked out in Keith's most broken tones yet: 'You look at me / I don't know what you see / A reflection of what I want to be.' The song goes out on a lengthy coda with Charlie's brushes sprinkling delicately against the stratospheric soprano sax of jazz legend Wayne Shorter, the man who also closed 'Waiting On A Friend'. It all comes to rest after a billowing free jazz crescendo which leaves the heart in mid-air. When it comes to using space in music, and taking soul into the cosmos, Keith is up there with greats like Norman Whitfield, the genius behind the Temptations.

Don Was says in *According to . . .*, 'Keith doesn't write songs by sitting alone with a sequencer. He likes to work live in the studio so he can explore the song's different corners and hidden passageways. We were playing "How Can I Stop", repeating the final four chords over and over like a mantra. I knew there was this ideal in music where you lose all self-consciousness and play in the moment, but I'd never experienced it. I was playing a Wurlitzer piano; Keith was playing an electric guitar on the other side of the room. It was a musical conversation, utterly effortless, like transcendental meditation.'

As Keith told Barney Hoskyns in *Mojo*, 'I wouldn't have been able to write songs like that ten, fifteen years ago. I wouldn't have been able to put it over with the right attitude. I guess a lot of the earlier stuff is just a hard shell. "Before They Make Me Run", and so on. Although never forget that one of the first ones was "Happy", which should explain some of the lines on this face. Even on the dope, when the cops are waking you up again, you somehow have to laugh.'

Keith also talked about the emergent tenderness in his songs in *Guitar Player*: 'they're more or less sort of just a feeling, really. They're little bits of your life that just come back to you, and suddenly you say, "Oh, that little situation. Yeah, now I can really finish it off, tail it off, because now I can write a song about it." But you don't think about it. It's something that maybe happened 20 years ago, ten years ago, whatever, just a little incident here or there, or somebody told you something. It's just in a way trying to transmit a certain feeling.'

There are also some tracks that Mick sings which obviously come from the Keith canon, usually with Waddy Wachtel playing guitar and Rob Fraboni mixing. 'Flip The Switch', with Keith's words about a convict on death row, now holds the title as the fastest track the Stones have ever done.

As a whole it's a bumpy ride, a game of three halves. The tracks with dance producers are pretty superficial, while the joint ventures hang faithfully to the Stones' essence. Meanwhile, Keith stays true to his personal quest. It's easy to dress up the Stones in trendy production gimmicks, but much harder to take it forward with subtlety and emotion.

'Our motto this time was *Vive la difference!*' Keith joked to Q, probably through gritted teeth.

In August, the Stones' machine started cranking up as the band gathered in Toronto to rehearse for the *Bridges To Babylon* tour. Several reports had Keith in fairly bad shape – drinking heavily, or even using smack. Bongo Jackie had died, closely followed by Patti's sister. Keith's rented house was dubbed 'Doom Villa' by tour personnel.

The pressure got to him in the rehearsal room the night before Patti's sister's funeral, where he was due to be a pallbearer. He'd asked Ronnie to hang out with him for a bit of moral support, but instead he was in the next room with a bunch of guys noisily watching a boxing match, having bet money on Julio Cesar Chavez. When Woody walked into Keith's room, he was almost strangled. Roadies had to drag off the raging Keith, who later admitted he lost it for a minute there – 'I made a mistake, I wasn't compos mentis.'

It was over as soon as it began, and Ronnie would once again be Keith's closest associate on the upcoming tour. Even if Keith constantly took the piss or playfully put him down, they'd now been best friends for nearly a quarter of a century.

Barney Hoskyns conducted his excellent interview at Doom Villa on the eve of the tour, putting the record straight about the state of Keith's head at the time. As they were in Toronto, Hoskyns asked about heroin – or rather, the fact that a new, more genial Keith had emerged after he'd kissed it goodbye.

'There's a demon in me, and he's still around. Without the dope, we have a bit more of a chat these days. It's more of a truce. It's been twenty-odd years, and there's been families not brought up under stress like the first lot ... Marlon, he's had a weird life. My upbringing compared to his was very mundane, it was a cap and a satchel, whereas his was buzzing around in a Bentley, waking his dad up with a broom because, y'know, he's got that shooter under the pillow ... I think he likes to kick back, but he saw there were some things you don't do. Let's face it, Anita and I were pretty fuckin' wild, hah! But we all get along today.'

The tour was launched with the customary big press conference in New York City on 18 August. This time the Stones arrived via the Brooklyn Bridge in a red '55 convertible. The tour was due to start in Chicago on 18 September, but first they played one of their 'secret' warm-ups at Toronto's tiny Horseshoe Tavern. Hoskyns was there, moved to ponder why Keith and Charlie get the shouts from the crowd: 'And I think to myself that the point is this: Mick Jagger wants to be black. Keith Richards is black. Mick wants to be loved, but Keith and Charlie are loved.'

Barney was there again a couple of weeks later for opening night in Chicago. Prepared for 'a hollow ritual', he commented on the amazing quality of the new $3 million sound system and reported that 'the heartening news is that the stadium-size Rolling Stones in late September actually sound like a band,' citing Keith's 'All About You' as a highlight: 'The whole band seems to be emotionally on board for this slice of transmuted Southern soul, and Bernard Fowler and Lisa Fischer flank him for the last verse, cushioning his fragile voice with their rich harmonies. I'm open-mouthed, astonished that anything like that can ever happen in the context of a Rolling Stones gig.'

The stage was another sprawling Mark Fisher creation, this time based on the exotic desert city on the album cover. It was dominated by the biggest video screen ever seen – a 1600-square-foot eye-shaped Jumbotron – and flanked by 40-foot inflatable goddesses. The *tour de force* this time was the debut of the Stones' second stage at the back of the crowd. The basic idea was nicked off of U2's Popmart tour, but the Stones' stage was reached by a protracting bridge which slowly arced over the heads of the crowd, building the suspense before the band loped over to recreate the spirit of the Crawdaddy circa '63 for three songs.

After major pyrotechnic eruptions, Keith strode on in a floor-length leopard-skin coat and shades to grin malevolently as he whipped the band into 'Satisfaction'. What followed was the usual mixture of old and new, with a section where punters at home could vote for a song on the Internet as Mick monitored a big screen. Keith played 'All About You' and 'Wanna Hold You' on the early part of the tour, before tackling 'Thief In The Night' and 'You Don't Have To Mean It' later on. He repeatedly referred to the gigs as 'time to let the tigers out of their cages!', charging into those opening chords with an almost demented glee.

The album was released on 23 September, reaching number six in the UK, number three in the US, and selling four million copies worldwide in its first year. Q were typical in headlining their review 'Capable', giving the album three stars and an average reception, while homing in on the Keith tracks. Stuart Maconie added, 'Perhaps the most genuinely likeable tunes here are both sung by Keith Richards and both, to varying degrees, are exercises in pastiche. "You Don't Have To Mean It" shows the band audibly kicking off their shoes and having fun with a featherweight but musically perfect recreation of a Trojan Records single, circa 1974. And better still is the concluding track, "How Can I Stop": beautifully moody, ersatz soul whose emotional punch is 100 per cent authentic.'

Asked about his health in David Sinclair's accompanying interview, Keith says, "I would suggest other people worry about their own health, quite honestly. I'm 54 and I kick ass . . . When I run out of energy I'll be the first to know it.' He was more forthcoming about how he'd always strived to stay true to the dark heart of the blues:

'You go to the crossroads and somewhere along the way, you make a deal with the Devil . . . . I have a little bottle of sand from Robert Johnson's crossroads. I carry it

'I'm 54 and I kick ass.' Keith starts up another Bridges To Babylon set, Holland 1998.

around in my pocket. It all depends on why you go into this thing in the first place. Me, I just want to be Muddy Waters, even though I'll never be that good or that black. My heart's there. If I was black nobody would talk about my age. It's almost racism in reverse.'

Amidst all the speculation about Keith's health at the time, it took a fan to find out the real score. In a readers' questions session for the January '99 Q, as the *Bridges To Babylon* world tour kept rolling on, one guy asked when was the last time he took smack. Keith was totally honest and frank in his reply, and, in his own way, shot down all the people who'd been waiting for him to fall off the wagon since the late seventies.

'Somewhere early on in this tour, somebody came through with a little taste, y'know. 'Cause in a way, you like to test yourself. Never say no. You can quit it, it's no big deal. but every now and then you go, OK. And my body says to me when I try it, "Uh-oh, been there, done that, I'm not getting the high." I was getting the bits I didn't like, the sweating and the itching. I loved it when I was doing it and developed a very strong relationship with the residue of the poppy in all its forms [grins].'

After the States, the tour juggernaut had rolled on to Japan and South America. In Rio, Keith and Ronnie went for a boat ride, but had to be rescued by diligent paparazzi when their ship caught fire and sank. Cap'n Keith saw the funny side.

It was also around this time that Liam Gallagher of Oasis famously threw down the gauntlet on live radio, offering out 'those old farts' Keith, George Harrison and Mick to a fight on Primrose Hill one Saturday morning. Keith had incurred his displeasure by reflecting on Oasis: 'I've been pretty mean in my time, but these guys [Liam and his brother Noel] are just obnoxious.' But perhaps the real verbal punch was his opinion of their music: 'I don't hear anything there, it's all just retro to me.'

'I will beat the fucking, living daylight shit out of them,' Liam crowed in reply. Keith was non-plussed, dismissing it as 'English showbiz pop-dom bullshit'. At that time, Oasis were enormous and enjoying their equivalent of the Stones' initial press-fuelled notoriety. It didn't faze ol' Keith none.

Asked about it in *Mojo*'s special, celebrating his 60th birthday in 2003, he said, 'my attitude was, "Come back when you grow up." It didn't rile me. I thought it was quite funny. But it says more about him than about anyone else. Having said that, we've all done it. I threw out a challenge to Billy Fury 40 years ago.'

The tour was supposed to hit Europe in summer '98, but had to be postponed by three weeks for the most unlikely of reasons. During his scheduled break in May, Keith was at home in Westin and got caught under a book avalanche in his library, breaking three ribs.

'It was actually Leonardo da Vinci's *Treatise on Anatomy*,' he explained in Q. 'The Guggenheim Museum called up and said, "Would you do a human figure for charity?" They sent me this parchment and charcoal and it was about two in the morning and I thought, "Well, if I'm going to do this, I'll check with the master." And it's on the top shelf, about eighteen feet up. So I get on this little ladder, a bit wobbly, and as I touched the top shelf the whole fucking thing just came down on me. Blitzed me. So you could say I did learn quite a bit about anatomy.' Four UK concerts were also postponed until June' 99 because of tax reforms that would have landed the Stones with a £12 million bill – affecting not just the band, but their entire 300-strong touring party.

The tour was plagued by rain and Mick developed laryngitis, postponing more gigs. In August, though, the Stones met another of Keith's long-term ambitions by playing Russia at the 83,000-capacity Luzhniki stadium. They'd been trying to play the country for 30 years but were always told by the authorities that their show was 'too decadent'. The tour wound up late August in Istanbul. The band had played 108 shows in 25 countries and were seen by 4.75 million people. This time they grossed nearly $300 million.

On 14 August, Keith's daughter Angela, who now worked on a stud farm, got married to carpenter Dominic Jennings at Chichester registrar's office. Keith couldn't attend because he was playing in Estonia, but had arranged a major bash, plus a blessing by the local priest, in the grounds of Redlands two days later. When he flew back he gave his daughter a day to remember.

Father of the bride. Keith leads daughter Angela to the altar, August 1998.

The ceremony was attended by the whole Richards family, plus Ronnie from the other family – Mick and Charlie had to stay out of the country for tax reasons. Bert flew in from Connecticut, where he now lived in a house in Keith's grounds, while Anita came with Marianne Faithfull. After Bernard Fowler read a love poem, the proud dad walked his daughter down the aisle to the strains of 'Angie', played by Bobby Keys. Lisa Fischer sang Keith's favourite, 'The Nearness Of You', as the couple were pronounced man and wife. Many guests had tears in their eyes by then.

The tabloids had fun with a story about Angela turning down Keith's kind offer of the Stones doing a few numbers – strange, considering how celebrity mag *OK!*, which carried eleven pages on the event, included a photo of Keith and Darryl Jones fronting the wedding band, who also included Bobby, Lisa and Ronnie. Keith, wearing a South American army jacket, took them through a selection of R&B covers, and the party went on until the early hours.

When the tour finished, Keith went straight back to Westin. In *According to . . .* he says he made 'a conscious effort to be back at home, and instead of getting up at three or four in the afternoon, I'd get up at seven in the morning and drive the kids to school . . .

'You can travel and move and still keep a family together. Otherwise there wouldn't have been gypsies or nomads . . . . I don't think a constant hands-on thing with families is necessary, as long as you know where the heart lies. They can always find me and I can always find them . . .'

In November, the Stones slid out a live album from the tour, called *No*

Security. Keith and Mick also appeared on three covers on an album called *Blues Blues Blues* by Chicago guitarist Jimmie Rogers – 'Trouble No More', 'Don't Start Me Talkin'' and 'Goin' Away Baby'.

In January '99, Keith popped up in another 'readers' questions'-style interview for *Q*. The interview took place at New York's Plaza Hotel, which got Keith reminiscing about the posh Fifth Avenue toy shop, FAO Schwarz, around the corner. In the mid-seventies, when the band played New York, Keith would embark on spending sprees to acquire all their Doctors and Nurses kits. 'The syringe. It would actually take a needle. Then I'd come back here, order a coffee, steal the spoon and I'd have the works . . .'

'Everyone seems surprised that you're still alive,' came a comment from one reader in Carlisle. Honesty prevailed again. 'I'm probably more surprised than most. But I never considered dying . . . one could perceive that I was hellbent . . . a lemming. But to myself, I was pretty much . . . experimenting. I'm not a pig in whatever it is I do. I looked upon myself, in a sort of romantic and silly way, as a laboratory . . . . Then after about ten years, I realised that this experiment had gone on far too long.'

Keith revealed that he carries a .38 revolver on the road – 'The .38's for business . . . I haven't actually used it in years, but I shoot hats with it, just to make sure it works.'

Once again, he was asked if the rumours were true that he'd shagged Mick. 'Never got around to it, but y'see, I don't fancy him. Otherwise, he'd be fair game. But when you've grown up with somebody from four years old, you're over it. Even in the most desperate situation . . . I'd rather fuck a puddle.'

When a girl from Berlin asked what he was saying to his guitar when she saw him talking to it onstage, the answer came, 'I love you.'

With postponed dates to fulfil and an album to promote, the Stones decided to keep on touring in 1999. 'How can I stop?' remarked Keith, referring to Bob Dylan's Never-Ending Tour which had been continuing since 1988.

On 25 January in Oakland, the *No Security* tour kicked off 33 dates in the States, finishing up on 12 April, in Chicago. Keith was happy that, as it was winter, they were playing indoor arenas. By now some ticket prices were hitting $250 and some gigs didn't sell out. But Keith was on a roll, still performing 'Thief In the Night' and 'You Don't Have To Mean It', or sometimes 'You Got The Silver', on the tour that Mick agonised over an expensive divorce from his second wife, Jerry Hall.

The *Oakland Chronicle* summed it up: 'The euphoric grin on Richards' face as he kneeled with his guitar said plenty. Too old to rock to rock 'n' roll? Let him flail at the strings until they lower him into the dirt.'

The rescheduled European leg of the tour opened in Stuttgart on 29 May and ran through June. They brought back the *Babylon* set, and also slotted in a 'secret' gig at the Shepherds Bush Empire on 8 June. (I was very pissed off to miss it because I was comatose in Ibiza.)

When the tour was over Keith went home to Connecticut, but made his presence felt again in London on 3 November, when he attended the annual *Q* awards ceremony at the Park Lane Hotel. He was presented with the Special Merit Award by Sir Bob Geldof.

The account in the January 2000 issue is hilarious. Keith was on the cover, being hoisted into the air by Tom Rowlands of the Chemical Brothers and Blur's Damon Albarn. Charms and tokens are hanging from his hair and he's laughing his arse off.

'Swaying like a man who may have drunk more than half of a bottle of Stolichnaya by midday, smelling like a man who most certainly had, the genuinely choked Keith Richards graciously accepted his Q Special Merit award. Or at least, that's what we thought the award was called,' said the report.

Keith's standup-style acceptance speech started, 'I love this breakfast thing. It's a novelty to me,' before he thanked everyone for his 'Man of the Year' award. When TV comedian Johnny Vaughn introduced the Best New Act, Keith nudged his companion, Ronnie, grabbed his coat and went to stand up, declaring, 'That'll be us then!'

Later, Keith was interviewed about the occasion. 'Man of the Year! At least for a year I can walk around and say, "Do you know who you're talking to?" I should wear it on my head! [puts award on head] See! I don't know whether to wear it as a halo or a cock ring . . . I feel shy . . . yeah, shy, overwhelmed. Proud too, but what can you say?'

They asked Keith about the stuff in his hair, which was becoming the subject of speculation. 'Yeah, the doctors are mystified! It's like, two years on the road – there's most of the band in there, heh heh. It's weaved in by Lisa Fischer and I said, "They'll fall out in a month or two," and they've been here for like a year and a half now. It's a fetish thing. I can't chop 'em off. I've got to wait for them to fall off.'

The rambling conversation got onto a TV show called *Stella Street*, where comedy actors Phil Cornwell and John Sessions played the proprietors of Mick 'n' Keith's corner shop. Mick's the efficient one, while Keith drinks half the stock.

'. . . a corner shop, yeah, and Mick keeps worrying about the "Seeee-ll by" date and I don't give a shit, right? I saw one episode that came over to the States and I thought, "How appropriate. I mean, basically Mick and I do run a corner store anyway."'

As the twentieth century drew to a close, Keith was in a decidedly happy frame of mind, announcing that he was going back 'into a bunker and see if this next millenium actually happens. I've got a few machine-guns, a stash of cash, some tinned food . . . and I'm waiting!'

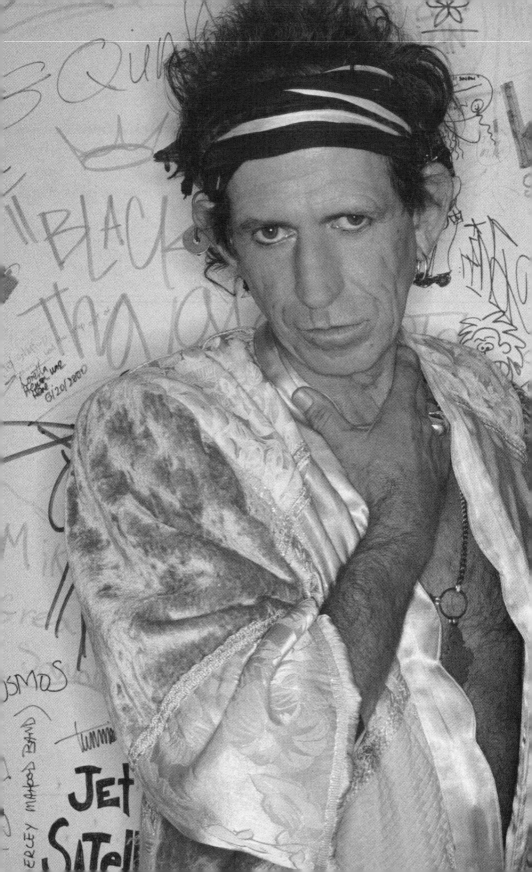

CHAPTER SEVENTEEN

UNLICKED

'The good die young . . . but hey, where does that leave me?' — Keith Richards.

Keith Richards entered the 21st century still kicking back after the incessant touring of the nineties. The previous decade had seen his public image transcend that of Mick Jagger's junkie-wildman sidekick, establishing him as the consummate rock 'n' roll icon. He'd also metamorphosised into a deep soul balladeer, who, if he ever gave up his day job, could have a lucrative career as a standup comedian. With mini-switchblades woven into his hair, as the new millennium dawned, Keith could safely emerge from his bunker.

Unfortunately, 2000 would also turn out to be a year of sadness, with a number of deaths: Jack Nitzsche, the brilliant arranger who'd worked with the Stones in the sixties; John Phillips, who'd just seen the album he'd recorded with the Stones in '78, *Pay, Pack And Follow*, finally released; Joe Seabrook, Keith's bodyguard of 26 years; George Harrison, whose death from cancer prompted Keith to pay tribute in *Rolling Stone*, saying, 'Miss you. Bless you. And we're still listening.' In May there was Mick's mum, Eva, who Keith had known ever since school days.

To cap it all, in December, Bert returned from a ripping week in the Caribbean with the family, and passed away himself. According to Keith, he winked at him just before he shuffled off the coil. I only met Bert a couple of times, but by all accounts he was a classic bloke. In many ways, his son was a chip off the old block, certainly in terms of his sense of humour, penchant for plain food – and, as old Bert got older and loosened up, a good drink. Patti may have had to prod Keith into contacting Bert again after twenty years apart, but they certainly made up for lost time.

Keith didn't talk much about Bert's passing, apart from a lovely passage in *According to the Rolling Stones*. 'My dad said to me on his death bed, "We never stop growing . . ." That was the last thing he said, and then I closed his eyes. He always said that younger people think older people know everything, but older people know they don't know shit from shit anyway. Nobody stops growing, otherwise there's no point in doing the trip in the first place.'

Keith spent that year alternating between Westin and Jamaica, but saw in 2001 at Redlands with family and friends like Alan Clayton. It was Keith's first New Year's Eve without his dad in nearly twenty years.

Keith spent much of 2001 in Connecticut, hatching plans for the return of the Stones and working in his L-shaped basement, which now included a pool room, studio and bar - his own permanent Voodoo Lounge. Here, he wrote songs and worked with collaborators, like the great Hubert Sumlin, who'd been Howlin' Wolf's guitarist, another personal hero. There were also reports that Keith was working on a Muddy Waters tribute album, which has yet to surface. He was asked to contribute to *Timeless*, the Hank Williams memorial record, choosing 'You Win Again', which the Stones had once recorded – with Mick singing – during the *Some Girls* sessions. As Keith told *Uncut* later, 'I cut it down in my basement and we got a Grammy! It just worked. I dunno, things just happen to me. I don't even go for it.'

Mick's fourth solo album, *Goddess In The Doorway* – or *Dogshit In The Doorway*, as Keith liked to call it - bombed spectacularly despite a massive promotional campaign. It came out around the time of the 11 September atrocities, and was hideously overshadowed by events. In late October, Keith and Mick appeared at Paul McCartney's Concert For New York benefit at Madison Square Garden, playing 'Salt Of The Earth' and 'Miss You'.

By now, the band had started talking about celebrating their fortieth anniversary in 2002. It would keep them touring the world until the end of 2003, on the back of a definitive greatest hits album with new songs, accompanied by a book put together by the band and a major DVD.

In the autumn of 2001, Keith received the most unusual honour of appearing on the cover of *Men's Fitness* magazine! Usually the domain of musclebound jocks outlining their exercise regimes, there was Keith, smoking a defiant Marlboro and being compared to Cliff Richard in a kind of who's-had-more-fun? scenario. The conclusion seemed to be that it was Keith, oddly enough.

In November, *The Sun's* Dominic Mohan reported in the *Bizarre* column, 'Pals fear for Ronnie Wood and Keith Richards' health as I'm told they are both partying heavily.' It hardly seemed like a hold-the-front-page exclusive, but in early 2002 Ronnie went off to rehab in Cottonwood, Arizona to conquer what had become his excessive drinking.

Ronnie talked about it in *According to . . .* 'It was a new era for me, an amazing period – not doing a bottle-and-a-half of vodka a day – even though it was very hard! There were times when I really would have loved a drink, but the feeling soon passed.'

It's also significant that Ronnie is Keith's best mate – his drinking partner of nearly 30 years, and the person he's closest to in the world outside of his family. Many people assumed Keith would lead Ronnie astray and he'd be back on the sauce within days of getting sober. Not so. Ronnie stuck to his new booze-free regime through thick and thin, with Keith's total support and, to Ronnie's surprise, the occasional word of praise.

As Keith says of his irrepressible partner in *According to . . .*, 'He had incredible stamina and tolerance, because most people would think, "Oh my God, Ronnie's going to stop doing all that stuff, but he's going to be the most boring person." . . . . He was just as funny, just as loony, but he looked in your eyes when you spoke to him, and when we were playing together, he was so much more imaginative. He got it together, like I did after my ten years in my personal laboratory.'

Keith encouraged Ronnie to take up reading, and gave him a book called *The Floating Brothel* – set in 1768 when the first convicts were transported to Botany Bay, with a bunch of whores on board to help set up the first Australian colonies.

Eighteen months later, he was still sober. Asked by *Q* if it was hard for Ronnie to hang out if he wasn't drinking, Keith replied, 'No, Ronnie's done what he had to do. I drink. Ronnie was a piss artist. He never stopped. After the last tour I stayed round his house and he'd wake up in the morning and go "sambuca and water!" No, no, no, Ronnie, no!'

In May 2002, the Stones revealed plans for a world tour that would start in September and go on for over a year, at a spectacular press conference in New York City featuring a massive yellow blimp painted with the tongue logo. 'If we'd have announced it in some other city, they'd have felt that we were cold-shouldering them,' said Keith in *Uncut*. 'New York is a good town for me, too. I can get a lift from the cops if it's raining and I'm walking down the street. "It's raining, Keith, get in" – "OK!" It's not often that you'd willingly get in the back of a police car, and go "OK guys."'

Despite the rumours, it was never billed as a farewell tour, even though both Keith and Mick would turn 60 in 2003. They were simply celebrating 40 years of being the Rolling Stones, by playing a stadium, arena and club in every city they visited.

Asked again how long they planned to keep on touring, Keith shot back, 'Until the undertaker pulls up to the door.'

For the accompanying album, the Stones had negotiated with Allen Klein to use some of their classic back catalogue. In June, they also gathered in a Paris studio with Don Was to record some new songs. Not for the first time, they hadn't even been in the same room together for three years. 'Our last sessions in Paris were similar to the way we used to record,' Keith said later in *Uncut*. 'Three microphones and let's go. Basically we got sick to death of the hi-tech. Recently we've been recording stuff while we've been on the road, in hotel rooms, whatever. Maybe a great Stones album will come out of that. Who knows?'

(The *Four Flicks* DVD gives a candid look at the Stones cranking into action. As they jam and experiment, Keith gets mad about the sound levels, later declaring, 'I make the riffs. I am the Riff Master!')

The following month was spent rehearsing at a private school near Toronto. With the newly-sober Ronnie on the rejuvenating high that you get from kicking booze, they ploughed into the back catalogue and also worked up soul nuggets like Otis Redding's 'That's How Strong My Love Is' and the O'Jays' 'Love Train'. Many of the Stones' tracks hadn't been performed for years, if ever. 'There's so many songs,' said Darryl Jones. 'I look at Keith sometimes and say, "What is this?", and he says, "I wrote it but I don't know it!"' At the same time, Decca had remixed and re-released all the Stones albums up to 1970. 'I've heard those mixes and I'm hearing guitar bits that I never knew I did on there,' said Keith.

But tragedy would strike again on 18 July, when backline mechanic Chuch McGee, who'd come to the Stones at the same time as Ronnie in '75, died of an aneurysm, aged 55. Mick flew the whole entourage to the funeral in his private plane. The *Licks* tour would be dedicated to McGee's memory, with his photo in the tour programme bearing the legend, 'This man was indeed the salt of the earth.'

When *Forty Licks* was released in October, reaching number two in both the UK and US, there were four new songs, including Keith's 'Losing My Touch', one of his traditional closing ballads. It's even softer and sadder than 'How Can I Stop', as he sings about a relationship breaking up amidst a definite air of paranoia,

The Stones announce the Forty Licks *tour to the press.*

dwelling on personal failings. It lays his old soul the barest it's ever been. The backing is piano-based and sublimely sensitive, with Ronnie on pedal steel. It can make you cry, under the right circumstances.

A storm broke out in 2002, when it was announced that Mick would be getting a knighthood. Keith went ballistic. He would have nearly two years to harangue and complain before Mick actually got patted by HM's sword.

In '95, the *Daily Telegraph* had carried a piece under the headline, 'Drugs, sex and rock 'n' roll: how about knighthoods?' Boris Johnson had written, 'Only one tribute remains to be paid by their native land to Michael Philip Jagger and Keith Richards . . . the most influential songwriting duo since Lennon and McCartney.' He rattles on about how the collective age of the Stones was now higher than that of the Tory cabinet, before getting to his point: '. . . were it not for his mascara Keith Richards would look like the kind of wheezing mendicant one might toss a pound coin to in a shopping mall; and while they are still on their pins, and while the cockiness that is their trademark still carries conviction, I say Her Majesty should be advised to give them all knighthoods.' In old-school posh dialect, Johnson held up the band's contribution to music, tut-tutted at past behaviour, but commended their contribution to the economy and people's general happiness, concluding, 'Arise Sir Mick. Arise Sir Keith. Nothing less will do.'

But in '97, Keith would bark to Q, 'To me, the monarchy is not that important, but I tell you, none of them are getting near me with a sword. I kneel for no-one.'

When Tony Blair later recommended Mick for a knighthood, and Mick accepted, Keith hit the ceiling.

'What did I feel when I heard about the knighthood?' said Keith when interviewed by *Mojo* before the tour. 'Cold, cold rage at his blind stupidity. It was enraging, I threatened to pull out the tour - went berserk, bananas! . . . I doubt they thought of offering me one. Because they know what I would've said. The idea that I'd take something from the people At Whose Pleasure I was banged up – they knew I'd tell them where to put it!'

But, as Charlie said, 'if Mick got one, Keith should have been offered one, and that would have *really* been something else.'

On the eve of the tour, the press started revving up again, with Paul Sexton from the *Daily Express* joining the band at rehearsals in Toronto. Once again, the Jagger-Richards love-hate relationship was at the forefront. Mick, who described Keith as having 'a big mouth,' claimed, 'He likes to make out he's still a very rebellious 59-year-old. That's all right. That's the role you play.'

Keith retorted with, 'Mick's got an ego. I insult the man. But he has the hide of a rhino, and he's just determined to be who he is . . . . I'm a bit of a moralist when it comes to the Stones, and Mick has been a bit flippant about them . . . .

'I don't know if there's some sort of inner competition, maybe that's the chemistry that keeps us going. The fact is that we're totally opposite people, but we're attracted to each other at the same time, and there's also the recognition that we can't get divorced. Even if we said "I never want to see you again," we'd be meeting in an office somewhere to divide up the babies.'

As usual, there was a club warm-up a few days before the tour started at Toronto's Palais Royale. The DVD shows a very nervous band in the dressing room before the gig. 'All I've got to do is remember a few chords,' mutters Keith as he paces about. The gig goes well in the small, hot and sweaty club. Afterwards in the van, the obviously relieved Stones are like a bunch of happy kids who've just slayed the local village hall, laughing and jostling each other.

Then they go to Boston on a private chartered plane to prepare for opening night on 4 September. Keith orders a drink from the bar: 'Screwdriver. Make it a tool-kit. Put the hammer in. A double.' When they first stroll onto the stage of the empty venue, he says, 'I feel at home already.'

The set was drawn from an arsenal of around a hundred songs. They delved into, dusted off and revamped back-catalogue classics that had never been performed before and changed the set each night depending on the venue. Stadiums got an across-the-board Greatest Hits selection, club audiences heard more obscure Stones tracks with soul covers thrown in, while arena shows had a different featured album every night that was either *Let It Bleed*, *Sticky Fingers* or *Exile*.

As the opening night was an arena show at the Fleet Centre, they decided on *Let It Bleed*, and trotted through 'Love In Vain', 'Live With Me', 'Monkey Man' and 'Midnight Rambler'. Keith changed his two-song spot as the tour progressed, starting in the US with 'Thru And Thru', which people now knew from *The Sopranos*.

'We call this the Y-Front Tour because the gigs come in small, medium and large,' said Keith in the London *Evening Standard*. 'The big gigs are always fun, but

'What happens next?' 'I don't know!' – Ronnie and Keith during a gig at MGM Grand Garden Arena, Las Vegas, 30 November 2002.

you don't have a lot of room to manoeuvre. You're locked into video screens, lighting - whatever it says on the list, that's what you're gonna play. The small gigs you get up there and suddenly you're back in Richmond . . . . After a year of nothing but stadiums you notice the band getting jaded. We couldn't just do stadiums ever again.'

The tour, which went on for four months until winding up at New York's Madison Square Gardens, grossed $120 million. To coincide, the Stones had also taken their highly-profitable merchandising to a new level by launching an expensive line in exotic lingerie. Under the name Fashion & Licks, it was launched at a reception in Beverly Hills. Two of the models were Keith's daughters, Theodora and Alexandra - by now seventeen and sixteen - who appeared suitably (and skimpily) attired on the front pages of the tabloids. Daddy's little girls had certainly grown up.

In February, the tour blitzed Australia and Japan, where banners blared, 'Banzai Keith'. 'It's nice to be at the Budokan,' declared Keith at the famous venue, launching into his Max Miller routine. 'It's nice to be anywhere!' The Stones visited India for the first time, and played in torrential monsoon conditions. But, while it had taken the Stones years to be allowed into China, those shows had to be cancelled because of the SARS epidemic.

Reviews set the tone for the entire *Licks* tour – revelling in the nostalgia and spectacle, while homing in on the role that Keith played in proceedings. 'To me, Keef is the star of the band,' wrote *The Sun*'s Dominic Mohan. 'Only the Gallaghers can match his dirty guitar riffs and stage-consuming presence.'

Vogue's May issue carried a lengthy tribute to the Stones, featuring past friends and acquaintances. 30 years on from the time he hung out with Keith as a wide-eyed cub reporter, Nick Kent could be more objective: 'On the one hand he seemed to represent a form of freedom, and on the other he was totally enslaved by heroin. He was in the middle of a major conflict. He wasn't alone in getting wasted. He was just more adamant about doing it, less apologetic about it. Others would do the same thing but behind closed doors. He's incredible. If I ever meet Keith Richards again, I'd say, "Listen, I don't want to talk to you, I want to interview your liver."'

Barbara Charone, who wrote one of the best early Keith biographies and still does press work for him, said, 'Keith Richards is a very, very funny man. He loves the Peter Cook and Dudley Moore *Derek And Clive* albums and shares their droll sense of humour . . . when he was on trial in Canada . . . his punishment was playing two concerts for the blind . . . The programmes were in Braille and when I asked him to autograph mine, he signed in dots.'

If You Grin, You In

The European leg of the *Licks* tour kicked off at Munich's Olympiahalle on 4 June. UK journos on the scene included the venerable Allan Jones of *Uncut*: 'The first time Keith Richards appears on the giant video screen at the back of the Olympiahalle stage, people around me jump, like they've just been frightened by something looming unexpectedly out of a cupboard in a horror film . . . . Keith, up there, a face carved out of Delta loam, chipped house-brick and fused alabaster, looks like he'd keep coming at you whatever you threw at him – undead, determined to stay that way.'

Keith's solo spot in Europe – which would usually feature 'Slipping Away' and either 'Happy' or 'Before They Make Me Run' – 'virtually steals the entire show', according to Jones.

The Sun reported that the Stones were nonplussed when German fans bombarded the stage with Y-fronts, although Keith would say in *According to . . .*, 'The fact is that I am 60 years old and twenty-year-old chicks are still throwing panties at me! It's ludicrous, really. What do I tell the old lady about these?' Ronnie added in *Jack* that the group got 'loads of bras and knickers on the little stage, which is funny. Keith collects them. I'm sure the roadies have got a special cess-tank for them.'

The Stones returned to the Paris Olympia on 10 July and filmed a riotous gig for the DVD. 'After Elvis Only Keith', said a fan's t-shirt. He started his solo spot with Hoagy Carmichael's 'The Nearness Of You', the song he most loved to play in the early hours. It had first appeared on a bootleg from the '77 Toronto sessions. He'd sung it to Patti at his wedding, and had Lisa Fischer sing it when his daughter Angela got married.

For 'Before They Make Me Run' he whipped out his faithful gold Telecaster and scrubbed the chords out for dear life. 'One love!' he shouted at the end.

It was the tour that saw Keith Richards finally eclipse Mick Jagger in terms of media coverage and public affection. During the weeks preceding the long-awaited UK leg, there was a glut of Keef interviews but only one feature on Sir Mick in *The Observer*, to coincide with the singer's 60th birthday on 26 July. Keith popped up in Q, *Uncut*, *Mojo*'s Stones special, the *Evening Standard* and *NME*. He was bearing the brunt of the demand for Stones interviews – and enjoying every minute of it.

They all took similar paths, starting with detailed descriptions of Keith's attire, hair, distinctive laugh and intake of fags and 'nuclear waste' – the man's term for his current favourite tipple of vodka and Sunkist orangeade. I was struck by how a lot of his answers reiterated what he was telling me in those Savoy hotel sessions in the eighties. Except now he'd become a wizened raconteur, dripping with dry wit and comic one-liners while putting on the persona that the writer wanted to see. Here was a man whose time had finally come.

Q stoked the fires in their September issue, catching up with Keith on the afternoon following the opening night at Munich's Olympiahalle in June. Ben Mitchell describes the press conference for local journalists where Keith apparently 'scratched his stomach to reveal a huge knife tucked down the waistband of his trousers'.

The interview is soaked in classic Keef mystique. A question about when he last pulled a gun on someone gets him reminiscing about scoring smack in New York, with some Wild West embroidery. 'You knew that when you went up to get the stuff they'd be downstairs ready to take it back off you at gunpoint, so you go downstairs and shoot out the lights. Boom! Boom! Boom! I went there when everything else was dry, only a couple of times, but it was quite interesting to see the way the ricochets go. Sometimes they shot back, I've been under fire.'

Mitchell seemed to be after the outlaw Keef, who customised his hotel rooms, carried weapons and was handed gifts of a chemical nature ('usually weed').

So does Keith think people are still scared of him?

'I don't go round trying to intimidate people, but you don't want to fuck with me,' he insists, though he'll admit to having a shy side to his personality.

Asked about the biggest misconception people have about him, he answers, 'Probably they imagine that I'm still doing this and doing that . . . orgies, that would be on the extreme end of it. You grow out of things. At the same time I still like to be on the loose. I'll hang out with guys playing guitar and that's always been basically my idea of fun. Ask any of my women. Music is first. If you know that about me, then you've got it.'

The food factor, a big theme in recent interviews, looms again, as he bemoans the fact that 'you can't find a good banger anywhere' outside of Britain. His favourite is pork, leek and ginger, plus the mighty chipolata. He likes kippers too. 'I was brought up on a very limited diet, really, because it was after the war and there weren't a lot about. Basically the same stuff over and over again. You get attached' – though he hates cheese. ('It's just milk gone off to me.')

Money?

'. . . I still wake up amazed by the whole thing. I grew up in a council house. No phone, no TV, no car. Hey, we just did our thing - you want to go somewhere, get on the bike. Money's a funny thing. I just see it as a gift to me. I'm not big on charity because I don't like the organised shit, but I take care of my mates and my folks and my extended family . . . without being taken to court [Laughs].'

Is he ever completely straight?

'Never! Not since I first tasted it. I mean, my father said to me, "Keith, there's a difference between scratching your arse and tearing it to bits." I've always borne that in mind. I do drink through the day, but I don't wake up in the morning and get stoned right away . . . . I guess it's because of heroin. If you've been through that one and got through it, the rest of it is really like gnat's piss.'

Mitchell sums up by asking the Stones themselves to sum up Keith in one word.

Mick raises his eyebrows ceilingwards.

'Help!' says Charlie.

'Wholesome,' adds Ronnie.

And Keith?

'Lucky.'

Mojo put out a '40th Anniversary Collector's Edition' devoted to the Stones, with Paul Trynka doing an 'at home with Keith' at the Devil's Den - apparently for the first time since 1965, when he showed the *Rolling Stones* fan monthly around the newly acquired Redlands!

Describing Keith as 'tanned, barefoot and radiant with health . . . dancing over with the energy of a spring lamb,' Trynka turns his attention to his pile of listening material. It includes the perennial *The Harder They Come*, the Chess 50th anniversary set, former Meter Zigaboo Modeliste, Mozart and Lee Perry. (Keith was also reading biographies of Rasputin, Andrew Oldham, Marie Antoinette, Ray Charles and Johnnie Johnson.)

When Trynka produced a copy of Robert Johnson's *King Of The Delta Blues Singers Volume Two*, Keith remarks, 'I still put that record on to scare myself,' and bounces off to return clutching a copy of the blues legend's death certificate. Procured mysteriously from the Mississippi records office, it needs a double-sided frame because 'the back's never been seen!' Here the doctor has written that Johnson - whose cause of death is a great mystery, the theories including murder and too much booze - 'died of syphilis'. Which deepens the mystery even more.

They go down to the basement to check out his vinyl. Keith drags out boxes which contain some of his 2,500 singles and albums. Apart from Blind Willie McTell, there's Charlie Watts' Orchestra, Kraftwerk, Stevie Wonder, George Benson, Ian McLagan, Bette Midler ('There's a load of crap here'), the Gladiators, The Clash, Gregory Isaacs, the Ramones and a sealed Rod Stewart album ('Rod must've sent me that himself').

NME chose a famous shot of Keith in '76 for the front cover of their 'Rock Decadence' issue. They also used the now tried-and-tested format of putting questions to him from fellow musicians and readers. Writer Steve Sutherland helpfully pointed out that Keith smoked six fags and sank four quarter pints of vodka and Tango in the ensuing hour, before going on to mention one e-mail which said he had 'the filthiest laugh in the world' – on a par with Sid James. Keith was delighted. 'What a fucking compliment, man!'

They ask Keith about his hair.

'These things just happen. Most of them are there because half the band are sitting around in my room and I crash out on the couch and they'll tie something in there and then I'll just wait for them to fall out. There is a little bit of superstition in there too: people throw stuff and say, "Hey, put this in your hair for good luck." So, y'know, while I have it, I'll hang it in!'

There's even good old shepherd's pie. Beans or gravy?

'Ah, now the baked beans. That's interesting . . . I usually leave them out of there. The more you get into a shepherd's pie, the more interesting it becomes. I've had it when you put the onions in at the end so that they don't cook too much. The shepherd's pie is an ongoing experiment - that's one of the reasons I love it - it's a different song each time you cook it.'

Robert Harvey of The Music asks, 'How are you still alive?' Keith laughs again. 'I hate to say it but hey, I'm just a bloke but I do come from good stock and I'll push it out here and there. I don't do it so much any more. The show's enough, y'know. The shows used to be twenty minutes long. Now they're two hours. It was easy then. Now we sweat a lot and it's a lot of action, especially if you're carrying a guitar round your neck for two hours and you gotta move.'

Do you plan to donate your body to science when you die?

'Yeah, but I'm afraid they'll turn it down.'

Holed up in Amsterdam the week before the Stones were due to hit London, Keith talked to Charles Shaar Murray for the *Evening Standard*. As Murray − once Nick Kent's partner-in-crime on *NME* − put it, 'Keith Richards is clearly having a wonderful time being Keith Richards . . .'. Murray knew the elegantly wasted Keith of old, but now saw him as 'rock and roll's archetypal wicked uncle . . . His raffish demeanour and chequered past add spice and edge to his jovial, benevolent demeanour.'

Keith spoke about the Stones' much-derided longevity: 'You're supposed to be around for two or three years and then goodbye. Hey, what about Jerry Lee Lewis and Little Richard? Those cats are still going. Mind you, they're all nuts, of course. Maybe that's what everybody likes. If a rock 'n' roll star's gonna live this long, let's watch 'em go nuts.'

Charlie Murray has always been a blues boffin, and if there's one thing Keith loves, it's talking about the blues.

'In a way, the blues is a constant wellspring which keeps bubbling up. I don't think there's any music made in the West, even the most banal pop songs, that don't owe something to the blues somewhere down the line. And it all comes from African music, which is why it's so exciting. There's something primal about it which we all recognise, because we're all African. Some of us just left and turned white.'

Murray also raises the point that Johnny Depp based his character Captain Jack Sparrow, in the movie *Pirates of the Caribbean*, on Keith.

'We met about five or six years ago and started swapping clothes. This is Johnny's shirt, by the way. He has an incredible guitar collection. We have dinner sometimes and get together: his kids and my kids. He's a good guy. I like him a lot. But I had no idea he was studying me. Everybody that's seen it is, like, "God, it's you." This is the only time I've been accepted by Disney!'

Depp himself admitted to *Uncut* that 'Keith became the main inspiration . . .

He has a way about him. A beautiful confidence. There's an elegance, a graceful quality that Keith has. A wisdom and a wit, certainly, that I thought would be useful for the character.

'When I first started out doing the research on the movie, it dawned on me that pirates were the rock 'n' roll stars of the eighteenth century. And for me the greatest rock 'n' roll star of all time is Keith Richards, hands down.'

Hello Stranger

Alan Clayton and I had kept in touch for a while after that night at the Savoy in '83. But we lost contact after I moved to New York, and I didn't see him again until a chance meeting on a London traffic island in early 2003. He told me he'd continued to keep in touch with Keith over the years, and that the man had given him a rather special guitar. We arranged to get together.

So I bowled round to the house in White City that Alan shares with his good lady, Jackie and son, Paul. He'd just got back after spending a couple of days with Keith in Milan, on the *Licks* tour. Alan had stayed in Keith's double suite, so it seemed like little had changed since the Savoy!

I was bursting to see this guitar. First, Alan played me some tracks by his new group, Monkey Sea. It was filthy rock 'n' roll with titles like 'Gold Cortina'. Then he disappeared upstairs – to reappear with a beautiful 1964 Gibson Hummingbird acoustic.

'There's a lot of spirits in that guitar,' said Alan, as he carefully took it out of its battered black case and handed it to me. I felt a few tingles as I held it and noticed the wear, notches and gauges on the body. 'Well, no one else has had it,' he said, noticing my expression as I weighed up a little history. Apparently, it was the guitar on which Keith wrote many of his late sixties and early seventies classics, including 'Wild Horses'. It's in the *One Plus One* film as the Stones work up 'Sympathy For The Devil'. Naturally, I asked how he ended up with it.

It was late 2000 and Monkey Sea had played a gig at the Croydon Greyhound. Afterwards, drummer George Butler and bass player John returned to London, while Alan and Jackie drove down to Redlands, where Mr. Richards was in residence and waiting.

'I'd told Keith about the new band and wanted to play him the demos,' he recalled. 'So we went down and I had my two Telecasters with me, so I left them in the hallway. It was a good night. I played Keith the new demos and he really liked them. In fact, he was playing along! Next morning I had to go and, as we were leaving, I picked up my two guitars. Keith came out of the dining room and handed me this one. "You left one," he said. "No, I didn't," I said. "No, *you left one*. It's yours," he said. And it turned out to be this guitar.

'I didn't know the history of it at the time but Alan Rogan, who's been guitar roadie for Pete Townshend, Eric Clapton and Keith, told me about it. He'd looked after the guitar for Keith when he was doing the Stones. When he left he gave it back to Keith and then Keith gave it to me. It's just so nice to have, and what's good about it is it's a working guitar.'

I asked Alan how he'd sum up Keith.

Keith and Alan Clayton discuss the Steptoe and Son *album on the European tour.*

'I love his enthusiasm. I went to see him in Milan and, where most people just come offstage and chill out, he's off there listening to tapes of the new stuff they've done in Paris. He never stops listening to music.

'And the guitar. I didn't own an acoustic guitar and it's not like he gave me a bit of junk! But that's what a nice bloke he is. It's a roots feeling.'

The feeling would grow throughout 2003 as Keith asked Alan to accompany him on bits of the tour. No work to do, none necessary. Alan ended up travelling around Europe with Keith. 'His little holiday,' Jackie calls it. Keith gave him his tour pass and itinerary so he could go to any gigs he fancied. Which included the London shows.

'You should write a book,' said Keith one night.

The UK dates were special. The Stones machine was at full throttle in the weeks before, during and after. They released 'Sympathy For The Devil', giving the unenviable job of remixing to dance giant Fatboy Slim – who kept all of the vocal and messed with the rhythm at the suggestion of Bernard Doherty, whose son is a big fan. With further mixes from the Neptunes, it went on to become the Stones' first number one in the US for years.

On the day of the Twickenham gig, *The Observer* carried a Rotterdam review by Molloy Woodcraft, who said he'd been talking to a woman who'd decorated her lavatory as a tribute to Keith Richards. He described Keith and Ron looking 'like nothing so much a as witchdoctor and his impish protégé', and wrote that Keith's 'Edith Piaf-meets-Geronimo dumbshow was really touching.'

Twickenham Rugby Stadium, Sunday 24 August, 2003 marked a return to the turf where the Rolling Stones were spawned.

The vibe before a Stones show is always special – especially when it's in or near London. They know they're coming home again, to poke that tongue at all the detractors, the press who've written them off in the past, the authority figures who've tried to break them, and the young pretenders who've stolen their template but can't hold a candle to them.

This one was doubly special. The Stones were just down the road to Richmond, the place where, 40 years previously, they'd been playing the Sunday lunchtime sets at the Station Hotel. Mick's punishing two-hour ritual, in which he's said to run about twelve miles, had taken its toll on this tour. Gigs had been postponed when he'd gone down with laryngitis or flu, but it's to his credit that he managed to pull it off.

If this was to be the last tour, as rumour suggested, then Twickenham was certainly the one to go out on. The tour didn't coincide with a new album which needed to be pushed, but a consolidation of their golden moments on *Forty Licks*.

Although the presentation and staging was often breathtaking, the band were concentrating on the music. There was a definite 'up' mood to the show. Compared to my first proper Stones gig at Wembley, nearly 30 years ago to the month, the difference was astounding.

Especially in Keith. The wasted pirate-ghost persona was truly a thing of the past. He wore his achievements and his endurance with a subtle, stately pride. Sporting a black, spangly bandanna and a succession of bright silk shirts, the man was a revelation – even for unashamedly biased souls such as I. Using a different guitar for each song, he alternated between caressing and squeezing out those riffs, almost bent double at the knees, to strutting and cruising the walkways while delivering killer-salvo solos.

Though following Charlie as usual, Keith was every inch the bandleader, kickstarting the songs, and bringing them to a close, often by flicking his plectrum – inscribed simply 'The Rolling Stones' – out into the crowd. The difference from the somnambulent spectre who glided through the seventies tours, while taking a quick nap against the amps, was beyond measure.

Before the gig Keith would be in his self-customised 'Camp X-Ray', playing snooker with the sobered-up Ronnie – Ronnie was on expresso. He revealed how Mr. Wood whipped his arse every night: '. . . he's been hanging out with Jimmy White and Ronnie O'Sullivan and picking up tips while he's at home. Me, I haven't touched a damned cue since I saw Ronnie last time, so maybe that's the secret . . . Usually I'm lucky to get a red and a colour down! And then there's always some cheating going on. "Ooh, sorry, I dropped the chalk in front of your ball!" We don't take it too seriously.'

Backstage, the Stones convene about five minutes before they go on, after wardrobe and 'perestroika – that's makeup . . . reconstruction,' says Keith. It was also, on the *Licks* tour, when they worked out what the first song was going to be. Thanks to Bernard Doherty and his assistant Lucy Hopkins, me and my girlfriend, Michelle, were perched in the press box. (It said £150 on the ticket. Blimey.)

My heart was in my mouth for the hour before the Stones went on. After a build-up which began with the lights going down and a bass rumble shaking the ground, there was a sudden explosion and there was Keith, lurching into 'Brown Sugar'. Nothing can match that impact. The stage was suddenly a hive of cavorting as they whacked their collective foot firmly down on the metal and made their presence known in the best way they know how.

'Brown Sugar' was a good chance for the audience to get limbered up for a bit of participation – 'Yeah, yeah, yeah, *Whooo!*' – which Mick seemed glad of at times. Maybe the next two songs were a tad unexpected – 'You Got Me Rockin'', from *Voodoo Lounge*, and the last single, 'Don't Stop' – but most of the crowd were too happy to be there to care.

Mick made a few announcements that emphasised what their homecoming meant to the Stones. 'No one has ever played here before. We are privileged, you and I. We started playing the other rugby club nearby and it's not far from here to there.'

There were five indisputable classics next: 'Rocks Off' from *Exile* came as a blaring party wake-up. It was followed by one of the most beautiful songs ever written, 'Wild Horses'. You could sense the communal shiver going down 70,000 spines as Keith plucked those plaintive opening notes and Mick sang that he was '*tarred of living*'. It was delivered perfectly, with sensitivity and grace, encouraging one of the biggest singalongs of the night. Even Mick was moved to say, 'that was sweet,' at its conclusion.

The mood was carried on by the next song, 'You Can't Always Get What You Want' – maybe a little earlier than usual, but as majestic as ever. 'Paint It, Black' was a rampant charger, before Keith put the brakes on to steer the evergreen 'Tumbling Dice' to a glorious climax.

Then it was the moment when Mick introduces the band. Charlie – 'the Wembley Whammer' – was showered with the usual lengthy ovation, before Ronnie was announced as 'the Hillingdon Harlot'. Then it was Keith's turn – 'the Sage of Sidcup' – before he stepped forward for his solo spot.

The guitarist was visibly overwhelmed, as he leant on the mikestand. I could swear he was brushing away a tear as he said, 'It's good to be back, know what I mean? It's good to be home.' Such a lot of water under the bridge since then. So many lifetimes crammed into so many years. Some lives lost. All of this could have been flashing before his welling eyes as he began a gorgeous version of 'Slipping Away', its reflections on lost love and lost life gaining an extra poignancy.

The whole night must have seemed like coming full circle. Maybe that's why, a few songs later, Keith strode proud and smiling along one of the walkways, side-by-side with his lifetime mate Mick Jagger, who also seemed moved by the occasion.

With not a dry eye left in the house, Keith led the band into a blazing version of 'Happy'. The set was approaching its climax as searing flames exploded into the heavens during a spellbinding version of 'Sympathy For The Devil', which saw the stage transformed into a red-glare approximation of Satan's living room.

Now for that catwalk. As a crunching drum kicked out, the band made their way to the small stage smack in the middle of the rugby pitch. Keith took longer than the others as he homed in on certain audience members to slap palms. Then the Rolling Stones joined ranks as a stripped-down bar band – singer playing harmonica, two guitars, bass, drums and piano.

'Starfucker' gave Keith a chance to vent his Chuck Berry licks with stinging

The Stones relax for a photo shoot during the Forty Licks *tour.*

aplomb, while a slo-mo trawl through 'I Just Wanna Make Love To You' revisited the first album. 'Street Fighting Man' was astounding, with Keith setting up a veritable wall of noise as he bent double over that insurrectional riff. When it was over, he took even longer to make it back to the main stage.

Then the home stretch: A sinister, dread-ridden rendition of 'Gimme Shelter', with Lisa Fischer turning in a sky-scraping vocal performance. 'Honky Tonk Women' throbbed along as great as ever, but this time accompanied by a cartoon projection inspired by Japanese Manga, depicting a naked girl being shown exactly what that infamous Stones tongue could get up to.

Keith cranked ferociously into 'Start Me Up', and I continued reflecting on the sex in the Stones' music. Sure, there'd always been Mick's hip-shake, pout and dirty words, but listen to those riffs. What are 'Honky Tonk Women' and 'Start Me Up' if not extensions of Keith's groin? The man has always been renowned as the harbinger of Drugs 'n' Rock 'n' Roll. What about the Sex? Keith's cruise-altitude guitar lungings have defined a grimy, lustful counterpart to Jagger's slavering for decades. But, at Twickenham, Keith was making love to that guitar, locating erogenous zones you never knew existed. The guitar responded accordingly.

'Satisfaction' took out the main set with its extended soul revue-hysteria coda, which recalled Otis Redding's cover version. Keith used the pink and black Telecaster given to him by ZZ Top. The final hit was 'Jumpin' Jack Flash', drawn-out, ultra-climactic, confetti-strewn and totally euphoric. Keith had so much power at his fingertips by now, he only had to tap his guitar to bring out a sheet of noise that must have shook the planes flying over from Gatwick Airport.

Then the customary bow, fireworks, and out into the night to face the cattle train.

The day after Twickenham, I bought all the papers. All the reviews featured words like 'triumph' and 'magic'. *The Independent*'s Gavin Martin got it: 'When it comes to stadium staging the Stones have few equals ... Richards can laugh, stumble and fall over as he attempts his own peculiar version of Chuck Berry's duck walk during "Tumblin' Dice", safe in the knowledge that he is playing his searing chords as well as at any time during the last 40 years, if not better.'

But the most refreshing review came from my girlfriend Michelle, twenty years my junior and the proverbial Stones concert virgin. Now she knew exactly what primeval force had motivated me for as long as I can remember. Later, when Michelle was pouring out her impressions, I thought it made an illuminating change and her rapt enthusing reminded me of myself after Wembley Arena 30 years before. So I got her to write some of it down ...

'This love of the Stones had always been in my blood and I never really shook it off. Just the way Keith came across, you wanted to be like him, because you just knew that your parents would totally disapprove. This was the moment I'd been waiting for all my life. Just being there, absorbing the whole atmosphere before they came on, was intoxicating enough. When they came on my jaw dropped in total amazement. I was lapping all this up, like a thirsty dog. Keith was just totally amazing – his dedication, his charisma. I just wanted to be there holding his hand. I came out of there a changed person, and it totally restored my faith in music.'

Another life pivoted around by the Stones.

The night we went to Twickenham, the BBC showed a rockumentary about the group called *The One and Only Rolling Stones*. Most of the Stones 'experts' they wheeled on – like Pierce Brosnan – seemed to agree that Keith 'epitomised rock 'n' roll'. As Pete Clark's review in the *Evening Standard* said, 'You show me a man who does not wish that he had – maybe just once – gone on a bender with Keith and I'll show you a mouse.'

The London Astoria on 27 August proved predictably impossible to get into, as they'd stuffed the balcony with celebs like Kate Moss, Cat Deeley, Fun Lovin' Criminal Huey Morgan, Andrew Lloyd Webber, Holly Valance, Jay Kay and Primal Scream's Bobby Gillespie. But we saw them at Wembley Arena – scene of the 1968 *NME* Pollwinners Concert dambuster – on Monday 15 September. Hats off to Bernard and Lucy again.

I wondered why it was 150 quid for twelve rows back in the stalls. I soon realised why when the Stones left the main stage, only to reappear again on a smaller stage about ten yards away. My 40 years of following the Stones reached its apex when Alan Clayton popped out and said, 'Follow me.' He'd had a word with Keith, and been told it was alright to come back and see him while support band The Darkness were squeaking away. Led by Alan, Michelle and I duly went through a few doors, up a corridor and into Keith's dressing room.

There was a big sound system, low lights and a well-stocked fridge. Michelle walked in and took her shoes off. She was nervous about meeting him for the first time.

When we walked in, Keith was in the centre of the room in conversation with

'Let the tigers out.' Keith and Mick in Munich on the Licks *tour.*

a guy making a biopic of Gram Parsons. It was a surreal atmosphere, with comedian Vic Reeves lurking in the corner, but very chilled.

Keith ambled over, extending his hand with a big grin. 'How ya doin', man?' He gave me a bear hug. People have said that you don't see Keith for years, but when you do it's like you saw him last week. He looked great, in a green military-style jacket and black bandana with all that stuff swinging about in his hair.

I introduced him to Michelle. 'Hi darling,' he said, as he kissed her hand with a gentlemanly flourish. Her nerves evaporated - to the point that Vic Reeves and the girls in the corner thought she worked for the Stones. Soon Ronnie came bouncing in, accompanied by his old mate Jeff Beck. A few minutes later Patti showed up. It turned into the best twenty-minute party I've ever been to.

I gave Keith my copy of Stanley Holloway's *Brahn Boots* album for old time's sake. He was impressed when Michelle presented him with a story written about him by her nine-year-old daughter Abbey. He scanned it, grinning to himself.

'Keith was sipping his Sunkist and smoking his fag. "Hey, Mick, come here!" Mick bent down and was on his hands and knees. Keith put his bottle on Mick's back and had a whiff of his fag. "Hey man, get up," he said to Mick, kicking him in the side. They burst outside of Keith's mansion and Mick threw his fag at Ronnie. Keith was left with his Sunkist bottle and found a water bomb in his coat pocket, and threw it at Mick. Keith came strolling down the hallway. He looked happy. "Right guys, where's my shepherd's pie?" "It's here," said Ronnie and Mick and Charlie, altogether. Keith snatched up his beloved pie and told the boys that he had managed to order 500 shepherd's pies. The End.'

Keith found this immensely funny. He signed, 'What a story!' on Abbey's autograph book. I remembered that I was nine too when I got into the Stones. Maybe I've passed it on.

It was great seeing him again, and he signed my programme, '20 years on, one love.' We chatted a bit, though he didn't really have to fill me in on what he'd been up to over the years. But the atmosphere was relaxed and friendly. It was one of those blurry, dream-like moments that go by in a flash.

Then it was approaching show-time so Keith and Ronnie had to get changed. There were cheery goodbyes and Mr. Clayton led us off on the nearest cloud. When Michelle asked Keith if she could give him a kiss, he duly obliged with a hug thrown in.

'That was fierce,' said a grinning Keith to Alan afterwards.

The Stones' set featured *Sticky Fingers* as the album for the night. 'Slipping Away' even excelled the Twickenham version, rearing and cathartic. They hotfoot-ed to the little stage and uncorked an uncanny treatment of 'Little Red Rooster'. Unlike Twickenham, we were out of the press box and in the thick of the crowd. It was electric. One of those nights you cherish forever. Thanks to Alan and Keith.

A lot of things seemed to come around on this tour. During the nineties I worked and DJed for Primal Scream. Stones fans to the hilt, they've been accused of copying the *Exile* period and have definitely followed that direction in terms of excessive behaviour. The Scream supported the Stones at a later Twickenham gig and on three dates in Spain and Portugal. A marriage made in heaven, I'd say.

The day after the Scream got back, I spoke to keyboard player Martin Duffy, who still seemed in shock from the events of the previous week. The rock-'n'-roll-*Carry-On*-film that's the-Scream-on-the-road fitted in well with the Stones. The two groups posed for a team photograph, with Keith sidling up next to Martin. Singer Bobby Gillespie and bass player Mani went to visit him before he went on. Apparently he didn't say much, but whacked on a Chuck Berry album and did some warm-up moves. 'Seems a bit like a dream now, but a good one,' said Duff.

Full Circle

Tour over. Mick was finally free to collect that knighthood. Again, the press seized on it as an excuse to stoke up war between him and Keith.

Keith's feelings on the matter hadn't been dulled by the camaraderie of the tour. In *Uncut*, he complained, 'It's not what the Stones is about, is it? I don't want to step out on stage with someone wearing a fucking coronet and sporting the old ermine. At the same time, I told Mick, "It's a fucking paltry honour. If you're into this shit, hang on for the peerage. Don't settle for a little badge." He defend-ed himself by saying that Tony Blair suggested he took the knighthood. Like that's an excuse . . . . Like it doesn't depend how you feel about it.'

Mick finally bent down in front of Prince Charles on 12 December, wearing trainers, and found time to take a swipe back at Keith.

'I think Keith would like to get the same honour,' he crowed outside the Palace. 'He's like a bawling child who hasn't got an ice cream. It's nothing new.

Keith likes to make a fuss.'

But Keith got more respect from his music business peers when he turned 60. Looking at the man careering around the stage as if shot through with some kind of alien electrical energy, I can see him perched on a stool playing 'How Can I Stop' in twenty years time. If he can get through what he's done and come out running, what *is* gonna stop him? He's reached a position in rock 'n' roll which no-one else ever has - the beloved elder statesman who hasn't lost a bit of his personal charisma. Hold him up alongside any of his peers – like McCartney, Townshend, or even Mick Jagger – and nobody comes close in terms of wisdom, passion, or simply being a bloody good bloke.

The tributes came flooding in. *Uncut* devoted 28 pages to him for the second time in a year. Jon Wilde kicked off by wishing Keith a happy 60th birthday.

'It's a funny place to be . . . There's a lot of people who thought I'd never make it this far, including myself. For a long time, it felt like being wished to death but I got over it. Of course, I saw the white light at the end of the tunnel a few times. But I proved I was sturdy. This body of mine, I pushed it as far as I could push. That was an interesting experiment. While it lasted.'

When did it stop?

'Oh, it never stops, old chap. At least it hasn't for me.'

Wilde quotes Keith as saying the Stones keep on touring for the same reason that a dog licks its own balls.

'Yeah, basically,' he laughs at his own metaphor. 'I might have put it a little more poetically. What I mean by that is it's part of nature for us . . . . You can call it habit. You can call it addiction.'

Keith's vision of the Stones' longevity seem to have replaced the venerable blues musicians with heroes of the seven seas as his role models. 'Since nobody has sailed this sea before, one expects some storms and some choppy waters . . . what do the critics know? They've never been on this sea before and nor have we. We're just floating out there and seeing where it can go.

'It's like we've now gone over the equator. We're Magellan. Or Sir Frankie Drake.'

Mick says he still doesn't fully understand his relationship with Keith. 'I think Keith is a very inward person. He was always a very quiet and meditative type, so to bring out what he really wants to say I think is quite a problem for him sometimes. I'm a very outgoing person and very gregarious. Keith isn't really. Although he's learnt to be more gregarious than he used to be.'

Ronnie's final word on his best mate? 'The funny thing about Keith is that even though he may be out of his brain, he still knows what the fuck he's doing all the time . . . He still plays great even if he's out of it. It's incredibly rare to have a playmate like Keith. We're lucky to have that rapport. Playing and working together is a gift. We seem to think exactly the same way and I've never found that with anyone else.'

And Charlie Watts?'

'Keith is the easiest person in the world to play with, and I've never wanted to play rock 'n' roll with anyone else. He's got a wonderful sense of timing. He's one of the best rhythm guitarists ever. And he's the greatest Chuck Berry player.

Time is on our side! Keith meets the missus at Wembley, September 2003.

That's the sound Keith really loves . . . I don't think Keith will ever stop. There's no reason why he should. He'll always be playing a guitar somewhere, won't he?'

Ex-guitar partner Mick Taylor said, 'His style and his sound have pretty much defined what the Rolling Stones are, at least from *Beggars Banquet* onwards . . . I was . . . in the audience at the London Astoria in August and I was impressed with Keith's charisma on stage and his playing and everything about him. He seemed very focused compared to the way he used to be. There's no reason why he shouldn't go on for a long time yet, given the kind of musician he is.'

Chrissie Hynde – a long-time Keef admirer, who once had a job as his house cleaner – also paid tribute: 'Keith has that air of danger. He's the total outlaw. He epitomises the alternative lifestyle. He doesn't give a fuck, which is why he's never had to reinvent himself. He's timeless and eternal and there's a deep sense of humanity about him.'

They even got a doctor in to give his verdict on Keith's resilient constitution – even if it was Hank Wangford, once a cod-country figure on the London pub-rock circuit.

'Keith is unusual. But he isn't unique. He's just the most visible example of serious abuse and living through it . . . Keith is the exception. Nobody can think that they can do what he's done and get away with it. He's got a very strong constitution. People like Gram Parsons didn't have it. Keith has a genetic strength and, just as importantly, he has an appetite for life. He wants to be here.'

'He's probably right,' responded Keith. 'As far as I'm concerned, life is all you get and I'll make the best out of it. There have been some friends of mine – Gram Parsons being one of them – about whom some people have said, "Oh, he made the mistake of trying to keep up with Keith." . . . . But . . . I've never forced anyone else to come along with me. In fact, believe it or not, there are certain guys I've told, "No, you go to sleep. I'm going to do this and you don't have to follow me . . ."'

Christopher Sandford, who recently published his own reserved take on Keith in *Satisfaction*, painted a picture of him in the *Daily Express* which might be termed the 'anti-Keef'. He described him as 'an all-round good egg' who'd been a model boy scout, good at sports, and sang 'Zadok The Priest' for the Queen. He also wrote that his greatest hero is World War Two flying ace Douglas Bader and described how he wrote a cheque for 30 grand to save the local church hall near Redlands.

Sandford expressed something approaching shock at the fact that Keith is close to his mum, likes kids and animals, and secretly donates to many charities. He even claims that Keith's much-toted 'nuclear waste' is iced tea and that Patti got him into churchgoing and an exercise regime, and banned him from swearing in the house.

Sandford describes him as an 'endearing figure . . . pottering around the Sussex countryside,' quoting Keith's in-laws who call him 'an enthusiastic disciple of Christ.' The point of the piece was clearly to debunk the Keef myths, and present a Keith Richards who was palatable to a conservative, middle-aged readership – the opposite to someone like John Blake, who presented Keith as the junk-fuelled, knife-wielding Prince of Darkness.

What Sandford doesn't mention is that Keith Richards still kicks severe ass. Alan Clayton travelled with Keith for those last European gigs too. (He also turned up at the launch party for my book on Primal Scream with a plectrum from Keith. What a boost!) A few weeks later, Michelle and I spent the weekend at Alan's. He'd just got back from a few days at Redlands, chilling with Keith after the tour finally wound up.

'People would ask me what I was doing on the tour,' recalled Alan. 'I could only say, "Nothing." I was there to keep Keith company. Oh, and rolling spliffs! Later on I started doing the chicken run, under the ramp to the second stage, carrying the guitars.'

I asked for his general impression of Keith. 'The celebrated lifestyle is still totally Keith, but tempered these days and a lot more private.'

As he'd said earlier, 'He's taking it easy these days. He's changed. He's a family man now.'

That isn't to say that Keith's joined the straight world. He just seems at peace with his own world and his music, and doesn't feel the need to blot anything out these days.

It's all still down to the music. 'He doesn't want to be a rock 'n' roll star. He just wants to be a rock 'n' roll player. There's a lot of people who like music but only a few people who are passionate about it like that.

'He showed me his fingers. They're all flat at the end. He calls 'em hammerhead sharks. They're unbelievable. Years of playing. It works though!'

Knowing Keith's love of classic Brit humour well, Alan had discovered a cache of *Steptoe and Son* albums and burnt him a CD. Hopefully he had a good laugh after the tour.

'When we were down at Redlands I said, "Have you listened to it yet?" He said, "When people give me something I put it to one side and when I get home and chill out, that's when I listen to it." He likes a lot of British comedy, all sorts of stuff. Do you remember that Max Miller stuff when we met him? He had loads of stuff like that.

'Keith is really funny. Off the cuff. Deadpan. Good delivery. But it's hard to remember it! Every time you see a good comedian you come away knowing you've had a great time but you can't remember it.'

I remarked on how friendly Keith was to Michelle and I when he took us backstage. 'That was fucking great! He loved it. He likes pleasing people. That's what's nice about him. He handles so much, really well. That's what amazes me too: how he can keep on being genuine for so long.'

As the years go on, despite all the trials and tribulations, Keith seems to get stronger. As does his playing.

Throughout this book, I've used my living memory to try and convey the effect that Keith Richards has had on my life and attitude. No apologies if it sometimes approaches blind fan-worship. To try and convey in words something so intangibly inspiring is daunting. When I first met Keith 27 years ago, I must have felt similar to how he did when he encountered Muddy Waters in '64.

I *want* him to still be up there in ten years time, playing 'Slipping Away'. Or, as Keith put it in GQ, 'I like the expanding vision of life, of what goes on. I find it's like a great book. I'm two thirds of the way through it and, I mean, I can't wait for the ending, but I can put it off for a while. It's life, isn't it? I couldn't have written this story, man.'

'Musically, I've never laid down a lie,' he mused in *According to the Rolling Stones*. 'I'll lie to everybody – especially judges! – but I won't lie to my audiences; what I put out I do in the hope that I can make your heart throb a little better or bring a little tear to your eye or make you smile . . . . I just wish to transmit the joy I feel to somebody else, and if I can do that, I've done my gig.'

As I write these final words, I notice that the February 2004 issue of dance music bible *Mixmag* has printed a list of the '25 Highest People in History'. Keith is number one, beating off competition from Timothy Leary, Charlie Parker, Ozzy Osbourne, Shaun Ryder – and yours truly at number fourteen, for some reason. It's the first time I've ever been in the same chart as Keith Richards.

'All the crap you go through, I mean, how bad is it really?' – *Keith Richards*

INDEX